The Usborne
Junior
Illustrated
English
Dictionary

Edited by
Felicity Brooks and Hannah Wood

Designed by
Kirsty Tizzard and Stephanie Jones

Illustrated by Nikki Dys

Additional editing by
Caroline Young and Mairi Mac

D1439236

Using your dictionary

You can use this dictionary to find out the meanings of words, see how they're used, or check spellings. All the words are listed in alphabetical order. Here's how to look up a word using "before" as an example:

1. Think of the first letter of your word. Use this strip to help you find the section with words that start with that letter.

2. Think of the next letters in your word. These two words tell you the first and last word on each page.

3. Look down the list of words that are in blue until find the word you are looking for.

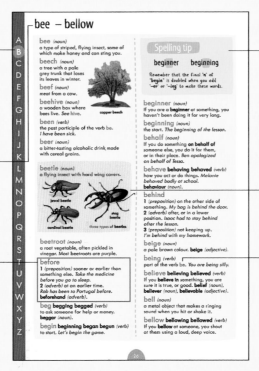

Boxes contain useful spelling tips, facts about where words come from, or information on how English works.

There are lots of **illustrations.** Some have labels showing you different parts of the picture.

A **blue word in a definition** means you can find out more by looking that word up.

When you have found the word you are looking for, here are some of the things you will see:

The main words, which are known as headwords, are all in blue.

This shows how to pronounce words that are tricky to say.

Different forms of the headword, such as parts of verbs or unusual plurals, are listed here.

An example in *italics* shows how a word can be used.

Words that are related to the headword are listed at the end.

diet (*die-ut*) dieting dieted
1 (noun) what you eat.
A healthy diet.
2 (verb) to eat less food, or stop eating certain foods, in order to lose weight.

difference (noun)
the way in which things are not the same. **different** (adjective), **differently** (adverb).

The definition tells you what the word means. There may be more than one.

The word class (see facing page) that a word belongs to is shown in brackets.

Word classes

Every word in English belongs to a **word class** (sometimes called a "part of speech"). Some belong to more than one. Here are the main word classes:

nouns

A noun is a word that **names a thing, an object, or a feeling**: I saw a yellow *boat*.

verbs

A verb is a "doing" word, and **tells you about an action, or something being done**: Louise *jumped* over the final hurdle.

adjectives

An adjective **tells you more about a thing or a person**: Sal's new puppy is very *cute*. Adjectives also have other versions:

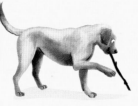

• the *comparative*, which compares something to something else: Mark's puppy is *cuter* than Sal's.

• the *superlative*, which means "the most" of that adjective: My puppy is *cutest* of all.

Most adjectives add '-er' and '-est' to make the comparative and the superlative, but some longer words add "more" or "most" before:

> expensive ⟶ more expensive ⟶ most expensive

There's more about **grammar and punctuation** at the back of the book. You'll also find lists of prepositions, conjunctions, pronouns, and other useful words.

adverbs

An adverb **tells you more about a verb, or how something is done**: Cheetahs run *quickly*.
Lots of adverbs end in '-ly', but some don't, for example: Cheetahs run *fast*.

prepositions

A preposition **tells you more about the other parts of a sentence.** Many prepositions tell you where someone or something is, for example: Sophie swam *under* the water.

conjunctions

A conjunction **joins parts of a sentence together**: I'd like a telescope *so that* I can study the planets.

pronouns

A pronoun is a **word you use instead of naming a person or a thing**: Alison is mean. *She* finished my pizza.

Aa

a, an *(determiner)*
one of something. You use **a** before a word that starts with a consonant, for example, "I wish I had a cat". You use **an** before a word that starts with a vowel, for example, "When we were at the zoo, we saw an elephant".

aardvark *(noun)*
an African animal with a long, sticky tongue, which it uses to search for insects.

large ears

long nose

long tail

sharp claws

sticky tongue

aardvark

abandon
abandoning abandoned *(verb)*
to leave someone or something forever.
We abandoned the broken-down car.

abbreviation *(noun)*
a short way of writing a word.
"Dr" is an abbreviation of "doctor".
abbreviated *(adjective)*.

ability abilities *(noun)*
1 If you have the **ability** to do something, you can do it. *I know I have the ability to win this tennis match.*
2 skill. *James has great ability in art.*

able *(adjective)*
1 If you are **able** to do something, you can do it. *I am able to swim.*
2 skilful, or clever. **ably** *(adverb)*.

abnormal *(adjective)*
unusual, or not normal.

aboard *(preposition)*
on or into a train, ship, or aircraft.
aboard *(adverb)*.

Aborigine *(ab-or-**ij**-in-ee) (noun)*
one of the native people of Australia, who lived there before Europeans arrived. **Aboriginal** *(adjective)*.

about *(preposition)*
1 to do with a particular subject.
This documentary is about penguins.
2 around, but not exactly. *I'll be finished in about five minutes.*

above
1 *(preposition)* higher than.
The cups are kept above the fridge.
2 *(adverb)* at a higher level or layer.
The plane flew above the clouds.
3 *(preposition)* more than.
My score was above Luke's.

abroad *(adverb)*
in or to another country. *We are going abroad this summer.*

abrupt *(adjective)*
1 sudden and unexpected. *The car came to an abrupt stop.* **abruptly** *(adverb)*.
2 rude and short-tempered.

absent *(adjective)*
If someone is **absent**, they are not in a place. **absence** *(noun)*.

absolute *(adjective)*
complete or total. *Kate looks an absolute idiot.* **absolutely** *(adverb)*.

absorb absorbing absorbed *(verb)*
to soak up liquid. **absorbent** *(adjective)*.

absurd *(adjective)*
silly or ridiculous. **absurdity** *(noun)*,
absurdly *(adverb)*.

abuse abusing abused
1 *(ab-**yuce**) (noun)* rude or unkind words or actions.
2 *(ab-**yooze**) (verb)* to treat a person or animal cruelly.

abyss abysses *(noun)*
a very deep hole that seems to have no bottom.

accelerate
accelerating accelerated *(verb)*
to get faster and faster.
acceleration *(noun)*.

accent *(noun)*
the way that you say words.
Jacques speaks with a French accent.

accept accepting accepted *(verb)*
to take something that someone has
offered you.

access accesses *(noun)*
a way into a place. *There is no
access to the building this way.*
accessible *(adjective)*.

accessory accessories *(noun)*
1 an extra part for something.
2 something, such as a belt or a scarf,
that goes with your clothes.

accident *(noun)*
something bad that happens by
chance. *Jess broke her arm in a
cycling accident.* **accidental** *(adjective)*,
accidentally *(adverb)*.

accommodation *(noun)*
a place where people live or stay.

**accompany accompanies
accompanying accompanied** *(verb)*
to go somewhere with someone.
Nina accompanied me to the picnic.

according to *(preposition)*
as someone has said or written.
According to Amy, this film is very funny.

account *(noun)*
1 something written or spoken that
tells you about something that has
happened. *Ricky gave his account
of the trip to the zoo.*
2 money you keep in a bank.

accurate *(adjective)*
correct and exact. **accuracy** *(noun)*,
accurately *(adverb)*.

accuse accusing accused *(verb)*
to say that someone has done
something wrong. **accusation** *(noun)*,
accuser *(noun)*.

ace *(noun)*
1 a playing card with only one symbol
on it. *The ace of spades.*
2 a serve in tennis that is impossible
to hit back.

Spelling tip   achieve

"Achieve" follows the spelling pattern:
**'i' before 'e' except after 'c', when
the letters make an 'ee' sound.**

ache *(noun)*
a dull pain that goes on and on. *I have
an ache in my neck.* **ache** *(verb)*.

**achieve
achieving achieved** *(verb)*
to do something by putting in a lot
of effort. **achievement** *(noun)*.

acid *(noun)*
a type of chemical. Some foods, such as
vinegar and lemons, contain acids which
make them taste sharp and sour. Some
acids are very strong and can burn your
clothes and skin. **acidic** *(adjective)*.

acid rain *(noun)*
rain that is polluted by gases from cars,
factories, and so on, that can harm
plants and animals.

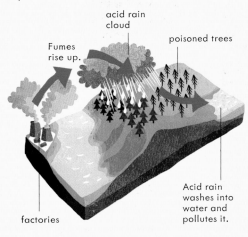

acid rain cloud

poisoned trees

Fumes rise up.

Acid rain washes into water and pollutes it.

factories

This picture shows how **acid rain** is made.

acorn *(noun)*
a nut that grows on oak trees.

acrobat *(noun)*
someone who does difficult balancing
and jumping tricks that are exciting
to watch. **acrobatic** *(adjective)*.

a b c d e f g h i j k l m n o p q r s t u v w x y z

acronym (noun)
a word made from the first, or first few, letters of the words in a phrase. "Radar" is an acronym for "**ra**dio **d**etecting **a**nd **r**anging".

act acting acted
1 (verb) to do something. *We must act now to save the rainforests.*
2 (verb) to have a part in a play, film, and so on.
3 (noun) something that you do. *That was a very selfish act.*
4 (noun) a short performance or a part of a play.

action (noun)
1 something that you do. *We took action to help the injured bird.*
2 things that are happening. *There was a lot of action in the film.*

active (adjective)
busy and always moving.

activity activities (noun)
1 things that are happening. *The playground was full of activity.*
2 something that you do for fun. *We do sports activities in the holidays.*

actor (noun)
someone who acts in a play, film, and so on.

Spelling tip   **actor**

Words that end with '-or' and '-er' often mean "a person who does something". Can you think of any more words that follow this pattern?

actual (adjective)
real, or true. *This is an actual dinosaur bone.* **actually** (adverb).

acute (adjective)
1 very sharp or strong. *Acute pain.*
2 An **acute** angle is less than 90°.

AD (abbreviation)
AD is used to show that a date comes after the birth of Jesus Christ, or the year 0. *AD2500.*

adapt adapting adapted (verb)
1 to change something so that it can be used for a different purpose. *We have adapted our garage to make it a games room.*
2 to get used to being in a new place. *It can be hard to adapt to a new school.*

add adding added (verb)
1 to put one thing with another. *Add the eggs to the flour.*
2 to put numbers together.

adder (noun)
a small, venomous snake.

addictive (adjective)
very hard to give up. *Smoking is addictive.* **addict** (noun), **addicted** (adjective).

addition (noun)
adding numbers or things together.

address addresses (noun)
1 the place where someone lives.
2 email address the set of letters, symbols, and sometimes numbers, that you type into the address bar to send someone an email.

adjective (noun)
a word that describes someone or something. "Tall", "angry" and "handsome" are all adjectives. *See* **word classes**, *page 3.*

adjust adjusting adjusted (verb)
1 to move or change something slightly. **adjustment** (noun).
2 to get used to something new and different. **adjustment** (noun).

admire admiring admired (verb)
1 to like and respect someone. **admiration** (noun).
2 to look at something and enjoy it. *Ella admired the mountain view.*

admit admitting admitted (verb)
1 to own up to doing something wrong. **admission** (noun).
2 to let someone or something enter a place. **admission** (noun).

adolescent *(noun)*
a young person who is more grown-up than a child, but is not yet an adult. **adolescence** *(noun)*, **adolescent** *(adjective)*.

adopt adopting adopted *(verb)*
When someone **adopts** a child, they take them into their family and become his or her parent. **adoption** *(noun)*.

adore adoring adored *(verb)*
to love someone or something very much.

adult *(noun)*
a fully-grown person or animal. **adulthood** *(noun)*, **adult** *(adjective)*.

advance
advancing advanced *(verb)*
to move forward. *The tiger advanced towards its prey.*

advantage *(noun)*
1 something that helps you or is useful to you. *I think my new trainers gave me an advantage in the race.*
2 If you **take advantage** of someone, you use them to help yourself do well.

Advent *(noun)*
the weeks leading up to Christmas in the Christian Church's year.

adventure *(noun)*
something exciting that you do, or that happens to you. **adventurous** *(adjective)*.

adverb *(noun)*
a word usually used to describe a verb. Adverbs tell you how, when, where, how often, or how much something happens. "Slowly", "usually" and "soon" are all adverbs. *See word classes, page 3.*

advertise
advertising advertised *(verb)*
to give information about something that you want to sell, often in a short film on television or the internet, or a picture with words on a poster, to try to make people want to buy it. **advertisement** *(noun)*, **advert** *(noun)*, **ad** *(noun)*.

advice *(noun)*
If you give someone **advice**, you tell them what you think they should do. *Shahid gave me good advice on how to mend my bike.*

advise advising advised *(verb)*
to tell someone what you think they should do. *Tom advised me to stay at home during the storm.*

aeroplane *(noun)*
a machine with wings and an engine, that flies through the air.

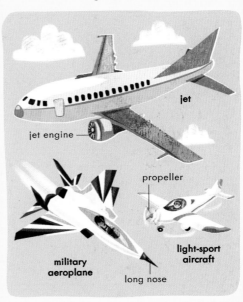

jet

jet engine

propeller

light-sport aircraft

military aeroplane

long nose

different types of **aeroplanes**

affair
1 *(noun)* a particular event or thing that has happened. *The food fight was a messy affair.*
2 affairs *(plural noun)* things which concern a lot of people. *Foreign affairs.*

affect affecting affected *(verb)*
to change someone or something in some way. *The bad weather affected our camping trip.*

affection *(noun)*
a strong liking for someone or something.

affectionate *(adjective)*
very loving. *My cat is very affectionate.*

A B C D E F G H I J K L M N O P Q R S T U V W X Y Z

afford **affording afforded** *(verb)*
1 If you can **afford** something, you have enough money to buy it.
2 to be able to do something, or to have enough time to do it. *We've walked so far, we can afford to take a long break.*

afloat *(adjective)*
floating on water.

afraid *(adjective)*
1 frightened, or worried.
2 sorry. *I'm afraid I can't come.*

after *(preposition)*
1 later than. *Let's play after lunch.*
2 following someone or something. *Cara's puppy ran after her.*

afternoon *(noun)*
the time of day between midday and about six o'clock in the evening.

again *(adverb)*
one more time. *Let's go again!*

against *(preposition)*
1 next to and touching. *Put your ear against the wall.*
2 on the opposite side to a person or team in a game or competition. *I played chess against Grandad.*
3 If you are **against** something, you do not agree with it. *I'm against killing whales.*

age **ageing** *or* **aging aged**
1 *(noun)* how old a person or thing is.
2 *(noun)* a time in history. *The Iron Age.*
3 *(verb)* to get older.

ageism *or* **agism** *(noun)*
treating people unfairly because of their age.

agent *(noun)*
1 someone who arranges things for other people. *A travel agent.* **agency** *(noun).*
2 a spy. *A secret agent.*

aggressive *(adjective)*
A person or animal that is **aggressive** behaves in a fierce, scary way. **aggression** *(noun)*, **aggressively** *(adverb).*

agile *(adjective)*
able to move quickly and easily. **agility** *(noun).*

agism *(noun)*
see **ageism**.

ago *(adverb)*
before now, or in the past. *We moved house three years ago.*

agony **agonies** *(noun)*
If you are **in agony**, you are in a lot of pain.

agree **agreeing agreed** *(verb)*
1 to say yes to something. *I agreed to Milly's plan.* **agreement** *(noun).*
2 to think that someone or something is right. *Dan and I agree that this book is interesting.* **agreement** *(noun).*

agriculture *(noun)*
farming. **agricultural** *(adjective).*

In medieval **agriculture**, large blades called scythes were used to cut crops.

ahead *(adverb)*
1 in front. *You walk ahead.*
2 in the future. *I'm thinking ahead to next week's camping trip.*

aid **aiding aided** *(verb)*
to help someone. **aid** *(noun).*

aim **aiming aimed** *(verb)*
1 to hit, throw or shoot something towards something else. **aim** *(noun).*
2 to try to do something. *I aim to become a chef.* **aim** *(noun).*

air *(noun)*
the invisible mixture of gases around us that we breathe.

aircraft **aircraft** *(noun)*
a vehicle that can fly.

air force *(noun)*
people and aircraft that can defend a country or attack another country from the air.

airline (noun)
a company that owns aircraft and organizes flights to transport people and goods.

airport (noun)
a place where aircraft take off and land, and where people get on and off planes.

aisle (noun)
the passage that runs between the rows of seats in a church, cinema, aircraft, and so on.

alarm **alarming alarmed**
1 (noun) something, such as a sound or flashing light, that wakes you up or warns you of danger.
2 (verb) to make someone afraid that something bad might happen. *I don't want to alarm you, but I can smell smoke.* **alarm** (noun).

album (noun)
1 a collection of songs by one singer or group that are all sold together.
2 a book in which you keep photographs, stamps, and so on.

alcohol (noun)
a liquid found in drinks such as wine or beer, which can make people drunk.

alert **alerting alerted**
1 (adjective) If you are **alert**, you pay attention to what is happening.
2 (verb) to warn someone that there might be danger. *Alert the fire brigade!*
3 (noun) a warning of danger. *A bomb alert.*

algae (noun)
small plants that grow without roots or stems in water or damp places.

alien (noun)
a creature from another planet.

alight (adjective)
burning. *Is the fire still alight?*

alike
1 (adjective) looking or acting the same. *The twins are very alike.*
2 (adverb) in a similar way. *The team all dress alike.*

alive (adjective)
living. *My goldfish isn't alive any more.*

alkali (noun)
a substance that turns litmus paper blue. Sea water is a weak alkali. **alkaline** (adjective).

all
1 (determiner) the whole of a particular group or thing. *Are you all ready?*
2 (pronoun) the whole of a particular group or thing that has been mentioned. *All are welcome to come.*

Allah (noun)
the Muslim name for God.

allergic (adjective)
If you are **allergic** to something, it makes you unwell. **allergy** (noun).

alligator (noun)
a large animal, similar to a crocodile, with strong jaws and very sharp teeth.

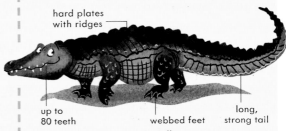

hard plates with ridges

up to 80 teeth

webbed feet

long, strong tail

American alligator

alliteration (noun)
the use of words that have the same sound at the beginning, for example, "The gruesome ghost gave a ghastly groan." **alliterative** (adjective), **alliterate** (verb).

allow **allowing allowed** (verb)
to let someone have or do something. *We're not allowed to leave school early.*

all right *or* alright
1 (adjective) quite good, but not great.
2 (adjective) not hurt, or not ill. *I'm amazed you're all right after that fall.*
3 (interjection) You say **all right** when you agree to do something.

almost (adverb)
very nearly. *I almost dropped the plate.*

a b c d e f g h i j k l m n o p q r s t u v w x y z

alone *(adjective)*
by yourself. *I was alone in the house last night.* **alone** *(adverb)*.

along
1 *(preposition)* from one end to the other. *We cycled along the path.*
2 all along the whole time. *I knew all along that Max was lying.*

aloud *(adverb)*
in a voice that other people can hear. *I read my story aloud to the class.*

alphabet *(noun)*
all the letters of a language arranged in order. **alphabetical** *(adjective)*.

$$\alpha \quad \beta \quad \gamma \quad \delta \quad \varepsilon$$

alpha beta gamma delta epsilon

first letters of the **Greek alphabet**

already *(adverb)*
before now. *I've seen that film already.*

also *(adverb)*
as well. *I like cats, but I also like dogs.*

alter altering altered *(verb)*
to change something. *We've altered our plans to include Jack.*

alternative
1 *(noun)* something that you can choose to have or do instead of something else. *If you don't want to eat fish, the alternative is chicken.* **alternative** *(adjective)*, **alternatively** *(adverb)*.
2 *(adjective)* different from what is usual. *Alternative medicine.*

alternative energy *(noun)*
energy that comes from nature, such as the Sun, waves, and wind.

although *(conjunction)*
1 even though. *Although we are lost, I think we'll find our way back.*
2 but. *Natalie is only nine, although she seems much older.*

altogether *(adverb)*
including all the people or things.

aluminium *(al-yoo-**min**-yum)* *(noun)*
a light, silver-coloured metal.

always *(adverb)*
If something is **always** happening, it happens all the time or very many times. *I always have cereal for breakfast.*

a.m. *(abbreviation)*
the time between midnight and midday. *I get up at 7 a.m.*

amateur *(noun)*
someone who does a sport or activity for fun, rather than for money.

amaze amazing amazed *(verb)*
If something **amazes** you, it makes you feel very surprised and impressed. **amazement** *(noun)*, **amazing** *(adjective)*, **amazingly** *(adverb)*.

ambition *(noun)*
something you really want to do. *My ambition is to be a film star.*

ambulance *(noun)*
a vehicle that takes people to hospital when they are injured or ill.

among or **amongst** *(preposition)*
1 in the middle of other people or things. *We hid among the trees.*
2 If something is shared **among** several people, they all get some of it.

amount *(noun)*
The **amount** of something is how much of it there is.

amphibian *(noun)*
an animal that can live on land and in water. **amphibious** *(adjective)*.

bumpy skin on back

dry, rough skin

webbed feet

The European common toad is an **amphibian**.

amuse amusing amused *(verb)*
1 to make someone laugh or smile. **amusing** *(adjective)*.
2 to keep someone happy and stop them from being bored. *The board game amused us for hours.* **amusement** *(noun)*.

anagram *(noun)*
a word or phrase made by changing the order of letters in another word or phrase. "Pea" is an anagram of "ape".

analyse analysing analysed *(verb)*
to look at something very closely and in great detail, so that you can understand and explain it. **analysis** *(noun)*.

ancestor *(noun)*
Your **ancestors** are members of your family who lived before you.

anchor *(noun)*
a heavy metal hook on a chain, which is lowered from a ship or boat to keep the boat still. **anchor** *(verb)*.

ancient *(adjective)*
very old. *Ancient ruins.*

and *(conjunction)*
a word used to join two or more words or phrases together. *I've read the book and seen the film.*

android *(noun)*
a robot that acts and looks like a human being.

angel *(noun)*
1 a messenger of God in the Bible. **angelic** *(adjective)*.
2 a very kind, gentle person. **angelic** *(adjective)*.

anger *(noun)*
the feeling of being very cross.

angle *(noun)*
the space between two lines at the point where they touch. Angles are measured in degrees, for example, 90°.

Spelling tip

angel   angle   angelic

Be careful not to get the spelling of these words mixed up. If you get confused, try to remember the adjective "**angelic**". When you say it aloud, you can hear that the 'e' comes **before** the 'l'.

angry angrier angriest *(adjective)*
If you are **angry**, you feel very cross. **angrily** *(adverb)*.

animal *(noun)*
a living creature that can breathe and move about. Fish, birds, insects and mammals are all animals.

animated *(adjective)*
An **animated** film is made by filming pictures very quickly, one after the other, so that the characters in the pictures seem to move. **animation** *(noun)*.

ankle *(noun)*
the joint that connects your foot to your leg.

anniversary anniversaries *(noun)*
a date which people remember because something important happened on that date in the past. *A wedding anniversary.*

Word family

anniversary
annual
These words both start with '**ann–**' and come from the Latin word for "year", "**annus**". They are to do with things that happen every year.

announce
announcing announced *(verb)*
to tell a lot of people about something important. **announcement** *(noun)*, **announcer** *(noun)*.

annoy annoying annoyed *(verb)*
to make someone feel angry. **annoying** *(adjective)*.

annual
1 *(adjective)* happening once every year. *An annual competition.* **annually** *(adverb)*.
2 *(noun)* a book that comes out once a year.

anonymous *(adjective)*
written, done or given by someone whose name is not known. *An anonymous letter.* **anonymity** *(noun)*.

a b c d e f g h i j k l m n o p q r s t u v w x y z

another
1 (determiner) one more, or a different one. *Have another piece of cake.*
2 (pronoun) a different one. *Lucy didn't like the dress, so she bought another.*

answer **answering answered**
1 (verb) to say or write something when you are asked a question. **answer** (noun).
2 (noun) a way of solving a problem. *Is there an answer to the problem of global warming?* **answer** (verb).
3 (verb) If you **answer back**, you say something rude or cheeky.

ant (noun)
a small insect that lives in a large group called a colony.

unhatched eggs

The queen has her own chamber.

queen

nursery for larvae and cocoons

food store

*Each chamber in an **ant** colony has a special purpose.*

Antarctic (noun)
the area around the South Pole. **Antarctic** (adjective).

anteater (noun)
a South American animal with a very long tongue that it uses to search for ants and other small insects.

long, sticky tongue

giant anteater

sharp claws for tearing open anthills

long tail

antelope (noun)
a large animal similar to a deer, that runs very fast and lives in Africa and parts of Asia.

antenna
antennas or **antennae** (noun)
a feeler on the head of an insect.

anthem (noun)
a song that has special meaning for a group of people. *I know all the words to the national anthem.*

anthology **anthologies** (noun)
a collection of poems or stories by different writers, which are all printed in the same book.

anti- (prefix)
Anti- is put before a word to mean against or the opposite of that word. *The school is very anti-bullying.* See **prefixes**, page 351.

antibiotic (noun)
a drug that kills bacteria and cures many infections.

anticipate
anticipating anticipated (verb)
to expect something to happen and be prepared for it. *The police anticipate trouble after the match.*

anticlockwise (adverb)
in the opposite direction to the hands of a clock. **anticlockwise** (adjective).

antique
1 (noun) a very old object that is worth money because it is rare or beautiful.
2 (adjective) very old. *An antique clock.*

antiseptic (noun)
a chemical that kills germs.

antler (noun)
one of the two branched horns on a deer's head. See **deer**.

anxiety **anxieties** (noun)
a feeling of worry or fear.

anxious (adjective)
worried. *Mum gets anxious when I'm late.* **anxiously** (adverb).

any
1 *(determiner)* one, some, or several. *Do you have any butter?*
2 *(pronoun)* one, some or several of a thing that has been mentioned. *We need some ketchup, did you buy any?*
3 *(determiner)* even the smallest amount. *I don't eat any fish.*
4 *(pronoun)* even the smallest amount of a thing that has been mentioned. *I don't want any.*
5 *(determiner)* whatever or whichever. *Come over at any time.*

anybody *(pronoun)*
any person. *Can anybody help me?*

anyone *(pronoun)*
any person. *Is anyone there?*

anything *(pronoun)*
any thing. *It's so noisy, I can't hear anything. Is anything the matter?*

anyway *(adverb)*
in any case. *I never liked him anyway.*

anywhere *(adverb)*
in any place. *I've looked but I can't find my phone anywhere.*

apart *(adverb)*
If two people or things are **apart**, they are not together. *The islands are too far apart to swim between.*

ape *(noun)*
a large animal similar to a monkey, but with no tail. Chimpanzees, gorillas, gibbons and orangutans are all apes.

gibbon
chimpanzee
gorilla

types of **apes**

apologize *or* apologise
apologizing apologized *(verb)*
to say that you are sorry about something. **apology** *(noun)*, **apologetic** *(adjective)*.

apostrophe *(noun)*
the punctuation mark (**'**). It is used to show belonging, for example, "Jane's bag", or to show that letters have been missed out, for example, "can't", which is short for "cannot". *See* **punctuation**, *page 349.*

app *(noun)*
a program on a computer, tablet or phone that does a particular job. *This is an app you can use to make music.*

apparatus *(noun)*
the equipment you use to do something.

appeal **appealing appealed** *(verb)*
1 to ask for something urgently.
2 If something **appeals** to you, you like it or find it interesting.

appear
appearing appeared *(verb)*
1 to come into sight. *A bird appeared at the window.* **appearance** *(noun)*.
2 to seem. *Emily appears nervous.* **appearance** *(noun)*.

appearance *(noun)*
1 the way that you look.
2 the act of appearing or arriving somewhere. *A sudden appearance.*

appendix **appendixes** *(noun)*
a small tube inside your body.

appetite *(noun)*
a desire for food. *Joe has a big appetite.*

applaud
applauding applauded *(verb)*
to show that you like something by clapping your hands. **applause** *(noun)*.

apple *(noun)*
a round, crisp fruit that grows on a tree.

application *(noun)*
If you make an **application** for something, such as a job, you ask for it in writing. **applicant** *(noun)*.

a b c d e f g h i j k l m n o p q r s t u v w x y z

apply
applies applying applied *(verb)*
1 to ask for something in writing.
2 to affect or involve. *The rules don't apply to us.*
3 to put something on something else. *Apply the cream to your skin.*

appointment *(noun)*
a meeting with someone at a fixed time. *A dentist's appointment.*

appreciate
appreciating appreciated *(verb)*
1 to think that someone or something is good. **appreciation** *(noun)*.
2 to understand something. *I appreciate your point of view.*

apprentice *(noun)*
someone who is learning a job or skill by working with someone who has skill and experience in doing that job. *Zoe is an apprentice electrician.* **apprenticeship** *(noun)*.

approach
approaches approaching approached *(verb)*
to move nearer to someone or something. *We could hear the dogs barking as we approached the house.*

appropriate *(adjective)*
suitable, or right. *Lucie's new hairstyle is not appropriate for school.* **appropriately** *(adverb)*.

approve
approving approved *(verb)*
to think that someone or something is good or suitable. *Mum doesn't approve of these shoes.* **approval** *(noun)*.

approximate *(adjective)*
almost correct, but not exact. *We were given an approximate price.* **approximately** *(adverb)*.

apricot *(noun)*
a small, soft fruit with orange skin.

April *(noun)*
the fourth month of the year.

apron *(noun)*
a piece of clothing that you wear to protect your clothes when you are cooking, painting, and so on.

aquarium
aquariums *or* **aquaria** *(noun)*
a glass tank in which you can keep fish and other underwater animals.

Arabic *(noun)*
a language spoken by many people in the Middle East and North Africa.

arc *(noun)*
a curved line.

arcade *(noun)*
1 a row of arches in a building.
2 amusement arcade a covered area with machines, such as video games, that you pay to play on.
3 shopping arcade a covered passageway with shops or stalls.

arch **arches arching arched**
1 *(noun)* a curved part of a bridge, building, and so on.
2 *(verb)* to curve. *The cat arched its back.* **arched** *(adjective)*.

archaeology
or **archeology** *(noun)*
a way of learning about the past by digging up old buildings and objects and looking at them carefully. **archaeologist** *(noun)*, **archaeological** *(adjective)*.

archery *(noun)*
the sport of shooting at targets, using a bow and arrow. **archer** *(noun)*.

architect *(noun)*
someone who draws plans for buildings.

architecture *(noun)*
1 the study or work of designing and creating buildings.
2 the style of a particular building or group of buildings.

Arctic *(noun)*
the frozen area around the North Pole. **Arctic** *(adjective)*.

area (noun)
1 the size of a surface.
2 part of a place. *This is a beautiful area of the country.*

arena (noun)
a large area, used for sports or entertainment.

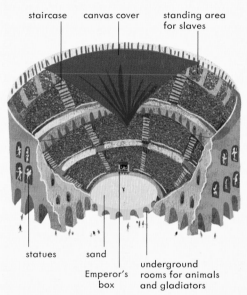

staircase   canvas cover   standing area for slaves

statues   sand   underground rooms for animals and gladiators
Emperor's box

The Roman Colosseum was used as an **arena**.

argue arguing argued (verb)
to say that you do not agree with someone, often in an angry way. *Rob and Chris were arguing about where to eat.* **argument** (noun).

arithmetic (noun)
sums with numbers. Adding, subtracting, multiplying and dividing are all types of arithmetic.

arm
1 (noun) the part of your body between your shoulder and your hand.
2 **arms** (plural noun) weapons.

armchair (noun)
a comfortable chair with supports for your arms.

armour (noun)
metal clothes worn by soldiers and knights long ago, to protect them in battle. *See* knight.

armpit (noun)
the area under your arm, where it joins your shoulder.

army armies (noun)
a large group of people trained to fight on land.

aroma (noun)
a nice smell. *The aroma of coffee.*

around
1 (preposition) surrounding, or in a circle. *All the children gathered around the magician.*
2 (preposition) in many different parts of a place. *We travelled around Spain.*
3 (adverb) more or less. *There were around 30 of us.*

arrange arranging arranged (verb)
1 to make plans for something to happen. *We arranged to meet at the cinema.* **arrangement** (noun).
2 to place things so that they look nice. *Mum arranged the flowers in the vase.* **arrangement** (noun).

arrest arresting arrested (verb)
If the police **arrest** someone, they take them to the police station. **arrest** (noun).

arrive arriving arrived (verb)
to reach a place. **arrival** (noun).

arrow (noun)
1 a sign showing the way to go.
2 a thin stick with a pointed end, which is shot from a bow.

art (noun)
1 the skill of creating something beautiful or with a special meaning, by drawing, painting, or making things with your hands.
2 the results of people being creative, including paintings, sculptures, theatre, and music.

artery arteries (noun)
one of the tubes that carry blood from your heart to all the other parts of your body.

arthritis (noun)
a disease which makes people's joints swollen and painful.

a b c d e f g h i j k l m n o p q r s t u v w x y z

article *(noun)*
1 a piece of writing in a newspaper or magazine, or on the internet. *Have you read this article about our school?*
2 an object or thing. *An article of clothing.*
3 a word, such as "a", "the", or "some", that goes in front of a noun.

artificial *(adjective)*
not real, or made by humans rather than being natural. *Artificial flowers.*

artist *(noun)*
someone who creates art, such as paintings. **artistic** *(adjective)*, **artistically** *(adverb)*.

Spelling tip   artist

Words ending with '**-ist**' often mean "**a person who does something**". For example, an "**artist**" makes art, a "**cyclist**" cycles, and a "**guitarist**" plays the guitar.

as *(conjunction)*
1 when. *The crowd watched as the plane came in to land.*
2 because. *As the electricity has gone off, we'll have to light candles.*
3 a word used in comparisons, for example, "The giant was as tall as a skyscraper".

ash ashes *(noun)*
1 the powder that is left after something has been burnt.
2 a type of large tree.

ashamed *(adjective)*
If you are **ashamed**, you feel sorry about something you have done.

ask asking asked *(verb)*
1 If you **ask** a question, you are trying to find something out.
2 If you **ask** someone for something, you try to get them to give it to you.

asleep *(adjective)*
sleeping. *"Ssshhh, the baby's asleep."*

aspirin *(noun)*
a drug that you can take to feel better if you are in pain or have a fever.

ass asses *(noun)*
a donkey.

assault *(noun)*
a violent attack against someone or something. **assault** *(verb)*.

assemble
assembling assembled *(verb)*
1 to come together in one place. *The whole school assembled in the hall.*
2 to put all the parts of something together. *Meg assembled the model car.*

assembly assemblies *(noun)*
a meeting of lots of people.

assist assisting assisted *(verb)*
If you **assist** someone, you help them. **assistance** *(noun)*.

assistant *(noun)*
1 a person who helps someone else to do a task or job. **assistance** *(noun)*.
2 someone who works in a shop.

assonance *(noun)*
the use of words with the same vowel sound in them. "Fly by in the sky" is an example of assonance.

assortment *(noun)*
a mixture of different things. **assorted** *(adjective)*.

assume assuming assumed *(verb)*
to think that something is true, without checking it. **assumption** *(noun)*.

assure assuring assured *(verb)*
to promise something, or say something positively. *Annie assured me that she would come to my party.*

asterisk *(noun)*
a mark (*) used in printing and writing.

asteroid *(noun)*
a very small planet that moves around the Sun.

asthma *(noun)*
If you have **asthma**, you sometimes have coughing fits or find it hard to breathe. **asthmatic** *(noun)*, **asthmatic** *(adjective)*.

astonish **astonishes**
astonishing astonished *(verb)*
to make someone feel very surprised.
astonishment *(noun)*.

astronaut *(noun)*
someone who travels in space.

astronomer *(noun)*
a scientist who studies the stars
and planets.

astronomy *(noun)*
the study of stars, planets, and space.

Word family

asterisk **astronaut** **astronomer** **astronomy**	These words all come from the Greek word "astron", meaning "star". An "asterisk" is a little star, and an "astronomer" studies the stars and space. The '-naut' part of "astronaut" comes from "nautes", meaning "sailor", so the word "astronaut" originally meant "star sailor".

asymmetrical *(adjective)*
A shape or picture that is **asymmetrical**
cannot be divided into two equal halves.

at *(preposition)*
1 in a place. *Rajesh is at home.*
2 when it is a particular time. *I'll meet
you at the cinema at seven o'clock.*

ate *(verb)*
the past tense of **eat**.

athlete *(noun)*
1 someone who does athletics.
2 someone who is very good at sports.
athletic *(adjective)*.

athletics *(noun)*
sports in which people run, jump,
or throw. **athletic** *(adjective)*.

atlas *(noun)*
a book of maps.

atmosphere *(noun)*
1 the mixture of gases around a planet.
2 the mood or feeling in a place. *I didn't
like the atmosphere in Alex's house.*
atmospheric *(adjective)*.

atom *(noun)*
the smallest part
of a substance.
Everything is made
up of atoms.

atom nucleus
(magnified)

electron

attach
attaches attaching
attached *(verb)*
to join or fix one thing
to another.

attachment *(noun)*
a file that you send to someone with
an email.

attack attacking attacked *(verb)*
1 to try to hurt someone or something.
attack *(noun)*, **attacker** *(noun)*.
2 to try to defeat an enemy or capture
a place where the enemy is. *The soldiers
attacked the castle.* **attack** *(noun)*.

attempt
attempting attempted *(verb)*
to try to do something. **attempt** *(noun)*.

attend attending attended *(verb)*
to go to a place or an event. *Thousands
of people attended the concert.*
attendance *(noun)*.

attention *(noun)*
1 concentration or thought.
2 the action of dealing with or taking
care of someone or something. *The cake
I'm baking needs my attention.*
3 If you **pay attention**, you concentrate
on something.
4 When soldiers **stand to attention**,
they stand up straight, with their feet
together and their arms down by
their sides.

attic *(noun)*
a room in the roof of a building.

attitude *(noun)*
your opinions and feelings about someone or something. *Aidan has a positive attitude towards his work.*

attract attracting attracted *(verb)*
1 If someone or something **attracts** you, you find them interesting or nice to look at. **attraction** *(noun)*.
2 If something **attracts** objects or people, it pulls them towards itself. *Magnets attract iron and steel.* **attraction** *(noun)*.

attractive *(adjective)*
pleasant, or pretty to look at. *My Uncle Tom lives in a very attractive little village.* **attractiveness** *(noun)*, **attractively** *(adverb)*.

auction *(noun)*
a sale where things are sold to the person who offers the most money for them. **auctioneer** *(noun)*.

audience *(noun)*
the people who watch or listen to something, such as a speech or show. *My parents are in the audience.*

audition *(noun)*
a short performance by an actor, singer, and so on, to see whether they are suitable to be in a play, concert, and so on. **audition** *(verb)*.

August *(noun)*
the eighth month of the year.

aunt *(noun)*
the sister of your mother or father, or the wife of your uncle.

auntie *or* **aunty aunties** *(noun)*
a friendly way of saying **aunt**.

author *(noun)*
the writer of a book, poem, and so on.

authority authorities
1 *(noun)* the right to do something or to tell other people what to do. *The detectives have the authority to search the house.*
2 the authorities *(plural noun)*
people, such as the police, who have a lot of power.

autistic *(adjective)*
Someone who is **autistic** has a condition that makes it difficult for them to communicate with other people, and to make sense of the way that people talk and behave. **autism** *(noun)*.

autobiography
autobiographies *(noun)*
a book that tells the story of the writer's own life. **autobiographical** *(adjective)*.

autograph *(noun)*
a famous person's signature.

automatic *(adjective)*
Something that is **automatic** works on its own, without someone controlling it. **automatically** *(adverb)*.

autumn *(noun)*
the season between summer and winter, when it gets colder and the leaves fall from the trees. **autumnal** *(adjective)*.

In **autumn**, the leaves of maple trees turn from green to reddish-gold.

available *(adjective)*
1 ready to be used or bought. **availability** *(noun)*.
2 not busy, and so free to see people. **availability** *(noun)*.

avalanche *(noun)*
a large mass of snow and ice that suddenly moves down the side of a mountain.

avenue *(noun)*
a wide road in a town or city, often with trees on either side.

average *(noun)*
1 In maths, you find an **average** by adding a group of numbers together and then dividing the total by the number of numbers you have added up. *The average of 2, 4 and 6 is 4.*
2 usual, or ordinary. *An average day.*

avocado *(noun)*
a fruit with a dark green skin and a large stone, often used in salads.

avocado cut in half
stone

avoid
avoiding avoided *(verb)*
1 to keep away from a person or place. *Avoid the cliff edge.*
2 to try to stop something from happening. *We must avoid making any mistakes.*

awake
awaking awoke awoken *(adjective)*
not asleep. *I felt wide awake after my nap.*

award *(noun)*
a prize. *Carlos got an award for his painting project.*

aware *(adjective)*
If you are **aware** of something, you know about it. *I wasn't aware that Joss had a dog.* **awareness** *(noun)*.

away *(adverb)*
1 moving from a place, person, or thing. *Rosie ran away from me.*
2 apart. *Our school is about three miles away from our house.*
3 not at home, or not present. *Lizzie is away this week.*

awesome *(adjective)*
very impressive and exciting. *That roller coaster looks awesome.*

awful *(adjective)*
terrible, or horrible. *Donna is such an awful singer.*

awkward *(adjective)*
1 difficult to do or use. *An awkward catch.* **awkwardly** *(adverb)*.
2 not able to relax and talk to people easily. *Jamie is a bit awkward.* **awkwardly** *(adverb)*.
3 causing difficulty or embarrassment. *There was an awkward silence when Danny came in.* **awkwardly** *(adverb)*.

axe axing axed
1 *(noun)* a tool with a sharp blade on the end of a long handle, used for chopping wood.
2 *(verb)* to get rid of something, or bring something to an end. *The programme will be axed after this series.*

axis axes *(noun)*
1 an imaginary line through the middle of an object, around which that object spins. *The Earth's axis.*
2 one of the two straight lines used to measure points on a graph.

> Notice that the plural of "**axis**" is irregular: "**axes**".

axle *(noun)*
a rod that goes through the centre of a wheel, so that the wheel can spin.

Aztec *(adjective)*
1 The **Aztec** people were groups of people who lived in Mexico around 600 years ago. **Aztec** *(noun)*.
2 to do with the Aztecs.

Aztec pattern

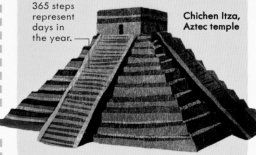
365 steps represent days in the year.

Chichen Itza, Aztec temple

The **Aztec** people are famous for their patterns and architecture.

a b c d e f g h i j k l m n o p q r s t u v w x y z

A
B
C
D
E
F
G
H
I
J
K
L
M
N
O
P
Q
R
S
T
U
V
W
X
Y
Z

Bb

babble babbling babbled *(verb)*
1 to speak really quickly, without making much sense.
2 to make the sound babies make before they can talk.

baboon *(noun)*
a large monkey that lives in Africa.

baby babies *(noun)*
a newly-born or very small child or animal. *My cousin had a baby yesterday.* **babyish** *(adjective)*.

cygnets
(baby swans)

piglets (baby pigs)

These are some **baby** animals with their parents.   **calf** (baby cow)

baby-sitter *(noun)*
someone who is paid to look after children while their parents or carers are out. **baby-sit** *(verb)*.

bachelor *(noun)*
a man who has never been married.

back backing backed
1 *(noun)* the opposite end or side to the front. *We always sit at the back of the bus.*
2 *(noun)* the rear part of your body, from your neck to your bottom.
3 *(adverb)* When a thing goes **back**, it returns to where it came from. *Our cat came back last night.*
4 *(verb)* to support someone or something. *Everyone is backing our team in the cup final.* **backing** *(noun)*.

5 If you **back down**, you admit you were wrong. *Mum never backs down.*
6 If you **back out** of something, you decide not to do it any more.

background *(noun)*
whatever is behind the main part of a picture or image. *There is a sunset in the background.*

backhand *(noun)*
a way of hitting a ball with a racket, with your arm across your body and the back of your hand facing outwards.

backpack *(noun)*
a bag you carry on your back when travelling, walking, or climbing. **backpacker** *(noun)*, **backpacking** *(noun)*.

backstroke *(noun)*
If you do the **backstroke**, you swim on your back.

backwards or **backward** *(adverb)*
1 towards the area that is behind you. *Ollie fell backwards.*
2 When you do something **backwards**, you do it in the opposite way to how it's usually done. *I can run backwards.*

bacon *(noun)*
thin, salty slices of the meat that comes from a pig.

bacteria *(plural noun)*
very small living things, some of which can make people ill. **bacterial** *(adjective)*.

bad worse worst *(adjective)*
1 not good. *I'm having a bad day.*
2 serious. *I have a bad headache.*
3 not fit to eat. *That fruit is bad.*

badge *(noun)*
a small plastic or metal sign that you wear. Badges often have pictures or messages on them.

badger badgering badgered
1 *(noun)* a wild animal with short legs, and often with stripes on its head. Badgers only come out at night.
2 *(verb)* to pester or nag someone about something. *Freya badgered her dad until he bought the comic.*

badly *(adverb)*
1 not very well. *Amy sings really badly.*
2 urgently. *I badly need some new shoes.*

badminton *(noun)*
a game in which players hit a cone-shaped object called a shuttlecock over a high net using rackets.

baffle baffling baffled *(verb)*
to confuse or puzzle someone. *The film baffled me.* **baffling** *(adjective)*, **baffled** *(adjective)*.

baggage *(noun)*
suitcases or other luggage.

baggy baggier baggiest *(adjective)*
large and loose-fitting. *Ali always wears baggy clothes.*

bait *(noun)*
a small amount of food used to tempt fish or other animals so that you can catch them.

bake baking baked *(verb)*
to cook bread, cakes or other food in an oven. **baker** *(noun)*, **bakery** *(noun)*.

balance balancing balanced
1 *(verb)* When you **balance** things, you make sure they are both equal in weight or importance. **balanced** *(adjective)*.
2 *(noun)* If you have good **balance**, you can stay steady and not wobble.

balcony balconies *(noun)*
a platform on the outside of a building, with railings around it.

bald *(rhymes with "called")*
balder baldest *(adjective)*
If you are **bald**, you have no hair on top of your head. *My dad is completely bald.*

ball *(noun)*
1 a round object, used in games such as football and golf.
2 a very smart party where people dance. *Cinderella went to the ball.* **ballroom** *(noun)*.

ballad *(noun)*
a slow song, which is usually about love.

Spelling tip   ballet

The 'et' at the end of "ballet" is pronounced 'ay': 'bal-**ay**'. This word comes from French. Other words that have this spelling pattern include "**bouquet**", "**buffet**" and "**sorbet**".

ballerina *(noun)*
a female ballet dancer.

ballet *(noun)*
1 a style of dance in which the dancers have to learn very exact movements and steps.
2 a performance that tells a story through dance and music, not words.

balloon *(noun)*
a small, coloured rubber bag that is blown up and used as a decoration.

bamboo *(noun)*
a tall plant with a hard, hollow stem.

ban banning banned *(verb)*
If you **ban** someone from doing something, you stop them from doing it. *Do you think smoking should be banned?* **ban** *(noun)*.

banana *(noun)*
a curved, yellow fruit that grows in hot places such as the Caribbean and parts of Africa. *See* **fruit**.

band *(noun)*
1 a group of people who play music together.
2 a flat, thin strip or loop of material.

bandage bandaging bandaged
1 *(noun)* a piece of cloth that you use to cover a wound.
2 *(verb)* to wrap a bandage around a wound.

bang banging banged
1 *(verb)* If you **bang** something, you hit it really hard.
2 *(noun)* a very loud noise.

bangle *(noun)*
a bracelet made of plastic or metal.

banish banishing banished *(verb)*
If you **banish** someone, you send them away and don't let them return.
banishment *(noun)*.

banister *or* **bannister** *(noun)*
the rail that you hold onto when you go up some steps or stairs.

bank banking banked
1 *(noun)* a business which looks after people's money, and also lends money.
2 *(noun)* the side of a river or canal.
3 *(verb)* If you **bank on** something happening, you rely on it doing so.

banknote *(noun)*
a piece of paper money.

banner *(noun)*
a long strip of cloth or plastic, which often has a message on it.

banquet *(noun)*
a huge feast, often held in a hall.

banter *(noun)*
friendly, teasing chat. *The pupils enjoy a bit of banter with their teacher.*

baptize *or* **baptise**
baptizing baptized *(verb)*
to make someone a member of the Christian Church in a special ceremony.
baptism *(noun)*.

bar *(noun)*
1 a long, thin metal pole.
2 a place where drinks are served, for example in a pub.
3 a flat, solid block. *A bar of chocolate.*

barbecue *or* **barbeque** *(noun)*
1 a meal of grilled meat and vegetables, cooked and eaten outside.
2 an outdoor grill used for cooking food, heated by gas or by hot coals.
barbecued *(adjective)*, **barbecue** *(verb)*.

barbed wire *(noun)*
wire with sharp spikes along it.

barber *(noun)*
someone who cuts men's and boys' hair.

bar code *(noun)*
the strip of lines and numbers printed on items in a shop, that is scanned at the till.

bare barer barest *(adjective)*
1 If you are **bare**, you have no clothes on.
2 When a room is **bare**, it is empty.

barefoot *(adjective)*
If you are **barefoot**, you are not wearing any socks or shoes.

barely *(adverb)*
only just. *We barely had enough money to pay for the meal.*

bargain bargaining bargained
1 *(noun)* something that is being sold very cheaply.
2 *(noun)* a deal, or an agreement.
3 *(verb)* to discuss prices with someone until you agree on how much something is worth.

barge barging barged
1 *(verb)* If you **barge** into someone, you bump into them roughly, or push them out of the way.
2 *(noun)* a long, flat-bottomed boat.

Ancient Egyptian royal barge

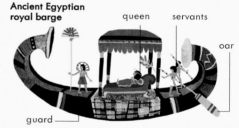
queen servants oar guard

bark *(noun)*
1 the loud sound dogs make when they are alarmed or excited. **bark** *(verb)*.
2 the rough covering on the outside of a tree.

barley *(noun)*
grains of a plant that are used to make different foods and drinks, including bread and beer.

bar mitzvah *(noun)*
a ceremony held when a Jewish boy reaches 13 years old, to celebrate that he has become an adult.

barn *(noun)*
a large farm building where crops, machinery or animals are kept.

barrel *(noun)*
1 a large container with curved sides that is used to hold liquids, such as water or beer.
2 the long part of a gun that looks like a tube.

barrier *(noun)*
a wall, fence or gate that stops things from going past it.

The Great Wall of China was built around 2,500 years ago as a **barrier** to keep out invaders.

base **basing based**
1 *(noun)* the lowest part of something. *The base of my cake was soggy.*
2 *(noun)* the place an army or business is controlled from.
3 *(verb)* If you **base** something on something else, you use it as your inspiration, or starting point. *I based my story on a dream I had.*

baseball *(noun)*
a game where two teams of nine players try to score points by hitting a ball with a bat and running around four bases.

basement *(noun)*
the part of a house that's beneath the ground floor. *My dad keeps all his tools in the basement.*

basic
1 *(adjective)* simple and straightforward. *This recipe is very basic.*
2 basics *(plural noun)* the main things you need to know or have.

basically *(adverb)*
on the whole, or essentially. *My painting is basically finished.*

basin *(noun)*
a small sink fixed to the wall, for washing your hands and face.

basket *(noun)*
a container, often with handles, which you use for storing or carrying things, such as shopping.

basketball *(noun)*
a game in which two teams try to get a ball into one of the hoops at each end of the court by bouncing and passing it.

bass **bass or basses** *(noun)*
1 *(rhymes with "case")* a musical instrument or part of a piece of music that has the lowest notes. *See* note.
2 *(rhymes with "case")* a man with a very low singing voice.
3 *(rhymes with "gas")* a kind of fish, some types of which can be eaten.

bassoon *(noun)*
a large, wooden musical instrument that you blow through to make a sound. *See* orchestra.

bat **batting batted**
1 *(noun)* a flying animal that only comes out at night.
2 *(noun)* You use a **bat** for hitting the ball in games such as cricket and baseball.
batsman *(noun)*.
3 *(verb)* to take a turn at hitting a ball and scoring points in a game. *Joe batted for over an hour.*

brown long-eared bat

South American leaf-nosed bat

Indian fruit bat (eating)

a b c d e f g h i j k l m n o p q r s t u v w x y z

batch **batches** *(noun)*
a group of things that have been made at the same time, or that arrive together. *Liz made another batch of cookies.*

bath *(noun)*
1 a large container which you fill with water, lie in, and wash yourself.
2 When you **have a bath**, you get into the bath and wash yourself.

bathe **bathing bathed** *(verb)*
to go for a swim in the sea, a pool, or a river. **bather** *(noun)*.

bathroom *(noun)*
a room in a house with a bath, shower, and sometimes a toilet in it.

bat mitzvah *(noun)*
a ceremony sometimes held when a Jewish girl reaches 12 years old, to celebrate that she has become an adult.

baton *(noun)*
1 a short, thin stick used by a conductor to help an orchestra or band play in time.
2 the piece of wood, metal or plastic which runners pass to each other in a relay race.

batter **battering battered**
1 *(verb)* If you **batter** something, you hit it over and over again.
2 *(noun)* a mixture of eggs, milk, and flour, used to make pancakes or cover food such as fish before it is fried. **battered** *(adjective)*.

battery **batteries** *(noun)*
a container of chemicals which produces electrical energy that makes things such as cars, phones, and some toys work.

battle *(noun)*
a violent fight, usually between two armies. **battlefield** *(noun)*, **battleship** *(noun)*.

bawl **bawling bawled** *(verb)*
1 to cry like a baby.
2 to shout at someone loudly and roughly. *"Get your feet off the chairs!" bawled the teacher.*

bay *(noun)*
1 a sheltered part of the coast, where the land curves inwards.
2 a special area for parking or unloading goods in a car park.
3 If you **keep something at bay**, you don't let it get too close to you. *Danny kept the big dog at bay.*

bazaar *(noun)*
a market with lots of small shops and stalls.

BBQ *(noun)* *(abbreviation)*
short for **barbeque**.

BC *(abbreviation)*
short for "Before Christ". **BC** is used to show that a date comes before the birth of Jesus Christ, or the year 0. *Julius Caesar died in 44BC.*

be **am are is; being; was were; been** *(verb)*
1 to exist. *There are no tigers in England.*
2 You use **be** when someone or something is doing something. *I am running. The monkey is sitting on the branch.*
3 to take place or happen. *My birthday is next week.*
4 You use **be** when you are describing something. *My cat is chubby. Peter is a musician.*
5 If you have **been** to a place, you have visited it. *I have been to Sweden.*

beach **beaches** *(noun)*
a strip of sand or pebbles, where the land ends and the sea begins.

bead *(noun)*
a small piece of glass, plastic or metal with a hole in the middle. Beads can be threaded onto a string to make necklaces and bracelets.

beak *(noun)*
the hard, pointed part of a bird's mouth.

beaker *(noun)*
1 a tall plastic or glass cup.
2 a plastic or glass jar used in scientific experiments.

beam **beaming beamed**
1 *(noun)* a ray of light, such as from the Sun or a car's headlights.
2 *(noun)* a long, thick piece of wood or metal, used to support the roof or floor of a building.
3 *(verb)* to smile widely.
The baby beamed at me.

bean *(noun)*
a large seed that you can eat, such as broad beans or baked beans. *Coffee beans are made into coffee.*

bear **bearing bore borne**
1 *(noun)* a big, furry wild animal.

Here are three types of **bears**:

sloth bear

Himalayan brown bear

spectacled bear

2 *(verb)* to carry or support something. **bearer** *(noun)*.
3 *(verb)* to accept a person, thing, or situation. *Mum can't bear rap music.* **bearable** *(adjective)*.
4 *(verb)* to produce something. *Apple trees bear apples.*

beard *(noun)*
hair that grows on a man's chin and cheeks.

beast *(noun)*
a fierce, uncontrollable wild animal.

beat **beating beat beaten**
1 *(verb)* to hit someone or something many times.
2 *(verb)* to win against someone.
3 *(verb)* to stir a mixture of foods quickly with a fork or whisk.
4 *(noun)* a rhythm, usually in a piece of music.

beautiful *(adjective)*
lovely, very attractive, or pleasing. *The view from the top of the hill is beautiful.* **beauty** *(noun)*, **beautifully** *(adverb)*.

beaver *(noun)*
an animal with a wide, flat tail that lives near water.

because *(conjunction)*
for the reason that. *I came over because I wanted to see you.*

become **becoming became** *(verb)*
to begin to be. *I am becoming nervous about the show.*

bed *(noun)*
1 a flat piece of furniture that you sleep on.
2 part of a garden in which you grow flowers.
3 the bottom of an ocean or river.

bedclothes *(noun)*
the duvet, or sheets and blankets, that you use on a bed.

bedding *(noun)*
1 another word for bedclothes.
2 straw, hay, and so on, used for animals to sleep on.

bedroom *(noun)*
a room in a house that people sleep in.

bedtime *(noun)*
when you usually go to bed. *Anwar's bedtime is 8 o'clock on school nights.*

Word family

bedclothes
bedroom
bedtime

These are all compound words (made up of two or more words joined together) with the root word "**bed**". Remember that none of them has a space between the words.

a b c d e f g h i j k l m n o p q r s t u v w x y z

bee – bellow

bee (noun)
a type of striped, flying insect, some of which make honey and can sting you.

beech (noun)
a tree with a pale grey trunk that loses its leaves in winter.

copper beech

beef (noun)
meat from a cow.

beehive (noun)
a wooden box where bees live. *See* hive.

been (verb)
the past participle of the verb be. *I have been sick.*

beer (noun)
a bitter-tasting alcoholic drink made with cereal grains.

beetle (noun)
a flying insect with hard wing covers.

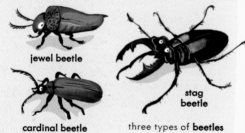
jewel beetle
cardinal beetle
stag beetle
three types of **beetles**

beetroot (noun)
a root vegetable. Most beetroots are purple. *See* vegetable.

before
1 (preposition) sooner or earlier than something else. *Take the medicine before you go to sleep.*
2 (adverb) at an earlier time. *Rob has been to Portugal before.*
beforehand (adverb).

beg begging begged (verb)
to ask someone for help or money. **beggar** (noun).

begin beginning began begun (verb)
to start. *Let's begin the game.*

Spelling tip
beginner   beginning

Remember that the final 'n' of "begin" is doubled when you add '-er' or '-ing' to make these words.

beginner (noun)
If you are a **beginner** at something, you haven't been doing it for very long.

beginning (noun)
the start. *The beginning of the lesson.*

behalf (noun)
If you do something **on behalf of** someone else, you do it for them, or in their place. *Ben apologized on behalf of Tessa.*

behave behaving behaved (verb)
how you act or do things. *Melanie behaved badly at school.* **behaviour** (noun).

behind
1 (preposition) on the other side of something. *My bag is behind the door.*
2 (adverb) after, or in a lower position. *Isaac had to stay behind after the lesson.*
3 (preposition) not keeping up. *I'm behind with my homework.*

beige (noun)
a pale brown colour. **beige** (adjective).

being (verb)
part of the verb be. *You are being silly.*

believe believing believed (verb)
If you **believe in** something, you are sure it is true, or good. **belief** (noun), **believer** (noun), **believable** (adjective).

bell (noun)
a metal object that makes a ringing sound when you hit or shake it.

bellow bellowing bellowed (verb)
If you **bellow** at someone, you shout at them using a loud, deep voice.

belly bellies *(noun)*
a friendly word for **stomach**.

belong belonging belonged *(verb)*
1 If something **belongs to** you, you own it. *The purple hat belongs to Aunt Betty.*
2 to be a member of a group. *I belong to a choir.*
3 to be in its proper place. *That plate belongs on this shelf.*

belongings *(plural noun)*
the things that someone owns.

beloved *(adjective)*
much loved. *Tom is my beloved brother.*

below *(preposition)*
1 lower than. *My score was below Lee's.*
2 in a lower place than. *Press the button below the screen to turn it off.*

belt *(noun)*
a strip of leather or material that you wear around your waist.

bench benches *(noun)*
a long seat, often made of wood, that several people can sit on.

bend bending bent
1 *(verb)* If you **bend** something, you change its shape, usually by making it curved.
2 *(verb)* If something **bends**, it becomes curved.
3 *(verb)* If you **bend down** or **bend over**, you lean over from your waist.
4 *(noun)* a curve. *There are lots of bends in this road.*

beneath *(preposition)*
If something is **beneath** something else, it is under it. *The cow is sleeping beneath the tree.*

berry
berries *(noun)*
a small, often round fruit which grows on some trees and bushes. Many berries can be eaten, and have a sweet taste.

edible berries

raspberries

strawberry

bilberries

beside *(preposition)*
next to, or at the side of. *My aunt lives beside the sea.*

besides
1 *(preposition)* apart from. *I have no pets besides my goldfish.*
2 *(adverb)* also. *I didn't like the food. Besides, the waiter was rude.*

best
1 *(adjective)* better than anyone or anything else. *Mel's the best singer here.*
2 *(noun)* the thing or person that is better than anyone or anything else.

bet betting bet *(verb)*
1 When you **bet**, you win money if you guess the result of a race, competition or game correctly. If you guess wrongly, you lose all of your money. **bet** *(noun)*.
2 to think something is very likely to happen. *I bet the dog will find that bone.*
3 to dare someone to do something. *I bet you can't eat that whole cake.*

betray betraying betrayed *(verb)*
If you **betray** someone, you let them down, or help their enemies. **betrayal** *(noun)*.

better *(adjective)*
1 of a higher quality or standard than something else. *This book is better than that one.*
2 not ill anymore. *Sophie is better now.*

between *(preposition)*
1 with people or things on either side. *I stood between Jack and Liam.*
2 from one to the other. *We passed the jar of sweets between us.*
3 somewhere in the middle of two points in time, or two points on a scale. *It'll take between two and three hours.*

beware *(verb)*
If someone tells you to **beware of** something, they warn you to be careful, as it could be dangerous.

beyond *(preposition)*
1 on the far side of something. *The lake is beyond those trees.*
2 If you say something is **beyond** you, you mean that you find it too difficult.

a b c d e f g h i j k l m n o p q r s t u v w x y z

biased (*by*–ust) (*adjective*)
If you are **biased**, you think one person, team or opinion is better than the other.

Bible (*noun*)
the holy book of the Christian religion.

biceps (*noun*)
the muscle that runs along the top of your upper arm.

bicycle (*noun*)
a machine you ride on and which moves when you push on two pedals with your feet. *See* mountain bike.

big **bigger biggest** (*adjective*)
1 large. *Holly has a big dog.*
2 important. *Pollution is a big problem.*
3 older. *Finn is my big brother.*

bike (*noun*)
short for bicycle.

bikini (*noun*)
a swimming costume for girls and women that is in two pieces.

bilingual (*adjective*)
If someone is **bilingual**, they can speak two languages very well.

bill (*noun*)
1 a piece of paper with how much money you owe on it, for example in a restaurant.
2 a bird's beak.

bin (*noun*)
a container for rubbish.

bind **binding bound** (*verb*)
to tie things together tightly.

binoculars (*plural noun*)
two metal and glass tubes that you look through, which make things that are far away look nearer.

biodegradable (*adjective*)
Something that is **biodegradable** can be broken down by bacteria, so it doesn't cause pollution.

biography **biographies** (*noun*)
a book that tells someone's life story.
biographer (*noun*),
biographical (*adjective*).

biology (*noun*)
the study of living things, such as plants and animals. People who study biology are called biologists.

bird (*noun*)
an animal that has wings, feathers, and a beak. Most birds can fly.

some different kinds of **birds**

peach-faced lovebird

herring gull

black woodpecker

goldfinch

red and green macaw

flamingo

birch **birches** (*noun*)
a tree which loses its leaves in winter and has thin, peeling bark.

birth (*noun*)
1 the time when a baby comes out of its mother's body.
2 When a woman or female animal **gives birth**, she has a baby.

birthday (*noun*)
the day on which you were born, which people usually celebrate.
My birthday is on 15th December.

biscuit (*noun*)
a small, thin cake which has been baked until it is crunchy.

bishop (*noun*)
1 a senior priest in the Christian Church.
2 a piece in the game of chess.

bison (*noun*)
a large, wild animal that looks a bit like a cow and is covered with shaggy hair.

bit
1 *(noun)* a small amount or piece of something.
2 *(noun)* the smallest piece of information in a computer's memory.
3 *(verb)* the past tense of bite.

bite biting bit bitten *(verb)*
1 If you **bite** something, you use your teeth to cut or break off a piece of it. **bite** *(noun)*.
2 If a venomous snake or insect **bites** you, it shoots venom into your body with its fangs. **bite** *(noun)*.

bitter *(adjective)*
1 tasting sharp and slightly sour. *Coffee has a bitter flavour.*
2 upset and annoyed. *Bob was bitter about coming second.* **bitterly** *(adverb)*.
3 very cold. *A bitter wind.*
bitterness *(noun)*, **bitterly** *(adverb)*.

black
1 *(noun)* the darkest of all colours, the colour of the night sky. **black** *(adjective)*.
2 *(adjective)* Someone who is **black** has naturally dark-coloured skin.

blackberry
blackberries *(noun)*
a dark purple fruit that grows wild.

blackberries

blackbird *(noun)*
a wild bird with black feathers and a yellow beak.

bladder *(noun)*
the place in your body where waste liquid is stored before you wee it out.

blade *(noun)*
1 the sharp edge of a knife or tool, used for cutting things.
2 a single piece of grass.

blame blaming blamed *(verb)*
If you **blame** someone for something, you say it is their fault. *I blame Gary for the accident.* **blame** *(noun)*.

bland blander blandest *(adjective)*
If a food is **bland**, it doesn't have much flavour.

blank blanker blankest *(adjective)*
If a page is **blank**, it has nothing written, drawn or printed on it.

blanket *(noun)*
1 a warm cover that you can spread over your bed.
2 a layer or coating. *The ground was covered with a blanket of snow.*

blare blaring blared *(verb)*
to make a loud, annoying noise. *The car alarm blared.*

blast blasting blasted
1 *(noun)* a loud explosion.
2 *(noun)* a sudden rush of air.
3 *(verb)* When a rocket or spacecraft **blasts off**, it takes off.

blaze blazing blazed *(verb)*
to burn very fiercely. **blaze** *(noun)*.

blazer *(noun)*
a type of smart jacket. *Some school uniforms include a blazer.*

bleach
bleaches bleaching bleached
1 *(noun)* a chemical that kills germs, and makes things go white.
2 *(verb)* to make something go paler, or white. *The sun in Greece bleached my hair.*

bleed bleeding bled *(verb)*
to lose blood, either inside your body or through a wound.

blend blending blended *(verb)*
to mix things together. **blender** *(noun)*.

bless blessing blessed
1 *(verb)* to ask God to look after someone or something. **blessing** *(noun)*.
2 *(interjection)* Some people say **bless you** when someone has sneezed.

blew *(verb)*
the past tense of blow.

blind
1 *(adjective)* A **blind** person or animal can't see anything. **blindness** *(noun)*.
2 *(noun)* a covering of material or strips of metal or wood that you pull down over a window.

blink – blush

blink blinking blinked *(verb)*
to quickly shut your eyes and open them again.

blister *(noun)*
a sore bubble of skin with liquid inside, made by something rubbing on it or from contact with heat. *My new shoes gave me blisters.*

blizzard *(noun)*
a heavy snowstorm.

blob *(noun)*
a small lump of something soft. *A blob of cream.*

block blocking blocked
1 *(noun)* a large piece of something hard. *A block of cheese.*
2 *(verb)* to stop something from passing or from happening. *The broken-down bus blocked the road.*

blog blogging blogged
1 *(noun)* a short word for "web log", which is an online diary.
2 *(verb)* to write a blog. **blogger** *(noun).*

blond or **blonde** *(adjective)*
Blond people have pale yellow hair.

blood *(noun)*
the red liquid that is pumped around your body by your heart.

bloom blooming bloomed
1 *(noun)* a single flower.
2 *(verb)* When a plant **blooms**, its flowers come out.

blossom *(noun)*
the flowers that appear on some fruit trees before the fruit grows.

cherry blossom (cutaway)

seed

This part becomes the fruit.

blotch blotches *(noun)*
a stain or mark. **blotchy** *(adjective).*

blouse *(noun)*
a shirt that girls or women wear.

blow blowing blew blown
1 *(verb)* to puff air out of your mouth.
2 *(verb)* to move in the wind. *The trees were blowing from side to side.*
3 *(noun)* a disappointment. *It was a blow not to get through to the finals.*
4 If something **blows up**, it explodes.

blue bluer bluest
1 *(noun)* the colour of the sky on a sunny day. **blue** *(adjective).*
2 *(adjective)* another word for **sad**. *I feel blue.*

bluebell *(noun)*
a small, blue wildflower that grows in woodlands.

bluff bluffing bluffed *(verb)*
to pretend you are going to do something when you aren't really. *David said he would tell Mum, but I knew he was only bluffing.*

blunt blunter bluntest *(adjective)*
1 not sharp. *This knife is blunt.*
2 If you are **blunt**, you say things without thinking about how others might feel. **bluntness** *(noun),* **bluntly** *(adverb).*

blur blurring blurred
1 *(verb)* to make something unclear, or smudge it. **blurred** *(adjective).*
2 *(noun)* a shape you can't see very clearly.

blurb *(noun)*
the words on the back of a book, DVD, packet, and so on, written to make people want to buy it.

blurt blurting blurted *(verb)*
to say something quickly, without thinking about it.

blush
blushes blushing blushed *(verb)*
When you **blush**, your face goes red, usually because you're ashamed or embarrassed.

board **boarding boarded**
1 *(verb)* to get onto a ship, train, or plane.
2 *(noun)* a flat piece of card or wood.

boarding school *(noun)*
a school where the students eat and sleep at the school instead of going home after lessons.

boast **boasting boasted** *(verb)*
If you **boast**, you tell everyone how good you are at something. **boast** *(noun)*, **boastful** *(adjective)*.

boat *(noun)*
a small vessel which you ride in to get across water.

four different types of **boats**

raft

sailing boat

motor

rudder

motor boat

paddle

canoe

bob **bobbing bobbed** *(verb)*
When something **bobs** on water, it floats and moves up and down gently.

body **bodies** *(noun)*
1 all the parts a person or animal is made of, including their head, limbs, organs, and skin.
2 a dead animal or person.

bodyguard *(noun)*
someone who is paid to protect a famous or important person from being attacked.

bog *(noun)*
a muddy, wet area of ground.

boil **boiling boiled** *(verb)*
1 When a liquid **boils**, it reaches such a high temperature that it starts to bubble.
2 When you **boil** something, you cook it in boiling water.

boisterous *(adjective)*
If you are **boisterous**, you enjoy rough, noisy games. **boisterously** *(adverb)*.

bold **bolder boldest** *(adjective)*
1 very brave and confident. *It was very bold of Kay to stand up to the teacher.* **boldly** *(adverb)*, **boldness** *(noun)*.
2 **Bold** text is thicker and darker than normal, **like this.**

bolt **bolting bolted**
1 *(verb)* If you **bolt** a door, you slide a metal bar across the back of it to keep it closed.
2 *(verb)* to run away suddenly. *The horse bolted.*
3 *(noun)* a thick metal pin for fixing things together.

bomb *(noun)*
a weapon that explodes.

bone *(noun)*
the hard, white parts in your body that form your skeleton. **bony** *(adjective)*. *See* **skeleton**.

bonfire *(noun)*
a large outdoor fire, often for burning garden waste.

bonnet *(noun)*
1 the metal covering over a car or truck's engine.
2 an old-fashioned hat, tied on with ribbons.

bonus **bonuses** *(noun)*
an extra, unexpected reward or treat. *We got a bonus game at bowling.*

book **booking booked**
1 *(noun)* a set of pages of writing joined together inside a cover.
2 *(verb)* to keep or reserve something. *Liz booked theatre tickets for us.*

a b c d e f g h i j k l m n o p q r s t u v w x y z

boost boosting boosted

1 (verb) When you **boost** something, you increase it, making it bigger or better. **booster** (noun).
2 (noun) If something gives you a **boost**, it makes you feel happier. *Seeing my Gran gave me a real boost.*

boot (noun)

1 a type of tough shoe that covers your foot and part of your leg.
2 the place in the back of a car where you can put things such as shopping or luggage.

border (noun)

1 the line that marks where one country or area ends and another one begins.
2 a narrow strip along the edge of something. *There's a white border around this page.*

bore boring bored (verb)

1 When someone or something **bores** you, you don't find them interesting at all. **boredom** (noun), **bored** (adjective), **boring** (adjective).
2 to drill a hole. *The workers bored into the rock.*
3 the past tense of **bear**.

born (adjective)

When someone is **born**, they come out of their mother's body and start their life.

borrow borrowing borrowed (verb)

to use something that belongs to someone else for a while, with their permission. *I borrowed Carl's book.*

boss bosses (noun)

the person in charge. *At home, Mum is boss.* **bossy** (adjective), **bossily** (adverb).

Spelling tip

Words that end with hissing sounds, such as '-s', '-ss', '-ch', '-tch', '-tz', '-x' or '-z', add '-es' in the plural.

boss → bosses

Can you spot any more words on these pages that follow this pattern?

both

1 (adjective) two of the same things. *I like both dresses.*
2 (pronoun) two things which have already been mentioned. *Which dress do I like? Both.*

bother bothering bothered (verb)

1 If something **bothers** you, you are annoyed about it. *The mess really bothered me.*
2 If you **can't be bothered** to do something, you don't feel like making the effort to do it. *I couldn't be bothered to go swimming.*

bottle (noun)

a tall glass or plastic container for holding liquid.

bottom (noun)

1 the lowest part of something. *There are some beans left in the bottom of the tin.*
2 the part of your body that you sit on.

bought (verb)

the past tense of **buy**.

boulder (noun)

a big rock.

bounce bouncing bounced (verb)

1 If something **bounces**, it springs back when it hits something hard.
2 to jump up and down again and again, usually on something springy.

bouncy

bouncier bounciest (adjective)
Something is **bouncy** if it springs back when you touch it.

bound bounding bounded

1 (verb) to leap. *The deer bounded away.*
2 (adjective) If something is **bound** to happen, it sure to do so. *Our teacher is bound to be cross.*
3 (verb) the past tense of **bind**.

boundary boundaries (noun)

a line which shows where the edges of an area or a piece of land are.

bouquet (boo-**kay**) (noun)

a big bunch of flowers.

bow bowing bowed
1 *(rhymes with "cow") (verb)*
to bend at the waist in front of an
important person, or at the end of a
show you have been performing in.
2 *(rhymes with "low") (noun)*
a knot made by looping ribbons,
laces, or string.
3 *(rhymes with "low") (noun)*
a weapon used for firing arrows.
4 *(rhymes with "low") (noun)*
a piece of wood with
horse hair stretched
across it, used for
playing violins,
cellos, and other
stringed instruments.
5 *(rhymes with "cow")*
(noun) the front of a ship.

violin

bow

bowl bowling bowled
1 *(noun)* a deep, open dish.
2 *(verb)* to throw a ball in games
such as cricket or baseball. *Eddie's
going to bowl first.* **bowler** *(noun)*.

bowling *(noun)*
a sport or activity that involves throwing
or rolling a ball towards a target.
Different types of bowling include
ten-pin bowling, bowls, and boules.

box boxes *(noun)*
a container with straight sides, often
made from cardboard.

boxers *(plural noun)*
men's underpants that are like shorts.

boxing *(noun)*
a sport in which two fighters wear
padded gloves and punch each other.
boxer *(noun)*.

boy *(noun)*
a male child.

boyfriend *(noun)*
the boy or man that someone is going
out with.

bra *(noun)*
a piece of clothing that many women
wear under their clothes, to support
their breasts.

bracelet *(noun)*
a piece of jewellery you wear
around your wrist.

braces *(plural noun)*
a wire frame fitted onto teeth
to straighten them.

bracket *(noun)*
Brackets are the punctuation marks ( ).
You use brackets to add extra
information when you are writing, for
example, "My dog (a golden retriever
called Sandy) loves to swim."

brag bragging bragged *(verb)*
to talk a lot about your achievements
in a boastful way.

Braille *(noun)*
a way of writing that uses raised dots,
so that blind people can feel them with
their fingers to read.

b   r   a   i   l   l   e

Each **Braille** letter is a different pattern of dots.

brain *(noun)*
the soft organ inside your head that
controls all your thoughts and movements.

brake braking braked *(verb)*
When you **brake**, you slow down
or stop the vehicle you are driving.
brake *(noun)*.

branch
branches branching branched
1 *(noun)* the part of a tree that grows
sideways out of its trunk.
2 *(noun)* a shop that is part of a big
chain of stores.
3 *(verb)* to split into two or more.
The road branches here.

brand *(noun)*
a particular product, or make
of thing.

brass *(noun)*
1 a yellowish metal.
2 musical instruments made of brass.
See orchestra.

a b c d e f g h i j k l m n o p q r s t u v w x y z

brave braver bravest (adjective)
If you are **brave**, you are not afraid
of doing difficult or dangerous things.
bravery (noun), **bravely** (adverb).

bread (noun)
a food made with flour
and baked in an oven.

different types
of **bread** from
around the
world

cornbread

rye
bread

bagel

pretzel

ciabatta

tortillas

tiger
bread

baguette

breadth (noun)
how wide something is.

break breaking broke broken (verb)
1 If you **break** something, you damage
it so that it's in pieces or won't work.
2 If you **break** a promise, you don't
keep it.
3 break down to stop working.

breakdown (noun)
If a car or other vehicle has a
breakdown, it stops working.

breakfast (noun)
the first meal you eat in the morning.

breakthrough (noun)
a sudden and very important discovery.

breast (noun)
a fleshy part on the front of a woman's
body, which can make milk for a baby.

breaststroke (noun)
a swimming stroke where you swim on
your front and move your arms in circles.

Spelling tip

breath   breathe

Be careful not to mix up "**breath**"
(noun) with "**breathe**" (verb). Try
remembering that there is an '**e**' at
the end of "**breathe**" because it is a
verb, whereas there is no '**e**' in "**noun**".

breath (noun)
1 air that you take into your lungs
and then let out again.
2 If you are **out of breath**, you are
finding it hard to breathe.
3 If you say something **under your
breath**, you say it very quietly.

breathe breathing breathed (verb)
to take air in and out of your lungs.

breathtaking (adjective)
If something is **breathtaking**,
it is very beautiful or impressive.
The view was breathtaking.

breed breeding bred
1 (noun) a type of animal. *What's
your favourite breed of dog?*
2 (verb) to have babies or young.

breeze (noun)
a gentle wind. **breezy** (adjective).

bribe bribing bribed (verb)
to dishonestly try to persuade someone
to do something for you, by offering
them money or other things.
bribe (noun).

brick (noun)
a hard block of baked clay, used
for building.

bride (noun)
a woman who is going to get married
soon, or has just got married.
bridal (adjective).

bridegroom (noun)
a man who is going to get married soon,
or has just got married. Bridegroom is
often shortened to "groom".

A
B
C
D
E
F
G
H
I
J
K
L
M
N
O
P
Q
R
S
T
U
V
W
X
Y
Z

bridesmaid *(noun)*
a girl or woman who helps a bride on her wedding day.

bridge *(noun)*
a link across a river, railway or road, so that people can get to the other side.

suspension bridge

cantilever bridge

beam bridge

arch bridge

brief **briefer briefest** *(adjective)*
not lasting very long. **briefly** *(adverb)*.

briefcase *(noun)*
a small case with a handle, that is used for carrying books, papers, and so on.

bright **brighter brightest** *(adjective)*
1 A **bright** light shines very clearly. **brightness** *(noun)*, **brightly** *(adverb)*.
2 A **bright** colour is strong and easy to see.
3 If the weather is **bright**, it is sunny.
4 A **bright** person is clever.
5 If you are feeling **bright**, you are happy and cheerful. **brightly** *(adverb)*.

brilliant *(adjective)*
1 excellent. *Faye is a brilliant actor.*
2 very bright. *A brilliant light.*

brim *(noun)*
1 the top of a cup or glass.
2 the edge of a hat, that sticks out from your head.

bring **bringing brought** *(verb)*
1 If you **bring** someone or something with you, they are with you when you arrive.
2 **bring in** to introduce something new.
3 **bring up** to start talking about a subject in a conversation.
4 **bring up** to care for a child until they can look after themselves.

brisk **brisker briskest** *(adjective)*
quick. *A brisk walk around the park.*

bristle *(noun)*
a short, stiff hair. **bristly** *(adjective)*.

brittle *(adjective)*
easily snapped or broken.

broad **broader broadest** *(adjective)*
wide. **broadly** *(adverb)*, **broaden** *(verb)*.

broadband *(noun)*
a way of sending large amounts of information through a single wire between computers, telephones, and televisions.

broadcast **broadcasting broadcast** *or* **broadcasted**
1 *(noun)* a television or radio programme.
2 *(verb)* to transmit a radio or television programme.

broccoli *(noun)*
a green vegetable with tree-shaped heads on stalks.

floret

stem or stalk

broccoli

brochure
(bro-sure) (noun)
a leaflet or book with information about something.

broke
1 *(verb)* the past tense of **break**.
2 *(adjective)* If you are **broke**, you have no money.

broken *(adjective)*
1 in pieces, or not working properly.
2 the past participle of **break**.

bronze *(noun)*
1 a reddish-brown metal.
2 If you get a **bronze medal**, it means that you came third in a competition.

a b c d e f g h i j k l m n o p q r s t u v w x y z

brooch brooches (noun)
a piece of jewellery you can pin to your clothes.

brook (noun)
a small stream.

broom (noun)
a brush with a long handle for sweeping floors.

brother (noun)
Your **brother** is a boy or man who has the same parents as you. **brotherly** (adjective).

brought (verb)
the past tense of **bring**.

brown (noun)
1 the colour of soil. **brown** (adjective).
2 **Brown bread** is made with the whole wheat grain, and is a darker colour than white bread.

browse browsing browsed (verb)
1 to look at something in a relaxed way.
2 to search for something on the internet. *Abby browsed the web to find the perfect bag.* **browser** (noun).

bruise (noun)
a dark mark that appears on your skin when you have been hit or hurt yourself. **bruised** (adjective), **bruise** (verb).

brush brushes brushing brushed
1 (noun) a tool with bristles which can be used for cleaning, painting, and so on.
2 (verb) to use a brush for sweeping up, cleaning teeth, and so on.
3 (verb) to touch very lightly. *Robert's hand brushed against me.*

brutal (adjective)
cruel and violent. **brutality** (noun).

bubble bubbling bubbled
1 (noun) a small ball of gas or air inside a liquid.
2 (verb) to make bubbles. *The water bubbled.* **bubbly** (adjective).

bucket (noun)
a container with a handle, usually used for carrying liquids.

buckle (noun)
the metal fastening on a shoe or bag.

bud (noun)
a small shoot on a plant that opens into a leaf or a flower.

Buddha (noun)
the name given to the teacher who started the Buddhist faith.

Buddhism (noun)
the religion of the followers of Buddha. **Buddhist** (noun), **Buddhist** (adjective).

statue of **Buddha**

Buddhism began 2,500 years ago and now has 350 million followers. Buddhists try to achieve **Enlightenment** (knowing the truth about life) by leading good lives and **meditating**. When Buddhists meditate, they clear their minds of everyday thoughts and reach a state of deep relaxation and concentration.

budge budging budged (verb)
to move. *William won't budge from the sofa.*

budgerigar or **budgie** (noun)
a small, brightly-coloured bird, often kept as a pet.

budget (noun)
the amount of money that's available to spend on something. *My daily budget for food is £4.* **budget** (verb).

buffalo buffalo or **buffaloes** (noun)
a type of ox with big, curved horns.

African buffalo   Asian water buffalo

buffet (buff-ay) (noun)
a selection of food, laid out so that people can help themselves.

bug bugging bugged
1 (noun) an insect.
2 (noun) an illness that's not serious. *Reshma has a tummy bug.*
3 (noun) a small problem in a computer program.
4 (verb) If someone **bugs** you, they annoy you.

buggy buggies (noun)
1 a pushchair for a young child.
2 a small vehicle, often with an open top. *A beach buggy.*

build building built (verb)
1 to make something, using other things such as stone, bricks, or wood. *We built a den in the woods.* **builder** (noun).
2 If something **builds up**, it gets bigger, stronger, or greater in number.

building (noun)
a structure, for example a house, church, or block of flats.

built-up (adjective)
An area that is **built-up** has lots of buildings in it.

bulb (noun)
1 the part of an electric light or lamp that light shines from.

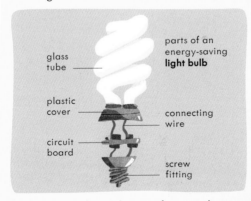

glass tube

parts of an energy-saving **light bulb**

plastic cover

connecting wire

circuit board

screw fitting

2 the onion-shaped part of some plants, that grows underground.

bulge bulging bulged (verb)
to swell outwards. *Mark's tummy bulged from all the cake.* **bulge** (noun).

Spelling tip   bulky

You have to **remove the 'y'** from words that end with a consonant and a 'y', such as "bulky", when you add '–ier' or '–iest': "bulkier", "bulkiest".

bulk (noun)
the main part of something. *We have finished the bulk of the gardening.*

bulky bulkier bulkiest (adjective)
big, and difficult to carry. *Please could you help me carry these bulky boxes?*

bull (noun)
a male cow, seal, whale, or elephant.

bulldozer (noun)
a powerful machine with a big blade fixed to the front that pushes earth and rocks away.

bullet (noun)
a small piece of metal that is fired from a gun.

bully bullies bullying bullied (verb)
to be unkind, and pick on other people. **bully** (noun).

bump bumping bumped
1 (verb) to knock into something by accident.
2 (noun) a lump or swelling.
3 (verb) If you **bump into** someone, you meet them by chance.

bumpy
bumpier bumpiest (adjective)
If something is **bumpy**, it has lots of ups and downs in it.

bun (noun)
1 a small, round cake or piece of bread.
2 hair fastened in a round shape on the top or back of someone's head.

bunch bunches (noun)
a group of things, such as flowers or grapes.

bundle (noun)
several things that are wrapped up together, often with string.

a b c d e f g h i j k l m n o p q r s t u v w x y z

bungalow – butcher

A
B
C
D
E
F
G
H
I
J
K
L
M
N
O
P
Q
R
S
T
U
V
W
X
Y
Z

Spelling tip boy buoy

The word "**buoy**" sounds the same as "**boy**". Remember, a "**buoy**" shows where things are underwater.

buoy

bungalow *(noun)*
a house without any upstairs rooms.

bunk *(noun)*
a bed with another bed above or below it.

bunting *(noun)*
little flags and other decorations, usually used at outdoor celebrations.

buoy *(noun)*
a floating marker, which shows where something is in the sea.

burden burdening burdened
1 *(noun)* a heavy load that has to be carried.
2 *(verb)* to weigh someone down with a heavy load or responsibility.

burglar *(noun)*
someone who breaks into another person's house, and steals their things. **burglary** *(noun)*, **burgle** *(verb)*.

burn burning burned *or* **burnt**
1 *(verb)* to damage or destroy something with heat or fire. *I burnt my hand on the kettle.*
2 *(noun)* a sore part of your skin, or a mark on something, caused by heat or fire.

burp burping burped *(verb)*
to let gas from your tummy out of your mouth, making a loud noise. **burp** *(noun)*.

burrow burrowing burrowed
1 *(noun)* a tunnel or hole under the ground where animals such as rabbits live.
2 *(verb)* to dig your way along, under the ground. *Moles have burrowed under our lawn.*

burst bursting burst
1 *(verb)* to pop or explode. *The balloon suddenly burst.*
2 *(noun)* a sudden rush. *Grace had a burst of energy.*

bury burying buried *(verb)*
1 to put something in a hole in the ground and cover it over. *The dog buried the bone.*
2 to put a dead body into the ground. **burial** *(noun)*.

bus buses *(noun)*
a large vehicle used for carrying lots of people around.

bush bushes *(noun)*
a plant with lots of leaves that looks like a small tree.

bushy bushier bushiest *(adjective)*
If something is **bushy**, it grows thickly. *Simon has bushy hair.*

business businesses *(noun)*
1 the kind of work a person does. *Dad is in the travel business.*
2 a company or shop that sells or supplies certain things. *A stationery business.*
3 If something is **none of your business**, it has nothing to do with you. *It is none of your business where I am going now.*

busker *(noun)*
someone who performs on the street for money.

bustle bustling bustled *(verb)*
to rush around, doing things. *Aunty Gina bustled around the kitchen.*

bustling *(adjective)*
busy. *The town has a bustling market.*

busy busier busiest *(adjective)*
If you are **busy**, you've got lots to do. **busily** *(adverb)*.

but *(conjunction)*
however. *I want to play hockey, but I've hurt my knee.*

butcher *(noun)*
someone who cuts up and sells meat.

butter *(noun)*
a smooth, yellow, fatty food made from cream. Butter can be spread on bread and used in cooking. **buttery** *(adjective)*.

buttercup *(noun)*
a small, yellow wildflower.

butterfly **butterflies** *(noun)*
an insect with brightly-coloured wings.

buttocks *(plural noun)*
the two rounded parts of your bottom.

button *(noun)*
1 a hard piece of plastic or metal sewn onto clothes to help you fasten them.
2 something that you press to turn a machine on and off, or to make something happen.

buy **buying bought** *(verb)*
to get something by paying money for it.

buzz **buzzes buzzing buzzed** *(verb)*
to make a low humming noise, like a bee does. **buzz** *(noun)*.

by *(preposition)*
1 near. *We live by the park.*
2 travelling in. *We're going by plane.*
3 You use **by** to say that someone did or made something. *The sandwiches were eaten by the children. This song is by Mozart.*

byte *(noun)*
A computer's memory is measured in **bytes.**

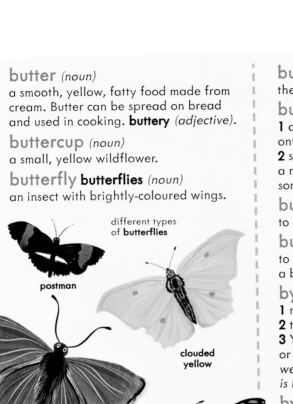

different types of **butterflies**

postman

clouded yellow

common blue

monarch

red admiral

peacock

tiger swallowtail

forewing

antenna

large white

head

meadow brown

orange tip

hindwing

high brown fritillary

proboscis (tongue)

a b c d e f g h i j k l m n o p q r s t u v w x y z

Cc

cab *(noun)*
1 the part of a lorry or other road vehicle where the driver sits.
2 another word for **taxi**, used especially in the US.

cabbage *(noun)*
a round vegetable with large leaves.

cabin *(noun)*
1 a room in a boat or on a ship.
2 a small house or hut.

cabinet *(noun)*
1 a piece of furniture with doors and shelves.
2 the Cabinet the most important people in the British government, chosen by the Prime Minister.

cable *(noun)*
1 a strong metal rope.
2 a wire that carries electricity, or telephone, television or computer signals.

cactus
cacti or **cactuses** *(noun)*
a plant that grows in dry places, can survive for a long time without water, and can be covered with spikes.

saguaro cactus

café *(noun)*
a place where you can buy hot drinks and simple meals.

caffeine *(noun)*
the substance in coffee and in some fizzy drinks that makes you feel wide awake and alert.

Spelling tip   caffeine

Watch out, because this word does not follow the spelling guideline: 'i' before 'e' except after 'c', where the letters make an 'ee' sound.

cage *(noun)*
a box of metal bars or wire, where you can keep birds or animals to stop them from escaping.

cake *(noun)*
a sweet, baked food, usually made with butter, sugar, flour, and eggs.

calcium *(noun)*
a substance, found in milk and dairy products, that is essential for healthy bones and teeth.

calculate
calculating calculated *(verb)*
to work something out, especially the answer to a maths problem, using facts and knowledge. *I calculated that Max would reach home ten minutes before I did.* **calculation** *(noun)*.

calculator *(noun)*
a small electronic machine that you can use to find the answers to maths problems.

calendar *(noun)*
a chart or list of days and dates, used to help plan future events.

calf calves *(noun)*
1 a young animal, most often a cow. *See* **baby**.
2 the part at the back of your leg, between your knee and your foot.

call calling called
1 *(verb)* to give something a name, or to describe someone as something. *Grandma called me a cheeky monkey.*
2 *(verb)* to get someone's attention or speak to them loudly. *Steven called to his friend across the street.*
3 *(verb)* to telephone someone. *Call me when you get to the station.*
4 *(noun)* a telephone conversation. *I had a call from my friend in Spain.*
5 *(noun)* a loud cry, or the noise an animal or bird makes.
6 If you **call someone back**, you telephone them to return a call that they made to you earlier.
7 If you **call something off**, you cancel it. *We had to call off the fun run.*

calm **calmer calmest**

1 (adjective) If someone is **calm**, they are quiet and unemotional. **calm** (noun), **calmly** (adverb).
2 (adjective) If the sea or weather is **calm**, it is peaceful and not very windy.
3 If you **calm down**, you become less excited or angry than you were before.

calorie (noun)

a measure of energy, especially the energy that you can get from food.

came (verb)

the past tense of come.

camel (noun)

a large animal, with four legs and one or two humps on its back, that can go for a long time without drinking.

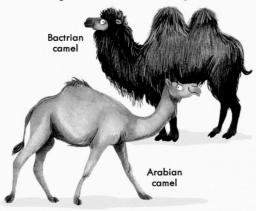

Bactrian camel

Arabian camel

camera (noun)

a machine that takes photographs, or records film or video.

These examples show how **cameras** have changed since they were first invented.

dry plate 1850s

box Brownie 1900s

medium format 1930s

35mm SLR 1940s

digital camera 2000s

camouflage (noun)

a pattern, either on an animal or on soldiers' uniforms and equipment, that makes it hard to be seen against its background. *A tiger's stripes act as camouflage.* **camouflage** (verb).

camp **camping camped** (verb)

to stay in a place for a short time, especially in a tent in the countryside. **camping** (noun), **camp** (noun).

campaign

campaigning campaigned (verb)
to try very hard to do something, or to get something done. *We campaigned to keep our local library open.* **campaign** (noun).

can **could** (verb)

1 to be able to do something. *I can swim.*
2 to be allowed to do something. *You can watch television when you've finished your homework.*
3 If something **can** happen, it is possible. *It can get quite cold at night.*

can (noun)

a container for food or drink made of thin metal.

canal (noun)

a man-made river, used for moving people and things around by boat.

cancel **cancelling cancelled** (verb)

If you **cancel** something that was arranged, you stop it from happening. *The singer was ill, so they had to cancel the concert.*

cancer (noun)

a serious and sometimes fatal illness.

candidate (noun)

someone taking an exam, applying for a job, or standing in an election. *There are eight candidates for one job.*

candle (noun)

a stick made of wax, with a string through the centre called a wick, that you burn to give light.

candy **candy** or **candies** (noun)

sweets, especially hard sweets. **candy** (adjective).

a b c d e f g h i j k l m n o p q r s t u v w x y z

cane (noun)
1 the hollow stem of some plants, such as bamboo.
2 a walking stick.

cannon cannon or cannons (noun)
a heavy and powerful gun that fires large stone or metal balls.

canoe (noun)
a small, narrow boat that is paddled by one or more people. See boat.

can't (verb)
a short way of writing cannot.
I can't carry on.

canteen (noun)
a large indoor area for eating, for example in a school or a large office.

canter cantering cantered (verb)
When a horse canters, it runs quite fast.

canvas canvasses (noun)
a strong, rough material used for making sails, tents, and working clothes, and as a surface for artists to paint on.

canyon (noun)
a large, deep, steep-sided valley that has been carved out by a river.

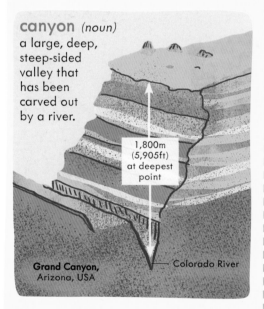

1,800m (5,905ft) at deepest point

Grand Canyon, Arizona, USA — Colorado River

cap (noun)
1 a type of hat, often with a peak that sticks out above your eyes. Baseball players often wear caps to keep the sun out of their eyes.
2 the top of a bottle or a pen.

capable (adjective)
1 able to do something. I'm sure that Hayley is capable of passing the exam.
2 If you are capable, you have skills and work well. Rajesh is a very capable rugby player.

capacity capacities (noun)
1 how much something can hold. This bottle has a capacity of two litres.
2 ability or intelligence. Lena doesn't have the capacity to understand the problem.

cape (noun)
1 a piece of clothing like a light cloak, worn over the shoulders and back.
2 a piece of land that sticks out into the sea.

capital (noun)
1 A country's capital is its most important city. Paris is the capital of France.
2 A capital or capital letter is a big letter, which you put at the beginning of a sentence, a name, and so on. A, B, C, D, and so on are capital letters. capital (adjective).

capsize capsizing capsized (verb)
When a boat capsizes, it turns on its side or upside down in the water.

capsule (noun)
1 a sealed container, which may contain medicine, or objects.
2 a sealed container that is a living and working space for astronauts.

captain (noun)
1 the person in charge of a ship, a plane, or a team.
2 an army or navy officer.

caption (noun)
a short piece of writing that describes or explains a picture.

captive (noun)
a prisoner, or someone or something that can't escape. captive (adjective), captivity (noun).

capture capturing captured (verb)
to catch and keep a person or animal. The criminal was captured this morning.

rear-view mirror, aerial, windscreen, sunroof, windscreen wipers, boot, fuel cap, bonnet, headlight, exhaust, number plate, wheel trim, bumper, wing mirror, door handle, tyre, indicator light

hatchback car

car *(noun)*
a wheeled vehicle with an engine, that is large enough to carry two or more people.

caramel *(noun)*
1 sugar cooked at a high temperature until it melts and turns brown.
2 soft toffee.
3 a light brown colour. **caramel** *(adjective)*.

caravan *(noun)*
a small home on wheels, which can be towed by a vehicle. *We are taking our caravan around the south of France next summer.*

carbohydrates *(plural noun)*
substances found in foods such as bread and pasta, that give you energy. Carbohydrates is often shortened to "carbs".

carbon *(noun)*
a very common chemical element. All living things on Earth contain carbon.

carbon dioxide *(noun)*
a gas that is breathed out by people and animals, and also produced by burning fuels such as petrol and coal.

carbon footprint *(noun)*
the amount of carbon dioxide a person produces through the way that they live and travel.

carcass **carcasses** *(noun)*
the dead body of an animal.

card *(noun)*
1 cardboard.
2 a folded, decorated piece of cardboard given or sent to someone, especially for a special event such as a birthday.
3 **Cards** are small pieces of card with pictures and numbers printed on them, used in games.
4 see **credit card**.

cardboard *(noun)*
thick, stiff paper.

cardigan *(noun)*
a knitted piece of clothing with sleeves, which opens up at the front.

There are four suits of **cards**: diamonds, hearts, clubs, and spades.

care **caring** **cared**
1 *(verb)* to be interested, concerned or worried about something. *I care about the environment.* **care** *(noun)*.
2 *(verb)* to look after a person or animal that needs your help. **caring** *(adjective)*.
3 *(noun)* If you **take care** of someone, you look after them.
4 *(noun)* If you **take care** when you are doing something, you do it carefully. *Take care while you're up the ladder.*

career *(noun)*
a job that you work towards and have for a long time.

carefree – carve

carefree *(adjective)*
If you are **carefree**, you have no worries.

careful *(adjective)*
1 taking time and doing things well.
carefully *(adverb)*.
2 avoiding danger. *Be careful when you cross the road.* **carefully** *(adverb)*.

careless *(adjective)*
Someone who is **careless** rushes and doesn't take care when doing things.
carelessly *(adverb)*, **carelessness** *(noun)*.

carer *(noun)*
a family member or a paid helper who looks after a child, or a sick, elderly or disabled person.

caretaker *(noun)*
someone who looks after a building, especially when it is not being used, for instance at night.

cargo cargoes *(noun)*
things being transported, especially by ship or by plane.

carnival *(noun)*
an outdoor festival with street parties, music, costumes, and dancing.
carnival *(adjective)*.

carnivore *(noun)*
an animal that eats meat.
carnivorous *(adjective)*.

carol *(noun)*
a religious song, sung at Christmas.

Wolves are **carnivores.**

carpenter *(noun)*
someone who makes things from wood, or uses wood in building.

carpet *(noun)*
1 a soft, thick mat or floor covering.
2 a thick layer of something.
A carpet of dust. **carpet** *(verb)*.

carriage *(noun)*
1 one of the parts of a train where the passengers sit.
2 a wheeled vehicle pulled by horses.

carrot *(noun)*
a long, thin root vegetable that is usually orange. *See* **vegetable**.

carry carries carrying carried *(verb)*
1 to bring something in your hands or arms. *When Amy was tired, her dad carried her.*
2 to transport something, or be a way for something to be passed on. *The rats were carrying a deadly disease.*
carrier *(noun)*.
3 If you **carry on** doing something, you keep doing it. *I carried on dancing after the music had stopped.*
4 If you **carry out** an action or task, you do it.

cart *(noun)*
a simple wheeled vehicle that can be pushed by a person or pulled by an animal to carry things.

carton *(noun)*
a small cardboard or plastic container, usually for food or drink. *A carton of apple juice.*

cartoon *(noun)*
1 a funny drawing, or a story told through drawings.
2 a film or television programme in which the story is told through animated pictures.

cartwheel *(noun)*
a gymnastics move in which you go sideways, balancing on your hands then landing on your feet.

steps showing how to do a **cartwheel**

carve carving carved *(verb)*
to cut something in a very exact way. *Mum carved the chicken for lunch. Jo carved the block of wood into a horse's head.* **carving** *(noun)*.

case – castle

case *(noun)*
1 a container used to transport or protect something. *I put my violin back in its case.*
2 an example of when something has happened. *A case of mistaken identity.*
3 an event that a detective or the police are investigating.
4 a trial in a court, where it is decided whether a person is guilty of a crime.
5 If you do something **in case** of something that might happen, you try to prepare or protect yourself against it. *I brought an umbrella in case it rains.*

cash *(noun)*
money. *I don't have much cash.*

cashier *(noun)*
the person who takes the money when you buy something in a shop.

cashpoint *(noun)*
a machine where you can take out money using a debit or credit card.

casino *(noun)*
a place where people go to play gambling games.

casserole *(noun)*
a food dish that usually contains meat and vegetables, and is cooked slowly.

cast *(noun)*
1 all the people in a performance, such as a play or film.
2 a stiff bandage that helps broken bones or sprained limbs to heal. *Molly had to wear a cast for six weeks.*

castle *(noun)*
a large, strong building built long ago and designed to keep enemies out.

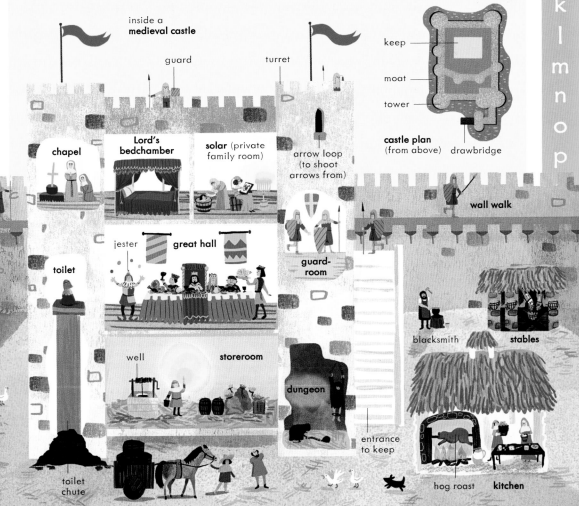

inside a
medieval castle

guard

turret

keep

moat

tower

chapel

Lord's
bedchamber

solar (private
family room)

arrow loop
(to shoot
arrows from)

castle plan
(from above)   drawbridge

wall walk

jester   **great hall**

guard-
room

toilet

well   **storeroom**

dungeon

blacksmith   **stables**

entrance
to keep

toilet
chute

hog roast   **kitchen**

casual *(adjective)*
relaxed and not smart or formal.
*Mum wears casual clothes when
she's not at work.*

cat *(noun)*
1 a small, furry animal often kept
as a pet.
2 Lions, tigers and leopards are all
big cats.

catalogue *(noun)*
a list of items, especially a book listing
things for sale. **catalogue** *(verb).*

catastrophe *(cat-**ass**-tro-fee) (noun)*
a terrible disaster. *The hurricane was
a catastrophe.* **catastrophic** *(adjective).*

catch catching caught
1 *(verb)* to take hold of something
that is moving. *My brother threw the
ball and I caught it.* **catch** *(noun).*
2 *(verb)* to find and trap someone or
something that is escaping. *The owl
caught the mouse.*
3 *(verb)* to get an illness. *I caught
chickenpox from Elin.*
4 *(verb)* to arrive on time to get
on a bus, train, or plane.
5 *(verb)* to notice or interrupt someone
who is doing something wrong. *Ashley
caught his little brother putting salt in
the sugar bowl.*
6 *(noun)* a hidden problem. *It sounds
too good to be true – what's the catch?*
7 *(verb)* If you **catch up with** someone,
you start off behind them but end up
in the same place as them.

category categories *(noun)*
a class or type. *James likes to put all
his DVDs into categories.*

Spelling tip

category → categories

To make a word that ends with
a consonant and then a 'y' plural,
you **remove the 'y'** and **add '–ies':**
categories; celebrities; ceremonies.

caterpillar *(noun)*
a worm-like animal with legs that is
the young form of a butterfly or moth.

These four stages show how a **caterpillar**
changes into a butterfly.

1 egg   2 caterpillar

3 **pupa** or **chrysalis**   4 **butterfly**

cathedral *(noun)*
a large, important church.

Catholic *(noun)*
a Christian who recognizes the
Pope as the head of the Church.
Catholic *(adjective).*

cattle *(noun)*
cows and bulls.

caught *(verb)*
the past tense of **catch.**

cauliflower *(noun)*
a vegetable with a large, round, white
centre. *See* vegetable.

cause causing caused
1 *(verb)* to make something happen.
2 *(noun)* the reason for something
happening. *Experts still disagree
over the cause of the explosion.*
3 *(noun)* a worthwhile aim. *We are
raising money for a good cause.*

cautious *(adjective)*
careful not to take risks. **caution** *(noun),*
cautiously *(adverb).*

cave *(noun)*
a large hole under the ground or inside
a mountain.

caveman *(noun)*
someone who lived in caves
in prehistoric times.

CCTV *(noun) (abbreviation)*
see **closed-circuit television**.

CD *(noun) (abbreviation)*
see **compact disc**.

ceiling *(noun)*
the surface across the top of a room.
*Bethany has stars painted on her
bedroom ceiling.*

celebrate
celebrating celebrated *(verb)*
to show that you are happy about
something, and make a special event
of it. *My parents celebrated their
twentieth wedding anniversary.*
celebration *(noun).*

celebrity celebrities *(noun)*
a famous person.

celery *(noun)*
a salad vegetable with crunchy green
or white stems.

cell *(noun)*
1 a room in a prison or police station
where someone is locked up.
2 one of the very small parts that
make up a living thing. *Red blood
cells carry oxygen around your body.*

cellar *(noun)*
a room below ground level in a house
or shop, often used for storage.

cello *(noun)*
a large musical instrument with four
strings. *See* **orchestra**.

Celsius *or* **centigrade** *(adjective)*
Temperature is measured in degrees
Celsius or **centigrade**. *Water boils at
100 degrees Celsius.*

cement *(noun)*
a building material which is mixed
and poured as a liquid, then sets solid.
cement *(verb).*

cemetery cemeteries *(noun)*
a place where dead people are buried.

Word family

centigrade
centimetre
century

These words all begin
with 'cent', which is
the Latin word for
"one hundred". There
are 100 **centimetres**
in a metre, and a
century is 100 years.
Water freezes at 0°C
and boils at 100°C,
which is what gives
the **centigrade** scale
its name.

centigrade *(adjective)*
see **Celsius**.

centimetre *(noun)*
a measure of length. A centimetre
is one hundredth of a metre.

centipede *(noun)*
a small animal with a long
body and many legs.

garden
centipede

centre *(noun)*
1 the middle of a shape or area.
central *(adjective).*
2 a place where people go to do
a particular activity. *A sports centre.*

century centuries *(noun)*
a hundred years.

cereal *(noun)*
1 a farm crop with grains, such as rice
and wheat, which is grown for food.
2 a breakfast food made from grains
and eaten with milk.

ceremony ceremonies *(noun)*
a formal event held to show the
importance of something. *A prize-giving
ceremony.* **ceremonial** *(adjective).*

a b **c** d e f g h i j k l m n o p q r s t u v w x y z

certain *(adjective)*
1 sure. *Ben is certain to be there. I am certain that this is the right place.* **certainly** *(adverb)*, **certainty** *(noun)*.
2 some, or particular. *Certain toys aren't suitable for young children.*

certificate *(noun)*
a document which proves something. *This is my birth certificate.* **certify** *(verb)*.

chain *(noun)*
1 metal rings connected in a line, which can be used to fasten something securely. **chain** *(verb)*.
2 a connected series of things. *In a food chain, each animal eats the thing below it.*

chair *(noun)*
a seat with a back for one person to sit on.

chairlift *(noun)*
a line of seats hanging from a moving cable, used to carry people up and down a mountain.

chalk *(noun)*
a soft white rock which can be used to write on surfaces and then be rubbed out. *A stick of chalk.*

challenge
challenging challenged *(verb)*
1 to take the opposite view to someone, or invite them to fight you. *Freya challenged George's claim that he could tame lions.*
2 to give someone a difficult task. *I challenge you to finish the whole pizza.* **challenge** *(noun)*, **challenging** *(adjective)*.

Spelling tip

challenge → challenging

When you add the endings '-ing' and '-ed' to a word that ends with a silent 'e', you remove the 'e' first.

chameleon *(noun)*
a type of lizard. Many types of chameleons can change the shade of their skin.

panther chameleon

champagne *(noun)*
a sparkling wine made in northern France, and often drunk at celebrations.

champion *(noun)*
the winner of a competition, or someone who is really brilliant at something. **championship** *(noun)*.

chance *(noun)*
1 If something happens **by chance**, it has not been planned, and is unexpected.
2 possibility. *Is there any chance you could come back this afternoon?*
3 opportunity. *I have the chance to go and study in America.*

change changing changed
1 *(verb)* to become different. *The frog changed into a prince.*
2 *(verb)* to make something different, or replace it with something else. *I changed my screensaver.*
3 *(verb)* to put on different clothes. *I'm going to change for PE.*
4 *(verb)* to get onto a different train or bus. *I need to change trains at the next station.*
5 *(noun)* the money that you get back when you pay more than the right amount for something.

channel *(noun)*
1 one of the stations on which you can watch television programmes. *I don't want to watch this, I'm changing channels.*
2 a passage that a liquid, such as water, can run along. **channel** *(verb)*.
3 a strip of water that connects two larger areas of water, especially two seas. *The English Channel.*

Chanukah
see **Hanukkah**.

chaos (noun)
a state of total confusion, with no order. *Traffic chaos.* **chaotic** (adjective).

chapel (noun)
a small church, or a room in a building used for Christian worship.

chapter (noun)
a section of a book.

character (noun)
1 a person in a book or a play.
2 a person. *Liam is a cheerful character.*

charcoal (noun)
a black substance, which can be burnt in barbecues or used for drawing.

charge charging charged (verb)
1 to rush forward with force. *The rhino charged.* **charge** (noun).
2 to make someone pay money for something. **charge** (noun).
3 If you are **in charge** of something, you organize or look after it.

charity charities (noun)
an organization that raises money for a good cause. *Imogen is raising money for a charity that rescues cats.*

charm (noun)
1 If someone has **charm**, they are polite and likeable. *Harry has lots of charm.* **charm** (verb), **charming** (adjective).
2 a small item that you carry with you, which is meant to bring good luck or protection. *A lucky charm.*

| ankh | eye of Horus | Bastlet |

Egyptian **charms**

chart (noun)
1 a map, especially one used for sea travel.
2 a set of information that is shown in a table or graph.

chase chasing chased (verb)
to hunt or follow someone or something, with the aim of catching them. **chase** (noun).

chat chatting chatted (verb)
to have a friendly conversation. *I love chatting to my friends.* **chat** (noun).

chatter chattering chattered (verb)
1 to talk a lot without saying anything important. **chatter** (noun).
2 If your teeth **chatter**, they knock together quickly because you are cold.

cheap cheaper cheapest (adjective)
If something is **cheap**, it doesn't cost much money, or costs less than you expect. **cheaply** (adverb).

cheat cheating cheated (verb)
to try to win a game, or get something that you want, by breaking the rules or being dishonest. **cheat** (noun).

check checking checked (verb)
to make sure that something has been done, is safe, or is correct. **check** (noun).

check in
checking in checked in (verb)
When you **check in** at a hotel or airport, you arrive and let someone in charge know that you are there.

checkout (noun)
the place in a shop, especially a supermarket, where you pay for your shopping.

checkup (noun)
a regular health check. *I'm going for a checkup at the dentist's.*

cheek (noun)
1 the soft part of your face between your eye and your chin.
2 rudeness. *You've got a lot of cheek, young man.* **cheeky** (adjective).

cheer cheering cheered (verb)
1 to shout to encourage a person or team, or to show that you are happy about something. **cheer** (noun).
2 If you **cheer up**, you start to feel happier than you did before.

cheerful – chicken

Spelling tip   cheerful

You will never see '**–full**' on the end of an adjective, always '**–ful**' with one 'l': "cheerful". When you add '–ly' to make an adverb, it has two 'l's: "cheerfully".

cheerful *(adjective)*
happy. *Nadine's always cheerful, even when things are difficult.*
cheerfully *(adverb)*.

cheese *(noun)*
a type of food made from milk. Cheese can be soft or hard.

cheetah *(noun)*
a large, spotted African wild cat that can run very fast.

Cheetahs can run up to 100km/h (60mph).

chef *(noun)*
a professional cook, who usually works in a restaurant.

chemical *(noun)*
a substance, usually one which has been man-made and is used for a particular purpose. **chemical** *(adjective)*.

chemist *(noun)*
1 a person or a shop that sells medicines and other health products.
2 a scientist who specializes in chemistry.

chemistry *(noun)*
the scientific study of what things are made of, and how they react with one another.

cheque *(noun)*
an official piece of paper from a bank that people sign and use to pay for things.

cherish
cherishes cherishing cherished *(verb)*
to love something very much, and look after it. *Mum cherishes her free time.*

cherry cherries *(noun)*
a small red or purple fruit with a seed called a stone inside. *See* **fruit**.

chess *(noun)*
a game played by two people, with pieces on a board with squares on it.

rook or castle   bishop   king   queen   knight

pawn   chesspieces

chest *(noun)*
1 the front part of your upper body, between your neck and waist.
2 a large wooden or metal container with a lid, that can be used to store things safely.

chest of drawers *(noun)*
a piece of furniture, used to store clothes or other items, with drawers that can be pulled out.

chew chewing chewed *(verb)*
to break down food with your teeth.

chewing gum *(noun)*
a stretchy, often mint-flavoured sweet, that you can chew but not swallow.

chick *(noun)*
a baby bird, especially a baby chicken.

chicken *(noun)*
1 a medium-sized bird that is kept for its eggs and meat. Also called a **hen**.
2 the meat from a hen.

chickenpox *(noun)*
an illness which gives you itchy spots like blisters on your skin.

chief
1 *(noun)* the leader of a group or tribe.
2 *(adjective)* most important.

child children *(noun)*
1 a young person, generally under sixteen years old.
2 a person's son or daughter.

childhood *(noun)*
the time in your life when you are a child. **childhood** *(adjective)*.

childish *(adjective)*
If someone is being **childish**, they are acting in a silly and immature way.

childminder *(noun)*
someone whose job is to look after other people's children, usually in their own home.

chill chilling chilled *(verb)*
to make something cool or cold. **chilled** *(adjective)*.

chilli chillies *(noun)*
a hot, spicy pod that grows on plants and is used to flavour food.

chilly chillier chilliest *(adjective)*
quite cold. *It's chilly outside.*

chime chiming chimed *(verb)*
When a bell or a clock **chimes**, it makes a ringing sound. **chime** *(noun)*.

chimney *(noun)*
a pipe that takes the smoke from a fireplace outside.

chimpanzee *(noun)*
a type of large African ape with dark fur and a pale face.

long, strong arms

Five toes on feet can grasp like hands.

chimpanzee

chin *(noun)*
the part of your face below your mouth.

china *(noun)*
1 a hard material used to make plates and cups.
2 a general word for cups, plates, and dishes. *Can you put the china away in the cupboard?*

chip *(noun)*
1 a stick of deep-fried potato.
2 a small piece that has broken off something. **chip** *(verb)*, **chipped** *(adjective)*.
3 A silicon **chip** is a small piece of silicon with electrical circuits on it, which makes computers work.

chlorine *(noun)*
a strong-smelling gas which is used to kill germs, especially to make the water in swimming pools safe.

chocolate *(noun)*
a sweet made from cocoa beans and sugar, and sometimes milk, that is usually brown in colour. **chocolate** *(adjective)*.

Chocolate is made from cocoa beans.

choice *(noun)*
1 a number of things that you can pick. *There's a choice of cereals, fruit, or a cooked breakfast.*
2 the act of choosing. *We need to make a choice soon.*
3 the person or thing you have picked. *Lowri is my choice for team captain.*

choir *(kwire) (noun)*
a group of people who sing together.

choke choking choked *(verb)*
1 to be unable to breathe, or find it difficult to breathe, because something is squeezing your neck or stuck in your throat.
2 to stop someone from breathing by squeezing or forcing something down their throat.

choose
choosing chose chosen *(verb)*
to pick one of several options. *Josh chose the green bike.*

chop **chopping chopped** *(verb)*
to cut something into small pieces.

chopsticks *(plural noun)*
thin sticks used for eating in countries such as China and Korea.

chord *(kord)* *(noun)*
two or more musical notes played together.

chore *(noun)*
a task that you don't enjoy. *Household chores.*

chorus **choruses** *(noun)*
the part of a song that is repeated after the verses.

christening *(noun)*
the ceremony in which someone, usually a baby, is named and welcomed into a church.

Christianity *(noun)*
the religion of followers of Jesus Christ. **Christian** *(noun)*, **Christian** *(adjective)*.

There are around 2 billion Christians in the world today. Christians believe that Jesus Christ is the Son of God, and that he died on the Cross so that humans wouldn't have to suffer for their sins. They worship in churches and follow the teachings of a book called the Bible.

The Cross is the sign of **Christianity**.

Christmas **Christmases** *(noun)*
the celebration of the birth of Jesus Christ, held on 25th December. **Christmas** *(adjective)*.

chrysalis *(kriss-a-liss)* **chrysalises** *(noun)*
the case that a caterpillar or other young insect makes around itself while it changes into its adult form. *See* **caterpillar**.

chubby **chubbier chubbiest** *(adjective)*
plump or slightly overweight.

chuck **chucking chucked** *(verb)*
to throw something carelessly.

chuckle **chuckling chuckled** *(verb)*
to laugh quietly. **chuckle** *(noun)*.

chunk *(noun)*
a thick or irregular-shaped piece of something. **chunky** *(noun)*.

church **churches** *(noun)*
a building where Christians meet to worship.

cigar *(noun)*
tobacco leaves which are tightly rolled together and then smoked.

cigarette *(noun)*
a paper tube containing tobacco, which is smoked.

cinema *(noun)*
a building where you go to watch films.

cinnamon *(noun)*
a reddish spice used in baking and in Middle Eastern and Asian cooking.

circle *(noun)*
1 a flat shape with a perfectly round edge. **circular** *(adjective)*.

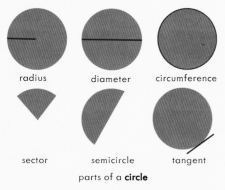

radius · diameter · circumference

sector · semicircle · tangent

parts of a **circle**

2 a group of people who know each other. *Becky has a large circle of friends.*

circuit *(noun)*
1 a track or path that starts and finishes in the same place.
2 joined-up wires for an electrical current to flow around.

circumference *(noun)*
the measurement around the edge of a circle.

Spelling tip

circuit   circle
citizen   circus   citrus

The letter '**c**' always makes a soft '**ss**' sound when it is followed by an '**i**' at the beginning of a word.

circumstance (noun)
a fact or situation that affects something else. *We were lucky to make it, considering the circumstances.*

circus circuses (noun)
a travelling group of entertainers, such as acrobats and clowns, that people go to see perform.

citizen (noun)
a person who belongs to a city or country.

citizenship (noun)
the status of being a citizen of a particular country.

citrus (adjective)
a type of fruit, which includes oranges and lemons.

Grapefruit is a **citrus** fruit.

city cities (noun)
a large, busy and important town.

civilization or **civilisation** (noun)
a group of people with their own culture, language, laws, and so on.

claim claiming claimed (verb)
1 to say something is true, even though some people may doubt it. *Bella claims she wrote it all by herself.* **claim** (noun).
2 to say that something belongs to you. *I claimed the reward.*

clammy
clammier clammiest (adjective)
unpleasantly damp. *My hands get clammy when I'm nervous.*

clamp clamping clamped (verb)
to hold something tightly and securely. **clamp** (noun).

clap clapping clapped (verb)
to hit the palms of your hands together, often to show that you enjoyed something. *The crowd clapped for a long time after the actors left the stage.*

clarinet (noun)
a woodwind instrument, often used in classical and jazz music. *See* **woodwind**.

clash clashes clashing clashed (verb)
1 to hit together with a ringing sound. *The soldiers' swords clashed.*
2 to disagree violently. *They clashed over how to spend the money.*
3 If colours **clash**, they look ugly together.

class classes (noun)
1 a group of people who have come together to learn something.
2 a period of time spent learning. *We have Spanish class this afternoon.*
3 a group of people or things that are similar in some way.

classic (adjective)
If something is **classic**, it is remembered as a great example of its kind. *This is a classic comedy film.* **classic** (noun).

clatter clattering clattered (verb)
to make a loud noise by hitting or falling on something again and again. *The tray clattered down the stairs.*

claw (noun)
Claws are sharp, curved nails on the feet of an animal or bird. **claw** (verb).

clay (noun)
thick, heavy mud. Some kinds can be moulded and baked to make bricks or pots.

clean cleaning cleaned (verb)
to remove dirt. **clean** (adjective).

clear clearer clearest (adjective)
1 see-through.
2 easy to see or hear. *The speech wasn't very clear from the back of the room.* **clearly** (adverb).
3 easy to understand. *It's not clear where we are supposed to go.*
4 not blocked. *The road ahead is clear.*

clear clearing cleared *(verb)*
to take away things that are not wanted or are in the way.

clench
clenches clenching clenched *(verb)*
to squeeze tightly. *Faye clenched her fist in anger.*

clergy *(plural noun)*
priests in the Christian Church.

clever cleverer cleverest *(adjective)*
1 intelligent and able to learn things easily. *Dolphins are very clever animals.*
2 well thought out. *That's a clever plan.*

click clicking clicked *(verb)*
1 to make a tapping sound. *The camera clicked as I took the photo.*
2 to select an icon or link on a web page.

cliff *(noun)*
a steep rock face, especially by the sea.

cliffhanger *(noun)*
an ending which leaves you really wanting to know the next part of the story.

climate *(noun)*
the kind of weather that an area usually has. *Norway has a cold climate.*

climax *(noun)*
the high point or the most exciting part in a story or event. *The climax of the film is the car chase through the city.*
climactic *(adjective)*.

climb climbing climbed *(verb)*
1 to go upwards, often up a hill or a slope. **climb** *(noun)*.
2 to go up a steep hill or cliff using your hands and feet. **climb** *(noun)*, **climbing** *(noun)*.

cling clinging clung *(verb)*
to hold onto someone or something tightly or anxiously. *Mark clung to the railings during the whole boat ride.*

clinic *(noun)*
a place where doctors and nurses see and treat their patients. **clinical** *(adjective)*.

clip clipping clipped
1 *(verb)* to trim or cut the edge of something.
2 *(noun)* something that is used to hold things in place, especially paper or hair.
3 *(noun)* a short part from a film or television programme.

cloak *(noun)*
a long piece of clothing without sleeves, that is fastened at the neck.

cloakroom *(noun)*
a place in a public building where you can leave your coat.

clock *(noun)*
something that shows the time.

clockwise *(adjective)*
in the direction that the hands of a clock move.

clockwork *(noun)*
the type of machinery found inside an old-fashioned clock.
clockwork *(adjective)*.

clone *(noun)*
an exact copy, especially of a living thing such as an animal. **clone** *(verb)*.

close *(close)* **closer closest** *(adjective)*
1 near. *I live close to the school.*
closely *(adverb)*.
2 If people are **close**, they are very friendly with each other and care about each other.

close *(cloze)* **closing closed** *(verb)*
1 to shut or seal something.
closed *(adjective)*.
2 to come to an end, or bring to an end. *The story closes when she moves to the city.*

Spelling tip   close

Notice that the word "**close**" (adjective) and the word "**close**" (verb) are pronounced differently, even though they are spelt exactly the same.

"Close" (adjective) has an 's' sound, but "close" (verb) has a 'z' sound.

closed-circuit television
or CCTV *(noun)*
a system used for security, where cameras record what is happening in a place, and someone can watch it and check everything is all right.

close-up *(noun)*
a picture taken very near the subject, especially in film or television where an actor's face is shown very large and in detail.

clot **clotting clotted** *(verb)*
When a liquid **clots**, it thickens and forms lumps. Your blood clots to stop cuts from bleeding. **clot** *(noun)*.

cloth *(noun)*
1 material, often made from cotton or wool.
2 a piece of material used for cleaning.

clothes *(plural noun)*
all the things that you wear on your body, such as shirts and jeans.

cloud *(noun)*
1 a mass of water vapour floating in the sky. **cloudy** *(adjective)*.
2 a large amount of smoke or dust.

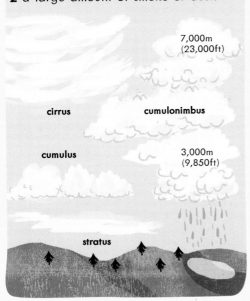

types of **clouds**

clown *(noun)*
1 a performer in a circus who wears funny clothes and make-up, and does silly things to make people laugh.
2 someone who often behaves in a silly way to make people laugh. *Akash is the class clown.*

club *(noun)*
1 a group of people who have a shared interest or hobby. *Penny has joined a volleyball club.*
2 a heavy stick used as a weapon. **club** *(verb)*.
3 a long stick with a metal head, used in golf. *See golf.*
4 **Clubs** is one of the four suits in a pack of cards, with a symbol that is black with three round leaves, like this ♣.

clue *(noun)*
1 a hint, or something that makes it easier for you to work something out. *I can't guess. Can you give me a clue?*
2 something that can help to solve a crime or mystery. *The glove in the kitchen is an important clue.*

clump *(noun)*
a small group of things or a lump of something. *A clump of plants.*

clumsy **clumsier clumsiest** *(adjective)*
Someone who is **clumsy** moves in an awkward way, and may break things. **clumsiness** *(noun)*, **clumsily** *(adverb)*.

cluster *(noun)*
a group of things close together. *There was a cluster of eggs in the bird's nest.* **cluster** *(verb)*.

clutch
clutches clutching clutched *(verb)*
to grip something tightly or anxiously with your hand.

clutter *(noun)*
a crowded and untidy mess. **clutter** *(verb)*.

co- *(prefix)*
Co- means with someone or something else. For example, to "co-operate" is to work together with someone.

coach – cod

coach coaches *(noun)*
1 a large bus used for taking passengers on long journeys.
2 a large carriage in a train where passengers sit.
3 someone who trains another person or a team in a sport. **coach** *(verb)*.
4 a carriage pulled by horses.

coal *(noun)*
a black rock that comes from under the ground, which is burnt to give heat.

coarse coarser coarsest *(adjective)*
rough and uneven. *Coarse salt.*

coast *(noun)*
the edge of the land, where it meets the sea or ocean. **coastal** *(adjective)*.

coastguard *(noun)*
a person or the people whose job is to watch for boats or people in trouble in the sea near the coast.

coat *(noun)*
1 a piece of clothing with sleeves, worn over other clothes outdoors.
2 an animal's hair or fur.
3 a layer of something. *A coat of paint.*
coat *(verb)*.

cobra *(noun)*
a type of snake with venomous fangs and a hood on its head. *See* **snake**.

cobweb *(noun)*
the net of sticky threads made by spiders to catch insects to eat.

cock *(noun)*
a male bird, especially a male chicken.

cockerel *(noun)*
a male chicken.

cockpit *(noun)*
the part of a plane where the pilot sits.

cocoa *(noun)*
a powder or a hot drink made from cocoa beans, with a strong chocolate taste. *See* **chocolate**.

coconut *(noun)*
a large nut that grows on a palm tree, with a hard, hairy brown shell, and white flesh that you can eat.

husk

flesh

coconut milk

The word "coconut" comes from the Spanish and Portuguese word, "coco", which means "grinning face". It was given this name because the three holes on a coconut look a little like a human face.

cocoon *(noun)*
the case that some young insects make around themselves before changing into their adult forms. *See* **caterpillar**.

cod *(noun)*
a large sea fish that is popular for cooking and eating.

These pictures show how a spider makes a **cobweb**:

sticky thread

The spider releases a sticky thread into the breeze towards another object.

The spider strengthens the sticky thread until it can hold another thread.

The spider pulls the new thread tight and attaches it to another object.

non-sticky thread

sticky thread

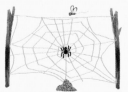

The spider adds some non-sticky threads.

The spider rests, then adds more sticky threads.

The spider waits on the web for insects.

code *(noun)*
1 a way of changing the letters or words in a message into a form that can only be understood by other people who know how to change it back into words. **code** *(verb)*.
2 the language of instructions in a computer program. **code** *(verb)*.
3 a set of rules or guidelines.

coffee *(noun)*
a bitter-tasting hot drink that makes people feel awake and alert, or the flavour of that drink. **coffee** *(adjective)*.

coffin *(noun)*
the box, usually made of wood, that someone is buried or cremated in.

cog *(noun)*
a piece of machinery, shaped like a wheel with teeth that link with another cog.

When a bigger **cog** turns a smaller **cog**, the speed increases and the direction changes.

coherent *(adjective)*
If something is **coherent**, it makes sense.

coil *(noun)*
something that is shaped into a series of loops. *A coil of rope.* **coil** *(verb)*.

coin *(noun)*
a round metal piece of money.

coincidence *(noun)*
A **coincidence** is when two things happen together by chance. **coincidental** *(adjective)*, **coincidentally** *(adverb)*.

colander *(noun)*
a bowl with holes in, used for draining water off food.

cold **colder coldest**
1 *(adjective)* low in temperature.
2 *(adjective)* unfriendly.
3 *(noun)* a common illness that causes sneezing, a runny nose, and a sore throat.
4 Cold-blooded animals can't change their body temperature themselves.

collage *(noun)*
a picture made by sticking paper or other objects onto a background.

collapse
collapsing collapsed *(verb)*
to fall down suddenly. *The whole building collapsed.* **collapse** *(noun)*.

collar *(noun)*
1 the part of a piece of clothing that goes around your neck.
2 a strap around the neck of a pet animal.

collect **collecting collected** *(verb)*
1 to bring things together, sometimes as a hobby.
2 to pick up someone or something and take them away with you. *We need to collect your sister on the way home.*

collection *(noun)*
1 a group of things that have been collected over time and have something in common. *I have a coin collection.*
2 an amount of money that has been raised for a good cause. *We had a collection for charity.*

college *(noun)*
a place where older children, teenagers or adults can go to learn.

collide **colliding collided** *(verb)*
If something **collides** with something else, it smashes into it. **collision** *(noun)*.

colon *(noun)*
the punctuation mark (:) used in writing before a list or explanation. *See* **punctuation**, *page 349*.

colony **colonies** *(noun)*
1 a group of people who have settled in a new place or another country.
2 a country which has been taken over by people from another country.

colossal *(adjective)*
enormous. *That mountain is colossal.*

colour *(noun)*
a shade, for instance red, yellow, green, or purple. **colour** *(verb)*, **colourful** *(adjective)*, **coloured** *(adjective)*.

a b c d e f g h i j k l m n o p q r s t u v w x y z

Spelling tip

column
comb

Watch out for the silent 'n' on the end of "column", and the silent 'b' on the end of "comb".

column *(noun)*
1 a pillar, usually part of a building.
2 a vertical strip of text on a page, especially a newspaper.
3 a vertical strip of numbers or other information in a table.

comb *(noun)*
a tool for untangling and smoothing hair. **comb** *(verb)*.

combine
combining combined *(verb)*
to bring or mix things together. *Combine the sugar with the eggs.* **combination** *(noun)*.

come **coming came** *(verb)*
1 to approach or go towards someone or something. *Come here.*
2 to arrive. *Rita's coming at six.*
3 The place that you **come from** is the place where you were born or grew up.

comedian *(noun)*
someone who entertains people by making them laugh.

comedy **comedies** *(noun)*
1 a type of entertainment which makes you laugh.
2 a play or film which is funny or light-hearted.

comet *(noun)*
an object in space which travels round the Sun, and looks like a star with a bright tail behind it.

comet

tail of dust and gas

nucleus made of dust, ice, and rock

coma (layer of water and dust)

comfort
comforting comforted *(verb)*
If you **comfort** someone, you make them feel better after something bad has happened to them. *My dog always comforts me when I'm feeling sad.* **comforting** *(adjective)*.

comfortable *(adjective)*
1 If something is **comfortable**, it feels nice and doesn't cause you any pain. *My new trainers are so comfortable.*
2 If you are **comfortable**, you are relaxed and not in any pain.

comic
1 *(noun)* a magazine or book in which the stories are told in cartoon strips.
2 *(adjective)* funny.
3 *(noun)* a comedian.

comma *(noun)*
the punctuation mark (,) used in writing. *See* **punctuation**, *page 349.*

command
commanding commanded *(verb)*
to order someone to do something. **command** *(noun)*.

comment *(noun)*
a spoken or written response or reaction to something. *Does anyone have any comments on the plan?* **comment** *(verb)*.

commentary **commentaries** *(noun)*
a spoken description or explanation of something that is happening. *Chris gave a commentary on the game.* **commentator** *(noun)*.

commercial
1 *(noun)* a radio, film or television advertisement.
2 *(adjective)* to do with buying and selling things.

commit
committing committed *(verb)*
1 If you **commit** to doing something, you promise that you will do it. *I've committed to helping at the summer fair.* **commitment** *(noun)*.
2 to do something wrong or illegal. *To commit murder.*

committed *(adjective)*
dedicated and serious. *Emily is a committed animal rights campaigner.*

committee *(noun)*
a group of people who are in charge of organizing something.

common
commoner commonest *(adjective)*
1 usual, or happening or found often.
2 shared. *Rob and I have many common interests.*

common noun *(noun)*
a word used to give a general name to a thing. "Ball", "truck" and "lion" are all common nouns.

common sense *(noun)*
If you have **common sense**, you can get on with everyday life without many problems, and you make good decisions or judgements about things.

commotion *(noun)*
a sudden noise, confusion, and fuss.

communicate
communicating communicated *(verb)*
to make someone understand something, or get a message to them, by speaking, writing, or using actions. *We communicate by email.*
communication *(noun).*

Communion *(noun)*
the service where Christians remember the death and rebirth of Jesus by sharing bread and wine.

community communities *(noun)*
a group of people who are linked by where they live, what they believe, or what they have in common. *The Jewish community.*

compact *(adjective)*
small and neat. *My bedroom is very compact.* **compact** *(verb).*

compact disc or **CD** *(noun)*
a disc where information, often music, can be stored.

companion *(noun)*
a friend or partner.

company companies *(noun)*
1 having someone with you. *I like company when I'm travelling.*
2 If you **keep someone company**, you stay with them.
3 a business. *A software company.*
4 a theatre or dance group.

comparative *(noun)*
the form of an adjective that means more but not most. "Bigger" and "more expensive" are comparatives.
comparative *(adjective). See* **word classes,** *page 3.*

compare
comparing compared *(verb)*
to judge two or more things and see how they are different, or which is better. *I compared the two offers.*
comparable *(adjective),*
comparison *(noun).*

compass compasses *(noun)*
1 an instrument with a needle which points north, and which helps you to find your way.

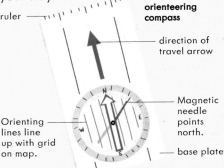

ruler

orienteering compass

direction of travel arrow

Magnetic needle points north.

Orienting lines line up with grid on map.

base plate

2 an instrument used for drawing circles. It's also called a pair of compasses.

Spelling tip

compass → compasses

Words that end with hissing sounds, such as 's', 'ss', 'ch', 'tch', 'tz', 'x' and 'z', add '-es' in the plural. For example, "compass" becomes "compasses" and "watch" becomes "watches".

a b **c** d e f g h i j k l m n o p q r s t u v w x y z

compassion *(noun)*
understanding how other people feel, or having sympathy for someone. **compassionate** *(adjective)*.

compatible *(adjective)*
1 well-matched, or able to get on with each other. *Tim and I decided not to work together because we weren't compatible.*
2 able to be used with another piece of equipment. *That charger isn't compatible with my phone.*

competent *(adjective)*
able to do something well. *Rhian is very competent at her job.*
competence *(noun)*.

competition *(noun)*
an event where many people try to do better than the rest to become the winner. *I won this medal in a diving competition.* **compete** *(verb)*.

competitive *(adjective)*
Someone who is **competitive** always wants to win or do better than others. *Gary ruined the rounders match because he got too competitive.*

complain
complaining complained *(verb)*
to make a fuss or say you are unhappy about something. **complaint** *(noun)*.

complete *(adjective)*
1 whole, with nothing missing. *This is a complete list of the books we sell.*
complete *(verb)*, **completely** *(adjective)*.
2 finished. *Is your homework complete?*
complete *(verb)*, **completion** *(noun)*.

complex *(adjective)*
complicated, with many different and connected parts. *This is a complex puzzle.*

complicated *(adjective)*
not simple or easy. *It's going to be very complicated to repair.* **complicate** *(verb)*.

complication *(noun)*
something that makes things difficult. *We got the train home without any complications.*

compliment *(noun)*
something nice that you say that makes someone feel good about themselves. **compliment** *(verb)*.

complimentary *(adjective)*
1 saying nice or positive things.
2 free. *The drinks are complimentary.*

compose
composing composed *(verb)*
to create a piece of writing or music. **composition** *(noun)*.

composer *(noun)*
someone who writes music.

compost *(noun)*
a mixture of rotted plants that is added to soil to help plants grow.

compound *(adjective)*
A **compound** word is one that is made of two or more words joined together, for example, "moonlight".

comprehensive
1 *(noun)* a secondary school that is free to attend and where students of all abilities are taught together.
2 *(adjective)* including everything that is needed. *A comprehensive list.*

compulsory *(adjective)*
If something is **compulsory**, you have to do it.

computer *(noun)*
a machine which can process information and carry out tasks. **computing** *(noun)*.

concave *(adjective)*
hollowed or curving inwards.

This skate ramp is **concave**.

conceal
concealing concealed *(verb)*
to hide something. *I concealed the stain on my top.* **concealed** *(adjective)*.

conceive
conceiving conceived *(verb)*
1 to think up a plan or idea in your mind, or to imagine something.
2 When a woman or female animal **conceives**, she becomes pregnant.
conception *(noun)*.

concentrate **concentrating**
concentrated *(verb)*
to focus all your attention on something.
concentration *(noun)*.

concept *(noun)*
1 an idea. *It's an interesting concept.*
2 an understanding or awareness of something. *Babies have no concept of time.*

concern **concerning concerned**
1 *(noun)* worry. *Bullying isn't a major concern in our school.* **concern** *(verb)*, **concerned** *(adjective)*.
2 *(verb)* to be about. *The story concerns a girl and her grandfather.* **concerning** *(preposition)*.
3 *(verb)* to involve or to be a worry to someone. *This problem concerns us all.* **concern** *(noun)*.

concert *(noun)*
a musical performance for an audience.

conclude
concluding concluded *(verb)*
1 to come to an end, or to bring something to an end. *Tim concluded his argument.* **conclusion** *(noun)*.
2 to use the facts to make up your mind about something. *I concluded that the sweets were for me.* **conclusion** *(noun)*.

concoct **concocting concocted** *(verb)*
to put together a mixture of things. **concoction** *(noun)*.

concrete *(noun)*
a very strong building material which is mixed as a liquid and sets solid. **concrete** *(adjective)*.

condense
condensing condensed *(verb)*
When steam **condenses**, it becomes liquid. **condensation** *(noun)*.

condition
1 *(noun)* the way that something is, for example how new or clean it is.
2 **conditions** *(plural noun)* the general weather and surroundings.
3 *(noun)* something that you must do before you can have or do something else. *You can go out on the condition that you tidy your room.* **conditional** *(adjective)*.

conduct **conducting conducted**
1 *(kon-**duct**)* *(verb)* to organize and carry out. *We conducted an experiment.*
2 *(kon-**duct**)* *(verb)* to direct an orchestra or choir. **conductor** *(noun)*.
3 *(kon-**duct**)* *(verb)* to transfer heat or electricity. *This pan conducts heat very well.* **conductor** *(noun)*.
4 *(**kon**-duct)* *(noun)* behaviour. *Alexa's conduct at the barbecue was awful.*

cone *(noun)*
1 a shape with a circular base at one end and a point at the other. **conical** *(adjective)*.
See shapes, page 348.
2 the fruit of an evergreen tree such as a pine or fir.

confess
confesses confessing confessed *(verb)*
to admit that you have done something wrong.
confession *(noun)*.

scale

seed

seed or pine nut

pine cone

Word origin — confetti

The word "confetti" is borrowed from Italian. In Italian, it is the word for little sweets which are thrown at weddings and other celebrations.

confetti (noun)
small paper or plastic shapes that are thrown at weddings and other celebrations.

confident (adjective)
1 If you are **confident**, you are happy with yourself and not shy or nervous. **confidence** (adjective).
2 If you are **confident**, you feel sure that you are able to do something, or that something will happen. **confidence** (adjective).

confidential (adjective)
Something that is **confidential** is supposed to be kept secret. *My diary is confidential.*

confirm
confirming confirmed (verb)
to say that something is true, or will happen. **confirmation** (noun).

conflict (noun)
an argument or battle.

confront
confronting confronted (verb)
to talk to someone about something bad that they have done. *I am going to confront Glyn about the missing phone.* **confrontation** (noun), **confrontational** (adjective).

confuse confusing confused (verb)
1 If something **confuses** you, you don't understand it or aren't sure what to do. **confused** (adjective), **confusing** (adjective).
2 to mistake one person or thing for another. *I was confusing Megan with her sister.* **confusion** (noun).

congratulate
congratulating congratulated (verb)
to praise someone for something they have done, or tell them you are pleased that something good has happened to them. **congratulation(s)** (noun).

congregation (noun)
the group of people at a religious service.

conjunction (noun)
a type of word which joins two words or parts of a sentence. "And", "because" and "but" are all conjunctions.

conker (noun)
the hard brown fruit of the horse chestnut tree. Conkers are sometimes used to play games.

connect
connecting connected (verb)
to join things together.

connection (noun)
a join or link.

connective (noun)
another word for a **conjunction**.

conquer
conquering conquered (verb)
to take control of a country or group of people by force. **conquest** (noun).

conscience (noun)
the part of your mind that knows whether the things you do are right or wrong. *I have a guilty conscience about finishing all the biscuits.*

conscientious (adjective)
taking care to do things well. **conscientiously** (adverb).

Spelling tip

conscientious
conscience   conscious

The letters 'sci' make a 'sh' sound in these words. Look out for this spelling pattern.

conscious (adjective)
If you are **conscious**, you are awake and know what is happening.
consciousness (noun).

consequence (noun)
something that happens because something else has happened. *You left the gate open and, as a consequence, the sheep got out.* **consequently** (adjective).

conservation (noun)
protecting valuable or important things, such as nature, wildlife, buildings, or art.

consider
considering considered (verb)
1 to think seriously about something. *You never consider my feelings!*
2 to make a judgement after thinking about something. *I consider that to be a wasted journey.*

considerate (adjective)
If you are **considerate**, you think about other people's feelings before you do or say things. *It was very considerate of you to save a place for me at the front.*

considering (conjunction)
taking into account. *The school fair was a success, considering the weather.*

consist consisting consisted (verb)
What something **consists of** is the things or parts that it is made up of.

consistent (adjective)
always the same. *Fatima's grades are consistent.* **consistently** (adverb).

console (noun)
a device that is connected to a screen and used for playing computer games.

consonant (noun)
a letter of the alphabet that is not one of the vowels **a**, **e**, **i**, **o** or **u**. There are twenty-one consonants in the alphabet.

constant (adjective)
continuous, not stopping, or always the same. **constantly** (adverb).

constellation (noun)
a group of stars that look like they are arranged in a pattern in the sky, and that have a name.

The **Big Dipper** and the **Little Dipper** can be seen near each other in the night sky.

The Little Dipper is also known as the **Little Bear**.

Little Dipper

the Big Dipper or Plough

The **Great Bear** is easy to spot – look for the seven stars that make the tail.

Taurus (The Bull)

Orion (The Hunter)

Orion's belt

Orion is a great hunter in Greek mythology. Look for the three bright stars called "Orion's belt".

Lepus (The Hare)

These are some famous **constellations**.

construct
constructing constructed *(verb)*
to build something or put it together.
construction *(noun)*.

constructive *(adjective)*
positive and helping someone or
something to improve. *Constructive
feedback.* **constructively** *(adverb)*.

consult **consulting consulted** *(verb)*
to ask someone for their opinion
or approval. **consultant** *(noun)*,
consultation *(noun)*.

consume
consuming consumed *(verb)*
1 to eat or drink something.
2 to use something up. *This car consumes
a lot of fuel.* **consumption** *(noun)*.

consumer *(noun)*
someone who buys goods, eats food,
or uses services.

contact **contacting contacted**
1 *(verb)* to communicate with someone,
for example by phone or email. *I'll
contact you next week.* **contact** *(noun)*.
2 If two things are **in contact**,
they are touching.

contact lens *(noun)*
a very thin piece of plastic that some
people wear on the surface of their
eye, to help them see better.

contagious *(adjective)*
If an illness is **contagious**, it can spread,
usually by people touching each other.
contagion *(noun)*.

contain
containing contained *(verb)*
to have or hold things inside. *This box
contains my pencils.* **container** *(noun)*.

content *(kon-**tent**) (adjective)*
If you are **content**, you are
feeling happy and comfortable.
contentedly *(adverb)*.

contents *(**kon**-tents) (plural noun)*
1 The **contents** of something, such
as a book or drawer, are the things
that are inside it.
2 a list, near the beginning of a book,
showing what is in it.

contest *(noun)*
a competition.

continent *(noun)*
a very large area of land, that is usually
made up of lots of different countries.

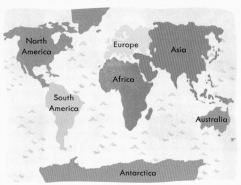

This map shows the seven **continents** of the world.

continual *(adjective)*
If something is **continual**, especially
a noise, it goes on and on without
stopping. **continually** *(adverb)*.

continue
continuing continued *(verb)*
to carry on. *The story continues
over the page.*

continuous *(adjective)*
Something that is **continuous** carries
on without being interrupted.
continuously *(adverb)*.

contract *(noun)*
a written agreement between two
people or organizations, which says
what each side must do.

contraction *(noun)*
two words which are shortened and
joined with an apostrophe. "Wouldn't"
is a contraction of "would not".

contradict
contradicting contradicted *(verb)*
to argue against something. *I said
the station was closed, but Charlie
contradicted me.* **contradiction** *(noun)*.

contrary *(adjective)*
opposite. *Contrary to what you may
have heard, school has not been
cancelled today.* **contrary** *(noun)*.

contrast (noun)
a strong and noticeable difference between two things, especially colours. *This sunshine is a nice contrast to the last two weeks of rain we've had.* **contrast** *(verb)*, **contrasting** *(adjective)*.

contribute
contributing contributed *(verb)*
to give money or things to help something. *Can you contribute anything for the cake stall on Sunday?* **contribution** *(noun)*, **contributor** *(noun)*.

control
controlling controlled *(verb)*
1 to make someone or something do exactly what you want. **control** *(noun)*.
2 to have power over someone or something. *Mrs Alexander controls the entire company.* **control** *(noun)*.

controls (plural noun)
the buttons, knobs, and so on, that you use to make a machine work.

controversial (adjective)
If something is **controversial**, not everyone agrees on it and it tends to cause arguments. *Nuclear power is a controversial subject.* **controversy** *(noun)*.

convenient (adjective)
1 easy to use or do, or requiring very little effort. *The drawer under my bed is a convenient place to store my shoes.*
2 close by. *Gran's house is very convenient for the shops.* **convenience** *(noun)*.
3 happening at a helpful time, or fitting in well with your plans. *The bus arrived just as we got to the station, which was convenient.* **conveniently** *(adverb)*.

convent (noun)
a place where nuns live.

conversation (noun)
two or more people talking about something. *Tara and I had an interesting conversation about pets.* **conversational** *(adjective)*.

convert converting converted (verb)
to change something into something else. *We converted our euros into dollars.* **conversion** *(noun)*.

convex (adjective)
bulging or curving outwards. **See lens**.

conveyor belt (noun)
a moving surface, for example at the tills in a supermarket.

convict convicting convicted (verb)
If someone is **convicted** of a crime, they have officially been found guilty of it in a court. **conviction** *(noun)*.

convince
convincing convinced *(verb)*
to make someone believe that something is true, or make them share your point of view. *It took years to convince my sister that there are no monsters under her bed.* **convincing** *(adjective)*.

cook cooking cooked (verb)
to prepare food, often by heating it. **cook** *(noun)*, **cookery** *(noun)*.

barbecuing　　　steaming　　　boiling

three ways of **cooking** food

cooker (noun)
a machine used for cooking food.

cookie (noun)
1 a sweet biscuit.
2 a piece of computer code that tracks how you use a website and sends information to the site's owner.

cool cooler coolest (adjective)
1 chilled, or slightly cold. *I need a cool drink after all that running around.*
2 calm, or not showing emotion. *Marcia always keeps cool in a crisis.*
3 Someone who is **cool** is well-liked and admired.
4 Something that is **cool** is exciting and interesting. *Jon has a cool new bike.*

A
B
C
D
E
F
G
H
I
J
K
L
M
N
O
P
Q
R
S
T
U
V
W
X
Y
Z

The prefix 'co-'

co-operative
co-ordinate
co-ordinated

The prefix 'co-' means "with someone or something else", and is often seen in words that have something to do with being or working together. Many of these words have a hyphen to make them easier to say.

co-operate
co-operating co-operated *(verb)*
to work with other people and be helpful.

co-operative *(adjective)*
Someone who is **co-operative** is helpful and works well with other people.

co-ordinate **co-ordinating co-ordinated** *(verb)*
1 to organize or arrange people, events, or activities. **co-ordination** *(noun)*.
2 to match colours and patterns. *I have co-ordinated my outfit.*

co-ordinated *(adjective)*
1 matching or going well together.
2 If you are **co-ordinated**, you move well and are not clumsy.

cope **coping coped** *(verb)*
to manage, especially when things are difficult. *We left Arun in charge of the younger children and he coped well.*

copper *(noun)*
a metal with a reddish-brown colour, which is often used for electrical wires. **copper** *(adjective)*.

copy **copies copying copied** *(verb)*
1 to make something that looks the same or is exactly the same as something else. **copy** *(noun)*.
2 to do something that is exactly the same, or in exactly the same way, as someone else.

coral *(noun)*
a hard, rock-like structure found in some warm, shallow areas of the sea, made by lots of tiny animals that group together.

brain coral

types of **corals**

Devonshire cup coral

cord *(noun)*
thick string or rope.

core *(noun)*
the central part of something, for example an apple or the Earth.

cork *(noun)*
1 a type of soft bark, used to make stoppers for bottles, and for mats and flooring.
2 a bottle stopper.

corkscrew *(noun)*
1 a tool used to remove corks from bottles.
2 a spiral shape.

corn *(noun)*
1 wheat grain, often used to make flour.
2 maize. It is also known as **sweetcorn**. *See* **vegetable**.

corner *(noun)*
the point at which two lines, surfaces or streets meet, usually at a right angle.

correct *(adjective)*
right, or true. *That's the correct answer.*
correctly *(adverb)*, **correct** *(verb)*, **correction** *(noun)*.

corridor *(noun)*
a long passage in a building or train.

corrode **corroding corroded** *(verb)*
to weaken, damage or destroy metal or other materials over a long period of time. *The rain has corroded my old bike.* **corrosion** *(noun)*, **corrosive** *(adjective)*.

corrupt *(adjective)*
1 If a person is **corrupt**, they are dishonest and unfair. **corrupt** *(verb)*, **corruption** *(noun)*.
2 If a computer file or piece of hardware is **corrupt**, it has become damaged and will not work properly.

cosmetic *(adjective)*
on the surface, or to do with how someone or something looks. *Cosmetic surgery.*

cosmetics *(plural noun)*
make-up and beauty products.

cost *(noun)*
how much you have to pay to buy something. **cost** *(verb)*.

costume *(noun)*
1 clothes worn by actors, or by people who are going to a special event.
2 clothing from a time in history. *Medieval costume.*

1450s   1550s   1630s   1750s   1850s

European costume

cosy **cosier cosiest** *(adjective)*
If a place is **cosy**, it is small, warm, and comfortable. *Putting pillows in our treehouse made it very cosy.*

cot *(noun)*
a small bed with high sides for a baby.

cottage *(noun)*
a small house, usually in the countryside. *My grandparents live in an old black-and-white cottage.*

cotton *(noun)*
1 a light material made from the fibres of the cotton plant, and used for making clothes. *Our school uniform includes a white cotton shirt.*
2 thin thread, used for sewing.

cotton wool *(noun)*
soft pads or balls of cotton, often used for cleaning skin.

couch *(noun)*
a long, comfortable seat with arms and a back, for two or more people.

cough **coughing coughed** *(verb)*
to make a sudden loud noise in your throat as you force air out of your lungs, often because you have a cold or other illness. **cough** *(noun)*.

could *(verb)*
1 the past or conditional form of **can**. *I could never work out where Fred went to on Friday nights.*
2 You use **could** to ask for something politely. *Could I have a drink of water?*

council *(noun)*
a group of people who meet and discuss how an organization or an area should be run. **councillor** *(noun)*.

counsellor *(noun)*
someone who is trained to help other people with their problems and give them advice. **counselling** *(noun)*.

count **counting counted** *(verb)*
1 to say numbers in order.
2 to find out how many there are of something. **count** *(noun)*.
3 **count on** to rely on someone to do something. *I was counting on Yolanda to bring the tickets.*

counter *(noun)*
1 a flat surface in a shop, a café, or a kitchen.
2 a small piece used in a board game.

countless *(adjective)*
too many to count. *Beth has had countless chances to apologize.*

country **countries** *(noun)*
1 an area of land or a nation that has its own government.
2 land away from towns and cities. **country** *(adjective)*.

Spelling tip

countries   **copies**

Remember that to make a word that ends with a consonant and then a 'y' plural, you remove the 'y' and then add '–ies'.

countryside (noun)
land away from towns and cities with few or no buildings in it.

county counties (noun)
an area of a country around a town or city, run by a council.

couple (noun)
1 two things or people, especially two people in a relationship.
2 a small number. *Sara says she'll be ready in a couple of minutes.*

coupon (noun)
a piece of paper or card that can be exchanged for something else, or that gets you money off the cost of something.

courage (noun)
bravery. *It took courage for Sam to disagree with his grandfather.* **courageous** (adjective), **courageously** (adverb).

courgette (noun)
a long, green vegetable.

course (noun)
1 the direction or path of something, such as a river.
2 a series of lessons or training sessions. *Dad is taking a course in Italian.*
3 a part of a meal. *I had soup for my first course.*
4 a piece of land set up for a sport. *A golf course.*
5 You say **of course** to emphasize what you are saying. *Of course you can stay.*

court (noun)
1 an area set up for playing a game such as tennis or squash.
2 the people who decide on legal cases, and the building where the cases happen.
3 the family and servants of a king or queen. **courtier** (noun).

courteous (adjective)
polite and formal. **courteously** (adverb), **courtesy** (noun).

cousin (noun)
the child of your uncle or aunt.

cove (noun)
a small area where the sea comes inland, often surrounded by cliffs.

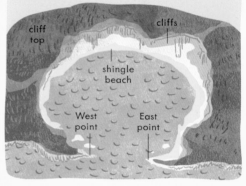

cliff top

cliffs

shingle beach

West point

East point

This picture shows **Lulworth Cove**, which is in Dorset in the south of England.

cover covering covered
1 (verb) to put something over something else to hide or protect it. **cover** (noun).
2 (verb) to learn about or teach a topic. *This term we've covered Ancient Greece and Rome.*
3 (noun) the outside of a book or magazine.

cow (noun)
1 a large farm animal that eats grass and is kept for its milk and meat.
2 the female of certain animals, including elephants, whales, and dolphins.

coward (noun)
someone who avoids doing brave or scary things. **cowardice** (noun), **cowardly** (adjective).

cowboy (noun)
a man whose job is to look after cattle on large farms, especially in the USA.

cowboy on horseback

crab (noun)

an animal that usually lives near the sea, that has a hard shell, eight legs, and two claws called pincers.

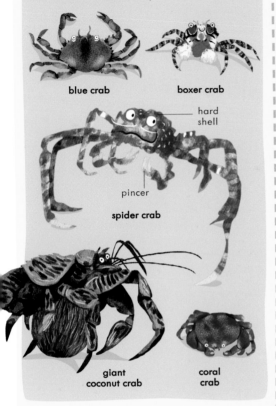

blue crab

boxer crab

hard shell

pincer

spider crab

giant coconut crab

coral crab

some different types of **crabs**

crack **cracking cracked** (verb)

1 to split or start to break, or to make something start to break. *I've cracked my phone screen.* **crack** (noun).
2 to make a loud, sharp sound. *The twigs cracked under my feet.* **crack** (noun).
3 to solve a puzzle or a mystery. *The police haven't yet cracked the case.*

cracker (noun)

1 a thin, crisp, savoury biscuit.
2 a Christmas decoration that can be pulled apart to make a loud bang, and that usually contains a small gift, a paper hat, and a joke.

crackle **crackling crackled** (verb)

to make lots of dry popping sounds.

cradle (noun)

a baby's bed which can be rocked gently.

craft (noun)

1 a skill learned over time.
2 making things with your hands for fun.

crafty **craftier craftiest** (adjective)

Someone who is **crafty** finds clever, but often dishonest, ways of getting what they want. **craftily** (adverb).

cram **cramming crammed** (verb)

to squeeze things into a small space.

cramp (noun)

muscle pain caused by exercise or by being in an uncomfortable position.

cramped (adjective)

uncomfortable, or lacking in space. *The back of the car was very cramped.*

crane (noun)

1 a machine for lifting heavy objects, especially at building sites or for loading and unloading ships.
2 a large bird with a long neck and long legs.

cranky

crankier crankiest (adjective)
If you are **cranky**, you are grumpy and impatient.

crash

crashes crashing crashed (verb)
1 to break or smash into pieces with a loud noise. *The cars crashed at the roundabout.* **crash** (noun).
2 to make a loud, jarring sound. **crash** (noun).
3 If a computer or computer program **crashes**, it stops working for a while and needs to be restarted. **crash** (noun).

crate (noun)

a wooden or plastic box used to hold and move things.

crater (noun)

a large circular hole in the ground made by an explosion or an asteroid, or the mouth of a volcano.

crave **craving craved** (verb)

to want something really badly. *I'm craving chocolate.* **craving** (noun).

A B **C** D E F G H I J K L M N O P Q R S T U V W X Y Z

crawl crawling crawled *(verb)*
1 to move on your hands and knees. *The baby has just learnt to crawl.* **crawl** *(noun).*
2 to move very slowly. *The traffic is crawling today.*

crayon *(noun)*
a coloured pencil or stick of wax for drawing and colouring.

craze *(noun)*
a sudden popular fashion.

crazy crazier craziest *(adjective)*
1 Someone who is **crazy** is wild and foolish. **crazily** *(adverb).*
2 If you are **crazy about** someone or something, you are extremely keen on them. *Zak is crazy about fantasy games.*

creak creaking creaked *(verb)*
to make a squeaking sound. *The floorboards creaked as Theo came downstairs.*

cream *(noun)*
1 a thick, white liquid food taken from the top of milk. **creamy** *(adjective).*
2 a yellow-white colour. **cream** *(adjective).*
3 a product that you rub into your skin.
4 the best of something.

crease creasing creased *(verb)*
to make a fold in a piece of paper or fabric, or to crumple it slightly. **crease** *(noun).*

create creating created *(verb)*
to make something. *Beth says she has created a time-travel machine.*

Spelling tip

create → creation

If you're struggling to remember whether a noun ends with '-tion' or '-sion', remember that if it is related to a verb that ends '**-ate**', the ending will always be '**-ation**': "create" → "creation"; "educate" → "education".

creation *(noun)*
1 the process of making something. *There are lots of different stories about the creation of the world.*
2 something that you have made. *Look at my wonderful creation.*

creative *(adjective)*
Someone who is **creative** is artistic and good at making things or thinking of new ideas. *Dara is very creative: all his Christmas presents are home-made.*

creature *(noun)*
a living being, especially an animal.

crèche *(noun)*
a place where small children are looked after while their parents are busy.

credible *(adjective)*
If someone or something is **credible**, you can believe or trust them. *It's a very credible story.*

credit *(noun)*
1 recognition or praise for doing something. *It was Marie's idea, but Chloe got all the credit.* **credit** *(verb).*
2 If you buy something **on credit**, you pay for it at a later date.

credit card *(noun)*
a card from a bank which lets people buy things and pay for them at a later date.

creep creeping crept *(verb)*
to move very slowly and quietly. *Mike crept into the kitchen and looked inside the biscuit tin.*

creepy *(adjective)*
Someone or something that is **creepy** is spooky and makes you feel nervous or frightened. *The old house was really creepy at night.*

crescent *(noun)*
1 a curved shape, like the shape of a new moon.
2 a curved street.

crew *(noun)*
a team of people who work together, especially on a boat, a ship, or a plane.

cricket (noun)

1 a game played on grass between two teams of eleven players. **cricketer** (noun).
2 an insect that makes a chirping sound.

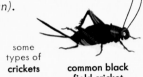

some types of crickets

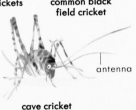

common black field cricket

speckled bush cricket

cave cricket

antenna

crime (noun)

1 an act which is against the law. *Stealing is a crime.* **criminal** (adjective).
2 illegal activities in general. *Too many people are victims of crime.*

criminal (noun)

someone who commits a crime. *The criminal will spend four years in jail.*

crisis crises (noun)

a dangerous or bad situation which needs to be dealt with quickly. *Amit is dealing with a family crisis.*

crisp crisper crispest

1 (noun) a very thin, crunchy slice of deep-fried potato, usually with salt or other flavourings added.
2 (adjective) dry and crunchy. *Crisp leaves.* **crispy** (adjective).
3 (adjective) stiff and not floppy. *A crisp white shirt.*
4 (adjective) icy and cold. *A crisp winter's morning.*

critic (noun)

1 someone who disagrees with another person, a decision, or an idea. *The new road plans have many critics.*
2 someone who gives their opinion about books, films, shows, or restaurants.

critical (adjective)

1 If you are **critical** of someone or something, you find faults in them.
2 extremely serious. *The patient is in a critical condition.* **critically** (adverb).

criticize or criticise

criticizing criticized (verb)
to point out the faults or bad points in someone or something. *Ahmed criticized my decision to dye my hair.* **criticism** (noun).

croak croaking croaked

1 (noun) the low, rough noise that a frog makes. **croak** (verb).
2 (verb) to make a rough, hoarse sound in your throat, like a frog.

crocodile (noun)

a large animal that lives in and around water, with strong jaws, sharp teeth, and a long body and tail.

crook (noun)

a dishonest person.

crooked (adjective)

1 not straight. *The picture was crooked, so Eddie straightened it.*
2 dishonest.

crop (noun)

a plant that is grown for food.

cross crosses (noun)

1 a shape made by two lines, such as **+** or **x**.
2 the symbol of the Christian Church.

cross crosses crossing crossed (verb)

1 to go from one side of something to the other. *We need to find a way to cross the river.* **crossing** (noun).
2 If you **cross** your arms or legs, you put one over the other.
3 If you **cross out** something you have written, you put a line through it.

cross (adjective)

angry or annoyed. *Jen's dad was cross that she hadn't done the washing-up.*

crossroads (plural noun)

a place where one road crosses another.

cross-section (noun)

a diagram that shows the inside of something by cutting through it.

crossword (noun)

a puzzle in which you have to put words into boxes by answering clues.

a b c d e f g h i j k l m n o p q r s t u v w x y z

crouch
crouches crouching crouched (verb)
to stand with your knees bent, low to the ground. *Cats often crouch before pouncing on their prey.*

crow (noun)
a large, black bird.

crowd (noun)
a large number of people gathered together. *We lost Polly in the crowd.* **crowd** (verb), **crowded** (adjective).

crown **crowning crowned**
1 (noun) a headdress made of gold or silver and jewels, worn by a king or queen.
2 (verb) to make someone a king or queen. *She was crowned in 1952.*

crucial (adjective)
essential, or most important. *The crucial ingredient is fresh basil.* **crucially** (adverb).

crude **cruder crudest** (adjective)
rude or offensive. *A crude joke.*

cruel **crueller cruellest** (adjective)
Someone who is **cruel** is unkind and deliberately makes other people suffer. **cruelty** (noun).

cruise (noun)
a relaxed trip taken for pleasure on a large ship. **cruise** (verb).

crumb (noun)
a tiny piece of food such as bread or cake.

crumble **crumbling crumbled** (verb)
to break down into tiny pieces. *My cake crumbled as I got it out of the oven.* **crumbling** (adjective).

crumple
crumpling crumpled (verb)
to crush paper or fabric to make it creased and untidy. **crumpled** (adjective).

crunchy
crunchier crunchiest (adjective)
If something is **crunchy**, it is dry and hard, and makes a noise when you chew it or step on it. *Crunchy cereal.* **crunch** (noun), **crunch** (verb).

crush
crushes crushing crushed (verb)
1 to squeeze something until it is damaged or liquid comes out of it. *I accidentally crushed a snail shell.* **crush** (noun).
2 to destroy. *James's hopes of playing in the team were crushed when he broke his leg.* **crushing** (adjective).

crust (noun)
the hard, dry outer part of something, such as a loaf of bread. **crusty** (adjective).

crutch **crutches** (noun)
a special stick that people use to help them walk when they have hurt their legs.

cry **cries crying cried** (verb)
1 When you **cry**, tears come from your eyes, usually because you are sad.
2 to shout, often because you are surprised or hurt. **cry** (noun).

cub (noun)
a young wild animal, especially a lion, a tiger, a wolf, a bear, or a fox.

cube (noun)
a solid shape with six square faces that are all the same size. *See* **shapes**, *page 348.*

cubic (adjective)
a word used to describe measures of volume. *Cubic centimetres.*

cubicle (noun)
a small enclosed area in a larger room, used for a particular purpose, such as getting changed or using the toilet.

cuckoo *(noun)*
a bird that lives in woodland and lays its eggs in other birds' nests.

cuckoo

cucumber *(noun)*
a long, green vegetable. *See* **vegetable**.

cuddle **cuddling cuddled** *(verb)*
to show affection by hugging someone. *Ellie cuddled the kitten for hours.* **cuddle** *(noun)*, **cuddly** *(adjective)*.

cue *(noun)*
1 words or something else which reminds you to speak or do something else. *When Ross leaves the stage, that's your cue to start playing the next song.*
2 a long pole used to play games such as pool or snooker.

cuff *(noun)*
the part of a sleeve that goes around your wrist.

cul-de-sac *(noun)*
a road or street which has only one way in or out.

culprit *(noun)*
someone who has done something wrong. *Somebody stuck a red nose on Mr Andrews' portrait, and they haven't found the culprit yet.*

culture *(noun)*
1 the arts, such as music, painting, theatre, and so on. **cultural** *(adjective)*.
2 a way of thinking or behaving, or a tradition. *This school has a culture of encouraging students to think for themselves.* **cultural** *(adjective)*.

cunning *(adjective)*
Someone who is **cunning** is clever, but may also trick people.

cup *(noun)*
1 a small container that you drink from.
2 a trophy given as a prize in a competition.

cupboard *(noun)*
a piece of furniture with doors, used for storing things.

cure **curing cured** *(verb)*
to make someone who has an illness or injury better. **cure** *(noun)*.

curious *(adjective)*
1 Someone who is **curious** wants to know or find out about things. *Eve was curious about the locked room.* **curiosity** *(noun)*, **curiously** *(adverb)*.
2 Something that is **curious** is strange or odd. *There's a curious smell coming from the fridge.* **curiously** *(adverb)*.

curl **curling curled**
1 *(noun)* a curved piece of hair. **curl** *(verb)*, **curly** *(adjective)*.
2 *(verb)* If you **curl up**, you make yourself into a rounded shape.

currant *(noun)*
1 a small, dried grape, used in cooking.
2 a soft black, red or white fruit, that grows on a bush.

three types of **currants**

blackcurrants

white currants   redcurrants

currency *(noun)*
the money used in a particular country. *Many countries in Europe share one currency, the euro.*

current
1 *(adjective)* happening or in place now. *The school has grown too large for its current site.* **currently** *(adverb)*.
2 *(noun)* a flow of air, water, or electricity. *Be careful when you swim here, because the current is very strong.*

Spelling tip

currant   current

One letter makes a big difference to the meanings of the words "currant" and "current", so take care when you spell them!

curriculum *(noun)*
a course of study that has been set out and agreed. *Maths is an important subject in the curriculum.*

curry *(noun)*
a type of dish that comes from Southeast Asia, which involves cooking vegetables and meat in spicy sauces.

coriander seeds

ground ginger

ground turmeric

cumin seeds

fenugreek

cardamom pods

black peppercorns

These spices can be used to make **curry.**

cursor *(noun)*
a small symbol which shows your position on a computer screen.

curtain *(noun)*
1 a piece of material at a window that can be pulled across to let in or block light from outside.
2 the large piece of material that is opened or raised at the start of a stage performance.

curve **curving curved** *(verb)*
to bend or have a rounded shape. *The road curved up the hillside.* **curve** *(noun)*, **curved** *(adjective)*.

cushion *(noun)*
a soft, padded object used to make a seat more comfortable.

custard *(noun)*
a sweet sauce made from egg yolks, sugar, and milk or cream.

custom *(noun)*
a habit or tradition. *In India, it is a custom to eat with the right hand.* **customary** *(adjective)*.

customer *(noun)*
a person buying something. *There was a long queue of customers at the till.*

Spelling tip   cutting

Notice that the '**t**' at the end of "**cut**" is doubled before you add '**-ing**', and that the past tense form is the same as the present tense form: "**cut**". Quite a few one-syllable words follow this pattern, such as "shut/shu**tt**ing/**shut**" and "hit/hi**tt**ing/**hit**".

cut **cutting cut** *(verb)*
1 to divide something using scissors or a knife. *I cut the paper in two.*
2 to be hurt by something sharp. *I cut my hand on the tin.* **cut** *(noun)*.
3 to reduce something. *The government has cut spending on the arts.*

cut and paste *(noun)*
selecting text or an image from one part of a computer document, deleting it, and placing it somewhere else.

cute **cuter cutest** *(adjective)*
sweet and nice to look at. *Your kitten is so cute.*

cutlery *(noun)*
knives, forks, and spoons.

cycle **cycling cycled** *(verb)*
to go somewhere by bicycle, or to exercise on a bicycle. *I cycled to Jamie's house.* **cycling** *(noun)*.

cygnet *(noun)*
a young swan. *See* **baby.**

cylinder *(noun)*
a solid shape with straight sides and circular ends. *See* **shapes**, *page 348.*

cymbal *(noun)*
a disc-shaped musical instrument made of metal. You play it by hitting it with a stick or another cymbal. *See* **percussion.**

cynical *(adjective)*
If you are **cynical**, you don't believe something and don't take it seriously. *Ben was cynical about the so-called miracle cure.* **cynicism** *(noun).*

Dd

dab dabbing dabbed *(verb)*
to touch something gently with something soft. *Amanda dabbed her eyes with a tissue.*

dabble dabbling dabbled *(verb)*
1 to dip something into water. *We dabbled our toes in the stream.*
2 If you **dabble in** something, you don't do it very seriously or very well.

dad *or* **daddy** *(noun)*
a friendly word for **father**. *My dad is funny.*

daffodil *(noun)*
a trumpet-shaped flower that blooms in the spring and can be yellow, white, or orange.

dagger *(noun)*
a short, pointed knife.

daily *(adjective)*
happening every day. *Robbie's daily journey to school takes an hour.* **daily** *(adverb)*.

The **daffodil** is the national flower of Wales.

dainty daintier daintiest *(adjective)*
elegant and delicate. *Jemma always wears dainty shoes.* **daintily** *(adverb)*.

dairy dairies
1 *(noun)* a place where milk is bottled and where things made from milk, such as butter, cheese, and yogurt, are made.
2 *(adjective)* **Dairy** foods are ones which contain milk, such as butter and cheese.

some types of **dairy foods**

cheese   yogurt

ice cream

Word origin   daisy

This word comes from the Old English words "**dæges eage**", which mean "**day's eye**", because daisies only open their petals during the day.

daisy daisies *(noun)*
a type of wild or garden flower with white petals and a yellow middle.

dam *(noun)*
a barrier built to hold back water.

damage damaging damaged
1 *(verb)* to harm someone or spoil something.
2 *(noun)* the harm that something does. *There was a lot of damage after the fire.*

damp damper dampest *(adjective)*
slightly wet. **damp** *(noun)*.

dance dancing danced *(verb)*
to move in time to music. **dance** *(noun)*, **dancer** *(noun)*, **dancing** *(noun)*.

dandruff *(noun)*
white flakes of dead skin in your hair.

danger *(noun)*
1 something that is not safe, or could harm you. **dangerous** *(adjective)*.
2 If you are **in danger**, you are not safe.

dangle dangling dangled *(verb)*
to hang loosely. *Simon's button was dangling by a thread.*

dare daring dared *(verb)*
1 If you **dare** someone to do something, you challenge them to do it. **dare** *(noun)*.
2 to be brave enough to do something. *I don't dare jump across the stream.* **daring** *(adjective)*.

dark darker darkest *(adjective)*
without any light. *The cave was very dark.* **darkness** *(noun)*.

a b c **d** e f g h i j k l m n o p q r s t u v w x y z

dart **darting darted**
1 (verb) to move quickly and suddenly. *The fox darted across the road.*
2 (noun) a small, pointed arrow that you throw at a board to win points.
3 (noun) In a game of **darts**, you aim and throw metal darts at a board to win points.

dash **dashes dashing dashed**
1 (verb) If you **dash** somewhere, you go there quickly. *Mum dashed into the shop on the way to work.*
2 (noun) the punctuation mark (–), used in writing. Be careful not to get it mixed it up with a hyphen, which looks similar, but is shorter.

Dashes

The main uses of dashes are:

1. to add extra information to a sentence: "Many children – like my brother – don't learn to walk until they are over a year old."

2. to show a break in a sentence, where you might also use a comma or semicolon: "We'll have to save up for it – unless, of course, we win the lottery."

data (noun)
information, or facts. *Our laptop has lots of data on it.*

database (noun)
a store of information on a computer.

date (noun)
1 the day of the month, and, sometimes, the year. *The date today is 5th February.*
2 a small, sweet fruit that grows on a palm tree.
3 If two people go on a **date**, they go out together. **date** (verb).

dates — date palm

daughter (noun)
A girl or woman is the **daughter** of her parents.

daughter-in-law (noun)
If you have a **daughter-in-law**, she is the woman married to your son.

dawn (noun)
the time when the Sun rises, at the beginning of the day. *We had to be up at dawn to catch our flight.*

day (noun)
1 a period of 24 hours, from midnight to midnight.
2 the part of the day when it is light. *I'm going to spend the day cycling.*

daydream **daydreaming daydreamed**
1 (verb) to let your mind wander off and think about other things. *I always daydream in maths lessons.*
2 (noun) a dream you have during the day, usually when you should be concentrating on something else.

daze (noun)
If you are **in a daze**, you are a bit confused and dreamy. *Mum and I were in a daze when we came out of the cinema.* **dazed** (adjective).

dazzle **dazzling dazzled** (verb)
1 If a bright light **dazzles** someone, it makes it hard for them to see properly. *The car's headlights dazzled me.* **dazzling** (adjective).
2 to impress or amaze someone. *The ballet dancer's beauty dazzled me.* **dazzling** (adjective).

dead (adjective)
not alive any more. *My pet goldfish is dead.*

deadline (noun)
the time something must be done by. *The deadline for your story is Tuesday.*

deadly **deadlier deadliest** (adjective)
If something is **deadly**, it is likely to kill you. *Some snake bites are deadly.*

deaf deafer deafest (adjective)
A **deaf** person can't hear anything,
or has trouble with their hearing.
deafness (noun).

deafening (adjective)
very loud. *The wardrobe fell with
a deafening crash.*

deal dealing dealt
1 (noun) a business arrangement
or agreement.
2 (verb) If you **deal with** someone
or something, you sort it out.
3 (verb) When you **deal** cards, you
hand them out to all the players.

dear dearer dearest (adjective)
1 If someone is **dear** to you, you care
about them very much. *A dear friend.*
2 If something is **dear**, it's quite
expensive to buy.
3 When you write a letter to someone,
you start with **Dear** and then their
name. *Dear Mr Brown.*

death (noun)
the end of life.

debate debating debated (verb)
to discuss something, considering
different views and possibilities.
debate (noun).

debt (noun)
1 a sum of money
that you owe
someone.
2 If you are
in debt to
someone, you
owe them something.

> Don't forget
> that the 'b' before
> the 't' in "debt"
> is silent, so it's
> pronounced "det".

decade (noun)
ten years. *I lived in Poland for a decade.*

decay decaying decayed (verb)
to rot or go bad. **decay** (noun).

deceive deceiving deceived (verb)
If you **deceive** someone, you don't
tell them the truth. **deceit** (noun),
deceitful (adjective).

December (noun)
the twelfth and final month of the year.

decent (adjective)
good, well-mannered, or acceptable.
decency (noun), **decently** (adverb).

deception (noun)
a trick. **deceptive** (adjective),
deceptively (adverb).

decide deciding decided (verb)
If you **decide** something, you make up
your mind about it. *Ollie decided to stay.*

deciduous (adjective)
A **deciduous** tree loses its leaves in winter.

decimal (adjective)
1 A **decimal system** of counting
uses units of ten.
2 A **decimal** or **decimal fraction** is a
whole number with a dot and more
numbers after it, such as 0.5, 6.25,
and so on. The numbers after the dots
are tenths, hundredths, and so on.

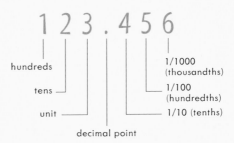

decimal fraction showing the different units

3 A **decimal point** is the dot in
a decimal fraction.
4 A **decimal place** is the position
of a number after a decimal point.
1.65 has two decimal places.

decision (noun)
When you make a **decision**, you make
up your mind.

decisive (adjective)
good at making decisions quickly.
decisively (adverb).

deck (noun)
1 the floor of a boat or a ship.
2 a wooden platform outside a building.

declare declaring declared (verb)
to announce something. *I declare that
Sol is the winner.* **declaration** (noun).

decline **declining declined** (verb)
1 If you **decline** something, you say "no" to it. *I had to decline the invitation.*
2 to get worse. *The weather declined after the weekend.* **decline** (noun).

decorate
decorating decorated (verb)
1 to make something look nicer, by arranging or adding things. *Let's decorate the cake.* **decoration** (noun).
2 to paint a room, or put up new wallpaper. **decorator** (noun), **decoration** (noun).

decrease
decreasing decreased (verb)
to get smaller, or less. *My appetite has decreased recently.* **decrease** (noun).

dedicate
dedicating dedicated (verb)
If you **dedicate** yourself to something, you give it a lot of your time and energy. **dedication** (noun).

deed (noun)
something you do. *Try to do a good deed every day.*

deep **deeper deepest** (adjective)
1 Something that is **deep** goes down a long way. *The lake is very deep in the middle.*
2 intense, or strong. *I have a deep hatred of sprouts.* **deeply** (adverb).

comparison of the highest and **deepest** points on Earth

Mount Everest 8,850m (29,035ft) above sea level

Mariana Trench 11,035m (36,204ft) below sea level

deer **deer** (noun)
a large wild animal that is shy and often lives in woods and forests. Some deer, usually the males, have big, branching horns on their heads called antlers.

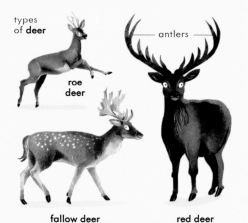

types of **deer**

antlers

roe deer

fallow deer

red deer

deface **defacing defaced** (verb)
to spoil the way something looks. *Vandals defaced the wall.*

defeat **defeating defeated** (verb)
to beat someone in a war or a competition. *The girls defeated the boys in the tug-of-war.*

defend **defending defended** (verb)
to protect someone or something from being attacked, damaged, or hurt. *I always defend my friends against bullies.* **defence** (noun).

defensive (adjective)
1 designed to protect or defend something, such as a building or goal. *There's a defensive wall around the city.*
2 If someone is **defensive**, they always act as if they are being criticized or attacked. **defensively** (adverb).

deficient (adjective)
lacking in something. *Junk food is deficient in goodness.* **deficiency** (noun).

define **defining defined** (verb)
to describe or explain something very clearly. *Please define exactly what you wish to do.*

The prefix 'de-'

deface
deflate
defrost

Many words that begin with 'de-' are to do with removing, undoing, or reducing something.

It comes from the Latin word 'de', meaning "**down from, away, or off**". For example, "**deflate**" is the opposite of "inflate".

definite (adjective)
certain or sure. *We need to make definite plans.* **definitely** (adverb).

definition (noun)
a phrase or sentence which explains what a word means. *Do you know the definition of the word "onomatopoeia"?*

deflate deflating deflated (verb)
to let the air out of something. *Everyone was disappointed when they deflated the bouncy castle.* **deflation** (noun).

deflect deflecting deflected (verb)
to make something change direction. *The boxer deflected the punch with his arm.* **deflection** (noun).

defrost defrosting defrosted (verb)
to let food that is frozen thaw out. *The chicken needs to defrost before we cook it.*

defy defies defying defied (verb)
If you **defy** someone, you refuse to do what they tell you to do. *Sam defied his dad by staying out past 7 p.m.* **defiant** (adjective), **defiantly** (adverb).

degree (noun)
1 temperatures and angles are measured in **degrees**. You use the symbol ° to show it. *The car skidded and turned round 180°. It is 30°C today.*
2 the qualification you get from a university or college. *She has a degree in French from York University.*

dehydrated (adjective)
If you are **dehydrated**, you do not have enough water in your body. **dehydration** (noun), **dehydrate** (verb).

delay delaying delayed (verb)
1 to make something happen later than it should have done. *Mum delayed the meal until Dad got home.* **delay** (noun).
2 to make someone or something late. *We were delayed by traffic.*

delete deleting deleted (verb)
to take something out of a piece of writing on a page, or on a computer screen. *I deleted the words I had spelt wrongly.*

deliberate (adjective)
If something is **deliberate**, someone has done it on purpose. *The player got sent off for a deliberate foul.* **deliberately** (adverb).

delicate (adjective)
1 easy to break. *Careful, that vase is old and very delicate.*
2 slender and graceful. *My friend Rosalind has such delicate hands and feet.* **delicately** (adverb).

delicatessen (noun)
a shop selling unusual foods from lots of different countries, especially meats and cheeses. It's often shortened to "deli".

delicious (adjective)
really tasty. *This sandwich is delicious.*

delight delighting delighted
1 (verb) to please someone very much. *Your singing delights me.*
2 (noun) a great pleasure. *It was a delight to watch the band playing.* **delightfully** (adverb).

deliver delivering delivered (verb)
to take something to someone. *The postman delivered the letters to our house.* **delivery** (noun).

demand
demanding demanded (verb)
to ask for something very firmly. *I demand that you stop laughing and listen to me!* **demand** (noun).

A B C **D** E F G H I J K L M N O P Q R S T U V W X Y Z

demanding (adjective)
A **demanding** person is always asking for things, and is never happy.

democracy **democracies** (noun)
a way of running a country or organization in which people vote for who they want to be in charge, in elections. **democratic** (adjective).

demolish
demolishing demolished (verb)
to knock something, such as a building, down. *They demolished my old school.*

demon (noun)
a devil, or evil spirit. **demonic** (adjective).

demonstrate
demonstrating demonstrated (verb)
1 to show someone how to do something, or how something works. *The teacher demonstrated how to do the experiment.* **demonstration** (noun).
2 When a group of people **demonstrate**, they get together in public to show that they are unhappy about something. **demonstration** (noun).

den (noun)
1 Some wild animals live in homes called **dens**.
2 a cosy, secret place.

denim (noun)
a strong material made from cotton that is used to make jeans, jackets, and other clothing. *See* **jeans**.

denominator (noun)
In maths, the **denominator** is the number under the line in a fraction, such as '4' in $\frac{1}{4}$.

dense **denser densest** (adjective)
thick. *There's a dense fog today.* **density** (noun).

dent **denting dented** (verb)
If you **dent** something, you make a dip where it was smooth before. *Dad dented the car door.* **dent** (noun).

dentist (noun)
someone who is trained to care for people's teeth. **dental** (adjective).

deny **denies denying denied** (verb)
to say that something is not true. *Roxy denies cheating.* **denial** (noun).

depart **departing departed** (verb)
to leave, especially if you are going on a journey. **departure** (noun).

department (noun)
part of an organization, such as a hospital or shop. *The toy department.*

depend
depending depended (verb)
If you **depend** on someone or something, you rely on them.

dependable (adjective)
If someone is **dependable**, you can rely on them and trust them.

dependence (noun)
a strong need for someone or something. **dependency** (noun), **dependent** (adjective).

Word family

depend
dependable
dependence

These words are all related. The ending '**-able**' is added to the verb "depend" to make the adjective "depend**able**", and the ending '**-ence**' is added to make the noun "depend**ence**".

depressed (adjective)
If someone is **depressed**, they have an illness that makes them feel very sad and helpless. **depression** (noun).

deprive **depriving deprived** (verb)
to stop someone from having something, or to take it away from them. **deprived** (adjective), **deprivation** (noun).

depth (noun)
1 how deep something is.
2 If you study something **in depth**, you study it in a lot of detail.

deputy **deputies** (noun)
A **deputy** helps a more senior person, and may stand in for them when they are not there. *Mrs Jones is the head teacher, and Ms Harvey is her deputy.*

descend
descending descended (verb)
to go down to a lower place. *The lift descended very quickly.* **descent** (noun).

describe
describing described (verb)
to talk about someone or something, and say what they are like. *Ravi described the place perfectly.*

desert **deserting deserted**
1 (***des**-ert*) (noun) a very dry, often sandy place, where there is hardly any rain.
2 (*des-**ert***) (verb) to leave a person or place behind. **deserted** (adjective).

deserve **deserving deserved** (verb)
If you **deserve** something, you have earned it. *Sally deserved to win first prize in the competition.*

design (noun)
the shape, colour and style of something. **designer** (noun), **design** (verb).

desire **desiring desired** (verb)
If you **desire** something, you want it very much. **desire** (noun).

desk (noun)
a table for working at.

desktop
1 (adjective) A **desktop** computer is kept on a desk or table all the time.
2 (noun) the home screen on a computer, which has icons that you click on to open files and programs.

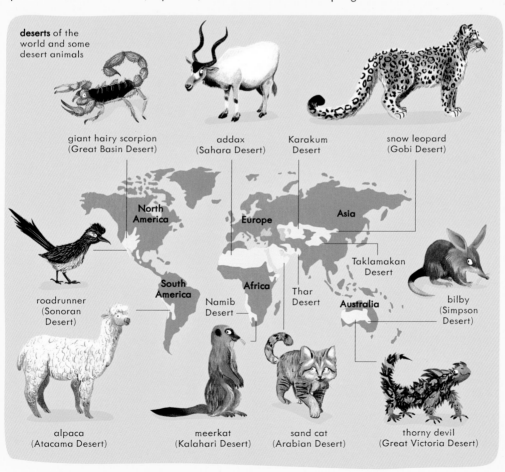

deserts of the world and some desert animals

giant hairy scorpion
(Great Basin Desert)

addax
(Sahara Desert)

Karakum
Desert

snow leopard
(Gobi Desert)

North America

Europe

Asia

Taklamakan
Desert

roadrunner
(Sonoran
Desert)

South
America

Africa

Namib
Desert

Thar
Desert

Australia

bilby
(Simpson
Desert)

alpaca
(Atacama Desert)

meerkat
(Kalahari Desert)

sand cat
(Arabian Desert)

thorny devil
(Great Victoria Desert)

a b c d e f g h i j k l m n o p q r s t u v w x y z

despair **despairing despaired** *(verb)*
to lose all hope. **despair** *(noun)*,
despairing *(adjective)*.

desperate *(adjective)*
1 When you are **desperate**, you will
do anything to make things better.
2 If a situation is **desperate**, it is very
urgent or dangerous. **desperately**
(adverb), **desperation** *(noun)*.

despise **despising despised** *(verb)*
to hate someone or something a lot.
Rachel despises mushrooms.

despite *(preposition)*
even though, or in spite of. *We won,
despite only getting one goal.*

dessert *(noun)*
a sweet dish eaten
after the main course
of a meal.

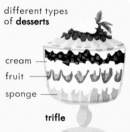

different types
of **desserts**

jelly

cream
fruit
sponge

trifle

fruit salad

destination *(noun)*
On a journey, the place you are going
to is your **destination**. *The destination
of this flight is Los Angeles.*

destiny **destinies** *(noun)*
Some people believe that your **destiny**
is the things that are supposed to happen
to you. *It's Freya's destiny to become
an astronaut.*

destroy
destroying destroyed *(verb)*
to ruin or spoil something. *That big
dog destroyed our sand castle.*
destruction *(noun)*.

destructive *(adjective)*
causing damage and unhappiness. *The
dog's behaviour was very destructive.*

detach
detaches detaching detached *(verb)*
to separate a part of something from
the rest of it. *The capsule detached
from the rocket.*

detached *(adjective)*
A **detached** house is not joined to any
other houses.

detail *(noun)*
a small part of something, or a fact
about it. *Please can you explain the
answer in more detail.*

detailed *(adjective)*
If something is **detailed**, it gives you lots
of information. *Farid gave a detailed
description of the creature he saw in
the forest.*

detective *(noun)*
someone whose job is to find out who has
committed a crime by looking for clues.

detention *(noun)*
a punishment which means you have
to stay in school when others are
allowed out.

determined *(adjective)*
If you are **determined** to do something,
you have made a firm decision to do it.
Verity is determined to run a marathon.

detest **detesting detested** *(verb)*
to hate someone or something very
much. *I detest cold cabbage.*

devastated *(adjective)*
1 very badly damaged, or almost
destroyed. *The village was devastated
by the earthquake.* **devastate** *(verb)*.
2 very shocked and upset. *Ben was
devastated when his toy boat sank.*

develop
developing developed *(verb)*
to grow, and gradually change. *Hugh's
talent for music developed over time.*
development *(noun)*.

device *(noun)*
a piece of equipment, or a tool. *A tin
opener is a device for opening tins.*

devil (noun)
1 an evil or wicked person.
2 In some religions, the **devil** is the most evil being that exists.

devious (adjective)
dishonest and nasty. *Aidan played a devious trick.* **deviousness** (noun).

devise devising devised (verb)
If you **devise** something, you make it up. *We devised a play at school.*

devoted (adjective)
loving and loyal. *My grandma's dog is devoted to her.*

devour devouring devoured (verb)
to eat something quickly and greedily.

dew (noun)
the droplets of water that you see on the grass and the ground in the early morning.

diabetes (noun)
an illness in which the body cannot control how much sugar there is in the blood. **diabetic** (adjective).

diagonal (adjective)
A **diagonal** line joins two opposite corners of a square or rectangle. **diagonally** (adverb).

diagram (noun)
a drawing or plan that shows the parts of something and explains it clearly.

dial dialling dialled
1 (noun) the round face of a clock, watch, or other measuring equipment.
2 (verb) to press buttons on a phone and call someone.

Spelling tip

dial → dialling → dialled

When you add an ending to the word "dial", you have to double the final 'l'. This is true for most other words ending in a short vowel and a single 'l'.

dialogue (noun)
1 a conversation between two people.
2 the words people say to each other in a play, television programme, or film.

diameter (noun)
You can find out the **diameter** of a circle by drawing a straight line across its centre, and measuring it. *See circle.*

diamond (noun)
1 a hard, clear, sparkly jewel that is very valuable and expensive. *See gem.*
2 a shape with four equal sides. *See shapes, page 348.*
3 **diamonds** one of the suits in a pack of cards. The symbol is a red diamond. *See card.*

diary diaries (noun)
a place or book with spaces to write notes about what has happened or will happen on every day of the year.

dice (noun)
a cube with six sides, with a different number of spots on each side. Dice are used in lots of games.

dictionary dictionaries (noun)
a book, like this one, that is full of words listed in alphabetical order, with their meanings.

did (verb)
the past tense of do.

die dying died (verb)
1 to stop living.
2 If someone says they are **dying** to do something, they mean they can't wait to do it. *I'm dying to see that film.*

diesel (*dee-zull*) (noun)
a type of fuel, used in many cars, trains, and trucks.

diet (*die-ut*) **dieting dieted**
1 (noun) what you eat. *A healthy diet.*
2 (verb) to eat less food, or stop eating certain foods, in order to lose weight.

difference (noun)
the way in which things are not the same. **different** (adjective), **differently** (adverb).

a b c d e f g h i j k l m n o p q r s t u v w x y z

A B C D E F G H I J K L M N O P Q R S T U V W X Y Z

difficult (adjective)
not easy. *This game is really difficult.*

difficulty difficulties (noun)
a problem, or something that is tricky to overcome.

dig digging dug (verb)
to break up and move soil. *The mole dug a hole.* **digger** (noun).

digest digesting digested (verb)
When you **digest** food, your body breaks it down and uses it.

digit (noun)
a single number. *22 is a two-digit number. 7 is a single digit.*

digital (adjective)
1 Digital information is transmitted and stored as a series of 0s and 1s.
2 A digital clock or watch shows the time using just numbers.
3 Digital televisions show pictures that are sent in digital form.

dignified (adjective)
calm and in control. **dignity** (noun).

dilemma (noun)
If you have a **dilemma**, you have to decide between two or more choices, none of which is very good.

diligent (adjective)
hard-working. *Anna is a diligent student.*

dilute diluting diluted (verb)
to make a liquid less strong, by adding water. *Aunty Kath always dilutes the squash too much.*

dim dimmer dimmest (adjective)
not very bright. *A dim light.*
dimly (adverb).

din (noun)
a lot of loud noise. *There was a din coming from the kitchen.*

dinghy dinghies (noun)
a small sailing boat.

dinner (noun)
the main meal of the day.

dinosaur (noun)
Dinosaurs were large animals that lived on Earth millions of years ago.

some types of **dinosaurs**

Triceratops

Tyrannosaurus rex

Velociraptor

Brachiosaurus

Word origin   dinosaur

The word **dinosaur** comes from the Ancient Greek words "**deinos**" and "**sauros**", which mean "**terrible lizard**".

plates

Stegosaurus

Iguanodon

spikes

Kentrosaurus

dip **dipping dipped**
1 *(verb)* If you **dip** something into a liquid, you put it in for a short time. *We dipped biscuits into our hot chocolate.*
2 *(noun)* If there is a **dip** in something, it goes down. *There is a dip in the road ahead.* **dip** *(verb)*.

There are many **dips** on this roller coaster.

direct **directing directed**
1 *(adjective)* The **direct** route is the shortest one. **directly** *(adverb)*.
2 *(verb)* to tell people the way to go. *The man directed us to the entrance of the football stadium.*
3 *(verb)* to be in charge of a film, play, or television programme. **director** *(noun)*.
4 *(adjective)* If you are **direct**, you make your feelings very clear. *Roy was direct with his instructions.* **directly** *(adverb)*.

direction *(noun)*
1 the way someone or something is going, or pointing.
2 If you give someone **directions**, you tell them which way to go when they are lost.

dirty **dirtier dirtiest** *(adjective)*
not clean. **dirt** *(noun)*.

disabled *(adjective)*
Disabled people have a condition or injury that makes it difficult or impossible for them to do certain things. **disability** *(noun)*.

disadvantage *(noun)*
1 a bad thing about something. *The main disadvantage of skiing is the cold.*
2 something which makes things more difficult. *It was a disadvantage to start the race after everyone else.*

disagree
disagreeing disagreed *(verb)*
to have a different opinion to somebody. *Laura disagreed with Alan about where they should go for dinner.* **disagreement** *(noun)*.

disappear
disappearing disappeared *(verb)*
to vanish, or go out of sight. *The mice all disappeared when we got a cat.* **disappearance** *(noun)*.

disappoint
disappointing disappointed *(verb)*
1 If you **disappoint** someone, you let them down, and don't do what they expect. **disappointing** *(adjective)*, **disappointment** *(noun)*.
2 If something **disappoints** you, it's not as good as you had hoped. *I was disappointed by the rides at the fair.* **disappointing** *(adjective)*, **disappointment** *(noun)*.

disapprove
disapproving disapproved *(verb)*
If you **disapprove of** something, you don't think it's a good thing. **disapproval** *(noun)*, **disapproving** *(adjective)*.

disaster *(noun)*
1 a terrible thing to happen, which causes suffering. *The hurricane was a disaster.* **disastrous** *(adjective)*.
2 a big failure. *The show was a disaster.* **disastrous** *(adjective)*.

disc *(noun)*
a flat, round shape.

Spelling tip disc disk

It's tricky to know whether to use the spelling "**disc**" or "**disk**", as they sound exactly the same. Remember that if you are talking about a shape, you should use the spelling "**disc**", and if you are talking about a computer, you should use the spelling "**disk**".

a b c d e f g h i j k l m n o p q r s t u v w x y z

A B C **D** E F G H I J K L M N O P Q R S T U V W X Y Z

discipline disciplining disciplined

1 (noun) control over your own behaviour. *It takes a lot of discipline to eat healthily.*
2 (verb) to have control over someone's behaviour, and punish them for being bad. *Teachers sometimes have to discipline their students.*

discount (noun)

If you get a **discount** on something, you buy it at a lower price than usual.

discourage

discouraging discouraged (verb) to try to stop someone from doing something. *We managed to discourage Saul from going down the slide headfirst.* **discouragement** (noun).

discouraged (adjective)

If you are **discouraged**, you are put off doing something or lose enthusiasm for it.

discover

discovering discovered (verb) to find, or find out about, something. *Kate discovered she had a hole in her tights.* **discovery** (noun).

discuss discussing discussed (verb)

to talk about something with other people. *We discussed where to go on our holiday this year.* **discussion** (noun).

disease (noun)

a serious illness. *Polio is a terrible disease.* **diseased** (adjective).

disgrace (noun)

something very bad, to be ashamed of. *This filthy room is a disgrace.*
disgraceful (adjective),
disgracefully (adverb).

disguise disguising disguised

1 (noun) something you wear to make yourself look different, so that people won't recognize you.
2 (verb) to make yourself look like someone else. *Jerry disguised himself as a clown.*

disgusting (adjective)

horrible, or really nasty. *There's a disgusting smell in here.*

The prefix 'dis-'

disinfect
dishonest
dislike

Words that begin with 'dis-' often mean "to get rid of" or "the opposite of" something. For example, if you are "dishonest", you are not honest, if you use a "disinfectant", you get rid of germs which might cause infection or illness, and if you "dislike" someone or something, you don't like them.

dish dishes (noun)

1 a bowl or plate, in which food can be served.
2 part of a meal. *We had a chicken dish and a lamb dish.*

dishonest (adjective)

1 If you are **dishonest**, you don't tell the truth. **dishonesty** (noun).
2 If you behave in a **dishonest** way, you trick people and cheat.

disinfectant (noun)

a liquid used to get rid of germs.

disintegrate

disintegrating disintegrated (verb) to break into small pieces. *Zoe's model plane disintegrated when it hit the ground.* **disintegration** (noun).

disk (noun)

a place where information is stored on a computer.

dislike disliking disliked (verb)

If you **dislike** someone or something, you don't like them at all. *I dislike marzipan.* **dislike** (noun).

dismay (noun)

deep sadness. **dismayed** (adjective).

dismiss

dismisses dismissing dismissed (verb) to send someone away. *The teacher dismissed the class early.*

disobedient *(adjective)*
If you are **disobedient**, you don't do as you are told. **disobedience** *(noun)*, **disobey** *(verb)*.

disorganized *or* **disorganised** *(adjective)*
1 not in order, or muddled up.
2 If you are **disorganized**, you are not good at being on time, having the things you need, and so on. *Phil is so disorganized.*

display **displaying displayed** *(verb)*
to show something. *The painter displayed his work.* **display** *(noun)*.

dispute *(noun)*
a quarrel or argument. *The player had a dispute with the referee.* **dispute** *(verb)*.

disqualify **disqualifies disqualifying disqualified** *(verb)*
to stop someone from taking part in a game or competition because they have broken a rule or done something wrong. **disqualification** *(noun)*.

disrupt **disrupting disrupted** *(verb)*
to interrupt something that is happening. *The cat disrupted my nap.* **disruption** *(noun)*.

dissolve **dissolving dissolved** *(verb)*
When something **dissolves** in a liquid, it mixes into it completely. *The sugar dissolved in Gran's tea.*

distance *(noun)*
1 the amount of space between two things. *What's the distance between your house and school?*
2 If something is **in the distance**, it is far away. *We could see the mountains in the distance.* **distant** *(adjective)*.

distinguish **distinguishes distinguishing distinguished** *(verb)*
to tell the difference between things. *Can you distinguish between an African and an Indian elephant?*

distort **distorting distorted** *(verb)*
to twist something out of its normal shape. *That photo distorts your face.*

distract
distracting distracted *(verb)*
to put someone off what they should be doing or looking at. **distraction** *(noun)*.

distress *(noun)*
great sadness or suffering. **distressed** *(adjective)*, **distressing** *(adjective)*.

distribute
distributing distributed *(verb)*
to deliver things to various places, or give things out. *Hamish distributed the books.* **distribution** *(noun)*.

district *(noun)*
an area. *I live in the busiest district of the city.*

disturb **disturbing disturbed** *(verb)*
If you **disturb** someone, you interrupt them, and stop them doing whatever they were doing. **disturbance** *(noun)*.

ditch **ditches** *(noun)*
a narrow channel by the side of a road or a field. Ditches are often full of water.

dive **diving dived** *(verb)*
1 to enter water headfirst, with your arms stretched above your head.
2 to swim in very deep water, wearing a special suit and a tank of air.
dive *(noun)*, **diver** *(noun)*, **diving** *(noun)*.

fin

buoyancy control device

wet suit

air tank

pressure gauge

snorkel

weight belt

diving glove

mask

scuba diving equipment

3 When a bird or a plane **dives**, it swoops downwards very quickly.

diversion (noun)
an alternative way of getting to a place, especially when a road is closed.

divide dividing divided (verb)
1 to split into parts. *Kelly divided the pizza into slices.*
2 In maths, if you **divide** a large number by a smaller one, you work out how many times the smaller number will go into the bigger one. *25 divided by 5 is 5.* **division** (noun).

divorce (noun)
the official end of a marriage, after which both people can marry someone else. **divorced** (adjective), **divorce** (verb).

Diwali (noun)
a festival celebrated by Hindus and Sikhs in the autumn. People give each other gifts, hold feasts and light lots of lamps.

At **Diwali**, Hindus decorate their doorsteps with rangoli patterns, like this one.

DIY (noun) (abbreviation)
This is short for "**do** **i**t **y**ourself", which means doing repairs and decorating around the house yourself instead of paying someone else to do them.

dizzy dizzier dizziest (adjective)
If you feel **dizzy**, your head feels funny, you can't focus properly, and you might feel like you are going to fall over. **dizziness** (noun).

do does doing did done (verb)
1 If you **do** something, you make it happen or take part in it. *I do the washing-up every day. I do karate on Mondays.*
2 to work on something. *I need to do my homework.*
3 **Do** is used to ask all sorts of questions. *Do you like my bag? What do you think?*
4 **Do** is used to make negative sentences. *I do not like riding scary roller coasters.*
5 If you say that something **will do**, you mean that it will be enough or good enough for what you need. *This piece of paper will do for our poster.*
6 If you ask someone "How are you **doing**?", you want to know if they are well at the moment.
7 If you ask someone "What **do you do**?", you want to know what their job is.
8 to fix or arrange something, so that it looks nice. *I'm going to do my hair before we leave the house.*
9 **Do** can be used to emphasize something. *I do like your new car. Do hurry, we're going to be late!*
10 If you **do something up**, you fasten it. *Bob can't do up his trousers.*

dock (noun)
1 the place where boats tie up, load, and unload. **dock** (verb).
2 the place in a court where the person on trial stands.

doctor (noun)
someone who is trained to treat people when they are ill.

document (noun)
1 a piece of paper with important or useful information on it. *You'll need your travel documents for the trip.*
2 a piece of work that is created and stored on a computer.

documentary
documentaries (noun)
a television programme or film about real situations and real people. *Did you see that documentary about whales last night?*

dodge dodging dodged *(verb)*
to move quickly out of someone or something's way.

doe *(noun)*
the female of some animals, such as deer, rabbits, and kangaroos.

does *(verb)*
a present tense form of do.

doesn't *(verb)*
a shortened version of "does not".
Natalie doesn't like mushrooms.

dog *(noun)*
a furry animal with four legs that barks, and that people often keep as a pet.

some breeds of **dogs**

pug

labrador retriever

dalmation

greyhound

poodle

Welsh terrier

doll *(noun)*
a toy that looks like a very small person.

dollar *(noun)*
the money used in some countries, including the United States and Canada.

dolphin *(noun)*
an animal that lives in the sea. Dolphins breathe air, so they are not fish, but they are excellent swimmers. *See echo.*

dome *(noun)*
a rounded roof. **domed** *(adjective)*.

St Paul's Cathedral, London, UK

dome

dominate
dominating dominated *(verb)*
to control someone or something. *The conversation was dominated by Maria.*
dominance *(noun)*, **domination** *(noun)*.

domino dominoes *(noun)*
a small rectangular block with spots on it. Dominoes are used to play games.

donate donating donated *(verb)*
to give something as a gift. *I am going to donate my old books to charity.*
donation *(noun)*.

donkey *(noun)*
an animal that looks a bit like a horse, but is smaller and has longer ears.

donor *(noun)*
someone who donates something to help others. Some donors donate parts of their body to people who are ill.

don't *(verb)*
a shortened version of "do not".

doodle *(verb)*
to draw without really thinking about it.
doodle *(noun)*.

door *(noun)*
a cover for an entrance into a room or a building, which has a handle to help you open and close it. **doorway** *(noun)*.

dormitory dormitories *(noun)*
a bedroom that lots of people sleep in at the same time.

dose *(noun)*
a measurement of medicine. *The correct dose is two spoonfuls.* **dosage** *(noun)*.

a b c d e f g h i j k l m n o p q r s t u v w x y z

dot (noun)
a small round point, like this full stop.

double doubling doubled (verb)
If you **double** something, you make it twice as big. *My wages have doubled over the last five years.* **double** (adjective).

doubt doubting doubted (verb)
If you **doubt** something, you aren't sure whether it's true. *Mum doubted that the cat had eaten all the bananas.* **doubtful** (adjective), **doubtfully** (adverb).

dough (doh) (noun)
a sticky mixture used to make bread.

doughnut (**doh**-nut) (noun)
a type of cake made from fried dough, either with a filling or a hole in the middle, and usually covered with sugar.

1. The dough is shaped into balls.

2. The balls are fried in oil.

3. The cooked doughnuts are filled with jam.

4. The doughnuts are covered in sugar.

These pictures show how jam **doughnuts** are made.

dove (noun)
a bird like a small pigeon that makes a soft, cooing sound.

down
1 (preposition) from a higher to a lower place. *Dad skied down the mountain.*
2 If you **put something down**, you stop carrying it and rest it somewhere. *I put my mug down.*
3 If you **put someone down**, you criticize them.
4 (adjective) If you feel **down**, you feel sad.
5 (noun) soft feathers.

download
downloading downloaded (verb)
to copy information or files from the internet or from another computer onto your computer. **download** (noun).

downstairs
1 (noun) the ground floor of a building, usually a house.
2 (adjective) on the ground floor. *The toilet is downstairs.*
3 (adverb) down a flight of stairs. *I tripped over the cat and fell downstairs.*

downward or downwards (adverb)
towards a lower place or level. *Ellen was lying face downward on her bed.*

doze dozing dozed (verb)
to sleep lightly. *Rachel dozed in the sunshine.* **doze** (noun).

dozen (noun)
twelve of something. *Cory ate a dozen hot dogs at the party.*

drab drabber drabbest (adjective)
very plain and dull. *That wallpaper is drab.* **drabness** (noun).

draft (noun)
a first rough copy of something, such as a letter or a story. *I lost the first draft of my story, so I have to start again.* **draft** (verb).

drag dragging dragged (verb)
to pull something heavy along. *Marcus dragged his suitcase behind him.*

dragon (noun)
a creature in stories and legends, that breathes fire and has wings and claws.

The flag of Bhutan has a **dragon** on it.

A B C D E F G H I J K L M N O P Q R S T U V W X Y Z

drain draining drained
1 *(verb)* to take the liquid out of something. *I drained the pasta when it was cooked.*
2 *(noun)* a pipe that carries water or other liquid waste away. **drainage** *(noun)*.

drama *(noun)*
1 **Drama** involves plays, the theatre, and acting. **dramatist** *(noun)*.
2 an exciting and interesting thing that happens.

dramatic *(adjective)*
1 If something is **dramatic**, everybody notices it. *A dramatic entrance.* **dramatically** *(adverb)*.
2 to do with plays, the theatre, and acting.

draught *(draft)* *(noun)*
a flow of chilly air.

draughts *(drafts)* *(noun)*
a game played with black and white counters on a board with squares on it.

draw drawing drew drawn *(verb)*
1 to create a picture of something using a pencil, pen, or crayons. **drawing** *(noun)*.
2 If two teams or players **draw** in a game, they both get the same number of points. **draw** *(noun)*.
3 If you **draw** the curtains, you pull them open or closed.
4 to pull something along. *Four horses draw the king's carriage.*
5 If you **draw back** from something, you decide not to do it at the last minute.
6 If you **draw up** a plan, you invent one. *Chris drew up a plan for sports day.*

drawback *(noun)*
a disadvantage. *Queues are the main drawback at theme parks.*

drawer *(noun)*
a box that slides in and out of a piece of furniture, in which you can store things.

dread dreading dreaded *(verb)*
If you **dread** something, you are scared and worried about it. **dread** *(noun)*.

dreadful *(adjective)*
very nasty or bad. **dreadfully** *(adverb)*.

Spelling tip

dreamed   dreamt

The past tense of "dream" can be spelt two ways: "dreamed" or "dreamt". Both are correct, but "dreamt" is more common in British English, and "dreamed" in American English.

The same is true for "burned/burnt", "spelled/spelt", and "learned/learnt".

---

dream
dreaming dreamed or **dreamt** *(verb)*
1 to imagine things happening when you are asleep. **dream** *(noun)*.
2 If you **dream** of doing something, you really want to do it. **dream** *(noun)*.

dreary
drearier dreariest *(adjective)*
dull and miserable. **drearily** *(adverb)*.

drenched *(adjective)*
very wet. *We were all drenched after the storm.* **drench** *(verb)*.

dress dresses dressing dressed
1 *(verb)* to put clothes on.
2 *(noun)* a piece of clothing that girls and women wear, which is a top and a skirt joined together as one.

dressing *(noun)*
1 a kind of bandage, put on wounds.
2 a sauce for salads.

dribble dribbling dribbled *(verb)*
1 to let spit trickle out of your mouth.
2 to run with a ball, controlling it all the time, in games such as football and basketball. *Pete dribbled the ball.*

drift drifting drifted
1 *(verb)* to move gently along, being carried by water or air. *The boat drifted down the river.*
2 *(noun)* a pile of snow or sand, created by the wind.

drill
a tool used for making holes. **drill** *(verb)*.

a b c d e f g h i j k l m n o p q r s t u v w x y z

drink **drinking drank drunk**
1 *(noun)* a liquid that you swallow.
2 *(verb)* to swallow liquid. *We all need to drink water.*

drip **dripping dripped** *(verb)*
When a liquid **drips**, it falls slowly, one drop at a time. **drip** *(noun)*.

drive **driving drove driven**
1 *(verb)* to be in control of a moving car, truck, train, and so on. **driver** *(noun)*, **driving** *(noun)*.
2 *(verb)* to make someone do or feel something. *Sarah's constant talking drove me to put my headphones in.*
3 *(noun)* the private lane that leads to someone's house.

drizzle *(noun)*
light rain. **drizzle** *(verb)*.

drool **drooling drooled** *(verb)*
to let saliva trickle from your mouth.

droop **drooping drooped** *(verb)*
to bend, sag, or hang downwards. *Those flowers are beginning to droop.*

drop **dropping dropped**
1 *(verb)* to let something fall. *I dropped the ball.*
2 *(verb)* to fall straight down, or get lower. *The temperature dropped this week.*
3 *(noun)* a small amount of liquid.
4 *(verb)* If you **drop out**, you decide not to do something any more. *Gareth dropped out of the army.*

drought *(rhymes with "shout")* *(noun)*
a long spell of very dry weather.

drown **drowning drowned** *(verb)*
to die because you have gone under water and can't breathe any more.

drowsy
drowsier drowsiest *(adjective)*
sleepy. *Sunshine makes me drowsy.*

drug *(noun)*
1 a mixture of chemicals used in medicines to make ill people better.
2 Some **drugs** are harmful substances that people can get addicted to.

drum **drumming drummed**
1 *(noun)* a musical instrument made of a round frame with a skin stretched tightly over it, which makes a loud sound when you hit it. **drummer** *(noun)*.
2 *(verb)* to play the drums.

crash cymbal   tom-toms   ride cymbal
snare drum
hi-hat
bass drum
drum kit   bass drum pedal   floor tom

drumstick *(noun)*
1 one of a pair of sticks, used for playing the drums.
2 part of a chicken leg, which can be cooked and eaten.

drunk *(adjective)*
If someone is **drunk**, they have drunk too much alcohol.

dry **drier driest** *(adjective)*
not wet. *My coat is dry.*

dry **dries drying dried** *(verb)*
If you **dry** someone or something, you remove liquid so they aren't wet any more. *We dried the dog after his bath.*

duck **ducking ducked**
1 *(noun)* a kind of bird that lives on water.

Mandarin duck   **Mallard duck**

two types of **ducks**

2 *(verb)* to bend your head low so that you don't hit something. *I ducked to avoid the branch.*

duckling *(noun)*
a young duck.

due *(adjective)*
1 expected, or about to arrive.
Our baby is due next week.
2 If something happens **due to** something else, it happens because of it. *The train was late this afternoon due to the cow on the tracks.*

duet *(noun)*
a song or piece of music for two people.

dull **duller dullest** *(adjective)*
1 not very interesting. *This afternoon's lesson was really dull.*
2 lacking in colour and brightness. *The weather is so dull today.*

dumb **dumber dumbest** *(adjective)*
1 If you are **dumb**, you are not able to talk.
2 a rather rude word for "stupid".

dump **dumping dumped**
1 *(verb)* to leave rubbish or waste somewhere.
2 *(noun)* a place where rubbish can be left.

dune *(noun)*
a hill of sand, on a beach or in a desert.

how **sand dunes** are formed

1. The wind builds up a peak.

2. The peak of sand collapses.

dungeon *(noun)*
an underground prison.

during *(preposition)*
1 at a particular time, or between particular times. *Please ring during the afternoon.*
2 while something else is going on or happening. *The tent blew down during the storm.*

Spelling tip

dwarf → dwarfs or dwarves

"Dwarf" can be spelt "dwarfs" or "dwarves" in the plural. Other words which end with an 'f' and follow this pattern are "hoof" → "hoofs"/"hooves" and "scarf" → "scarfs"/"scarves".

dusk *(noun)*
the end of the day, just before night falls.

dust *(noun)*
tiny bits of dirt and fluff.
dusty *(adjective)*.

duty **duties** *(noun)*
things that someone has to do, or should do. *My duties include walking the dog and washing up.*

duvet (**doo**-vay) *(noun)*
a thick cover that goes over your body when you are in bed.

DVD *(noun)* *(abbreviation)*
a disc that stores information, films, or music. DVD is short for "**d**igital **v**ideo **d**isc" or "**d**igital **v**ersatile **d**isc".

dwarf **dwarfs** or **dwarves** *(noun)*
a very small person, animal, or plant.

dwindle **dwindling dwindled** *(verb)*
to become smaller or less.

dye **dyeing dyed** *(noun)*
If you **dye** your hair or your clothes, you use a liquid or powder to make it go a different colour.

dynamic *(adjective)*
full of energy, and good at getting things done. *My Great Aunt Gwen is very dynamic.*

dyslexia (dis-**lek**-see-er) *(noun)*
If you have **dyslexia**, you find reading and spelling tricky, as you mix up the order that the letters come in.
dyslexic *(adjective)*.

Ee

each *(determiner)*
every individual one. *Each person gets one cupcake.*

eager *(adjective)*
keen and enthusiastic. *Jack was eager to leave for the party.* **eagerness** *(noun)*, **eagerly** *(adverb)*.

eagle *(noun)*
a large bird of prey with a curved beak and claws.

ear *(noun)*
the part of your body that you use for hearing.

early
earlier earliest
(adjective)
1 before the usual time, or before expected. *We had an early start to make sure we got to the match on time.* **early** *(adverb)*.
2 near the beginning of a period of time. *An early 20th-century house. We went to the early showing of the film.*

bald eagle

earn earning earned *(verb)*
1 to be paid money for work. *I wash my dad's car to earn money for a new bike.* **earnings** *(plural noun)*.
2 to work hard to get something. *You have earned your reward.*

earnest *(adjective)*
1 serious and keen.
2 showing great feeling. *She made an earnest promise.*

earphones *(plural noun)*
small speakers that you wear inside your ears to listen to music.

earrings *(plural noun)*
pieces of jewellery that you can wear on your ears. *Diamond earrings.*

earth *(noun)*
1 Earth the planet we live on.
earthly *(adjective)*.

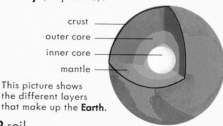

crust
outer core
inner core
mantle

This picture shows the different layers that make up the **Earth**.

2 soil.

earthquake *(noun)*
When an **earthquake** happens, the ground shakes because some of the huge pieces of rock that make up the Earth's surface are moving.

easel *(noun)*
a folding wooden stand for a painting.

east
1 *(noun)* one of the four main points of the compass. *See* **compass**.
2 *(adjective)* in or towards the east of a place. *The east coast.* **east** *(noun)*, **eastern** *(adjective)*.
3 *(adjective)* from the east. *An east wind.*

Easter *(noun)*
the festival when Christians celebrate Jesus Christ coming back from the dead.

easy easier easiest *(adjective)*
If something is **easy**, you do not need much skill or effort to do it. *I found the test today quite easy.* **easiness** *(noun)*, **easily** *(adverb)*.

Spelling tip

easy   easier   easiest

When you add the endings '-er' and '-est' to "early" and "easy" to make the comparative (meaning "more") and superlative (meaning "most") forms, remember to change the final 'y' to an 'i'.

eat eating ate eaten (verb)
to take in food through your mouth.
I feel terrible if I don't eat breakfast.

ebook or **e-book** (noun)
a book that comes as an electronic
file which you can download or read
online, using an e-book reader, tablet,
computer, or smartphone.

eccentric (ek-**sen**-trick) (noun)
someone with unusual habits.
eccentric (adjective).

echo echoes (noun)
a sound that bounces, usually in a large,
empty space. **echo** (verb).

clicks
sent out

echo returns

solid object

*Dolphins use **echoes** to help them
find their way underwater.*

eclipse (noun)
1 In an **eclipse** of the Moon, the Earth
comes between the Sun and the Moon,
so that all or part of the Moon's light
is blocked out.
2 In an **eclipse** of the Sun, the Moon
comes between the Sun and the Earth,
so that all or part of the Sun's light is
blocked out.

eco-friendly (adjective)
not harmful to the environment. *Our
new washing powder is eco-friendly.*

ecology (noun)
1 the study of the relationship between
plants, animals, and their environment.
2 the study of how human activity
affects the Earth.

economical (adjective)
not wasteful. *Our car is very economical
on petrol.* **economically** (adverb).

Word family

eco-friendly
ecology
economical
economy
ecosystem

These words come
from the same
Ancient Greek
word, "oikos",
meaning "house"
or "place of living".

economy economies (noun)
The **economy** is everything to do with
how people, businesses and countries
make and spend money.

ecosystem (noun)
a group of animals and plants in
a particular environment, who rely
on one another to survive.

ecotourism (noun)
going on holiday to a wild, exotic place
to look at wildlife and help protect it.

ecstasy ecstasies (noun)
a feeling of great happiness.
We danced around in ecstasy.
ecstatic (adjective).

eczema (**ex**-ma) (noun)
a condition that can make your skin
dry, rough, and itchy.

edge edging edged
1 (noun) the end or side of something.
The edge of the lake.
2 (verb) to move very slowly and
carefully. *We edged along the
steep path.*
3 If you are **on edge**, you are nervous
or anxious. **edgy** (adjective).

edible (adjective)
suitable or safe to eat.

edit editing edited (verb)
1 If you **edit** something you have
written, you check it again and make
changes to it, so that it is correct.
2 If you **edit** a film, television
programme, and so on, you choose
the parts that you want to keep in, and
the parts that you want to leave out.

edition *(noun)*
a version of a book or newspaper that is available at a particular time. *A new paperback edition.*

editor *(noun)*
the person in charge of a book, newspaper, magazine, or television programme, who checks everything that goes in it.

educate educating educated *(verb)*
to teach people facts or skills over a long period of time. **education** *(noun).*

eel *(noun)*
a long, thin, snake-like fish.

eerie eerier eeriest *(adjective)*
Something that is **eerie** makes you feel nervous and scared. *The abandoned fairground was eerie.* **eerily** *(adverb).*

effect *(noun)*
If something has an **effect**, it causes some sort of change. *Drinking more water has had a great effect on my health.*

Spelling tip

effect   affect

Be careful not to mix up "**effect**", which is a **noun**, and "**affect**", which is a **verb**.

- This rain is going to have a bad **effect** on my hair.
- This rain is going to **affect** my hair badly.

effective *(adjective)*
If someone or something is **effective**, they do their job very well. *This painkiller is very effective.* **effectively** *(adverb).*

efficient *(adjective)*
If someone or something is **efficient**, they work very well and do not waste time or energy. **efficiency** *(noun),* **efficiently** *(adverb).*

effort *(noun)*
If you **make an effort** or **put in effort**, you try hard.

e.g. *(abbreviation)*
the initials, used in writing, of the Latin phrase "exempli gratia", meaning "for example". *We make all sorts of things at knitting class, e.g. hats, scarves, jumpers, and gloves.*

egg *(noun)*
an oval or rounded object produced by female birds, reptiles, insects, and fish, in which the young develop. Some types of eggs are eaten by humans.

egg
turtle hatching from an **egg**

Eid al-Adha *(noun)*
a Muslim festival during the last month of the Islamic year when many Muslims make a pilgrimage to Mecca. Some Muslims celebrate the festival by sacrificing animals.

Eid al-Fitr *(noun)*
the Muslim festival to celebrate the end of the Ramadan period of fasting.

either
1 *(conjunction)* **Either** can be used to show a choice. *You can either stay or go.*
2 *(pronoun)* one of two. *Which mug should I take? Either.* **either** *(adjective).*
3 *(determiner)* one of two. *I don't like either painting.*
4 *(adverb)* also, or similarly. *If Ed's not going, I'm not either.*

eject ejecting ejected *(verb)*
to push something out. *Eject the DVD when you've finished watching the film.*

elaborate elaborating elaborated
1 *(el-**ab**-or-ut)* *(adjective)* complicated and detailed. *An elaborate pattern.* **elaborately** *(adverb).*
2 *(el-ab-or-**ate**)* *(verb)* to give more details. *Please elaborate on your plans for the trip.*

elapse **elapsing elapsed** *(verb)*
When time **elapses**, it passes.

elastic *(noun)*
a rubbery material which stretches and then goes back to its original size. **elasticity** *(noun)*, **elastic** *(adjective)*.

elbow *(noun)*
the joint that connects the upper and lower parts of your arm.

elder *(adjective)*
older. *My elder sister.*

elderly *(adjective)*
An **elderly** person is old. *An elderly gentleman was sitting on the bench.*

elect **electing elected** *(verb)*
to choose someone by voting. *Robert was elected as the new head boy.* **election** *(noun)*.

electrician *(noun)*
someone whose job is to install and repair electrical systems in buildings, towns, and so on.

electricity *(noun)*
a form of energy that is used for lighting, heating, and making machines work. *The storm cut off the electricity last night.* **electric** *(adjective)*, **electrical** *(adjective)*.

electrocute
electrocuting electrocuted *(verb)*
to kill or injure someone with an electric shock. **electrocution** *(noun)*.

electronic
1 *(adjective)* **Electronic** machines work by using electricity. Computers, televisions and radios are all electronic. **electronically** *(adverb)*.
2 *(adjective)* done or accessed by a computer or other electronic device. *My dad reads the electronic edition of the newspaper.* **electronically** *(adverb)*.
3 electronic book *(noun)* see **ebook**.
4 electronic mail *(noun)* see **email**.

electronics *(plural noun)*
the technology that makes electronic machines work.

elegant *(adjective)*
graceful and stylish. *Louise is an elegant dancer.* **elegance** *(noun)*, **elegantly** *(adverb)*.

element
1 *(noun)* In chemistry, an **element** is a pure substance that cannot be broken down into other substances. Oxygen and copper are elements.
2 *(noun)* one of the simple, basic parts of something. *Claude taught me the elements of cooking.*
3 the elements *(plural noun)* the weather. *If you go camping, you have to be prepared to face the elements.*

elementary *(adjective)*
simple, or basic. *Elementary maths.*

elephant *(noun)*
a large, grey animal with a long trunk and ivory tusks that lives in southern Asia and Africa.

There are two types of **elephants**: Asian and African. The pictures below show the main differences.

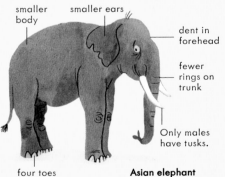

smaller body
smaller ears
dent in forehead
fewer rings on trunk
Only males have tusks.
four toes
Asian elephant

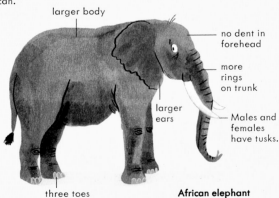

larger body
no dent in forehead
more rings on trunk
larger ears
Males and females have tusks.
three toes
African elephant

A B C D **E** F G H I J K L M N O P Q R S T U V W X Y Z

elf → el**ves**

To make the word "elf" plural, you remove the 'f' and add '-ves'.

Other words that follow this pattern are "half" → "hal**ves**", "shelf" → "shel**ves**", and "leaf" → "lea**ves**".

elf **elves** *(noun)*
a small, magical, mischievous person from legends and fairy stories.

eligible *(adjective)*
If you are **eligible** for something, like a job, you have the right qualifications for it. **eligibility** *(noun)*.

eliminate
eliminating eliminated *(verb)*
to get rid of someone or something. *Rebecca was eliminated from the game.*

eloquent *(adjective)*
An **eloquent** person speaks clearly, and has interesting things to say.

else *(adverb)*
1 other, or different. *They have gone somewhere else.*
2 more. *Tell me if you need anything else.*

elusive *(adjective)*
very hard to find, catch, or understand.

email *(noun)*
a message sent over the internet, often from one computer to another.

embark
embarking embarked *(verb)*
1 to go on board a ship or an aeroplane.
2 to begin something. *The boys embarked upon an adventure.*

embarrass **embarrasses**
embarrassing embarrassed *(verb)*
to make someone feel awkward and uncomfortable, often because they have accidentally done something that other people find funny. **embarrassment** *(noun)*, **embarrassing** *(adjective)*.

embrace
embracing embraced *(verb)*
to hug someone. *Mum embraced me when I got off the train.* **embrace** *(noun)*.

embryo (**em**-bree-oh) *(noun)*
an unborn human or animal that has just started to grow inside its mother's body.

emerald *(noun)*
1 a bright green precious stone.
2 a bright green colour.
emerald *(adjective)*.

emerge **emerging emerged** *(verb)*
If you **emerge** from somewhere, you come out into the open. *The rabbit emerged from its burrow.*
emergence *(noun)*.

emergency **emergencies** *(noun)*
a sudden and dangerous situation that must be dealt with quickly. *This is an emergency!* **emergency** *(adjective)*.

emit **emitting emitted** *(verb)*
to release or send out something, such as heat, light, or sound. *The spaceship emitted a strange beeping sound.*

emotion *(noun)*
a strong feeling, such as happiness, love, anger, or grief.

emotional *(adjective)*
1 to do with your feelings. *Emotional problems.*
2 When someone becomes **emotional**, they show their feelings, especially by crying. **emotionally** *(adverb)*.

emperor *(noun)*
a male ruler of an empire.

emphasize or emphasise
emphasizing emphasized *(verb)*
If you **emphasize** something, you make sure that people notice it, because you think it is important. **emphasis** *(noun)*, **emphatic** *(adjective)*.

empire *(noun)*
a group of countries that all have the same ruler. *The Roman Empire.*

employ
employing employed *(verb)*
to pay someone to work for you.
employer *(noun)*.

employee *(noun)*
someone who works for a person or
for a company, and is paid by them.
employment *(noun)*.

empress **empresses** *(noun)*
the female ruler of an empire, or the
wife of an emperor.

empty
emptier emptiest *(adjective)*
If something is **empty**, there is nothing
inside it. *The room was empty.*

empty
empties emptying emptied *(verb)*
to take the contents out of something.
*Gordon emptied the cereal box into
his bowl.*

enable **enabling enabled** *(verb)*
to make it possible for someone to do
something. *Getting birthday money
from my Aunt enabled me to buy
a telescope.*

enchanted *(adjective)*
A place or thing that is **enchanted** has
been put under a magic spell, or seems
magical. **enchant** *(verb)*.

encounter
encountering encountered *(verb)*
to meet or come across someone or
something, especially when you're not
expecting them. *We encountered a
storm in the mountains.* **encounter** *(noun)*.

encourage
encouraging encouraged *(verb)*
to praise or support someone so that they
continue to try. **encouragement** *(noun)*,
encouraging *(adjective)*.

encyclopedia *or* encyclopaedia
*(en-sy-klo-**pee**-dee-a) (noun)*
a book or set of books, or a website,
with information about many different
subjects. **encyclopedic** *(adjective)*.

end **ending ended**
1 *(noun)* the last part of something.
We reached the end of the race.
ending *(noun)*.
2 *(noun)* one of the two points furthest
from the middle of an object. *Hold the
end of this rope.*
3 *(verb)* to finish something. *We had
to end our meeting early.*

endangered species *(noun)*
a type of animal that may soon
become extinct.

endless *(adjective)*
Something **endless** has no end, or seems
to have no end. **endlessly** *(adverb)*.

endure **enduring endured** *(verb)*
1 If you **endure** something unpleasant
or painful, you put up with it.
endurance *(noun)*.
2 If something **endures**, it lasts for
a long time. **enduring** *(adjective)*.

enemy **enemies** *(noun)*
1 someone who really hates you and
wants to harm you or cause you trouble.
2 a country or army that you are
fighting against in a war.

energetic *(adjective)*
lively and active. *Alex has a very
energetic puppy.* **energetically** *(adverb)*.

energy **energies** *(noun)*
1 the strength to do things without
getting tired.
2 power which makes things happen,
such as making a machine work and
producing heat.

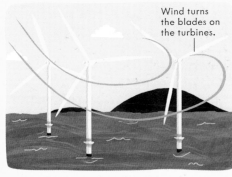

Wind turns
the blades on
the turbines.

Energy from the wind can be
used to produce electricity.

a b c d e f g h i j k l m n o p q r s t u v w x y z

A B C D **E** F G H I J K L M N O P Q R S T U V W X Y Z

engaged *(adjective)*
1 If two people are **engaged**, they have decided that they will get married. **engagement** *(noun)*.
2 If a telephone number or toilet is **engaged**, it is being used by someone else.

engine *(noun)*
1 a machine that makes things move.
2 the front part of a train that pulls all the carriages.

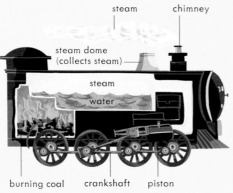

steam   chimney

steam dome
(collects steam)

steam

water

burning coal   crankshaft   piston

This picture shows the inside
of a steam **engine**.

engineer *(noun)*
someone who designs and builds machines, vehicles, bridges, and so on.

engrossed *(adjective)*
If you are **engrossed** in something, you give it all your attention.

engulf **engulfing engulfed** *(verb)*
to cover or swallow up someone or something. *A huge wave engulfed the swimmers.*

enjoy **enjoying enjoyed** *(verb)*
If you **enjoy** something, you like it very much. **enjoyment** *(noun)*, **enjoyable** *(adjective)*.

enlarge **enlarging enlarged** *(verb)*
to make something bigger.

enormous *(adjective)*
very large indeed.

enough *(determiner)*
as much as is needed. *I've had enough chocolate for today.* **enough** *(pronoun)*.

enquire *or* inquire
enquiring enquired *(verb)*
to ask about someone or something. *We enquired about the price.*

enquiry *or* inquiry *(noun)*
1 the act of asking for information.
2 an official investigation.

enrage **enraging enraged** *(verb)*
to make someone very angry.

ensure
ensuring ensured *(verb)*
to make sure that something happens. *Please ensure that you lock the door.*

enter **entering entered** *(verb)*
1 to go into a place.
2 to say that you want to take part in something, such as a competition, race, or exam.
3 to put information into a computer. *Enter your password.*

entertain
entertaining entertained *(verb)*
to amuse and interest someone. **entertainment** *(noun)*, **entertaining** *(adjective)*.

enthusiastic *(adjective)*
If you are **enthusiastic** about something, you are very keen to do it, or like it very much. **enthusiasm** *(noun)*, **enthusiast** *(noun)*.

entire *(adjective)*
whole. **entirely** *(adverb)*.

entrance (**en**-*trunss*) *(noun)*
the way into a place.

entrant *(noun)*
someone who takes part in a competition, race, or exam.

entry **entries** *(noun)*
1 a way into a place.
2 a picture, story, answer, and so on, that you send into a competition.
3 a piece of information put into a diary, computer, and so on.

envelope *(noun)*
a paper cover for a letter or card.

enviable *(adjective)*
If someone has something that is **enviable**, you would like to have it. *Jared has enviable style.*

envious *(adjective)*
If you are **envious**, you wish that you could have something that someone else has. **enviously** *(adverb)*.

environment
(noun)
1 the natural world, which includes the land, sea, and air. **environmental** *(adjective)*.

> Try thinking of the "natural matter" in the environment to remember the 'nm' in the middle.

2 all the things about your life that can have an effect on you, such as where you live, your family, and the things that happen to you.

envy envies envying envied *(verb)*
to wish that you could have something that someone else has. *I envy Claire's ability to concentrate.* **envy** *(noun)*.

epic
1 *(noun)* a long story, poem or film about heroic adventures and great battles. **epic** *(adjective)*.
2 *(adjective)* heroic, or impressive. *The team's performance was epic.*

epidemic *(noun)*
When there is an **epidemic**, an infectious disease spreads quickly to many people.

epilepsy *(noun)*
a condition that affects the brain and causes a person to have blackouts or fits. **epileptic** *(noun)*, **epileptic** *(adjective)*.

episode *(noun)*
one of the programmes in a radio or television serial. *Apparently we're going to find out who the killer is in the next episode.*

equal *(adjective)*
the same as something else in size, value, or amount. *Mix together an equal amount of sugar and flour.* **equal** *(verb)*.

equality *(noun)*
the same rights for everyone. *Racial equality.*

equals sign *(noun)*
In maths, the **equals sign** (=) means that the numbers on each side of it have the same value.

equation *(noun)*
The numbers on each side of the equals sign in an **equation** have the same value, for example, $4 \times 4 = 16$, or $3 + 5 = 4 \times 2$.

equator *(noun)*
an imaginary line around the middle of the Earth, halfway between the North and South Poles. The hottest parts of the Earth are around the equator.

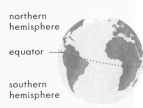

northern hemisphere

equator →

southern hemisphere

This picture shows the line of the **equator**.

equilateral *(adjective)*
An **equilateral** shape has sides that are the same length. *See shapes, page 348.*

equip equipping equipped *(verb)*
to provide someone with all the things that they need.

equipment *(noun)*
the tools, machines, and so on that you need to do something. *We need a lot of equipment for our sailing trip.*

Word family

equality
equals
equation
equator
equilateral
equivalent

Notice that these words beginning with 'equa–' or 'equi–' are to do with things being the same. They all come from the Latin word "aequalis", meaning "identical".

equivalent (adjective)
If one thing is **equivalent** to another, it is the same as the other in amount, value, or importance. **equivalent** (noun).

era (noun)
a period of time in history. *The Jurassic era.*

erase erasing erased (verb)
1 to rub out something. *I erased the mistake that I made.*
2 to delete something stored on a computer, camera, smartphone, and so on.

eraser (noun)
a small piece of rubber used for getting rid of mistakes in pencil.

erosion (noun)
the gradual wearing away of something, such as a cliff, by water or wind. **erode** (verb).

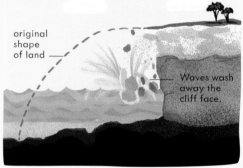

original shape of land

Waves wash away the cliff face.

Cliff **erosion** happens when waves wear away the land.

errand (noun)
If someone sends you on an **errand**, they ask you to go somewhere nearby to take a message or to deliver or collect something.

error (noun)
a mistake.

erupt erupting erupted (verb)
When a volcano **erupts**, it throws out rocks, hot ash, steam, and lava. **eruption** (noun). *See volcano.*

escalator (noun)
a moving staircase.

escape escaping escaped (verb)
1 to break free from somewhere. *The criminals escaped from prison.* **escape** (noun).
2 to avoid something. *We escaped the rain.*

escort escorting escorted (verb)
to go somewhere with someone, especially to protect them.

especially (adverb)
in particular, or mainly. *Jen is especially good at singing. Josh loves sport, especially tennis.*

essay (noun)
a long piece of writing about a particular subject.

essential (adjective)
very important and necessary. *Concentration is essential if you want to be a pilot.*

establish establishes establishing established (verb)
1 to set up a business, society, or organization.
2 to settle somewhere. *Bob is established in his new flat.*

estate (noun)
1 a large area of land owned by one person or family.
2 an area of land with houses, factories or offices on it. *I live on a housing estate.*

estimate estimating estimated
1 (ess-tim-**ate**) (verb) to work something out roughly. *We estimated that the journey would take 45 minutes.*
2 (ess-tim-**ut**) (noun) a rough guess.

Spelling tip

estimate   evaluate
evaporate

Remember to remove the final 'e' of these words before you add the ending '**-ing**'.

estuary (*est-yur-ee*) **estuaries** (*noun*)
the widest part of a river, where it joins the sea.

etc. (*abbreviation*)
a short form of the Latin phrase "et cetera", which means "and the rest". Etc. is used at the end of lists, for example, "On the farm there were chickens, sheep, pigs, etc."

eternal (*adjective*)
lasting forever. **eternally** (*adverb*).

ethnic (*adjective*)
to do with different racial groups. **ethnically** (*adverb*).

EU (*noun*) (*abbreviation*)
short for European Union.

euro (*noun*)
a unit of money, with the symbol €. Euros are used in many countries in Europe, such as the Republic of Ireland and Spain.

Europe (*noun*)
one of the seven continents of the world. Countries such as the UK, Sweden and Italy are all in Europe.

European (*adjective*)
from Europe, or to do with Europe. **European** (*noun*).

European Union (*noun*)
a group of countries in Europe who work together to improve things, such as job opportunities and the environment.

evacuate
evacuating evacuated (*verb*)
to move away from an area because it is dangerous. *Evacuate the building!*

evaluate
evaluating evaluated (*verb*)
to decide how good something is, after thinking carefully. *I evaluated the results of the science experiment.* **evaluation** (*noun*).

evaporate
evaporating evaporated (*verb*)
When a liquid **evaporates**, it changes into a gas. **evaporation** (*noun*).

even
1 (*adjective*) An **even** number can be divided exactly by two.
2 (*adjective*) equal. *An even score.* **evenly** (*adverb*).
3 (*adjective*) smooth and level. *An even surface.*
4 (*adverb*) You say **even** when something is rather surprising. *Mo carried on running even after his legs began to hurt.*

evening (*noun*)
the time of day between the late afternoon and the time you go to bed.

event (*noun*)
1 something that happens, especially something interesting or important.
2 an activity, such as a race, that is held during a sports competition. *The next event will be the 200m sprint.*

eventually (*adverb*)
finally, or at last. *Eventually we found the car in the car park.*

ever (*adverb*)
at any time. *Have you ever been on a jet ski?*

evergreen (*noun*)
a bush or tree which has green leaves all year round. **evergreen** (*adjective*).

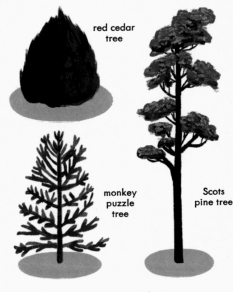

red cedar tree

monkey puzzle tree

Scots pine tree

some **evergreen** trees

a b c d e f g h i j k l m n o p q r s t u v w x y z

103

every *(determiner)*
1 all the people or things in a group. *Every guest gets a goody bag.*
2 every other one in every two. *I have a bath every other night.*

everybody *(pronoun)*
every person. *Everybody in the queue looked annoyed.*

everyday *(adjective)*
usual, or normal. *Everyday activities.*

everyone *(pronoun)*
every person. *Everyone clapped when I finished my solo.*

everything *(pronoun)*
all things. *I want to eat everything on the menu.*

everywhere *(pronoun)*
in all places. *I've looked everywhere for my glasses, but I can't find them.*

evict **evicting evicted** *(verb)*
to force someone to move out of their home. **eviction** *(noun).*

evidence *(noun)*
information and facts that help to prove something, or make you believe that something is true.

evident *(adjective)*
clear and obvious. *It was evident that Harriet found the lesson boring.*

Spelling tip

evidence   evident

"**Evidence**" is a noun and "**evident**" is an adjective. Other pairs of words follow this pattern, such as "**confidence**" (noun) and "**confident**" (adjective), and "**distance**" (noun) and "**distant**" (adjective).

Notice that if the noun ends '-ence', the adjective ends '-ent', and if the noun ends '-ance', the adjective ends '-ant'.

evil *(adjective)*
very wicked and cruel. **evil** *(noun).*

evolution *(noun)*
1 the gradual change of animals and plants over thousands of years. **evolve** *(verb).*
2 gradual change into a different form. *The evolution of mobile phones.*

ewe *(noun)*
a female sheep.

ex- *(prefix)*
Ex- means former. For example, "ex-wife" means "former wife".

exact *(adjective)*
totally correct and accurate.

exaggerate
exaggerating exaggerated *(verb)*
to make something seem bigger, better, or more important than it really is. *Andy exaggerated the size of the fish he had caught.* **exaggeration** *(noun).*

exam *(noun)*
an official test that you take to show how much you know about a subject. Exam is short for "examination".

examination *(noun)*
1 *see* **exam**.
2 a careful check.

examine
examining examined *(verb)*
1 to look carefully at something. *The pirates examined the map.*
2 When doctors **examine** you, they check your body carefully to see what is wrong.

example *(noun)*
1 one thing that shows what the others are like. *The flute is an example of a woodwind instrument.*
2 You say **for example** before you give an example of something. *Al loves team sports, for example hockey and football.*

exasperated *(adjective)*
If you are **exasperated**, you are annoyed or fed up. **exasperate** *(verb).*

exceed exceeding exceeded *(verb)*
1 to be greater or better than something else. *My birthday presents exceeded my expectations.*
2 to do more than is allowed or expected. *Drivers who exceed the speed limit will be fined.*

excellent *(adjective)*
very good indeed.

except *(preposition)*
apart from. *Everyone except Hannah went home.* **except** *(conjunction).*

exception *(noun)*
something that is not included in a general rule. *Caroline hates rock songs, with just a few exceptions.*

exceptional *(adjective)*
really excellent, or rare. *The teacher said my geography project was exceptional.*

excess *(adjective)*
too much, or more than the usual amount. **excess** *(noun).*

excessive *(adjective)*
too much. *Miss Peel wears an excessive amount of perfume.* **excessively** *(adverb).*

exchange
exchanging exchanged *(verb)*
to give one thing and receive another. *Tim and I exchanged presents.* **exchange** *(noun).*

excite exciting excited *(verb)*
to make someone enthusiastic and interested. **excitement** *(noun)*, **exciting** *(adjective)*, **excited** *(adjective).*

exclaim
exclaiming exclaimed *(verb)*
to say something loudly, especially because you are surprised or excited. **exclamation** *(noun).*

exclamation mark *(noun)*
the punctuation mark (!), used in writing to show that something has been shouted. *"Oh no!" cried the wizard as his wand fell into the lake.*

Spelling tip

exceed   excite
      exclaim   excuse

Notice that if a 'c' is followed by an 'e' or an 'i', it makes a soft 'ss' sound, as in "**exceed**" and "**excite**". If it is followed by a 'u', an 'o', or a consonant, it makes a hard 'ck' sound, as in "**exclaim**" and "**excuse**".

exclude excluding excluded *(verb)*
1 If you **exclude** something, you leave it out. *The list excludes prices.*
2 to stop someone joining in with something. *George was excluded from school.* **exclusion** *(noun).*

excuse excusing excused
1 *(ex-**kyooze**) (verb)* to forgive someone for doing something.
2 *(ex-**kyuse**) (noun)* a reason you give to explain why you have done something wrong. *Tom's excuse for being late was that there was a giraffe in the road.*
3 *(ex-**kyooze**) (verb)* to give someone permission not to do something. *The instructor excused Lydia from games.*
4 excuse me *(interjection)* You say **excuse me** when you want to get someone's attention or apologize for a small mistake.

execute executing executed *(verb)*
to kill someone as a punishment. **execution** *(noun).*

exercise *(noun)*
1 an activity that you do to keep fit and healthy. **exercise** *(verb).*
2 a piece of work that you do to get better at something. *I do piano exercises every night.*

exhale exhaling exhaled *(verb)*
to breathe out. **exhalation** *(noun).*

exhausted *(adjective)*
very tired. *Cross-country running makes me exhausted.*

exhibition *(noun)*
a collection of things that are put on show for people to look at, such as works of art and historical objects.

exist **existing existed** *(verb)*
to live, or to be real. *Do fairies exist?* **existence** *(noun)*.

exit **exiting exited**
1 *(verb)* to leave, or to go out.
2 *(noun)* the way out of a place.

exotic *(adjective)*
1 from a foreign, faraway country. *An exotic plant.*

For Europeans, these plants and animals are **exotic**.

rafflesia flower

Venus flytrap

Madagascan moth

King bird of paradise

pineapple fish

2 strange and fascinating. *That is an exotic perfume.*

expand
expanding expanded *(verb)*
to get bigger. **expansion** *(noun)*.

expect **expecting expected** *(verb)*
1 to think that something will happen. *I expect that it will rain later.* **expectation** *(noun)*.
2 to wait for someone to arrive. *We're expecting visitors.*
3 to think that something ought to happen. *Aunt Rita expects you to visit.* **expectation** *(noun)*.
4 If a woman is **expecting**, she is pregnant.

expedition *(noun)*
a long journey done for a special reason, such as exploring.

expel **expelling expelled** *(verb)*
If someone is **expelled** from a school, they have to leave as a punishment for breaking the rules. **expulsion** *(noun)*.

expensive *(adjective)*
costing a lot of money. *An expensive watch.* **expensively** *(adverb)*.

experience *(noun)*
1 something that you do, or that happens to you. *Going to India was an amazing experience.* **experience** *(verb)*.
2 the knowledge and skills that you gain by doing something. *I have a lot of experience of looking after animals.* **experienced** *(adjective)*.

experiment *(noun)*
a test that is done to find out whether an idea is true, or whether something works. **experiment** *(verb)*.

expert *(noun)*
someone who is very skilled at something, or knows a lot about a particular subject. **expertise** *(noun)*.

explain **explaining explained** *(verb)*
1 to talk about something so that other people understand it. **explanation** *(noun)*.
2 to give a reason for something. **explanation** *(noun)*.

explode **exploding exploded** *(verb)*
If something **explodes**, it bursts or blows apart with a loud bang.

explore **exploring explored** *(verb)*
to travel around a place in order to find out more about it. **exploration** *(noun)*, **explorer** *(noun)*.

Spelling tip

explode → explosion

Look at how the verb "**explode**" changes when it becomes the noun "**explosion**". Many other words follow this pattern, such as "exclu**de**" → "exclu**sion**".

explosion *(noun)*
a sudden, loud bang that is made when something bursts or blows up.

explosive
1 *(noun)* a substance that can blow up.
2 *(adjective)* able or likely to explode.

expose
exposing exposed *(verb)*
to uncover something so that people can see it. *Everyone gasped when the painting was exposed.* **exposure** *(noun)*.

express
expresses expressing expressed *(verb)*
to show what you feel or think by saying, doing or writing something. *Henry expressed his joy by dancing.*

expression *(noun)*
1 the act of showing your feelings.
2 the look on someone's face. *James had a blank expression.*

extend
extending extended *(verb)*
to make something longer or bigger. *We are extending our house.* **extension** *(noun)*.

extinct *(adjective)*
If a type of animal or plant is **extinct**, it has died out and does not exist anymore. **extinction** *(noun)*.

Dodos are **extinct**.

extinguish **extinguishes extinguishing extinguished** *(verb)*
to put out a flame, fire, or light.

extra *(adjective)*
more than the usual amount. *Carl had an extra helping of chips.* **extra** *(adverb)*.

extract *(noun)*
a short section taken from a book, speech, piece of music, and so on.

extraordinary *(adjective)*
very unusual or special. *George has extraordinary strength.* **extraordinarily** *(adverb)*.

Word family

extra   extraordinary   extraterrestrial

Words that begin with 'extra' are often to do with things that are unusual. The Latin word "extra" means "outside" or "beyond". "Extraordinary" means "out of the ordinary", and an "extraterrestrial" lives outside of our planet.

extraterrestrial *(noun)*
a creature from outer space. **extraterrestrial** *(adjective)*.

extreme *(adjective)*
1 very great. *The extreme cold makes it difficult for people to survive in Antarctica.*
2 furthest. *I reached the extreme edge of the woods.*

extrovert *(noun)*
someone who enjoys being with other people and is talkative. *Robbie is quite an extrovert.* **extroverted** *(adjective)*.

eye *(noun)*
1 one of the two organs in your head that you use for seeing.
2 the small hole in a needle.

eyebrow *(noun)*
the line of hair that grows above each of your eyes.

eyelash **eyelashes** *(noun)*
one of the short, curved hairs that grow on your eyelids.

eyelid *(noun)*
the upper or lower fold of skin that covers your eye when it is closed.

eyesight *(noun)*
the ability to see. *My gran's eyesight is getting worse.*

Ff

fable *(noun)*
a story that has a moral or lesson.

Probably the most famous **fables** were those written over 2,500 years ago, by a Greek man called Aesop. They include "The Goose that Laid the Golden Egg", "The Boy Who Cried Wolf", and "The Hare and the Tortoise".

fabric *(noun)*
material, or cloth.

fabulous *(adjective)*
If something is **fabulous**, it is amazing or brilliant. *Cara wore a fabulous dress to the ball.*

face **facing faced**
1 *(noun)* Your **face** is at the front of your head. It has two eyes, a nose and a mouth on it.
2 *(verb)* If something **faces** something else, it looks towards it, or is opposite it. *Our house faces the sea.*

Facebook *(noun)* *(trademark)*
a website where you can create a profile, talk to friends, and put up pictures.

fact *(noun)*
a piece of information that is true. **factual** *(adjective)*.

factory **factories** *(noun)*
a big building where products are made in large numbers.

fade **fading faded** *(verb)*
to get paler or less strong. *My new jeans faded in the wash.*

fail **failing failed** *(verb)*
1 If you **fail** an exam or test, you don't pass it. *Sue failed her driving test again.* **failure** *(noun)*.
2 If you **fail** to do something, you don't do it. *Henry always fails to arrive on time.* **failure** *(noun)*.

faint **fainting fainted** *(verb)*
to get really dizzy, and fall down. *Dean fainted after he gave blood.* **faint** *(adjective)*.

faint **fainter faintest** *(adjective)*
weak, or not very loud or strong. *The sound was too faint from the back.*

fair *(noun)*
a collection of different stalls where you can buy things or play games, or go on rides.

fair **fairer fairest** *(adjective)*
1 If you are **fair**, you treat everyone equally and reasonably. *It wasn't fair of Yolanda to get her brother into trouble.* **fairness** *(noun)*, **fairly** *(adverb)*.
2 Fair hair is a light yellow colour.

fairly *(adverb)*
quite, or rather. *This curry is fairly hot.*

fairy **fairies** *(noun)*
a tiny magical creature with wings, that you may read about in stories.

faith *(noun)*
1 If you **have faith in** someone or something, you trust them and have confidence in them. *I have faith in Mum's advice.*
2 a religious belief. *Aaron's faith helps him through hard times.*

faithful *(noun)*
loyal and trustworthy. **faithfully** *(adverb)*.

fake **faking faked**
1 *(noun)* a copy of something made to fool people. *The designer jacket was a fake.* **fake** *(adjective)*.
2 *(verb)* If you **fake** something, you only pretend to do it or feel it. *I faked surprise when I opened my present from Grandma.*

fall **falling fell fallen** (verb)
1 to drop to the floor or ground. *Emma fell off the monkey bars.* **fall** (noun).
2 to go lower. *Sales fell after the price went up.* **fall** (noun).
3 If you **fall asleep**, you go to sleep.
4 If you **fall in love**, you start loving someone. *We all fell in love with the puppy.*

false (adjective)
not true, real, or right. *Gran has false teeth.* **falsely** (adverb).

famous (adjective)
A **famous** person or thing is very well-known. *This church is famous for its statues.* **fame** (noun).

fan (noun)
1 someone who likes someone or something very much, especially a team, band, or celebrity. *Fans of the band waited by the exit to meet them.*
2 an object or machine that you use to blow or wave air onto you, to keep cool. *This electric fan is great in summer.*

fancy
fancies fancying fancied (verb)
to be keen to do or have something. *I fancy pasta for supper.*

fancy **fancier fanciest** (adjective)
very smart and special. *We wore fancy clothes to the wedding.*

fancy dress (noun)
clothes that you dress up in, to make you look like someone or something else. *Jake asked everyone to come in fancy dress.*

fang (noun)
a sharp tooth, for example on a snake.

fantastic (adjective)
extremely good, or wonderful. *That was a fantastic show.*

fantasy **fantasies**
1 (noun) something in your imagination, that does not exist or happen in real life.
2 (adjective) A **fantasy** film or book is about magical things and different worlds. *I enjoy reading fantasy books.*

Spelling tip

farther
further

The words "**further**" and "**farther**" mean just about the same thing, and although "further" tends to be much more commonly used, people will understand you whichever word you use. If you are using "farther", make sure you remember the 'r', as "father" means "dad".

far
farther farthest or **further furthest**
1 (adverb) at, to, or from a long way away. *Have you come far?*
2 (adverb) a lot. *This route is far shorter.*
3 (adjective) in the place that is not as near. *We live on the far side of town.*

fare (noun)
the price you pay for a ticket to travel somewhere.

Far East (noun)
the area of the world that includes countries such as China, Japan, Indonesia, and Thailand.

farewell (interjection)
a slightly old-fashioned word for **goodbye**.

farm (noun)
a place where crops are grown and animals are kept. **farm** (verb), **farmer** (noun), **farming** (noun).

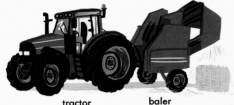

tractor   baler

plough

some machines used on **farms**

fascinate – feature

Spelling tip fascinate

If the letters 'sc' are followed by an 'i' or an 'e', they usually make a soft 'ss' sound, like here in "fascinate". If 'sc' is followed by the letters 'a', 'o' or 'u', they make a hard 'sk' sound, for example in "scare", "scold", and "discuss".

fascinate
fascinating fascinated *(verb)*
If someone or something **fascinates** you, you are very interested in everything about them. **fascination** *(noun)*.

fashion *(noun)*
1 a style or trend. *Are shorts in fashion this summer?*
2 the business of designing, selling and buying clothes in the latest styles.

fashionable *(adjective)*
If you are **fashionable**, you know what is stylish, and wear it.

fast **faster fastest**
1 *(adjective)* moving or able to move very quickly. *A fast car.*
2 *(adverb)* quickly. *Don't drive so fast!*

fast **fasting fasted** *(verb)*
to stop eating for a period of time. *Many people fast for religious reasons.*

fasten *(fass-un)*
fastening fastened *(verb)*
to close, fix, or do up. *Fasten your coat.*

fat **fatter fattest**
1 *(adjective)* If a person or animal is **fat**, they weigh more than is healthy.
2 *(noun)* the white, chewy part of meat.
3 *(noun)* Butter, margarine and oil are all **fats**.

fatal *(adjective)*
If something is **fatal**, it kills you. **fatally** *(adverb)*.

fate *(noun)*
1 what your future will be.
2 a force that some people believe controls and shapes our lives.

father *(noun)*
Your **father** is your male parent.

fault *(noun)*
1 something wrong. *This lamp has a fault.* **faulty** *(adjective)*.
2 If something bad is **your fault**, you did it, or made it happen. *It was my fault we lost the match.*

favour **favouring favoured**
1 *(noun)* a helpful thing you do for someone. *I walk the dogs as a favour to our neighbour.*
2 *(verb)* If you **favour** someone or something, you prefer them. *I favour mint ice cream over vanilla.*
3 If you are **in favour of** something, you like or support it.

favourite *(adjective)*
Your **favourite** person or thing is the one you like best. **favourite** *(noun)*.

fawn *(noun)*
1 a young deer.
2 a light brown colour. **fawn** *(adjective)*.

fear **fearing feared** *(verb)*
to be scared of something. *I fear snakes.* **fear** *(noun)*, **fearful** *(adjective)*, **fearfully** *(adverb)*.

feast **feasting feasted**
1 *(noun)* a large and special meal.
2 *(verb)* to eat lots of good things. *We feasted on strawberries.*

feather *(noun)*
one of the light, fluffy things that a bird has all over its body.

peacock feather

guinea fowl feather

macaw tail feather

Different types of birds have different **feathers**.

feature *(noun)*
1 Your **features** are the parts of your face, such as your eyes and nose.
2 an item in a newspaper or magazine.

February *(noun)*
the second month of the year, which has only 28 days, or 29 in a leap year.

> Remember both the 'r's in "February".

fed
1 *(verb)* the past tense of **feed**.
2 **fed up** *(adjective)* If you are **fed up**, you are bored and a bit miserable.

fee *(noun)*
the charge for something. *The fee for this job is £100.*

feed **feeding fed** *(verb)*
to give someone or something food. *I need to feed the cat.*

feedback *(noun)*
the things people say about something, often after it's happened. *There was lots of good feedback about the school show.*

feel **feeling felt** *(verb)*
1 to touch something with your fingertips. *Feel how soft this rug is.*
2 to sense something with part of your body. *Ruby felt the baby move.*
3 to experience an emotion. *I feel so angry.* **feeling** *(noun)*.

fell *(verb)*
the past tense of **fall**.

felt *(verb)*
the past tense of **feel**.

female *(noun)*
a person or animal of the sex that can have babies. **female** *(adjective)*.

feminine *(adjective)*
1 to do with women.
2 having qualities that are supposed to be typical of women.

fence *(noun)*
a barrier, usually made of wood or wire.

ferocious *(adjective)*
very fierce and violent. *Lions are ferocious hunters.* **ferociously** *(adverb)*.

ferry **ferries** *(noun)*
a ship that carries people across a stretch of water. **ferry** *(verb)*.

fertile *(adjective)*
1 Land that is **fertile** is good for growing crops.
2 If a woman or female animal is **fertile**, she can have babies.

festival *(noun)*
a big celebration, when lots of events happen. *There is a food festival in town this weekend.*

fetch **fetches fetching fetched** *(verb)*
to go and get someone or something. *I fetched Josh's coat.*

fête *or* **fete** *(noun)*
an outdoor event with games and stalls, held to raise money.

fever *(noun)*
If you have a **fever**, your temperature is high and you feel hot and sweaty. **feverish** *(adjective)*.

few **fewer fewest** *(adjective)*
not many. *I only ate a few biscuits.*

fiancé *(fee-on-say)* *(noun)*
a man who is engaged to be married.

fiancée *(fee-on-say)* *(noun)*
a woman who is engaged to be married.

fib *(noun)*
a little lie, usually one that isn't about something serious. **fib** *(verb)*.

fibre *(noun)*
a thread of something, such as cotton or muscle.

fiction *(noun)*
stories that are made up, and not about real things. **fictional** *(adjective)*.

fiddle **fiddling fiddled** *(verb)*
If you **fiddle** with something, you touch or play with it, often because you are nervous or bored.

fidget **fidgeting fidgeted** *(verb)*
to move around constantly, often because you are nervous or bored.

field *(noun)*
a piece of land, often with a fence or hedge around it, used for growing crops or keeping animals in.

a b c d e **f** g h i j k l m n o p q r s t u v w x y z

Spelling tip — fierce

This word follows the spelling guideline: 'i' before 'e' except after 'c', when the letters make an 'ee' sound.

fierce fiercer fiercest *(adjective)*
very violent or aggressive. **fierceness** *(noun)*, **fiercely** *(adverb)*.

fight fighting fought *(verb)*
1 to attack and try to hurt someone. **fight** *(noun)*, **fighter** *(noun)*.
2 to try to prevent or get rid of something. *We're fighting the plans to cut down the forest.* **fight** *(noun)*.

figure *(noun)*
1 the name for a number. *Tim drew the figure 6 on the board.*
2 the shape of a person's body, especially a woman's.

file filing filed
1 *(noun)* a collection of information on a computer, or in a box or folder.
2 *(verb)* to organize things into files and keep them safe.
3 *(noun)* a tool, used for making things smoother.
4 If people walk **in single file**, they walk one behind the other.

fill filling filled *(verb)*
to make full. *I filled my bowl with cereal.*

filling
1 *(noun)* the stuff that goes inside something such as a cake or a pie.
2 *(adjective)* If a food is **filling**, it makes you feel full quickly.

film filming filmed
1 *(noun)* a story told by moving pictures on a screen.
2 *(verb)* to record something with a camera. *Mum filmed the entire parade yesterday.*

filter *(noun)*
a device that cleans liquids or gases as they pass through it. **filter** *(verb)*.

filthy filthier filthiest *(adjective)*
very dirty. *Your trousers are filthy.* **filth** *(noun)*.

fin *(noun)*
a flap that sticks out of a fish or other sea animal's body, and helps it to swim.

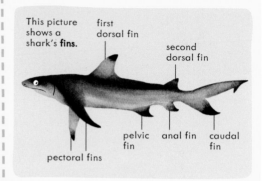

This picture shows a shark's **fins**.
first dorsal fin
second dorsal fin
pelvic fin
anal fin
caudal fin
pectoral fins

blacktip reef shark

final
1 *(adjective)* last in a series of things. *The final episode is on tonight.*
2 *(noun)* The **final** of a competition is the last round, when the winner is decided.

finance financing financed
1 *(noun)* money, or things that are to do with money. **financial** *(adjective)*.
2 *(verb)* to pay for something. *Our health service is financed by taxpayers.*

find finding found *(verb)*
1 to discover or see something, especially something that is lost. *I found my PE kit under my bed.*
2 to think or realize something. *I find Neil very unkind.*
3 If you **find something out**, you discover it. *I found out about it on the internet.*

fine finer finest
1 *(adjective)* feeling well. *I'm fine.*
2 *(adjective)* very good. *A fine meal.*
3 *(adjective)* delicate or thin. *Her dress was made of fine silk. I have fine hair.*
4 *(adjective)* If the weather is **fine**, it is bright and quite warm and sunny.
5 *(noun)* money you must pay if you do something wrong. *A parking fine.* **fine** *(verb)*.

finger (noun)
one of the four long, thin parts of your hands that you can move. The fifth, shorter one is your **thumb**.

fingerprint (noun)
a mark on a surface made by the lines on the tips of your fingers.

finish **finishes finishing finished**
1 *(verb)* to end or complete something. *I finished my homework at 7 p.m.*
2 *(noun)* the end of something, such as a race. *My family were waiting at the finish to cheer me on.*

fir (noun)
a type of tree that is cone-shaped and has very thin leaves called needles that don't fall off in the winter.

fire **firing fired**
1 *(noun)* the flames, heat and smoke made when something burns. *There's a fire in the barn!*
2 *(verb)* to send a bullet from a gun.
3 *(verb)* to tell someone they have lost their job. *My boss fired me yesterday.*

fire engine (noun)
a large truck that takes firefighters and the equipment they need to put out fires and rescue people.

fire extinguisher (noun)
a metal or plastic case which contains water or chemicals that can be used to put out small fires.

firefighter (noun)
someone whose job is to put out fires and help people escape from them.

firework (noun)
a tube or container filled with chemicals that makes lots of colourful sparks, and sometimes a loud noise, when you light it.

firm **firmer firmest** *(adjective)*
1 If something is **firm**, it is quite hard and solid. *A firm mattress.* **firmness** *(noun).*
2 If someone is **firm**, they are strict and don't change their mind easily. **firmly** *(adverb).*

first
1 *(adjective)* earliest, or before all the others. *I was the first person to finish the test.*
2 *(adverb)* If you do something **first**, you do it before anything else.

first aid (noun)
treatment given to someone who has been injured or taken ill, before they see a doctor.

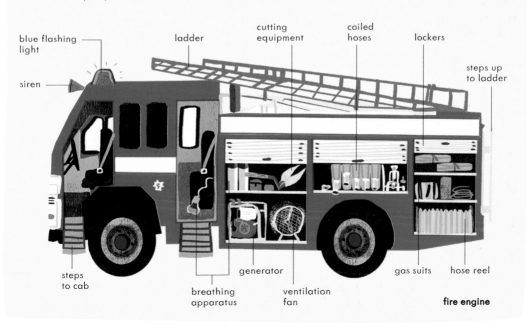

blue flashing light

siren

ladder

cutting equipment

coiled hoses

lockers

steps up to ladder

steps to cab

generator

breathing apparatus

ventilation fan

gas suits

hose reel

fire engine

A B C D E F G H I J K L M N O P Q R S T U V W X Y Z

fish fish *or* **fishes** *(noun)*
an animal that lives in water. Fish have scales and fins, and breathe through slits in their sides called gills. *See* **tropical**.

fish fishes fishing fished *(verb)*
to try to catch fish using a rod or net. *My uncle likes to fish.* **fishing** *(noun)*.

fist *(noun)*
a tightly closed hand.

fit fitting fitted *or* **fit** *(verb)*
If something **fits**, it is the right size and shape. *This dress fits me well.*

fit fitter fittest *(adjective)*
1 well, strong, and healthy. *Janet plays badminton to stay fit.* **fitness** *(noun)*.
2 good-looking or attractive.

fix fixes fixing fixed *(verb)*
1 to mend something. *Grandad fixed the broken gate.*
2 to join something to something else. *I fixed the new charm to my bracelet.*

fizzy fizzier fizziest *(adjective)*
with lots of bubbles in it. *I prefer fizzy water.*

flabby flabbier flabbiest *(adjective)*
a bit fat. *Our dog is getting a bit flabby.* **flab** *(noun)*.

flag *(noun)*
a piece of cloth with a design on, which may be fixed to a pole. Each country has its own flag.

flake flaking flaked
1 *(noun)* a small, thin piece of something. *The salad has flakes of tuna on top.*
2 *(verb)* If something **flakes**, thin bits of it peel off. *The paint on the door is flaking.* **flaky** *(adjective)*.

flame *(noun)*
a flickering tongue of fire. *There were flames coming out of the window.*

flamingo
flamingos *or* **flamingoes** *(noun)*
a long-legged pink or orange bird.

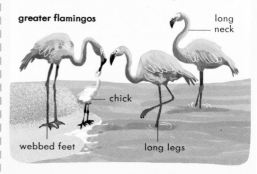

greater flamingos — long neck — chick — webbed feet — long legs

flap flapping flapped
1 *(verb)* to move or be moved up and down or from side to side. *The bird flapped its wings and took off.*
2 *(noun)* something flat that is attached to something else on only one side. *The cat got too fat for the cat flap. I opened the flap of the envelope.*

United Nations

Olympic Games

European Union

International Red Cross

Nepal

United States of America

Spain

Brazil

France

United Kingdom

Flags usually represent a country or organization.

flare flaring flared
1 (noun) a bright light, often used in an emergency to attract help.
2 (verb) If something **flares up**, it suddenly gets worse. *Zoe's eczema flared up on holiday.*

flash flashes flashing flashed
1 (noun) a short, sudden burst of light.
2 (verb) When a light **flashes**, it goes on and off quickly.
3 (verb) to show something very quickly. *The picture flashed on the screen.*

flashback (noun)
a scene in a film or story that is set in an earlier time than the main story.

flashy flashier flashiest (adjective)
If something is **flashy**, it looks expensive. *I hate flashy cars.*

flask (noun)
a container that you can put liquids in to keep them hot or cold.

flat flatter flattest
1 (adjective) smooth, with no bumps. *Let's find somewhere flat to sit.*
2 (adjective) without power, or without air. *My bike's got a flat tyre.*
3 (noun) a set of rooms for living in, usually part of a larger building.

flavour (noun)
the way something tastes. *A sour flavour.* **flavoured** (adjective), **flavouring** (noun).

flaw (noun)
a fault or weakness in something. **flawed** (adjective).

flea (noun)
a small, biting insect that sucks the blood of animals.

flee fleeing fled (verb)
to run away from something dangerous.

fleece (noun)
1 a warm jacket, made of soft material. **fleecy** (adjective).
2 a sheep's woolly coat.

flesh (noun)
the soft parts of your body, between your bones and your skin.

Spelling tip flexible

It can be tricky to know whether to use the ending '-ible' or '-able'. The ending '-able' is much more common. If you can remove the ending and the word makes sense, it's more likely to be '-able', for example: "enjoyable", "dependable". Some words, such as "flexible" and "accessible", you will just have to learn, though.

flexible (adjective)
1 Someone or something that is **flexible** can bend and change shape easily. **flexibility** (noun), **flexibly** (adverb).
2 If you are **flexible**, you are able and happy to change your plans.

flick flicking flicked (verb)
to strike or move something quickly, often with your thumb and finger.

flicker flickering flickered (verb)
If a light **flickers**, its brightness keeps changing. *The lamp keeps flickering.*

flight (noun)
1 a journey in an aeroplane or other type of aircraft.
2 A **flight** of stairs takes you from one floor to the next.

fling flinging flung (verb)
to throw something roughly.

flip flipping flipped (verb)
to turn something over quickly.

flipper (noun)
1 a wide, flat limb that some sea animals have to help them swim.
2 one of two wide, flat pieces of rubber you wear on your feet to help you swim.

float floating floated (verb)
1 to stay on the surface of a liquid and not sink.
2 to hover in the air without touching the ground.

flock (noun)
a big group of birds or animals.

flood flooding flooded *(verb)*
When something **floods**, it is so full of water that the water starts to spill out. *The river has flooded.* **flood** *(noun)*, **flooding** *(noun)*.

floor *(noun)*
1 the flat surface inside a building, that you walk on.
2 a level of a building. *The office is on the top floor.*

floppy floppier floppiest *(adjective)*
not stiff. *Our dog has a floppy tail.*

florist *(noun)*
a shop or a person that sells flowers.

> The words **"flour"** and **"flower"** sound almost exactly the same, so take care.

flour *(noun)*
a powder made by grinding grains. Flour is used to make bread and cakes.

flow flowing flowed *(verb)*
When something **flows**, it moves easily and smoothly. **flow** *(noun)*.

flower *(noun)*
the part of a plant that has colourful petals.

some types of **flowers**

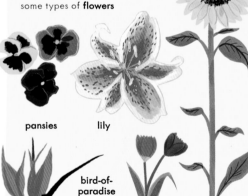

pansies   lily

bird-of-paradise flower

tulips   sunflower

flown *(verb)*
the past participle of **fly**. *The swallows have flown south for the winter.*

flu *(noun) (abbreviation)*
an illness which makes you feel very hot and achy. Flu is short for "influenza".

fluent *(adjective)*
If you are **fluent** in a language, you can speak it very well. **fluently** *(adverb)*.

fluffy fluffier fluffiest *(adjective)*
Something that is **fluffy** is light and soft. *My rabbit has a fluffy coat.* **fluff** *(noun)*.

fluid *(noun)*
a liquid. **fluid** *(adjective)*.

flute *(noun)*
a long musical instrument that you blow into to make sounds, with keys that you press to change the note. *See* woodwind.

flutter fluttering fluttered *(verb)*
to wave or flap gently. *The clothes on the line fluttered in the breeze.*

fly flies flying flew flown
1 *(verb)* to move through the air.
2 *(noun)* an insect with wings.

common housefly

foal *(noun)*
a young horse.

foam foaming foamed
1 *(noun)* lots of small bubbles. *A bath full of foam.* **foamy** *(adjective)*.
2 *(verb)* to make bubbles.

focus focuses focusing focused
1 *(verb)* to look carefully at something.
2 *(verb)* to concentrate on something.
3 *(verb)* to make sure a camera, microscope or telescope shows you things clearly.
4 *(noun)* the thing you care about most. *My focus is my work.*

fog *(noun)*
a thick cloud of water droplets close to the ground, that makes it hard to see. **foggy** *(adjective)*.

fold folding folded *(verb)*
to bend one part of something over another part. *Peter folded the piece of paper in half.* **fold** *(noun)*.

folk *(noun)*
1 people, especially your family. *Where do your folk live?*
2 a style of music that includes many traditional songs. **folk** *(adjective)*.

follow **following followed** *(verb)*
1 to go after someone. *I followed Will into the treehouse.*
2 If you **follow** instructions, you do as they say.
3 If you **follow** a road or path, you go down it.
4 If one thing **follows** another, it comes after it. **following** *(preposition)*.

fond **fonder fondest** *(adjective)*
If you are **fond of** someone or something, you like them. *Darren is very fond of his cousins.* **fondness** *(noun)*.

font *(noun)*
a style of lettering.

food *(noun)*
what you eat to stay alive and well.

food chain *(noun)*
a set of plants and animals that are linked because each one is eaten by the one above it in the food chain.

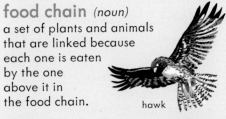

hawk

grass   cricket   mouse

The hawk is at the top of this **food chain.**

fool **fooling fooled**
1 *(noun)* someone who is silly, and makes bad decisions. **foolish** *(adjective)*, **foolishness** *(noun)*.
2 *(verb)* to trick someone.

foot **feet** *(noun)*
1 Your **feet** are the two parts of your body at the end of your legs, which you stand and walk on.
2 a measure of length equal to 12 inches (about 30cm).

Spelling tip

football   footprint   footstep

These are all **compound nouns**, made from the word "**foot**" and another word. Remember that there is no space or hyphen in them.

football *(noun)*
1 a game in which two teams of eleven players have to score goals by kicking a ball into a net. **footballer** *(noun)*.
2 the ball used for football.

footprint *(noun)*
the mark left by a person or animal's foot.

footstep *(noun)*
the sound of someone or something walking. *We heard footsteps in the hall.*

for *(preposition)*
1 If something is **for** someone, they are going to have it. *This cake is for you.*
2 to get or to have. *Most people work for money.*
3 What something is **for** is what it does. *What's that machine for?*

forbid
forbidding forbade forbidden *(verb)*
to tell someone that they are not allowed to do something. **forbidden** *(adjective)*.

force **forcing forced**
1 *(verb)* to make someone do something.
2 *(noun)* strength or power. *The force of the wind blew the trees down.*

forecast *(noun)*
A weather **forecast** tells you what the weather is going to be. **forecast** *(verb)*.

foreground *(noun)*
the part of a picture that looks nearest the front.

forehead *(noun)*
the part of your face that's above your eyebrows.

a
b
c
d
e
f
g
h
i
j
k
l
m
n
o
p
q
r
s
t
u
v
w
x
y
z

A B C D E F G H I J K L M N O P Q R S T U V W X Y Z

foreign *(adjective)*
from another place or country.
foreigner *(noun)*.

foresee
foreseeing foresaw foreseen *(verb)*
to predict something or be aware of something before it happens. *It's a good job we foresaw that hailstorm.*

forest *(noun)*
a large area with lots of trees growing closely together.

forever *(adverb)*
for always, or for the rest of time. *I will love you forever.*

forget
forgetting forgot forgotten *(verb)*
If you **forget** something, you don't or can't remember it. **forgetful** *(adjective)*.

forgive
forgiving forgave forgiven *(verb)*
to stop being angry or blaming someone for something. *Martha forgave me for ripping her dress.* **forgiveness** *(noun)*.

Spelling tip

forgive   forgave

forgiving   forgiven

Remember that you make the tenses of the verb "**forgive**" in exactly the same way as for the verb "**give**": "giving", "gave", "given".

fork *(noun)*
1 a small tool with three or four sharp points called prongs, which you use for eating.
2 a large tool with three or four sharp prongs, which you use for digging.
3 If there is a **fork** in a road or path, it branches in two or more different directions. **fork** *(verb)*.

forked *(adjective)*
shaped like a fork, with a split or pronged end. *Snakes have forked tongues.*

form forming formed
1 *(noun)* a type or kind. *The tango is a form of dance.*
2 *(noun)* a shape. *I could see the form of a person coming up the drive.*
3 *(verb)* to create something. *The company was formed in 1985.*
4 *(verb)* to make into a particular shape. *The soldiers formed a straight line outside the palace.*
5 *(noun)* a class in school. *Sixth form.*
6 *(noun)* a sheet with questions on it which need to be filled in.

formal *(adjective)*
smart, and not relaxed. *We had to wear formal clothes to the ball.*

format *(noun)*
the way something is set up or arranged into a pattern or plan. *I can't read these numbers in this format.* **format** *(verb)*.

formation *(noun)*
1 the process of making something. *The formation of this valley took millions of years.*
2 the way things are arranged into a pattern or shape. *The dancers were in a star formation.*

former *(adjective)*
from the past. *Mike is a former history teacher at our school.*

formula
formulas or **formulae** *(noun)*
1 a rule in science or maths written in numbers or symbols.
2 a recipe, or secret. *What's your formula for a successful family day out?*

fort *(noun)*
a building, similar to a castle, that has been strongly built to survive attacks.

forthcoming *(adjective)*
happening or coming up soon. *Raoul has a part in a forthcoming film this summer.*

Word origin   fortnight

This word is a shortened version of the Old English words **"feowertyne niht"**, meaning **"fourteen nights"**.

fortnight *(noun)*
two weeks. *Aunt Dorothy stayed with us for a fortnight.*

fortress *(noun)*
a place, such as a castle, which is strengthened against attacks.

fortunate *(adjective)*
lucky, or bringing good luck.
fortunately *(adverb)*.

fortune *(noun)*
1 a lot of money. *It cost a fortune.*
2 If you have **good fortune**, you have good luck.
3 If someone tells your **fortune**, they tell you what they think will happen to you in the future.

forward *or* **forwards** *(adverb)*
1 towards the place that is in front of you. *I walked forward.*
2 If you **look forward** to something, you are happy and excited that it is going to happen.

fossil *(noun)*
the stony remains of an ancient plant or animal.

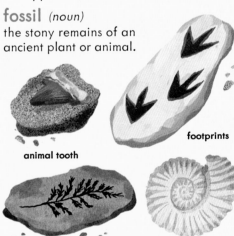

animal tooth

footprints

leaf

ammonite

four different types of **fossils**

foster **fostering fostered** *(verb)*
to care for a child that is not your own for a while.

foul **fouler foulest** *(adjective)*
smelly, dirty, and disgusting.

found *(verb)*
the past tense of **find**.

foundation *(noun)*
1 Foundations are the bottom part of a building, on which everything else is built. *The builders have finished the foundations of our new house.*
2 the basis or most important part of something. *The foundation of a good friendship is trust.*

fountain *(noun)*
a shooting jet or spray of water.

fowl *(noun)*
birds such as chickens, ducks, and geese, that people keep for their eggs and meat.

fox **foxes** *(noun)*
a wild animal that is a little smaller than a medium-sized dog, and has a pointy snout and ears, and a bushy tail.

fraction *(noun)*
1 a part of a whole number. $\frac{1}{2}$ and $\frac{1}{4}$ are fractions.
2 a very small part of something. *Only a fraction of the stolen money was ever found.*

fracture *(noun)*
a crack or break in something, especially a bone. **fracture** *(verb)*.

fragile *(adjective)*
very delicate and easily broken.

fragment *(noun)*
a small piece of something. *Hal had a fragment of glass in his knee.*

fragrance *(noun)*
a perfume or scent. **fragrant** *(adjective)*.

frail **frailer frailest** *(adjective)*
weak and delicate. *My great aunt is getting frail in her old age.*

A B C D E **F** G H I J K L M N O P Q R S T U V W X Y Z

Spelling tip

frame → framing → framed

Remember to remove the final, silent 'e' at the end of "frame" before you add the ending '-ing'.

Many other words with a silent 'e' on the end follow this pattern, including:

bake → baking → baked

smile → smiling → smiled

frame framing framed
1 (noun) the part that surrounds a window, picture, or a pair of glasses.
2 (verb) If you **frame** something, you put it in a frame. *Heather framed a photo of herself.*

framework (noun)
1 the structure that supports a building, car, object, and so on. *The framework of our greenhouse is made of wood.*
2 the basic outline or plan for something. *The framework for the wedding is in place.*

fraud (noun)
the crime of tricking other people in some way, usually involving getting their money by telling lies about who you are and what you do.

freckle (noun)
a light brown spot on your skin.
freckly (adjective).

free freer freest (adjective)
1 If a person or animal is **free**, they can go wherever they want to, and do whatever they like. **freedom** (noun).
2 If something is **free**, you don't have to pay for it. *A free meal.*

free freeing freed (verb)
to let a person or animal go after they have been trapped somewhere. *We freed the butterfly by opening the window.* **freedom** (noun).

freeze freezing froze frozen (verb)
1 When a liquid **freezes**, its temperature gets so low that it becomes solid. *Water freezes at 0°C.* **frozen** (adjective).
2 When you **freeze** foods, you put them in a freezer so that they will last longer. **frozen** (adjective).
3 to stop moving very suddenly. *I froze when I heard the doorbell.*

freezer (noun)
a very cold cabinet which can keep food frozen for many months.

freezing (adjective)
very cold. *It's freezing in here.*

frequency (noun)
how often something happens. *We lose the remote with great frequency.*

frequent (adjective)
If something is **frequent**, it happens often. **frequently** (adverb).

fresh fresher freshest (adjective)
1 **Fresh** food has not been cooked or treated in any way to last longer, but has been picked or made recently. *I love fresh fruit salad.* **freshness** (noun), **freshly** (adverb).
2 clean, cool, or new. *I need fresh air.*
3 new, or interesting. *Our maths teacher has lots of fresh ideas.*
4 **Fresh water** is found in rivers and lakes, but not in the sea.

fret fretting fretted (verb)
to worry about something. *Dad frets when I stay out late.*

friction (noun)
the force which is produced when two surfaces rub together.

fridge (noun)
a cabinet for keeping food cool. Fridge is short for "refrigerator".

friend (noun)
someone you know, like, and trust. *Chris is my friend.* **friendship** (noun).

friendly
friendlier friendliest (adjective)
kind, pleasant, and helpful to other people. **friendliness** (noun).

fright (noun)
If something gives you a **fright**, it shocks you and makes you feel scared. **frightened** (adjective).

frighten
frightening frightened (verb)
to scare someone. *Loud bangs frighten me.* **frightening** (adjective), **frightened** (adjective).

fringe (noun)
the hair that covers your forehead.

frizzy **frizzier frizziest** (adjective)
If hair is **frizzy**, it is not smooth at all, and has lots of tight curls.

frog (noun)
an animal that lives in or near water and has bulging eyes and long back legs which help it to jump a long way.

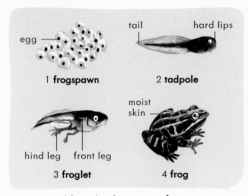

egg
tail
hard lips

1 **frogspawn**
2 **tadpole**

moist skin

hind leg   front leg
3 **froglet**
4 **frog**

life cycle of a **common frog**

from (preposition)
1 the place someone or something comes from or starts at. *The road goes from London to Liverpool. I'm from Australia.*
2 If you take something **from** someone, you take it away.
3 because of. *I'm out of breath from running.*
4 If a present is **from** someone, that person gave it to you.

front (noun)
1 the part that faces forwards. *The front of our house is blue.* **front** (adjective).
2 If someone or something is **in front of** you, they are before you.

frost (noun)
powdery ice that covers things when it's very cold outside.

frosty **frostier frostiest** (adjective)
1 covered with frost.
2 unfriendly. *Harriet gave Alex a frosty look.* **frostily** (adverb).

froth (noun)
lots of small bubbles in a liquid. *There's froth on my drink.* **frothy** (adjective).

frown **frowning frowned** (verb)
to pull your eyebrows together and wrinkle your forehead. You may frown because you are worried, annoyed, unsure, or concentrating hard. **frown** (noun).

fruit **fruit** or **fruits** (noun)
foods that are usually sweet, and which grow on plants or trees. **fruity** (adjective).

different types of **fruits**

apple

black cherries

pears

bananas

figs

oranges

honeydew melon

pineapple   kiwis   pomegranate

star fruits

dragon fruits

persimmons

lychees   mango

lime

peaches   plum   tangerine   watermelons

frustrated *(adjective)*
You feel **frustrated** if someone or something is stopping you from doing what you want to do. *Dad gets really frustrated when the car doesn't work.* **frustration** *(noun)*, **frustrate** *(verb)*.

fry **fries frying fried** *(verb)*
to cook something in a fat such as oil, butter, or margarine. **frying pan** *(noun)*.

fuel *(noun)*
something you burn to make energy or power. Some types of fuel include oil, gas, and coal.

fulfil **fulfilling fulfilled** *(verb)*
1 to do something that you promised or were expected to do.
2 to achieve a goal or desire. *I fulfilled my dream of going to China.*

fulfilled *(adjective)*
If you are **fulfilled**, you are happy in what you are doing. **fulfilment** *(noun)*.

full **fuller fullest** *(adjective)*
unable to fit anything more inside. *The car is full.* **fullness** *(noun)*, **fully** *(adverb)*.

full stop *(noun)*
the mark (.) that you put at the end of a sentence, or sometimes to show that you have shortened a word. *See* **punctuation**, *page 349.*

full-time *(adjective)*
If you have a **full-time** job, you do it every day of the working week.

fumble **fumbling fumbled** *(verb)*
to touch or handle something in a clumsy way. *I fumbled in my bag for the key.*

fun *(noun)*
When you have **fun**, you enjoy yourself.

Spelling tip · function

You will never see the ending '**–sion**' after a '**c**', only the ending '**–tion**', as here in "func**tion**", and also in "affec**tion**" and "collec**tion**".

---

function **functioning functioned**
1 *(noun)* Something's **function** is the thing that it does. *This book's function is to help you understand what words mean.*
2 *(verb)* If something **functions**, it works, or does its job. *This oven only functions half the time.* **functional** *(adjective)*.
3 *(noun)* an event. *There's a function going on in the village hall.*

fund **funding funded**
1 *(noun)* a sum of money, often raised to do something special, or to help other people. *The school is raising funds for a new hockey pitch.* **fundraising** *(noun)*, **fundraiser** *(noun)*.
2 *(verb)* If you **fund** something, you pay for it. *The trip was funded by the school.*

funeral *(noun)*
the special ceremony or service that is held soon after someone has died.

funfair *(noun)*
an outdoor event with rides, stalls, and games.

fungus **fungi** or **funguses** *(noun)*
a living thing, such as mould or a mushroom, that doesn't have leaves or flowers, and which reproduces by releasing tiny bodies called spores.

some types of **fungi**

fly agaric	**sulphur tuft**	**turkey tail**	**purple brittlegill**	**orange peel fungus**	**ink cap**

funnel (noun)
1 a tube which is wide at the top and narrow at the bottom, used to help you pour liquids.
2 a chimney on a ship or steam train.

funny funnier funniest (adjective)
1 If someone or something is **funny**, they make you laugh.
2 If something seems **funny**, it is strange, or worrying. *That fish looks a bit funny, so I won't eat it.* **funnily** (adverb).

fur (noun)
the soft, warm coat of an animal. **furry** (adjective).

furious (adjective)
1 very angry. **furiously** (adverb).
2 very fast. *The bus driver went at a furious speed.* **furiously** (adverb).

further
see far.

furthermore (adverb)
in addition, or besides. *Cycling is good for your health. Furthermore, it is more eco-friendly than driving.*

fury furies (noun)
a massive rage. *The head teacher was in a fury about the mess.*

fuse fusing fused
1 (noun) a safety device in electrical equipment which cuts off the power if there is too much electricity going through it.
2 (noun) the thing that is lit, or turned on, to make a bomb explode.
3 (verb) to join together. *Dave's broken bones fused quite quickly.* **fusion** (noun).

fuss fusses fussing fussed
1 (noun) If you **make a fuss about** something, you complain about it.
2 (noun) If you **make a fuss of** someone, you take great care of them and pay them a lot of attention.
3 (verb) If you **fuss** about something, you worry about it too much.

fussy fussier fussiest (adjective)
very choosy, especially about food. *Megan is a fussy eater.*

The future tense

The **future tense** is used to talk about things happening some time from now. There are two ways of forming it:

will + verb

I **will talk** to Lucas tomorrow.
I **will do** my homework tonight.

am/is/are + going to + verb

I'm **going to take** a picture of the view.
I'm **going to spend** my summer holidays in Greece.

Generally, you can use either of these forms, but here is how they are usually used:

"Going to" is more often used for talking about a plan.

I am **going to** invite all my friends to my birthday party.

I will give them invitations tomorrow.

"Will" is usually used for promising that you will do something.

future (noun)
the time that is ahead of us. *I'd like to visit Asia and Africa in the future.* **future** (adjective).

fuzzy fuzzier fuzziest (adjective)
1 A picture or sound that is **fuzzy** is not very clear. *The sound on this DVD is fuzzy.*
2 not smooth, or frizzy. *Fuzzy fur.*

Gg

gabble gabbling gabbled *(verb)*
to talk too fast for people to understand you easily.

gadget *(noun)*
a small machine that does a particular job. *A gadget for slicing eggs.*

gag gagging gagged *(verb)*
to tie something around someone's mouth to stop them from talking.
gag *(noun)*.

gain gaining gained
1 *(verb)* to get something good or useful. *I gained a lot of new friends from my netball team.*
2 *(noun)* an increase in the amount of something.
3 *(verb)* If you **gain weight**, you get heavier.
4 *(verb)* If you **gain on** someone that you are chasing, you get closer to them.

gala *(noun)*
a special event. *A swimming gala.*

galaxy galaxies *(noun)*
a large group of stars and planets.
galactic *(adjective)*.

Earth (28,000 light years from centre)

spiral arm

hot gas and dust

The Milky Way is a **spiral galaxy.**

gale *(noun)*
a very strong wind.

galleon *(noun)*
a large sailing ship used hundreds of years ago.

gallery galleries *(noun)*
a place where pieces of art, such as paintings, sculptures, photographs, and so on, are displayed for people to look at.

gallon *(noun)*
a unit used for measuring liquids. A gallon is about 4 $\frac{1}{2}$ litres.

gallop galloping galloped *(verb)*
When a horse **gallops**, it runs as fast as it can. **gallop** *(noun)*.

gamble gambling gambled *(verb)*
to bet money on the result of a race or game, or on something that might happen. **gambler** *(noun)*, **gamble** *(noun)*.

game *(noun)*
1 a fun activity with rules, that can be played by one or more people. *We invented a new game at the sleepover.*
2 wild animals, including birds such as pheasants and grouse, which are hunted for sport and for food.

gang ganging ganged
1 *(noun)* a group of people who do things together, usually with a leader.
2 *(verb)* If a group of people **gang up on** you, they all treat you unfairly and pick on you.

gaol *(noun)*
another way of spelling jail.

gap *(noun)*
a hole, or a space between things. *Mollie jumped over the gap in the floorboards.*

garage *(noun)*
1 a small building where one or more cars can be kept. *I can't get to my bike because the garage is full of junk.*
2 a place that sells petrol or repairs cars and other vehicles. *We had to take our car to the garage to be fixed.*

garden (noun)
land next to a house or other building where grass, flowers, vegetables, and so on, can be grown. **gardener** (noun), **gardening** (noun), **garden** (verb).

gargle **gargling gargled** (verb)
to move a liquid around your throat without swallowing it.

gargoyle (noun)
an ugly stone head or figure, found below the roof of old buildings, such as churches.

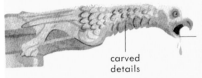

hole in mouth to allow rainwater to drain away

carved details

gargoyle on Notre-Dame Cathedral in Paris, France

garish (**gair**-ish) (adjective)
brightly coloured and not nice to look at. *I thought Louisa's bright blue dress was garish.* **garishly** (adverb).

garlic (noun)
the small white bulb of a plant similar to an onion, that has a strong flavour and smell. Garlic is very often used in cooking.

garment (noun)
a piece of clothing.

gas **gases** (noun)
1 a substance that is not liquid or solid. Gases will spread to fill any space. *The air that we breathe is a mixture of gases.*
2 a gas that is used as a fuel.

gash **gashes** (noun)
a long, deep cut.

gasp **gasping gasped** (verb)
to take in a short, quick breath, because you are surprised or in pain. *The cold water made me gasp.* **gasp** (noun).

gate (noun)
a metal or wooden barrier in a wall or fence, at the entrance to a building, garden, or field.

gateau (**gat**-oh) **gateaux** (noun)
a rich cake, usually containing cream.

gather **gathering gathered** (verb)
1 to collect things from different places. *We gathered blackberries today.*
2 to come together in a group. *A crowd gathered in front of the stage.*
3 to learn or understand. *I gather you didn't like your meal.*

gauge (rhymes with "page") (noun)
an instrument for measuring something. *A pressure gauge.*

gave (verb)
the past tense of **give**.

gay **gayer gayest** (adjective)
1 Someone who is **gay** has romantic relationships with people of the same sex.
2 an old-fashioned word for happy and lively.

gaze **gazing gazed** (verb)
to stare at someone or something for a long time. **gaze** (noun).

gear (noun)
the things or clothes that you need to do something. *Swimming gear.*

gel (noun)
a jelly-like substance.

gem (noun)
a precious stone, such as a diamond, ruby, or emerald.

ruby

sapphire

diamond

different types of **gems**

gender (noun)
the sex (male or female) of a person or animal.

gene (noun)
one of the parts of the cells of all living things. Genes are passed from parents to children, and control how you look. **genetic** (adjective).

general
1 (adjective) to do with everybody or everything. *General knowledge.* **generally** (adverb).
2 (adjective) not detailed or specific.
3 (noun) an army officer of very high rank.

generation *(noun)*
all the people born around the same time. *The next generation of children will be much better at using computers than us.*

generator *(noun)*
a machine which produces electricity.

generous *(adjective)*
Someone who is **generous** is happy to use their time and money to help others. **generosity** *(noun)*.

genie *(noun)*
In stories from the Middle East, a **genie** is a spirit who grants people's wishes.

genius *(**jee**-nee-us)* **geniuses** *(noun)*
an extremely clever or talented person. **genius** *(adjective)*.

gentle **gentler gentlest** *(adjective)*
1 careful and not rough. *Be gentle when you stroke the hamster.* **gentleness** *(noun)*.
2 kind and sensitive. *Eva is a gentle girl.* **gentleness** *(noun)*.

gentleman **gentlemen** *(noun)*
1 a polite name for a man.
2 a man with good manners.

genuine *(**jen**-yoo-in)* *(adjective)*
real and not fake. *A genuine diamond.*

geography *(noun)*
the study of the Earth, including its people, weather, and things such as mountains, deserts, and rivers. **geographer** *(noun)*, **geographical** *(adjective)*.

gerbil *(noun)*
a small, furry animal with long back legs and a long tail. Gerbils are often kept as pets.

small ears   whiskers

long, furry tail

Mongolian gerbil

germ *(noun)*
a very small living thing that can sometimes cause disease. *That dirty table must be covered in germs.*

germinate
germinating germinated *(verb)*
When seeds **germinate**, they start to grow shoots and roots.

gesture **gesturing gestured**
1 *(verb)* to move your head or hands as a way of saying something. **gesture** *(noun)*.
2 *(noun)* an action which shows a feeling. *That was a kind gesture.*

get **getting got** *(verb)*
1 to be given something. *I got some boots for my birthday.*
2 to fetch something. *I'll go and get the tennis rackets from the car.*
3 to own something. *Have you got a pet?*
4 to become. *The pond got fuller after it rained.*
5 to arrive somewhere. *After a long journey, we finally got home.*
6 to travel on. *I get the bus to school.*
7 to pay for something. *I'll get the meal.*
8 If you **have got** something, you own it.
9 **get over** to recover from something. *I only got over the shock the next day.*

geyser *(**gee**-zer)* *(noun)*
a hole in the ground through which hot water and steam shoot up in bursts. Geysers are found in volcanic areas.

ghastly
ghastlier ghastliest *(adjective)*
very bad or unpleasant.

ghetto **ghettos** *or* **ghettoes** *(noun)*
a poor area of a city, often the home of people of the same minority group.

ghost *(noun)*
a spirit of a dead person, believed to haunt people or places.

Spelling tip

ghastly   ghost

Be careful when spelling the words "ghastly" and "ghost": they both contain a **silent 'h'** after the 'g'.

giant

1 (noun) In stories, a **giant** is a very large, strong creature.
2 (adjective) very large. *I bought a giant pencil from the gift shop.*

giddy **giddier giddiest** (adjective)

If you feel **giddy**, you feel dizzy and unsteady. **giddiness** (noun).

gift (noun)

1 a present.
2 a special talent. *Rupert has a gift for painting.* **gifted** (adjective).

gig (noun)

At a **gig**, a musician or band plays live for the public.

gigantic (adjective)

huge. **gigantically** (adverb).

giggle **giggling giggled** (verb)

to laugh in a high-pitched way. **giggle** (noun).

gill (noun)

one of the two parts on the sides of a fish, through which it breathes.

ginger

1 (noun) a plant root used in cooking, which has a strong, spicy taste.
2 (adjective) **Ginger** hair is a reddish-orange colour.

gingerly (adverb)

slowly and carefully. *The dogs approached each other gingerly.*

gipsy (noun)

see **gypsy**.

giraffe (noun)

an African animal with a very long neck and long legs.

short horns
long neck

giraffe

girl (noun)

a female child.

girlfriend (noun)

the girl or woman that someone is going out with. *Sam has a new girlfriend.*

give **giving gave given** (verb)

1 to hand something over to someone else, or to provide something for someone. *Give me that book! The plane journey gave me a chance to sleep.*
2 to pay. *What will you give me for this?*
3 If you **give something away**, you let someone have it for free.
4 give in or **give up** to stop trying.

glacier

(**glass**-ee-er or **glay**-see-er) (noun)
a huge frozen river of ice that moves very slowly down a mountain valley.

glad **gladder gladdest** (adjective)

pleased or happy. *I'm glad you came.* **gladness** (noun).

gladiator (noun)

an Ancient Roman warrior who fought other gladiators or fierce animals to entertain people.

javelin

Roman gladiator

glamorous (adjective)

attractive and exciting. *Gemma told us all about the glamorous party.*

glance **glancing glanced** (verb)

1 to look at something for a very short time. **glance** (noun).
2 to hit something and slide off it at an angle. *The ball glanced off the goal post into the net.*

glare **glaring glared** (verb)

1 to look at someone in a very angry way. **glare** (noun).
2 If a light **glares**, it is very bright. *The Sun was glaring.* **glare** (noun).

glaring (adjective)

very obvious. *A glaring error.* **glaringly** (adverb).

glass **glasses** (noun)

1 a hard, see-through material used in windows, bottles, and so on.
2 a container for drinking, made from glass.

a b c d e f g h i j k l m n o p q r s t u v w x y z

glasses *(plural noun)*
two pieces of glass, called lenses, in a frame. Glasses are worn by some people to help them see better.

gleam **gleaming gleamed** *(verb)*
to shine. *The car gleamed in the sunlight.*

glee *(noun)*
great delight. **gleeful** *(adjective).*

glide **gliding glided** *(verb)*
to move smoothly and easily. *I glided over the ice.*

glider *(noun)*
a very light aircraft, which flies by floating and rising on air currents instead of using engine power.

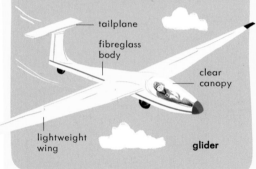

tailplane

fibreglass body

clear canopy

lightweight wing

glider

glimmer
glimmering glimmered *(verb)*
to shine faintly. *The ocean glimmered in the moonlight.* **glimmer** *(noun).*

glimpse **glimpsing glimpsed** *(verb)*
to see something very briefly. *I glimpsed the fox before it went through the hedge.* **glimpse** *(noun).*

glint **glinting glinted** *(verb)*
to sparkle, or to flash. *Mum's watch glinted in the sunlight.* **glint** *(noun).*

glisten **glistening glistened** *(verb)*
to shine in a sparkling way. *The dog's wet fur glistened.*

glitter **glittering glittered** *(verb)*
to sparkle brightly. **glitter** *(noun).*

gloat **gloating gloated** *(verb)*
to take great pleasure in your own good luck, or in someone else's bad luck.

global warming *(noun)*
a gradual rise in the Earth's temperature, caused by pollution in the atmosphere.

globe *(noun)*
1 a round model of the world.
2 the world. **global** *(adjective).*

gloomy
gloomier gloomiest *(adjective)*
1 If a place is **gloomy**, it is dull and dark. *A gloomy dungeon.* **gloom** *(noun).*
2 If a person is **gloomy**, they are sad and not hopeful. **gloom** *(noun).*

glory **glories** *(noun)*
1 fame and honour. *Joel enjoyed the glory of winning the talent contest.*
2 a beautiful and impressive sight. *The glory of the Taj Mahal.*

gloss *(noun)*
a shine on a surface. **glossy** *(adjective).*

glossary **glossaries** *(noun)*
A **glossary** explains the meaning of difficult words used in a book.

glove *(noun)*
a piece of clothing worn on your hand, which keeps it warm or protects it.

glow **glowing glowed** *(verb)*
If something **glows**, it gives off a steady light, often because it is hot. **glow** *(noun).*

glow-worm *(noun)*
a small beetle whose tail gives off a green light in the dark.

yellowish-green glowing tail

beetle body

The tail of a female **common glow-worm** glows to attract a male.

glue *(noun)*
a liquid used to make one surface stick to another. **glue** *(verb).*

glum **glummer glummest** *(adjective)*
gloomy and miserable. **glumly** *(adverb).*

Spelling tip

gnarled   gnaw   gnome

Take care to remember the silent 'g' in these words. A silent 'g' will usually appear before an 'n', as in these words, and in "si**g**n".

gnarled *(adjective)*
twisted, rough and lumpy with age. *A gnarled oak tree.*

gnaw
gnawing gnawed or **gnawn** *(verb)*
to keep biting something. *The dog gnawed the bone.*

gnome *(noun)*
In fairy stories, **gnomes** are creatures like very small old men.

go goes going went gone
1 *(verb)* to move away from or towards a place. *I'm going home.*
2 *(verb)* to work properly. *The car won't go for some reason.*
3 *(verb)* to become. *The class went quiet.*
4 *(verb)* If you are **going** to do something, you will do it in the future. *See* future.
5 *(verb)* If something **goes well**, it is a success.
6 go away *(verb)* to leave.
7 *(noun)* a turn. *It's my go.*

goal *(noun)*
1 something that you hope to do. *Tim's goal is to play rugby for Ireland.*
2 the net into which you try to kick, throw or hit the ball in sports such as football and netball.
3 When a player gets the ball into the net, they **score a goal.**

goat *(noun)*
a farm animal with horns and a beard, whose milk can be drunk or made into cheese.

gobble gobbling gobbled *(verb)*
to eat food quickly and greedily.

goblin *(noun)*
In fairy stories, **goblins** are small, ugly creatures who like to make trouble.

god *(noun)*
1 a being that people worship.
2 In Christianity, Islam, and Judaism, **God** is the creator and ruler of the universe.

goddess goddesses *(noun)*
a female being that people worship.

godparent *(noun)*
someone who promises to help bring up a child as a Christian.

goggles *(plural noun)*
special glasses that fit tightly round your eyes to protect them, for example when swimming.

go-kart *(noun)*
a very low, small, open car, built for racing.

gold *(noun)*
1 a yellowish metal, which is very valuable. **gold** *(adjective)*.
2 the colour of gold. **gold** *(adjective)*.

goldfish
goldfish or **goldfishes** *(noun)*
an orange-coloured fish, often kept as a pet.

golf *(noun)*
a game in which players use long sticks called clubs to hit a small, white ball around a course and into holes in the ground.

golf equipment

golf ball

wood for long shots

iron for medium and short shots

tee (holds ball)

wedge for hitting high in the air

putter for tapping the ball into the hole

gone *(verb)*
the past participle of **go**.

good better best *(adjective)*
1 of high quality, or deserving praise. *That is a really good idea.*
2 kind and honest. *A good deed.*
3 enjoyable or pleasant. *Have you had a good day?*
4 If you are **good at** something, you do it well. *Beth is good at hockey.*
5 suitable. *This camera will be good for our art project.*
6 well-behaved. *Mark is a good child.*
7 fit and well. *I'm feeling good today.*

goodbye *(interjection)*
a word you say to someone who is leaving, or when you leave them.

goodnight *(interjection)*
a word you say when someone is going to bed or when you go to bed.

goods *(plural noun)*
things that people buy and sell.

gooey gooier gooiest *(adjective)*
sticky. *Gooey mud.* **gooeyness** *(noun).*

goose geese *(noun)*
a large bird with a long neck and webbed feet. *See* **poultry.**

goose bumps or **goose pimples** *(noun)*
tiny bumps on your skin that you get when you are cold or frightened.

gorgeous *(adjective)*
very beautiful, attractive, or pleasant.

gorilla *(noun)*
a very large, strong ape with dark fur, that lives in Africa.

gossip gossiping gossiped *(verb)*
to talk with enjoyment about other people and their lives. **gossip** *(noun).*

western lowland gorilla

got *(verb)*
1 the past tense of **get**.
2 You can use **have got** instead of "have". *We have got a cat.*
3 You can use **have got to** instead of "have to". *We have got to finish washing the car.*

government *(noun)*
the group of people who rule a country or state and make important decisions which affect everyone who lives there.

> Remember the first 'n' in "government" when you spell it.

GP *(noun) (abbreviation)*
a family doctor, who treats common illnesses and sends patients to hospital if needed. GP is short for "general practitioner".

grab grabbing grabbed *(verb)*
to take hold of something suddenly and roughly. *Kevin grabbed the money.*

graceful *(adjective)*
Someone who is **graceful** moves easily and smoothly. *Ruth is a graceful dancer.* **grace** *(noun),* **gracefully** *(adverb).*

grade *(noun)*
a mark given for work done in school, college, and so on. *I got a grade B for maths.*

gradual *(adjective)*
happening slowly but steadily. *A gradual slope.* **gradually** *(adverb).*

graffiti *(plural noun)*
things that people write or draw in public places.

grain *(noun)*
1 the seeds of plants such as corn or wheat, that are used for food.
2 a very small piece of salt, sand, and so on. *A grain of sand.*

gram *(noun)*
a unit of weight. A paperclip weighs about a gram. There are 1,000 grams in a kilogram.

grammar *(noun)*
the rules of writing or speaking a language. **grammatical** *(adjective)*.
See grammar, page 349.

grand grander grandest *(adjective)*
large and impressive. *A grand cathedral.* **grandly** *(adverb)*.

grandad *or* **grandpa** *(noun)*
a friendly name for grandfather.

grandchild grandchildren *(noun)*
Someone's **grandchild** is the child of their son or daughter.

grandfather *(noun)*
Your **grandfather** is the father of one of your parents.

grandma *(noun)*
a friendly name for grandmother.

grandmother *(noun)*
Your **grandmother** is the mother of one of your parents.

grandparent *(noun)*
Your **grandparents** are your parents' parents.

granny grannies *(noun)*
a friendly name for grandmother.

grant granting granted *(verb)*
1 to give something or allow something. *We were granted permission to leave.*
2 If you **take something for granted**, you assume that you will get it, or you are not grateful for it.

grape *(noun)*
a small, juicy fruit that can be eaten fresh, dried to make currants, raisins, and so on, or crushed to make wine.

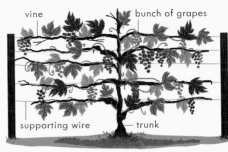

vine
bunch of grapes
supporting wire
trunk

grapes on a vine

grapefruit
grapefruit *or* **grapefruits** *(noun)*
a large fruit with a sour taste.

graph *(noun)*
a picture which shows how two sets of numbers or information are related.

graphics *(plural noun)*
the pictures in a computer game.

grasp grasping grasped *(verb)*
1 to hold onto something tightly. **grasp** *(noun)*.
2 to understand an idea. **grasp** *(noun)*.

grass grasses *(noun)*
a green plant with long, thin leaves that grows wild and is often used for lawns. **grassy** *(adjective)*.

grasshopper *(noun)*
a jumping insect with long back legs.

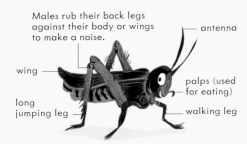

Males rub their back legs against their body or wings to make a noise.

antenna

wing

palps (used for eating)

long jumping leg

walking leg

brown grasshopper

grate grating grated
1 *(verb)* to shred food into small, thin pieces. *Grate the cheese.*
2 *(noun)* a grid of metal bars in a fireplace.

grateful *(adjective)*
thankful for something. *I am grateful for my presents.* **gratefully** *(adverb)*.

gratitude *(noun)*
a feeling of being thankful.

grave graver gravest
1 *(noun)* a place where a dead person is buried.
2 *(adjective)* very serious and worrying. *Grave danger.* **gravely** *(adverb)*.
3 gravestone *(noun)* a piece of carved stone that marks someone's grave.

a b c d e f **g** h i j k l m n o p q r s t u v w x y z

gravel *(noun)*
small, loose stones used for paths
and roads.

gravity *(noun)*
the force that pulls things down towards
the surface of the Earth and stops them
from floating away into space.

gravy *(noun)*
a hot, brown sauce, usually served
with meat.

graze grazing grazed *(verb)*
1 to scrape your skin against something
so that it bleeds. *I grazed my knee when
I fell off my skateboard.* **graze** *(noun)*.
2 When animals **graze**, they eat the
plants growing in an area.

grease *(noun)*
1 an oily substance found in animal fat,
and in hair and skin. **greasy** *(adjective)*.
2 a thick, oily substance used on
machines to help the parts move easily.
grease *(verb)*.

great greater greatest *(adjective)*
1 very good, or wonderful. *We had
a great time.*
2 very large in size or amount. *There
was a great storm last night.*
3 very important or famous. *Nelson
Mandela was a great man.*
greatness *(noun)*.

greedy
greedier greediest *(adjective)*
If you are **greedy**, you want more
of something than you need. *It was
greedy of Olivia to eat all the crisps.*
greed *(noun)*, **greedily** *(adverb)*.

green greener greenest
1 *(noun)* the colour of grass or leaves.
green *(adjective)*.
2 *(adjective)* to do with protecting the
planet. *Green energy.*
3 *(noun)* an area of ground often used
for activities or sport. *A village green.*

greengrocer *(noun)*
someone who sells fruit and vegetables
in a shop. **greengrocer's** *(noun)*.

greenhouse *(noun)*
a glass building used for growing plants
because it traps lots of heat inside.

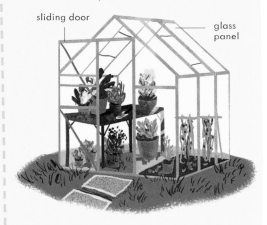

sliding door

glass
panel

greenhouse with plants inside

greenhouse effect *(noun)*
the warming of the Earth's atmosphere,
caused by gases which stop the Sun's
heat from escaping.

greet greeting greeted *(verb)*
to say something friendly or welcoming
to someone when you meet them.
greeting *(noun)*.

grew *(verb)*
the past tense of **grow**.

grey *(noun)*
the colour you get when you mix black
and white, like the colour of rain clouds.
grey *(adjective)*.

grid *(noun)*
a set of lines that cross at right angles
to make squares.

grief *(noun)*
a feeling of great sadness.

grieve grieving grieved *(verb)*
to feel very sad, usually because
someone you love has died.

grill *(noun)*
1 the part of a cooker that heats food
from above. **grill** *(verb)*.
2 a set of bars that you put food on
to cook over a fire. **grill** *(verb)*.

Spelling tip

grim   grime

Notice that the 'i' sound in "grim" is short (it rhymes with "him"), but when you add a silent 'e' to make "grime", it is long (it rhymes with "time").

grim grimmer grimmest *(adjective)*
1 If a situation or piece of news is **grim**, it is worrying and unpleasant.
2 If someone looks **grim**, they look gloomy and serious.

grime *(noun)*
thick dirt. *Everything in the shed was covered in grime.* **grimy** *(adjective)*.

grin *(noun)*
a big, cheerful smile. **grin** *(verb)*.

grind grinding ground *(verb)*
to crush something into a powder.

grip gripping gripped *(verb)*
to hold something very tightly. *Tina gripped the steering wheel.* **grip** *(noun)*.

groan groaning groaned *(verb)*
to make a long, low sound, showing that you are in pain or are unhappy. **groan** *(noun)*.

groceries *(plural noun)*
food and basic household goods such as cleaning products that you buy. **grocer** *(noun)*, **grocer's** *(noun)*.

groom grooming groomed
1 *(noun)* a man who is about to get married, or has just got married.
2 *(verb)* to brush and clean an animal, such as a horse or dog.
3 *(noun)* someone who looks after horses.

groove *(noun)*
a long cut in the surface of something.

gross grosser grossest *(adjective)*
unpleasant and disgusting.

ground
1 *(noun)* the surface of the Earth, or land. *Eliza lay on the ground.*
2 *(noun)* a piece of land used for playing a game or sport.
3 grounds *(plural noun)* land around a large house, castle, and so on.
4 *(verb)* the past tense of **grind**.

group *(noun)*
a number of things or people that go together or are similar in some way. *Josh is in the same maths group as me.*

grow growing grew grown *(verb)*
1 to get bigger in size, length, or amount. *I have grown 2cm this year.*
2 to plant something and look after it so that it lives and gets bigger. *My dad grows strawberries in the garden.*
3 When a plant **grows**, it develops and gets bigger. *Nothing grows in my garden.*
4 to become. *Simon is growing lazier and lazier!*

growl growling growled *(verb)*
When an animal **growls**, it makes a low, deep noise, usually because it is angry.

grown-up *(noun)*
an adult. **grown-up** *(adjective)*.

growth *(noun)*
the process or stages of getting bigger. *Dad marks our growth on the wall.*

grubby
grubbier grubbiest *(adjective)*
covered with dirt. *Keep your grubby fingers off my phone.*

grudge *(noun)*
If you **hold a grudge** against someone, you feel angry towards them because they have done something bad to you. *Helen held a grudge against Ed for a few weeks.*

gruesome *(adjective)*
disgusting and horrible. *The film was really gruesome.*

gruff gruffer gruffest *(adjective)*
rough and bad-tempered. *My Uncle Sam has a gruff voice.*

A B C D E F **G** H I J K L M N O P Q R S T U V W X Y Z

grumble
grumbling grumbled *(verb)*
to complain about something in a bad-tempered way. *Dad grumbled about the traffic all the way home.*

grumpy
grumpier grumpiest *(adjective)*
bad-tempered and unhappy. *Rachel was grumpy all day.* **grumpily** *(adverb)*.

grunt **grunting grunted** *(verb)*
to make a deep, rough sound, like a pig. *Luke grunted as he was woken up.* **grunt** *(noun)*.

guarantee
guaranteeing guaranteed
1 *(noun)* a promise that if something you have bought breaks or goes wrong, the makers will mend or replace it for you. *Our washing machine has a five-year guarantee.* **guarantee** *(verb)*.
2 *(verb)* to promise that something will definitely happen. *I guarantee we will be there by 5 o'clock.* **guarantee** *(noun)*.

guard **guarding guarded** *(verb)*
1 to keep a person or place safe. *Soldiers guard Buckingham Palace.* **guard** *(noun)*.
2 to watch a person or animal carefully so they cannot escape. **guard** *(noun)*.

guess
guesses guessing guessed *(verb)*
If you **guess** an answer, you think it may be right, but you are not totally sure. *I had to guess the quiz question.* **guess** *(noun)*.

guest *(noun)*
1 someone who has been invited to visit you or to stay in your home. *I can't come out at the weekend as we have guests.*
2 someone visiting a hotel or restaurant.

guide **guiding guided**
1 *(verb)* to help someone by showing them around or to a place. *The steward guided us to our seats.* **guide** *(noun)*.
2 guide dog *(noun)* a dog trained to lead a blind person around safely.

Spelling tip

guarantee guard guess
guest guide guilty

Remember the '**u**' after the '**g**' when you spell these words.

guidebook *(noun)*
a book that gives you information about a place.

guilty **guiltier guiltiest** *(adjective)*
1 If you are **guilty**, you have done something wrong. *The woman was found guilty of theft.* **guilt** *(noun)*.
2 If you feel **guilty**, you feel bad because you have done something wrong. *I felt guilty about losing Oli's football.* **guilt** *(noun)*.

guinea pig (**gin**-ee pig) *(noun)*
a small animal with smooth fur, short ears, and a very short tail, which is often kept as a pet.

guitar *(noun)*
a musical instrument with strings, which you play with your fingers or with a piece of plastic called a plectrum.

electric guitar

tuning peg

screw for strap — neck — head

bridge

fret marker

fingerboard

tremolo

volume and tone controls

output jack (leads to amplifier)

gulf *(noun)*
a large area of sea that stretches a long way into the land. *The Persian Gulf.*

gullible *(adjective)*
Someone who is **gullible** believes things you tell them that aren't true, and is easy to trick.

gulp **gulping gulped**
1 *(verb)* to swallow something quickly and noisily.
2 *(noun)* a large mouthful of a drink. *Ellie took a big gulp of water, then carried on dancing.*

gum
1 gums *(plural noun)* the areas of firm, pink flesh around your teeth.
2 *(noun)* a soft, chewy sweet.
3 *(noun)* a soft, chewy sweet that you don't swallow, which is often mint-flavoured.

packet of **bubblegum**

gun *(noun)*
a weapon that fires bullets through a metal tube.

gunpowder *(noun)*
a powder that explodes easily when lit, used in fireworks and some guns.

gurdwara *(noun)*
a Sikh temple.

gurgle **gurgling gurgled** *(verb)*
1 When water **gurgles**, it makes a low, bubbling sound. **gurgle** *(noun)*.
2 to make a sound like gurgling water. *The baby gurgled.* **gurgle** *(noun)*.

guru *(noun)*
1 a leader in the Hindu religion.
2 someone who knows a lot about a subject. *My cousin thinks he's a bit of a music guru.*

gush **gushes gushing gushed** *(verb)*
If a liquid **gushes**, it flows quickly and in large amounts. **gush** *(noun)*.

gust *(noun)*
a sudden, strong blast of wind. *The sign was knocked over by a gust of wind.*

guts *(plural noun)*
1 the organs inside your body, especially your stomach and intestines.
2 courage. *It takes a lot of guts to bungee jump.*

gutter *(noun)*
a pipe or channel at the edge of a roof or road where rain collects and drains away.

guzzle **guzzling guzzled** *(verb)*
to eat or drink something quickly and noisily. *Dave guzzled his pizza.*

gym *(noun) (abbreviation)*
a room with special equipment for doing exercises. Gym is short for "gymnasium".

gymnasium
see **gym**.

gymnastics *(noun)*
special exercises, which involve difficult and carefully controlled body movements such as flips, stretches, and rolls.

parallel bars   pommel horse

vault

This picture shows some different kinds of **gymnastics**.

gypsy *or* gipsy *(**jip**-see)* **gypsies** *(noun)*
someone who usually lives in a caravan and travels from place to place.

Hh

habit *(noun)*
something you do regularly, without really thinking about it. *Harry's habit of leaving the top off the toothpaste annoys me.* **habitual** *(adjective)*.

habitat *(noun)*
An animal or plant's **habitat** is where it lives. *The polar bear's habitat is the ice and snow of the Arctic.*

hack hacking hacked
1 *(verb)* If you **hack** something, you chop or cut it very roughly.
2 *(verb)* If you **hack into** a computer or computer system, you get into it without permission. **hacker** *(noun)*.

haggard *(adjective)*
looking worried and very tired. *Poor Mrs Jay looked haggard after the school trip.*

haggle haggling haggled *(verb)*
When a buyer and a seller **haggle**, they discuss the price of something. *You often need to haggle in the market.*

haiku *(noun)*
a Japanese poem with three lines and a very strict rhythm.

hail hailing hailed *(verb)*
1 When it **hails**, small balls of ice fall from the sky. **hail** *(noun)*.
2 If you **hail a taxi**, you make a sign for it to stop and pick you up. *I will go outside and hail a taxi to take us home.*

hair *(noun)*
1 the soft, fine threads that grow on your head and other parts of your body. Some animals have hair, too.
2 one thread of hair from someone's head or body.

haircut *(noun)*
If you have a **haircut**, someone cuts your hair. *Mum keeps telling me I need to get a haircut.*

hairdresser *(noun)*
someone who cuts and styles people's hair. **hairdressing** *(noun)*.

hairgrip or **hairpin** *(noun)*
a small, thin, flexible piece of metal or plastic, used for fastening someone's hair in place.

hair-raising *(adjective)*
very scary. *The new roller coaster ride was hair-raising.*

hairstyle *(noun)*
the way you have your hair.

mohican   ponytail   beehive   afro

some types of **hairstyles**

hairy hairier hairiest *(adjective)*
If a person or animal is **hairy**, they have lots of hair on their body. *Orangutans are very hairy.*

Hajj *(noun)*
a journey to Mecca, in Saudi Arabia, made by every Muslim who is fit and healthy enough at least once in their life. It happens during the final month of the Islamic calendar.

A cube-shaped building called the Kaaba is the final destination of the **Hajj**. Muslims walk anticlockwise around the Kaaba seven times.

halal *(adjective)*
Halal food is produced and cooked following the rules of the Muslim faith.

Spelling tip

half ⟶ halves

Some words that end with an '**f**' or '**fe**', such as "hal**f**", remove the 'f' or 'fe' and add '**–ves**' in the plural: "hal**ves**".

Other examples include:
"kni**fe**" → "kni**ves**" and "wi**fe**" → "wi**ves**".

half **halves**
1 *(noun)* one of the two equally-sized parts of something.
2 *(adverb)* not completely done or finished.
3 *(adverb)* When telling the time, if you say it is **half past** an hour, you mean that it is 30 minutes past the hour.

half-heartedly *(adverb)*
without much enthusiasm. *Mike played half-heartedly.* **half-hearted** *(adjective)*.

half-time *(noun)*
the break in the middle of a game such as football.

halfway *(adverb)*
1 in the middle, between two different places. *Paul suddenly stopped when he was halfway up the ladder.*
halfway *(adjective)*.
2 in the middle of a period of time. *Halfway through the night, we were woken by a loud clap of thunder.*

hall *(noun)*
1 the part of a house that you come into when you open the front door, that leads to all the other rooms.
2 a big room, where people meet or hold important events. *A school hall.*

Halloween or **Hallowe'en** *(noun)*
the evening of 31st October, which some people celebrate by dressing up as ghosts, witches, or other spooky things.

halo **haloes** *(noun)*
a glowing circle of light that is shown around the heads of angels and holy people in many old paintings.

halve **halving halved** *(verb)*
1 If you **halve** something, you divide it into two equal parts. *Halve the onion.*
2 to cut something down so that there is only half as much as there was. *They halved the number of buses to our village.*

ham *(noun)*
meat from a pig's back legs that has been salted or smoked, and is often eaten cold.

hammer **hammering hammered**
1 *(noun)* a heavy head on a long handle, used for hitting nails.
2 *(verb)* to hit something very hard. *Jamie hammered on the door.*

hammock *(noun)*
a piece of netting or strong cloth that is hung up from both ends, so that you can lie in it.

hamster *(noun)*
a small animal similar to a mouse, but with a short tail, that people often keep as a pet.

golden hamster

hand
handing handed
1 *(noun)* the part of your body on the end of your arm, with four fingers and a thumb.
2 *(verb)* to give or pass something to someone. *Ian handed me the box of chocolates.*
3 *(noun)* The **hands** of a clock point to the numbers on it, and tell you the time.
4 If you **give someone a hand**, you help them.

handbag *(noun)*
a bag which women use to carry their purse, keys and other things around.

handbook *(noun)*
a book which tells you how to do something. *Check the handbook.*

handcuffs *(plural noun)*
metal rings joined by a chain, which are fixed around prisoners' wrists to stop them from escaping. **handcuff** *(verb)*.

A
B
C
D
E
F
G
H
I
J
K
L
M
N
O
P
Q
R
S
T
U
V
W
X
Y
Z

handful (noun)
1 A **handful** of something is the amount of it that you can hold in your hand. *A handful of rice.*
2 a few. *There was only a handful of people at the concert.*

handicap (noun)
something that makes it difficult for you to do something. *Having no money is a handicap if you want to travel the world.*

handkerchief (noun)
a piece of cloth or paper that you use for blowing your nose.

handle **handling handled**
1 *(verb)* to pick something up and touch it. *You must handle the glasses carefully.*
2 *(noun)* the part of something you hold onto to pull it, carry it, or open it. *Push down on the door handle to open.*

handlebars (noun)
the part of a bike that you hold onto to steer it.

handshake (noun)
holding and shaking someone's hand, as a greeting.

handsome (adjective)
attractive or good-looking. Handsome is usually used about men or boys.

handwriting (noun)
the style you use to form letters and words. *My handwriting is very untidy.*

handy **handier handiest** (adjective)
1 useful. *That's a handy box to keep your pencils in.*
2 skilful. *Dad is handy with a power drill.*
3 nearby. *Is there a cloth handy, to mop up this spill?*

hang **hanging hung** (verb)
1 When you **hang something up**, you fix it to a hook, or the wall, so that it dangles down and doesn't touch the floor. *We hang our coats up in the hall.*
2 If you **hang on**, you wait. *Let's hang on until it's stopped raining.*
3 If you **hang up** on someone, you end a telephone conversation with them.

hangar (noun)
a very large shed, usually used for storing planes and other aircraft.

hanger (noun)
a shaped piece of metal, plastic or wood that you can hang clothes on.

Hanukkah or Chanukah (noun)
a Jewish festival that happens in November or December, when Jews light candles on a nine-branched candlestick called a menorah.

Hanukkah celebrates the time that a group of Jews called the Maccabees recaptured the Temple in Jerusalem, where they found a container with enough oil to last for one day. However, when they lit the lamp, it burned for eight days. This is why Hannukah lasts for eight days. Each day, another candle on the menorah is lit, so that by the final day all the candles are burning.

menorah

haphazard (adjective)
If something is **haphazard**, it has not been carefully organized or planned. *The shop layout was rather haphazard.* **haphazardly** *(adverb)*.

happen
happening happened (verb)
1 If something **happens**, it takes place. *The fair is happening on Saturday.*
2 to be experienced by someone. *The same thing happened to me.*
3 If you **happen to** do something, you do it by chance. *I happened to see Jessica in town.*

happy **happier happiest** (adjective)
When you are **happy**, you feel really good. *Sunshine always makes me feel happy.* **happiness** *(noun)*, **happily** *(adverb)*.

harass
harasses harassing harassed (verb)
to pester, follow or annoy someone.
She harassed all her guests until they'd had enough and left.
harassment (noun).

harbour (noun)
a safe place where boats and ships can tie up, when they are not at sea.

hard **harder hardest**
1 (adjective) firm and solid. *The ground is hard in winter.* **hardness** (noun).
2 (adjective) difficult. *Helen finds maths very hard.*
3 (adverb) with a lot of effort. *Ashwin worked hard to get good grades.*

hard disk (noun)
see **hard drive**.

hard drive (noun)
the part of a computer that contains a hard disk on which information is stored, including the information which tells the computer how to work.

hardly (adverb)
only just. *I can hardly see because my fringe is so long.*

hardship (noun)
difficulty, especially the difficulty of not having enough money. *That family copes with great hardship.*

hardware (noun)
1 the parts inside a computer that make it work.
2 nails, screws and other tools you need for doing jobs around the house.

hardy **hardier hardiest** (adjective)
tough. *The sheep that live in the mountains are very hardy animals.*

hare (noun)
an animal similar to a large rabbit, but with longer ears, which can run very fast.

harm **harming harmed** (verb)
If you **harm** someone, you hurt them.
harm (noun), **harmful** (adjective).

harmless (adjective)
Something that is **harmless** can't hurt you.

harmonica (noun)
a small, rectangular instrument that you blow and breathe through to make sounds. It is also called a mouth organ.

harmony **harmonies** (noun)
musical notes that sound nice when played or sung together. *The choir sang in harmony.* **harmonious** (adjective).

harness **harnesses** (noun)
1 leather straps around an animal's body, which are used to control it.
2 straps around someone's body that attach to safety ropes and keep them safe.

harp (noun)
a big, triangular musical instrument that you play by plucking its strings.
harpist (noun).

strings

harp and harpist

harsh **harsher harshest** (adjective)
1 unkind or nasty. *The coach's criticism of the match was too harsh.*
2 rough and unpleasant. *Harsh weather.*

harvest **harvesting harvested**
1 (noun) the time when farmers pick or gather in their crops.
2 (verb) When farmers **harvest** their crops, they cut them and bring them in from the fields.

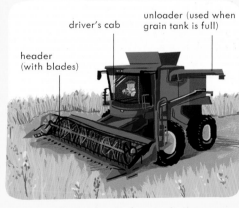

driver's cab

unloader (used when grain tank is full)

header (with blades)

Grain crops are **harvested** using a **combine harvester**.

A B C D E F G H I J K L M N O P Q R S T U V W X Y Z

hassle **hassling hassled**
1 *(verb)* to pester someone. *The salesman hassled me the whole time I was in his shop.*
2 *(noun)* a bother, or a nuisance. *Having to walk the dog is a real hassle.*

hasty *(adjective)*
quick or hurried. *I made a hasty dash to the bathroom when I started feeling ill.*

hat *(noun)*
a piece of clothing you wear on your head.

cowboy hat

Panama

trilby

boater

bowler hat

top hat ushanka

baseball cap

cloche fedora

woolly hat

types of **hats**

hatch
hatches hatching hatched *(verb)*
When an egg **hatches**, a baby bird, reptile or fish breaks out of it.

hate **hating hated** *(verb)*
to dislike someone or something very much. *"I hate cricket," said Toby.* **hatred** *(noun)*.

hat-trick *(noun)*
When a sports player scores a **hat-trick**, they score three goals in one match.

haul **hauling hauled** *(verb)*
to struggle, trying to pull something very heavy. *We hauled the chest upstairs.*

haunt **haunting haunted** *(verb)*
1 If a ghost **haunts** a place, it appears there often. **haunted** *(adjective)*.
2 If you are **haunted by** something, or if something **haunts** you, you can't forget about it and are worried by it.

have **having had** *(verb)*
1 to own or possess something. *I have a new mobile phone.*
2 to do or experience something. *We had a great holiday in San Francisco.*
3 to receive or get something. *Have you had your lunch yet?*

hawk *(noun)*
1 a bird of prey that has a hooked beak and sharp claws. *See **food chain**.*
2 If you **watch someone like a hawk**, you watch them very closely.

hay *(noun)*
dried grass, which is fed to some pets and farm animals.

hay fever *(noun)*
People who have **hay fever** are allergic to the powder called pollen that's in many types of grasses and flowers. It causes a runny nose, itchy eyes, and sneezing.

hazard *(noun)*
something that could be dangerous. *All this paper is a fire hazard.* **hazardous** *(adjective)*.

hazel *(noun)*
1 a small tree, on which hazelnuts grow.
2 a greenish-brown colour. *Hazel is my favourite eye colour.* **hazel** *(adjective)*.

head **heading headed**
1 *(noun)* the top part of your body, which contains your brain, eyes, mouth, and so on.
2 *(noun)* the person in charge. *Josh is head of the group.* **head** *(adjective)*.
3 *(verb)* to go towards somewhere. *Claire headed home after the party.*

headache *(noun)*
a pain in your head.

heading *(noun)*
a title, written above a piece of writing.

Spelling tip

headlouse ⟶ headlice

The plural of "**louse**" is "**lice**", so the plural of "headlouse" is "headlice". These are some other unusual plurals:

child ⟶ children

grandchild → grandchildren

headline
1 (noun) the large type at the top of an article in a newspaper or magazine.
2 (plural noun) **Headlines** are the most important subjects in the news. *Here are today's headlines.*

headlouse headlice (noun)
a tiny insect with a hard body that can live in your hair.

headphones (plural noun)
a pair of small speakers that you wear in or over your ears so that you can listen to music, podcasts, and so on.

headquarters (noun)
the place a company or organization is run from. *Our headquarters is in London.*

head teacher (noun)
the teacher in charge of a school.

heal healing healed (verb)
If you **heal** someone, you make them better when they are ill or hurt.

health (noun)
Your **health** is how fit and well you are. *Uncle Jack is in good health at the moment.*

healthy
healthier healthiest (adjective)
1 If you are **healthy**, you are fit and well. *Josephine looks healthy.*
2 Something **healthy** is good for you. *This salad is really tasty, and it's also very healthy.*

heap heaping heaped
1 (noun) a pile of something. *There's a heap of dirty dishes in the sink.* **heaped** (adjective).
2 (verb) to pile something up. *Just heap all the rubbish over there.*

hear hearing heard (verb)
If you **hear** something, your ears pick up the sound it makes.

heart (noun)
1 the part of your body that pumps blood all around it, and keeps you alive.
2 This shape ♥ is a **heart** shape.
3 one of the cards in a pack of playing cards with a heart shape on it. *See* **card**.
4 If you learn something **off by heart**, you can remember it all easily.

heartbroken (adjective)
If you are **heartbroken**, you are very unhappy. *Sophia is heartbroken that her team lost.*

heat heating heated
1 (noun) great warmth. *Can you feel the heat from the fire?*
2 (verb) to warm something up, or cook it. *I heated some soup.*
3 (noun) a stage in a competition. *We won the first heat.*

heaven (noun)
1 a wonderful place, feeling, or thing. *I was in heaven when I tasted the dessert.* **heavenly** (adjective).
2 Some people believe that God lives in **heaven**, and that people's souls go there when they die.

heavy heavier heaviest (adjective)
1 If something is **heavy**, it weighs a lot.
2 a lot or a large amount of. *Heavy rain.* **heaviness** (noun), **heavily** (adverb).

Hebrew (noun)
the language people speak in Israel. **Hebrew** (adjective).

hectic (adjective)
very busy. *Our house is always hectic.*

hedge (noun)
a row of bushes that marks the edges of a garden or a field.

a b c d e f g h i j k l m n o p q r s t u v w x y z

hedgehog – helpless

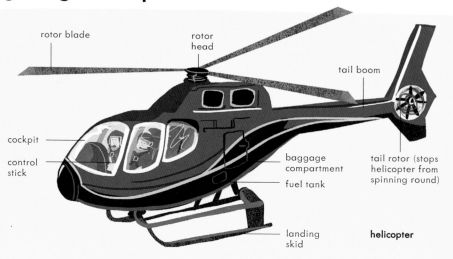

rotor blade

rotor head

tail boom

cockpit

control stick

baggage compartment

fuel tank

tail rotor (stops helicopter from spinning round)

landing skid

helicopter

hedgehog *(noun)*
a small animal that is covered with spines and only comes out at night.

heel *(noun)*
1 the back part of your foot.
2 the back part of a shoe, that supports your heel. *Mum never wears high heels.*

height *(noun)*
how tall or high off the ground something is. *Dad measures my height every month.*

heir *(noun)*
Someone's **heir** is the person who will get their money and property after they die. *The king died without an heir.*

heiress *(noun)*
the girl or woman who will be left money and property after someone's death.

Spelling tip

height   heir   heiress

These words follow the spelling guideline: **'i' before 'e' except after 'c' when the letters make an 'ee' sound**, because the 'ei' does not make an 'ee' sound in any of them. In "height" it makes an 'i' sound (to rhyme with "tight"), and in "heir" and "heiress" it makes an 'ai' sound (like in "air").

helicopter *(noun)*
a machine that can fly and hover, because it has rotor blades on its roof which spin around very fast.

hell *(noun)*
1 a horrible place or situation. *Getting the bus to school in the summer is hell.* **hellish** *(adjective)*.
2 the place where some people believe your soul will go when you die, if you have been wicked.

helmet *(noun)*
a hard hat that protects your head. *Cyclists should wear a helmet.*

help helping helped
1 *(verb)* If you **help** someone do something, you do some of it to make it easier for them. *I helped Tina to make some cakes for the bake sale.*
2 *(noun)* If you give someone **help**, you support them and make things easier for them. *The classroom assistant gave me a lot of help with my reading.* **helper** *(noun)*.

helpful *(adjective)*
Helpful people are very friendly and happy to help others. **helpfulness** *(noun)*, **helpfully** *(adverb)*.

helpless *(adjective)*
If you are **helpless**, you can't look after yourself or cope on your own. *Jimmy was helpless without Hannah.*

hemisphere *(noun)*
one half of a sphere. The Earth is divided into the northern hemisphere and the southern hemisphere. *See* equator. *See* shapes, *page 348.*

hen *(noun)*
1 a female chicken, which is often kept by people for the eggs that it lays.
2 a female bird.

her
1 *(pronoun)* a word used to talk about a girl, woman or female animal who has already been mentioned. *I like Eleanor, but I wouldn't want to make her angry.*
2 *(determiner)* a word which shows that something belongs to a girl, woman, or female animal. *That's her coat.*

herb *(noun)*
a plant with a particular flavour, which you can use in cooking.

some types of **herbs**

sage

chives

coriander

rosemary

herd *(noun)*
a large group of animals that live and feed together. *The farmer was proud of his herd of cows.*

here *(adverb)*
in this place. *Sit down here.*

hero heroes *(noun)*
1 a very brave person. **heroism** *(noun)*, **heroic** *(adjective)*.
2 the most important character in a film or story.

heroine *(noun)*
1 a very brave woman.
2 the main female character in a film or story. *I cried when the heroine died at the end.*

heron *(noun)*
a large bird with long legs that lives near water and eats fish.

hesitate hesitating hesitated *(verb)*
If you **hesitate**, you pause before you do or say something. **hesitation** *(noun)*.

hibernate
hibernating hibernated *(verb)*
When an animal **hibernates**, it goes into a long, deep sleep for most of the winter. **hibernation** *(noun)*.

hiccup hiccupping hiccupped or **hiccuping hiccuped**
1 *(verb)* If you **hiccup**, you make a short, gulping noise in your throat.
2 *(noun)* If you have **hiccups**, you can't stop hiccupping.

hide hiding hid hidden
1 *(verb)* When you **hide**, you make it difficult for someone to see or find you.
2 *(verb)* If you **hide** something, you keep it secret. *Becky hid her disappointment.*
3 *(noun)* the skin of an animal.

hideous *(adjective)*
very ugly. *That is a hideous shirt.* **hideously** *(adverb)*.

high higher highest *(adjective)*
1 very tall. *A high fence.*
2 far off the ground. **high** *(adverb)*.
3 how much something measures from top to bottom, or how far it is off the ground. *That wall is ten metres high.*
4 greater than normal. *I have a high temperature.*
5 If you are **on a high**, you are really excited and happy.
6 **High tide** is the time when the sea comes farthest up the beach.

highlight highlighting highlighted
1 *(noun)* the best or most interesting part of something.
2 *(verb)* If you **highlight** something, you make it obvious so that other people will look at it.

hijack hijacking hijacked *(verb)*
to take control of a plane, car or ship and make it go somewhere it isn't supposed to. **hijacker** *(noun)*.

a b c d e f g h i j k l m n o p q r s t u v w x y z

hike (noun)
a long walk. *We went on a hike through the forest at the weekend.* **hike** *(verb)*.

hilarious (adjective)
very funny. *The pantomime was hilarious.* **hilarity** *(noun)*, **hilariously** *(adverb)*.

hill (noun)
a mound of land that is higher than the land around it. **hilly** *(adjective)*.

him (pronoun)
a word used to talk about a man, boy or male animal who has already been mentioned. *I've only met Jacob once, but I already like him.*

Hindu (noun)
someone who follows Hinduism. **Hindu** *(adjective)*.

Hinduism (noun)
a religion which has lots of different gods and holy books, and is the main religion in India and Nepal.

Brahma
the creator

Shiva
the destroyer

Vishnu
the maintainer

These are the three main gods in **Hinduism**.

hinge (noun)
a piece of metal attached to a door and the wall next to it, which lets the door open and close.

hint (noun)
1 a clue or tip, which helps you to find out or understand something. *Give me a hint where you've hidden my keys.*
2 a tiny bit. *There's a hint of garlic in this dish.*

hip (noun)
one of the two joints at the top of your leg bones, which join your legs to the rest of your body. *See* skeleton.

hip-hop (noun)
a style of music, in which the words are often spoken rather than sung.

hippopotamus hippopotamuses or hippopotami (noun)
a very large African animal that can swim well and lives in or near water. They are often called "hippos".

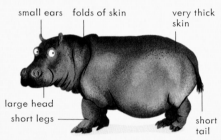

small ears folds of skin very thick skin

large head
short legs

short tail

common hippopotamus

hire hiring hired (verb)
1 If you **hire** something, you pay to use it for a while. *We hired a car.*
2 If you **hire** someone, you give them a job.

his (pronoun)
a word that tells you something belongs to a boy, man, or male animal. *It's his house, so you should behave yourself.*

hiss hisses hissing hissed (verb)
to make a 'ssss' sound. *The snake hissed.*

historic (adjective)
important in history. *A historic event.*

history histories (noun)
the study of things that happened in the past. **historian** *(noun)*, **historical** *(adjective)*.

hit hitting hit
1 *(verb)* If you **hit** something, you strike it hard. *Josh hit the ball over the wall.*
2 *(noun)* a big success.

hi tech (adjective) (abbreviation)
using the latest technology. Hi tech is short for "high technology".

hive *(noun)*

a special box that bees live in. They make honey in their hive and beekeepers collect it. *See* honey.

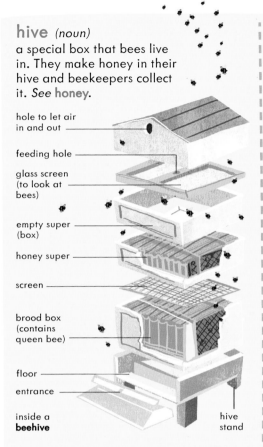

hole to let air in and out

feeding hole

glass screen (to look at bees)

empty super (box)

honey super

screen

brood box (contains queen bee)

floor

entrance

inside a **beehive**

hive stand

hoard **hoarding hoarded** *(verb)*

If you **hoard** things, you don't throw them away, even if you don't really need them. **hoarder** *(noun)*, **hoard** *(noun)*.

hoarse **hoarser hoarsest** *(adjective)*

If you are **hoarse**, your voice is very croaky. **hoarseness** *(noun)*.

hoax **hoaxes** *(noun)*

a trick or practical joke. *We heard there was free ice cream, but it was a hoax.*

Spelling tip

hoax → hoaxes

"Hoax" adds '-es' to become plural: "hoax**es**". Most words that end with a hissing sound, such as '-ch', '-tch', '-s', '-ss', '-tz', '-x' or '-z', do this, except "ox", which becomes "ox**en**" in the plural.

hobble **hobbling hobbled** *(verb)*

to walk unevenly because you are injured or in pain. *The player hobbled off the pitch.*

hobby **hobbies** *(noun)*

something you do in your spare time, because you enjoy it. *Grandad's hobby is collecting old war medals.*

hockey *(noun)*

a game played by two teams of eleven players. They use long sticks that are curved at the end to try to hit a very hard ball into a goal.

hold **holding held** *(verb)*

1 If you **hold** something, you have it in your hand or your arms. *Do you want to hold the baby?*
2 to be able to contain or carry something. *This jug holds two litres. I doubt this branch will hold my weight.*
3 If you **hold** a party, meeting, or other event, you organize it, and make the event happen.
4 to keep or reserve something for someone. *Could you hold my place?*
5 If you **hold back**, you don't do or say something that you want to, in case you cause trouble.
6 If you **hold someone or something down**, you use your arms to stop them from getting up or flying away.
7 If you **hold on**, you wait. *Can you hold on for five minutes, please?*
8 If something **holds you up**, it delays you. *We were held up by traffic.* **hold-up** *(noun)*.

hole *(noun)*

an opening, or a gap. *There's a hole in my sock.*

holiday *(noun)*

1 time when you don't have to go to school or work. You will often see it in the plural, "holidays". *Our Christmas holidays start tomorrow.*
2 a trip away, taken for fun. *We're going on holiday to Malta.*

hollow **hollower hollowest** *(adjective)*

If something is **hollow**, it's empty inside, and has nothing in it. *A hollow Easter egg.*

a b c d e f g h i j k l m n o p q r s t u v w x y z

holly hollies *(noun)*
a tree or bush with shiny green, prickly leaves, small white flowers, and red berries.

— prickly leaf

— berries

holly

holy holier holiest *(adjective)*
to do with God, or religion.

home *(noun)*
1 the place where you live, or where you are from. *My home is in Oxford.*
2 If you feel **at home**, you feel comfortable and relaxed. *I feel at home when I visit my friend's house.*

home page *(noun)*
the main page of a website, which has links to lots of other parts of the website and information. *Click to return to the home page.*

homesick *(adjective)*
If you feel **homesick**, you miss your home and family when you are away. *Judy felt homesick on the school trip to France.* **homesickness** *(noun)*.

homework *(noun)*
work you have to do after school, when you get home. *I have lots of homework to do tonight.*

homosexual *(adjective)*
Someone who is **homosexual** has romantic relationships with people who are the same sex as they are.

honest *(adjective)*
An **honest** person tells the truth and doesn't lie or steal. *It was very honest of you to admit you broke my sunglasses.* **honesty** *(noun)*.

honey *(noun)*
a sweet, sticky, golden food that is made by bees from the nectar they collect from flowers.

A honeybee collects nectar and uses it to make **honey**.

honeymoon *(noun)*
the holiday that a couple takes straight after their wedding. *Pete and Tina are on honeymoon in the Caribbean.*

honour *(noun)*
Something that is an **honour** makes you feel very proud to have done it. *It was an honour to meet the Queen.* **honoured** *(adjective)*.

honourable *(adjective)*
If you are **honourable**, you keep your promises and behave well. *My great-grandfather was an honourable man: he got medals for bravery in the war.* **honourably** *(adverb)*.

hood *(noun)*
the part of a coat that goes over your head. *Put your hood up if it rains to keep your hair dry.*

hoof hoofs or **hooves** *(noun)*
the hard part of some animals' feet. Horses, donkeys and cows have hooves. *Horses need to wear horseshoes to protect their hooves from damage.*

hook *(noun)*
a curved piece of metal or plastic that you use to grab, catch or hang something on. *Put your coat on the hook in the hallway.*

hooked *(adjective)*
1 curved. *The witch had a hooked nose.*
2 If you are **hooked on** something, you can't get enough of it. *I'm hooked on this comedy series.*

hoop *(noun)*
a big, round ring.

hoover *(noun)*
a machine that sucks up dirt from the floor and other surfaces. **hoover** *(verb)*, **hoovering** *(noun)*.

hop hopping hopped *(verb)*
1 to jump, usually on one leg. **hop** *(noun)*.
2 to move quickly from one place to another. *I hopped in the bath as soon as I got home.*

Spelling tip · hop hope

Notice that the 'o' sound is short in "hop" (it rhymes with "stop"), but when you **add a silent 'e'** to make "hope", it is long (it rhymes with "rope").

When you add the endings '**-ing**' and '**-ed**' to these words, "hop" doubles the final 'p', whereas "hope" removes the final 'e'. These are regular spelling patterns that it's very useful to learn.

hope **hoping hoped**
1 (verb) If you **hope** something happens, you wish for it, and want it to happen. *I really hope Ranjeet wins.*
2 (noun) a good, positive feeling or expectation. *My hope is that Tilly will make a full recovery.*

hopeless (adjective)
1 If you are **hopeless**, you are in despair, and feel very sad. **hopelessly** (adverb).
2 If you are **hopeless** at something, you are bad at it. *Dad's a hopeless dancer.*

horizon (noun)
The **horizon** is the line you can see in the distance, where the sky meets the land or the sea. *As we looked out to sea, we could see ships on the horizon.*

horizontal (adjective)
A line that is **horizontal** is flat, level, and goes from side to side rather than top to bottom. **horizontally** (adverb).

hormone (noun)
a chemical in our bodies that causes changes to happen. **hormonal** (adjective).

horn (noun)
1 a hard, pointed thing that grows on the heads of some animals, such as bulls. **horned** (adjective).
2 a musical instrument made of brass that you blow into. *My grandad plays the French horn.*
3 the part of a car that makes a loud noise to warn people you're coming.

horoscope (noun)
Some people believe that your **horoscope** is a prediction of your future, which is made by looking at where the stars and planets were when you were born.

Aquarius (21st Jan – 19th Feb)
Pisces (20th Feb – 20th Mar)
Aries (21st Mar – 20th Apr)
Taurus (21st Apr – 21st May)
Gemini (22nd May – 21st June)
Cancer (22nd June – 22nd July)
Leo (23rd July – 22nd Aug)
Virgo (23rd Aug – 23rd Sep)
Libra (24th Sep – 23rd Oct)
Scorpio (24th Oct – 22nd Nov)
Sagittarius (23rd Nov – 21st Dec)
Capricorn (22nd Dec – 20th Jan)

Your **horoscope** depends on your sign of the zodiac, or "star sign". These are the twelve star signs.

horrendous (adjective)
really terrible, unpleasant, or upsetting. *When I had the measles I felt horrendous.* **horrendously** (adverb).

horrible (adjective)
nasty and unpleasant. *There's a horrible smell in the cellar.* **horribly** (adverb).

horrid (adjective)
very unpleasant. *Aled was horrid to me today.*

horrific (adjective)
shocking or terrible. *The journey in the rain was horrific.* **horrifically** (adverb).

Spelling tip

horrify → horrifying

When adding '-ing' to words that end with a consonant and then a 'y', such as "**horrify**", you keep the 'y'. If you're adding an ending that starts with a different letter, you change the 'y' to an 'i', for example: "horrified".

horrify
horrifies horrifying horrified (verb)
If something **horrifies** you, it shocks and disgusts you. *Samantha's behaviour at the party horrified me.*

horse (noun)
a large animal with hooves, a mane, and a tail. People ride horses as a hobby or in races, and people also use horses for pulling things such as carts.

hose (noun)
a long, flexible tube that water can go through. *The firefighters used their hose to put out the blaze.*

hospital (noun)
a place where nurses and doctors care for people when they are ill.

host (noun)
someone who has invited people to a party or other social event. *Alex was a brilliant host.* **host** (verb).

hostage (noun)
a person who is kept prisoner by someone who demands certain things in exchange for setting the hostage free. *The pirates took the captain as hostage.*

hostel (noun)
a place where people can stay very cheaply. *We always stay in a youth hostel on school holidays.*

hostess hostesses (noun)
a woman who has invited people to a party or other social event.

hostile (adjective)
1 Someone who is **hostile** is very unfriendly and angry. *Jack was hostile towards us because we arrived late to his party.* **hostility** (noun).
2 Somewhere that is **hostile** is hard to survive in. *The Antarctic is a very hostile environment.*

hot hotter hottest (adjective)
1 very warm. *This bath is too hot.*
2 spicy. *Anika's curries are always too hot for me.*

hot-air balloon (noun)
a large bag which is filled with heated air so that it floats, with a basket hanging underneath that can carry people.

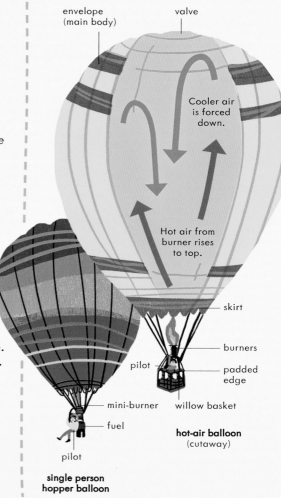

envelope (main body)

valve

Cooler air is forced down.

Hot air from burner rises to top.

skirt

burners

pilot

padded edge

mini-burner

willow basket

fuel

hot-air balloon (cutaway)

pilot

single person hopper balloon

hotel (noun)
a place where people can pay to stay overnight and have their meals.

hound hounding hounded
1 (noun) a dog.
2 (verb) to chase or pester someone. *The press hound the movie star all the time.*

hour (noun)
a measure of time. There are 60 minutes in an hour, and 24 hours in a day. **hourly** (adverb).

house housing housed
1 (noun) a building that people live in. *Our house is always full of noise.*
2 (verb) to provide a home for a person or animal. *We house our rabbit in an old shed.*

housework (noun)
all the jobs that have to be done to keep a house clean and tidy. *We have a lot of housework to do before we can go out.*

hover hovering hovered (verb)
If something **hovers** in the air, it stays in the same place. *We watched the bird hover over the field.*

hovercraft (noun)
a vehicle which has a cushion of air underneath it, and can move over the surface of both water and land.

how (adverb)
1 a word used to ask in what way something is done or happens. *How did you get here so quickly?*
2 a word used to ask many kinds of questions. *How do you feel today? How far is it to walk?*

however
1 (conjunction) a word that can be used between two parts of a sentence, or two separate sentences, that say opposite things. *I don't really like lamb, however I do like beef.*
2 (adverb) a word that can mean "no matter how". *You have to do it, however much you don't want to.*

howl howling howled (verb)
to make a noise like a wolf or a dog. *I howled in pain when I stubbed my toe on the doorframe.* **howl** (noun).

HQ (abbreviation)
short for **headquarters**.

huddle huddling huddled
1 (noun) a small, tight group. *A huddle of fans waited by the stage door.*
2 (verb) When people or animals **huddle** together, they stand very close to each other. *Penguins huddle together for warmth.*

huff (noun)
If you are **in a huff**, you are in a childish, sulky mood.

hug hugging hugged (verb)
to hold someone or something close to you because you care for them. *Roland hugged his dog.* **hug** (noun).

huge huger hugest (adjective)
very large indeed. *Max wears huge boots.* **hugely** (adverb).

hulk (noun)
the main body of a ship or boat, including the bottom, sides, and deck, but not the rigging or other fittings.

hum humming hummed (verb)
1 If you **hum**, you sing with your mouth closed. *Annie hums when she's happy.*
2 If something, such as a machine, **hums**, it makes a low, buzzing noise all the time.

human
1 (noun) a person.
2 (adjective) to do with people or human beings.

humane (adjective)
kind and merciful. **humanely** (adverb).

humanity (noun)
1 all the people in the world.
2 kindness and sympathy. *They showed such humanity when my dog died.*

humankind (noun)
humans in general.

humble
humbler humblest *(adjective)*
If you are **humble**, you don't show off or think you're better than everyone else, even if you achieve great things. *Jane was humble about her award.*
humbly *(adverb)*, **humbled** *(adjective)*.

humid *(adjective)*
warm and damp. **humidity** *(noun)*.

humiliate
humiliating humiliated *(verb)*
to make someone look and feel foolish. **humiliation** *(noun)*.

humorous *(adjective)*
funny. *Russell made a humorous speech.*

humour *(noun)*
1 all the things that make people laugh. *The show was full of humour.*
2 If you have a **sense of humour**, you enjoy laughing at things. *Peter has a great sense of humour.*

hump *(noun)*
a small hill, or a lump. *Camels have humps on their backs made of fat.*

hunch
hunches hunching hunched
1 *(noun)* a suspicion, or an idea. *I have a hunch Phil's hiding in there.*
2 *(verb)* to bring your shoulders forwards and lower your head. *Lily hunched over her homework.* **hunched** *(adjective)*.

hungry
hungrier hungriest *(adjective)*
If you are **hungry**, you want to eat something. *Dave is always hungry.*
hunger *(noun)*, **hungrily** *(adverb)*.

Spelling tip

hungry → hungrier

When you are adding the endings '**-er**' and '**-est**' to adjectives that end with a consonant and a 'y', such as "hungry" and "husky", you change the 'y' to an 'i' first: "hungrier", "huskiest".

hunk *(noun)*
a large piece. *I ate a hunk of bread.*

hunt **hunting hunted** *(verb)*
1 to chase something so that you can kill and eat it. *Many animals learn to hunt when they are young.*
2 to search for something. *Gran is always hunting for her glasses.*

hurdle **hurdling hurdled**
1 *(verb)* to jump over something. *John hurdled over the barrier.*
2 *(noun)* a small fence that you jump over in a race. **hurdler** *(noun)*, **hurdling** *(noun)*.

hurdling

3 *(noun)* a problem or obstacle. *There are always hurdles to overcome on the way to success.*

hurl **hurling hurled** *(verb)*
to throw something as hard as you can. *Jess hurled the javelin.*

hurt **hurting hurt**
1 *(verb)* If you **hurt** someone, you cause them pain or unhappiness. **hurtful** *(adjective)*.
2 *(verb)* If you **hurt yourself**, you give yourself an injury somehow. *Johnny hurt himself when he tried to climb over the fence.*
3 *(adjective)* If you are **hurt**, you are injured, or upset because of something someone has done or said. *I was hurt by Terry's comment.*

husband *(noun)*
Someone's **husband** is the man they are married to.

hush **hushes hushing hushed**
1 (noun) a sudden period of quietness. *There was a hush when the winner was announced.*
2 (interjection) You say "**hush!**" to tell people to be quiet.
3 hush up (verb) to keep something a secret.

husky **huskier huskiest** (adjective)
If your voice is **husky**, it is croaky and hoarse. **huskily** (adverb).

husky **huskies** (noun)
a dog with a thick, furry coat that was bred to pull sledges across snow, but is now often kept as a pet. *See* sledge.

hut (noun)
a small wooden building.

hutch **hutches** (noun)
a cage for rabbits and other small pets. *A rabbit hutch.*

hydrogen (noun)
a gas, which is the most common substance in the universe.

hyena (noun)
a wild animal, similar to a dog, that mostly comes out at night and hunts in groups, in Africa and parts of Asia.

hygienic (hi-**jee**-nik) (adjective)
Something **hygienic** will keep you healthy and not make you ill, because it is clean and germ-free. *It is hygienic to wash your hands before eating.* **hygiene** (noun), **hygienically** (adverb).

hymn (noun)
a song that Christians sing in church.

hype (noun)
the exaggerated things people say about something to make everyone excited about it. *The hype about the film was unbelievable.*

hyper (adjective) (abbreviation)
If someone is **hyper**, they are very restless and can't stop rushing around. It's short for "hyperactive". *The sweets at the birthday party made me hyper.*

Hyphens

Hyphens are used in three main ways:

1. **In compound words**, to join together the two (or more) parts of the word, for example:

half-hearted
daughter-in-law

2. **To separate letters** that would be tricky to say together in a word, especially when a prefix has been added to a word, such as in "re-enter".

"Co-ordinate" would be difficult to pronounce without a hyphen.

3. **To show that a word has been split** and then carries on on the line below, as this one does because "below" won't fit.

hyphen (noun)
the punctuation mark (-).

hypnotize or **hypnotise**
hypnotizing hypnotized (verb)
If you **hypnotize** somebody, you make it seem as if they are asleep, but they are still able to do things that you tell them to. **hypnotism** (noun), **hypnotist** (noun).

hypocrite (noun)
someone who pretends to feel or believe something that is different from their true feelings or beliefs. **hypocrisy** (noun).

hypothesis **hypotheses** (noun)
an idea or theory about how something will happen. **hypothetical** (adjective).

hysterical (adjective)
If you are **hysterical**, your emotions are out of control because you are very scared or excited about something. **hysteria** (noun), **hysterically** (adverb).

a b c d e f g h i j k l m n o p q r s t u v w x y z

Ii

ice *(noun)*
water that has frozen solid. *Careful on the ice!* **iced** *(adjective)*.

ice age *(noun)*
a period of time when a large part of the world is covered in ice.

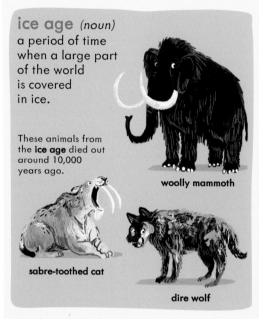

These animals from the **ice age** died out around 10,000 years ago.

woolly mammoth

sabre-toothed cat

dire wolf

iceberg *(noun)*
a huge piece of ice that is floating in the sea.

ice cream *(noun)*
a very cold, sweet food made from frozen milk or cream and flavourings.

ice hockey *(noun)*
a game played on ice by two teams. Players skate around and try to hit a flat disc called a puck into a goal, using long sticks.

ice rink *(noun)*
a place where people skate on a specially frozen area of ice. *Wayne had his birthday party at the ice rink.*

ice-skate
ice-skating ice-skated *(verb)*
to glide around on ice, wearing ice skates. **ice-skater** *(noun)*.

ice skate *(noun)*
a boot with a metal blade on the bottom, for skating on ice.

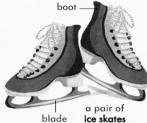

boot

blade

a pair of **ice skates**

icicle *(noun)*
a long finger of ice that hangs down.

icing *(noun)*
a sweet covering that people put on top of cakes. **ice** *(verb)*.

icon *(noun)*
1 a person or thing that people really respect. *He's a football icon.*
2 a small picture on a screen that you click on to make something happen.

ICT *(noun) (abbreviation)*
the use of computer systems and technology to help people and organizations communicate and use information. ICT stands for "**I**nformation and **C**ommunications **T**echnology".

icy **icier iciest** *(adjective)*
1 covered with ice. *The path is very icy.*
2 very cold. *There is an icy wind today.*

ID *(noun) (abbreviation)*
see **identification** and **identity**.

idea *(noun)*
1 a thought, or a plan. *My idea was to pack the car the night before.*
2 what you know about something, or your awareness of something. *I had no idea Paul kept goats.*

ideal
1 *(adjective)* perfect, or most suitable. *This pen is ideal.* **ideally** *(adverb)*.
2 *(noun)* something you think would be perfect. *My ideal is a world without war.*

identical *(adjective)*
If two or more things are **identical**, they are exactly the same. **identically** *(adverb)*.

identification *(noun)*
something that proves who you are. It's often shortened to "ID".

identify
identifying identified *(verb)*
to say who someone is, or what
something is. *Dad identified the
wallet as his.*

identity **identities** *(noun)*
Your **identity** is who you are. It's often
shortened to "ID".

idiot *(noun)*
a stupid person. **idiotic** *(adjective)*.

idle *(adjective)*
If you are **idle**, you don't like being
active or working hard.

idol *(noun)*
1 someone who is greatly admired.
My Aunt Ruth is my idol.
2 a picture or statue of a god that
people worship.

i.e *(abbreviation)*
i.e. is used in writing before an
explanation. *Jenny's latest idea seems
a lot like her last one, i.e. crazy.*

if *(conjunction)*
1 You use **if** when you are talking about
something that might happen. *If I win
the competition, I'm going to spend the
prize money on new clothes.*
2 on the condition that. *You can play
computer games if you finish all your
science homework.*

igloo *(noun)*
a dome-shaped house made out
of blocks of snow and ice.

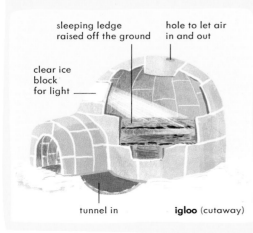

sleeping ledge
raised off the ground

hole to let air
in and out

clear ice
block
for light

tunnel in **igloo** (cutaway)

ignorant *(adjective)*
If you are **ignorant** about something,
you don't know anything about it.
ignorance *(noun)*, **ignorantly** *(adverb)*.

ignore **ignoring ignored** *(verb)*
If you **ignore** someone or something,
you take no notice of them. *I saw Lauren
at the party, but I ignored her.*

ill **worse worst** *(adjective)*
unwell or sick. *That food made me ill.*

illegal *(adjective)*
against the law. *It is illegal to drive
on the pavement.* **illegally** *(adverb)*.

illegible *(adjective)*
If a piece of writing is **illegible**, it is
impossible to read. *His handwriting is
almost illegible.* **illegibly** *(adverb)*.

illiterate *(adjective)*
unable to read or write. *Sadly, many
people around the world are illiterate.*
illiteracy *(noun)*.

illness **illnesses** *(noun)*
something that makes you unwell.

illogical *(adjective)*
If something is **illogical**, it doesn't make
sense. *Rob's decision to walk home
barefoot was completely illogical.*

illuminate
illuminating illuminated *(verb)*
to light something up. *The living room
was illuminated by the lights on the
Christmas tree.* **illumination** *(noun)*.

illusion *(noun)*
something which appears to exist or be
real, but is not. *These lines look bent,
but it's just an optical illusion.*

illustrate
illustrating illustrated *(verb)*
to add pictures to a story in a book
or magazine. **illustrator** *(noun)*,
illustrated *(adjective)*.

illustration *(noun)*
a picture in a book or magazine,
that has something to do with what
the text says.

a b c d e f g h i j k l m n o p q r s t u v w x y z

Spelling tip

image   imaginary   imagine

The letter 'g' usually makes a soft 'j' sound when it is followed by an 'e' or an 'i', as in "image", "imaginary" and "imagine".

image (noun)
1 a picture in a book or film, or on the screen of a phone, television, and so on.
2 a picture you have in your mind. *I have an image of a cottage by the sea.*
3 Your **image** is the way other people see you. *Lucia has a very cool image.*

imaginary (adjective)
Something that is **imaginary** has been made up, and doesn't really exist. *My little sister has an imaginary friend.*

imagine
imagining imagined (verb)
to picture something in your mind. *Imagine what it would be like to be a millionaire.* **imagination** (noun).

imam (noun)
someone who leads Islamic services in a mosque.

imitate
imitating imitated (verb)
to copy someone or something. *The parrot imitated Granny.* **imitation** (noun).

immature (adjective)
1 If someone is **immature**, they often behave childishly. **immaturity** (noun).
2 If something is **immature**, it's not yet fully grown or developed.

immediately (adverb)
now, or at once. *Stop that immediately!* **immediate** (adjective).

immense (adjective)
very, very big. *Blue whales are immense.* **immensely** (adverb).

immerse
immersing immersed (verb)
1 If you **immerse** something, you put it underwater. **immersion** (noun).
2 If you **immerse yourself in** something, you get deeply involved in it.

immigrant (noun)
someone who comes from their country to live and work in another one. **immigration** (noun).

imminent (adjective)
happening very soon. *An alien invasion is imminent.* **imminently** (adverb).

immoral (adjective)
1 Someone who is **immoral** is wicked.
2 An act that is **immoral** is unfair and wrong. **immorality** (noun).

immune (adjective)
If you are **immune** to an illness, you won't catch it. **immunization** or **immunisation** (noun), **immunity** (noun).

impact (noun)
1 the effect something has. *Winning the lottery had a massive impact on our lives.*
2 An **impact** happens when something hits something else very hard.

impatient (adjective)
1 not happy to wait. **impatience** (noun), **impatiently** (adverb).
2 easily annoyed.

imperfect (adjective)
not perfect, or faulty in some way. **imperfection** (noun), **imperfectly** (adverb).

The prefix 'im-'

immature
immoral
impolite
impossible

When the prefix 'im-' is added to the front of a word, it often makes that word mean its opposite. For example, "impolite" means "not polite" and "impossible" means "not possible".

impersonate
impersonating impersonated *(verb)*
If you **impersonate** someone, you talk and act like them. **impersonation** *(noun)*.

imply
implies implying implied *(verb)*
If you **imply** something, you try to make people realize it without saying it out loud. *Heather's expression implied that she wanted to leave.* **implication** *(noun)*.

impolite *(adjective)*
rude. *It's impolite to jump the queue.* **impolitely** *(adverb)*.

import **importing imported** *(verb)*
to bring things into your own country from abroad. *Britain imports lots of goods from China.* **import** *(noun)*.

important *(adjective)*
1 Something **important** needs to be taken seriously. *It's important to have a smoke alarm.*
2 An **important** person has a lot of power or fame. **importance** *(noun)*, **importantly** *(adverb)*.

impossible *(adjective)*
If something is **impossible**, it can't be done by anyone, or it can't happen. *It's impossible for humans to live underwater.* **impossibly** *(adverb)*.

impractical *(adjective)*
not sensible, or not right for the job you are trying to do. *Natalie's high-heeled shoes were very impractical for a camping weekend.*

impress
impresses impressing impressed *(verb)*
to make people think that you are good, skilled, or deserving of respect. *Anthony impressed me very much at his interview.* **impressive** *(adjective)*.

impression *(noun)*
1 a feeling, or an idea. *I got the impression that Kofi liked me.*
2 If you **do an impression** of someone or something, you talk and act like them. *Uncle Dan does a fantastic impression of a squeaky door.*

imprison
imprisoning imprisoned *(verb)*
If someone is **imprisoned**, they are put into jail. **imprisonment** *(noun)*.

improve **improving improved** *(verb)*
to get better, or make something better. *The chef improved his recipe.*

improvement *(noun)*
1 a thing that makes something better. *Home improvements.*
2 the act of becoming better. *I've seen an improvement in your maths this term.*

impulsive *(adjective)*
If you are **impulsive**, you do things suddenly, without thinking them through. **impulse** *(noun)*, **impulsively** *(adverb)*.

in *(preposition)*
1 inside. *Greg is in his room.*
2 wearing. *Sita is in her uniform.*
3 into. *Laura fell in the pond.*
4 You use the word **in** to show the state or condition of someone or something. *Jake was reading in silence.*

inaccurate *(adjective)*
not right, or not correct. *Carolyn's guesses were totally inaccurate.* **inaccuracy** *(noun)*, **inaccurately** *(adverb)*.

inappropriate *(adjective)*
not right for the situation you are in. *It's inappropriate to sing in the library.* **inappropriately** *(adverb)*.

inbox *(noun)*
the place in your computer that all your emails come into.

incapable *(adjective)*
If you are **incapable** of doing something, you can't do it. *My sister is incapable of swimming 25m.*

inch **inches** *(noun)*
a unit of measurement, equal to about 2.5 centimetres. There are 12 inches in a foot.

incident *(noun)*
an event, or something that happens. *There's been an incident at the match.*

a b c d e f g h i j k l m n o p q r s t u v w x y z

include including included (verb)
If you **include** someone or something, you make them a part of a bigger group. *We included the pets in our family photo.* **inclusion** (noun).

incoherent (adjective)
If something that someone says is **incoherent**, you can't hear it properly or it doesn't make sense.

income (noun)
Your **income** is the money you earn or receive.

incomplete (adjective)
not finished, or not whole. *The guest list for the party is incomplete.*

inconsiderate (adjective)
Someone who is **inconsiderate** does not think about other people's needs. *It's inconsiderate to leave all this mess!* **inconsiderately** (adverb).

inconvenient (adjective)
If something is **inconvenient**, it makes things difficult for other people. *It was so inconvenient that Belle arrived at dinner time.* **inconvenience** (noun).

incorrect (adjective)
not right. *4 + 2 = 7 is incorrect.* **incorrectly** (adverb).

increase
increasing increased (verb)
to get bigger, either in size or in number. *We increased the price of our house.* **increase** (noun).

incredible (adjective)
unbelievable, or amazing. *The special effects in the film were incredible.* **incredibly** (adverb).

incurable (adjective)
An **incurable** illness can't be made better. *Our dog has an incurable limp.* **incurably** (adverb).

indeed (adverb)
a word used to make what you say stronger. *The film we watched was very sad indeed.*

independent (adjective)
1 If something is **independent**, it rules itself. **independence** (noun).
2 If you are an **independent** person, you don't need or want help from anyone else. **independently** (adverb).

indestructible (adjective)
impossible to destroy.

index indexes (noun)
an alphabetical list of words at the end of a book, which shows you on which pages you can find out about the things mentioned in the book.

index finger (noun)
the finger next to your thumb.

indication (noun)
a sign, or proof. *Matthew gave no indication he felt ill until it was too late.*

indifferent (adjective)
If you are **indifferent** to something, you are not interested in it. *I am indifferent to where we go at the weekend.* **indifference** (noun).

indigestion (noun)
a pain in your stomach or chest that you can get after eating. *Annie ate so fast that she had indigestion.*

indignant (adjective)
If you are **indignant**, you are angry because someone has done or said something unfair. **indignantly** (adverb).

individual
1 (adjective) separate or special. *Every room has its own individual charm.* **individually** (adverb).
2 (noun) a person. *Lawrence is such a strange individual.*

indoors (adverb)
inside a building. *I always prefer to eat indoors.* **indoor** (adjective).

industry industries (noun)
all the factories and companies that make a particular thing. *The computer industry is booming.* **industrial** (adjective), **industrially** (adverb).

inefficient *(adjective)*
disorganized, wasteful, or not well-run.
inefficiency *(noun)*, **inefficiently** *(adverb)*.

inequality **inequalities** *(noun)*
unfairness. If you experience inequality,
you are not treated in the same way as
other people.

infant *(noun)*
a baby, or a very young child. *The play
area is for infants only.* **infancy** *(noun)*,
infant *(adjective)*.

infection *(noun)*
an illness caused by germs.

infectious *(adjective)*
If you have an **infectious** illness, other
people can catch it from you. **infect** *(verb)*.

inferior *(adjective)*
not as good as something else.
inferiority *(noun)*.

infinite *(adjective)*
going on forever, or having no limits.
infinitely *(adverb)*.

infinitive *(noun)*
the basic, unchanged form of a verb,
for example "to walk" or "to dance".

infinity *(noun)*
a place or a number that has no end.

inflammable *(adjective)*
Something **inflammable** catches fire
very easily.

inflatable *(adjective)*
able to be filled with air and then used.
inflatable *(noun)*.

inflatable life raft
(cutaway)   first-aid kit   cover

flares

paddles

inflatable
base

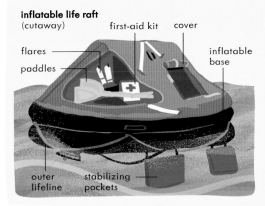

outer
lifeline

stabilizing
pockets

Spelling tip

inflate ⟶ inflation

Look at how the verb "inflate" changes
to become the noun "inflation". Another
word that follows this pattern is:

illustrate ⟶ illustration

inflate **inflating inflated** *(verb)*
to blow up with air.

inflation *(noun)*
a general increase in the price of things.

influence **influencing influenced**
1 *(noun)* If you have **influence** over
someone, you can persuade them
to do things. **influential** *(adjective)*.
2 *(verb)* to have an effect on something.
*My Australian teacher influenced my
decision to do a project on koalas.*

influenza *(noun)*
an illness which makes you feel very hot
and achy. It's often shortened to "flu".

inform **informing informed** *(verb)*
to tell someone about something. *Our
guide informed us about the castle.*

informal *(adjective)*
relaxed and casual. *The wedding was
very informal.* **informally** *(adverb)*.

information *(noun)*
facts and knowledge. *The information
the receptionist gave us was very hard
to understand.*

information technology
or **IT** *(noun)*
computers and other electronic
equipment that people use, and the
study or use of them.

informative *(adjective)*
giving lots of helpful information.
The guidebook was very informative.

infrequent *(adjective)*
not happening very often. *The buses here
are infrequent.* **infrequently** *(adverb)*.

a b c d e f g h i j k l m n o p q r s t u v w x y z

infuriate
infuriating infuriated (verb)
to make someone extremely angry.
Sunni was infuriated when he couldn't log on to the website.
infuriating (adjective),
infuriatingly (adverb).

ingredient (noun)
one of the things that is used to make something, usually food.

inhabit
inhabiting inhabited (verb)
If a person or animal **inhabits** a place, they live there.

inhale **inhaling inhaled** (verb)
to breathe in. **inhalation** (noun).

inhaler (noun)
a device used by people who have breathing problems to spray a drug into their mouths so they can breathe it in.

inherit **inheriting inherited** (verb)
to receive something, such as money or property, from someone who has died.
inheritance (noun).

initial
1 (adjective) first. *My initial reaction when I saw his costume was to laugh.*
initially (adverb).
2 (noun) the first letter of a name.
My initials are B.S.N.

initiative (noun)
If you use your **initiative**, you do things without having to be told. *Joe used his initiative and went ahead with his plan.*

inject **injecting injected** (verb)
to use a needle to put medicine into someone's body. **injection** (noun).

injure **injuring injured** (verb)
to hurt someone. *My grandad was injured in the war.*

injury **injuries** (noun)
a wound, or damage to someone's body, or their feelings.

injustice (noun)
unfairness. *There's so much injustice in the world.*

ink (noun)
coloured liquid, usually used for writing and printing. Some sea animals squirt out a dark liquid, also known as ink, to defend themselves. **inky** (adjective).

reddish-brown ink

Ink irritates fish's eyes.

cuttlefish

Some sea animals, such as the broadclub cuttlefish, squirt **ink** to confuse attackers while they escape.

inland (adverb)
away from the sea. *Oxford is a long way inland.* **inland** (adjective).

in-law (noun)
someone related to you by marriage.
Our in-laws are coming for a barbecue.

inner (adjective)
on the inside. *My coat has a secret inner pocket.*

innocent (adjective)
An **innocent** person has not done anything wrong. **innocence** (noun),
innocently (adverb).

input (noun)
what a person adds to something.
My brother's input to the party planning was useless.

inquire or enquire
inquiring inquired (verb)
to ask about someone or something.
Inquire can also be spelt "enquire".

inquiry or enquiry (noun)
1 the act of asking for information.
2 an official investigation. *The police have begun an inquiry into the attack.*

inquisitive (adjective)
curious and eager to know about things. *Our new kitten is very inquisitive.* **inquisitiveness** (noun),
inquisitively (adverb).

insane *(adjective)*
mad, or crazy. **insanity** *(noun)*.

inscription *(noun)*
a message that has been carved, engraved, or written on something.

insect *(noun)*
a small animal with six legs and a body that has three separate parts. Many insects also have wings.

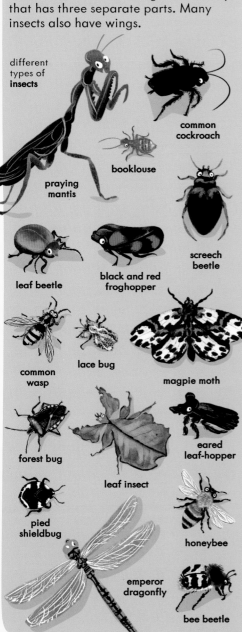

different types of **insects**

praying mantis

common cockroach

booklouse

leaf beetle

black and red froghopper

screech beetle

common wasp

lace bug

magpie moth

forest bug

leaf insect

eared leaf-hopper

pied shieldbug

honeybee

emperor dragonfly

bee beetle

insecure *(adjective)*
1 not safe. *That door is insecure, as the lock is broken.* **insecurely** *(adverb)*.
2 not very confident. **insecurity** *(noun)*.

insensitive *(adjective)*
1 An **insensitive** person does not think about other people's feelings.
2 If you say or do something that is **insensitive**, it might hurt other people's feelings. **insensitively** *(adverb)*.

insert inserting inserted *(verb)*
to put something into something else. *You need to insert the key into the lock to open the door.* **insertion** *(noun)*.

inside
1 *(adverb)* into a building. *We went inside when it started to rain.*
2 *(noun)* the inner part of something. *I love the inside of jam doughnuts.*
3 *(adjective)* found on or in the inner part of something. *An inside door.*
4 *(preposition)* within. *I always wear my scarf inside my coat.*
5 *(preposition)* in less than a certain amount of time. *We need to get home inside 15 minutes.*

insignificant *(adjective)*
not important. **insignificance** *(noun)*, **insignificantly** *(adverb)*.

insist insisting insisted *(verb)*
If you **insist** on doing or having something, you demand to do or have it. *Mum insisted that I have the final slice of her birthday cake.* **insistence** *(noun)*, **insistent** *(adjective)*.

inspect inspecting inspected *(verb)*
to look at something very closely and carefully. **inspection** *(noun)*.

inspector *(noun)*
someone who examines things to see if they are as they should be. *The inspector checked our train tickets.*

inspire inspiring inspired *(verb)*
If someone or something **inspires** you, they give you ideas and make you want to do as well as you can. *My dad inspired me to play the piano.* **inspiration** *(noun)*, **inspiring** *(adjective)*.

a b c d e f g h i j k l m n o p q r s t u v w x y z

A B C D E F G H **I** J K L M N O P Q R S T U V W X Y Z

install **installing installed** (verb)
1 to put something, such as a machine, in place and get it working. *Our new washing machine will be installed today.* **installation** (noun).
2 to load a program onto your computer.

instant
1 (noun) a moment.
2 (adjective) happening straight away. *The medicine had an instant effect.* **instantly** (adverb).

instead (adverb)
in the place of. *Dad was ill, so Mum went to the supermarket instead.*

instinct (noun)
something you know to do, or know how to do, without being told or shown. *The cat's instinct is to hide from strangers.* **instinctive** (adjective), **instinctively** (adverb).

instruct **instructing instructed** (verb)
to tell someone what to do, or how to do something. **instruction** (noun), **instructor** (noun).

instructions (plural noun)
the information that tells you how to do something. *The instructions on the packet said to cook the pie for an hour.*

instrument (noun)
1 a tool or small machine that does a particular job. *The paramedic had lots of instruments in his bag.*
2 something that is used to play music.

insulate **insulating insulated** (verb)
to cover something with special material to stop heat, electricity or sound escaping from it. **insulation** (noun).

insult **insulting insulted** (verb)
to say something rude to someone. **insult** (noun), **insulting** (adjective).

insurance (noun)
protection that you can buy for something, in case something goes wrong with it and you need money to sort out the problem. **insure** (verb), **insured** (adjective).

intact (adjective)
whole, or not broken. *Incredibly, the goldfish bowl was intact at the end of the journey.*

intellectual
1 (adjective) to do with thinking and using your brain. **intellect** (noun).
2 (noun) someone who is very intelligent, reads a lot, and knows a lot about a subject.

intelligent (adjective)
clever, and quick to understand things. *Chimpanzees are very intelligent.* **intelligence** (noun), **intelligently** (adverb).

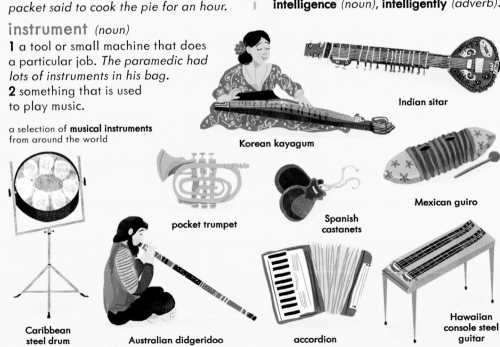

a selection of **musical instruments** from around the world

Indian sitar

Korean kayagum

Mexican guiro

pocket trumpet

Spanish castanets

Caribbean steel drum

Australian didgeridoo

accordion

Hawaiian console steel guitar

intend **intending intended** (verb)
to mean or aim to do something. *I intend to eat more fish from now on.*

intense (adjective)
very powerful or strong. *The flavour of chillies is very intense.* **intensely** (adverb).

intention (noun)
something you mean or aim to do. *My intention is to get full marks in next week's maths exam.*

intentional (adjective)
done on purpose. *That foul looked intentional.* **intentionally** (adverb).

interactive (adjective)
An **interactive** video game, computer program, and so on, lets the user influence how it works and what happens. *The screens in the art gallery are interactive.*

intercept
intercepting intercepted (verb)
to stop someone or something from getting from one place to another. *I intercepted the letter before it got to Phil.* **interception** (noun).

interest **interesting interested**
1 (verb) If something **interests** you, you want to know about it. *Chemistry really interests me.*
2 (adjective) If you are **interested in** something, you like it and want to do it or know more about it. *I'm very interested in tennis.*

interesting (adjective)
If something is **interesting**, it holds your attention and makes you want to know about it. *This museum is very interesting.*

interfere
interfering interfered (verb)
to get involved in something that doesn't really concern you. *Dan always interferes and ruins our games.* **interference** (noun).

interior (noun)
the inside of something. *The interior of Dad's car is full of dirt and rubbish.* **interior** (adjective).

interjection (noun)
a word you can use as a greeting, or to show surprise, pain, or other feelings.

Often interjections are used on their own, as a response to something, for example, "Wow!", "Hooray!", and so on. They can also be used within a sentence, separated by commas, for example: "Joe came over yesterday and, **bless him**, he brought brownies for us."

Hey!

Phew!

Ow!

intermediate (adjective)
between the beginner stage and the advanced stage. *Leah got her intermediate swimming badge today.*

internal (adjective)
inside someone or something, especially a human body. *Michael's injuries were all internal.* **internally** (adverb).

international (adjective)
involving people from many different countries. *The World Cup is an international football competition.* **internationally** (adverb).

internet (noun)
the huge computer network used to share messages and information around the world. **internet** (adjective).

interrupt
interrupting interrupted (verb)
1 to start talking before someone else has finished speaking.
2 to stop something happening for a while. *The storm interrupted our picnic.* **interruption** (noun).

interval (noun)
the break in the middle of a play or concert.

interview (noun)
a meeting where you are asked questions, often to see if you are right for a job. *My job interview lasted for three hours.*

a b c d e f g h i j k l m n o p q r s t u v w x y z

intestines *(plural noun)*
the organs that your food passes through after it has left your stomach. *See* organ.

intolerant *(adjective)*
Intolerant people do not accept views or beliefs that are different to their own. **intolerance** *(noun)*.

introduce
introducing introduced *(verb)*
If you **introduce** people to each other, you help them get to know each other.

introduction *(noun)*
1 the opening part of a book, article, song, and so on. **introductory** *(adjective)*.
2 meeting someone or doing something for the first time. *An introduction to yoga.*

introvert *(noun)*
someone who is shy. **introverted** *(adjective)*.

intrude **intruding intruded** *(verb)*
to push your way into a place or situation where you are not wanted or allowed to go. **intrusion** *(noun)*, **intruder** *(noun)*, **intrusive** *(adjective)*.

intuition *(noun)*
the ability to understand or know something without having to think about it. **intuitive** *(adjective)*.

Inuit *(noun)*
one of a group of people who live in the very cold, far northern areas of the world, including Canada and Alaska.

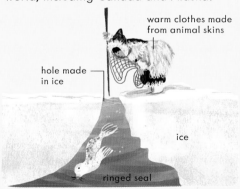

warm clothes made from animal skins

hole made in ice

ice

ringed seal

This picture shows how an **Inuit** hunts.

invade **invading invaded** *(verb)*
to go into a place and take it over. **invader** *(noun)*, **invasion** *(noun)*.

invalid
1 (**in**-va-lid)
(noun) someone who is very ill, and may have to stay in bed all the time.
2 (in-**va**-lid) *(adjective)* If something is **invalid**, it can't be used. *Jim's library card is invalid.*

> Remember, the meaning of the word "invalid" changes depending on how you pronounce it.

invent **inventing invented** *(verb)*
1 to make something up. *Tim invented a story about an alien invasion.*
2 to create a new machine or device.

invention *(noun)*
something new, that has never been made or thought of before. **inventor** *(noun)*.

inverted commas *(plural noun)*
the symbols (**" "**) or (**' '**) used in writing. They are sometimes called speech marks or quotation marks. *See* punctuation, *page 349.*

invest **investing invested** *(verb)*
to give money or time, or put effort into something. *Tony has invested a lot of money in the new restaurant.* **investment** *(noun)*.

investigate
investigating investigated *(verb)*
to try to find out all about something. *The police are investigating the crime.* **investigation** *(noun)*.

invisible *(adjective)*
Something **invisible** can't be seen.

invite **inviting invited** *(verb)*
to ask someone to do something or go somewhere. **invitation** *(noun)*.

involve **involving involved** *(verb)*
to include someone or something as a very important part. *Football involves trying to get the ball into the goal.*

involved *(adjective)*
If you are **involved in** something, you take part in it. *I was involved in organizing the camping trip.* **involvement** *(noun)*.

inwards or **inward** (adverb)
towards the inside. *Sweep the rubbish inwards towards the centre of the room.*

iron (noun)
1 a strong, hard metal used to make things such as gates and railings. Iron is also found in small quantities in some foods, and in your blood.
2 a machine that gets hot and is used to smooth the creases out of clothes.
ironing (noun), **iron** (verb).

irregular (adjective)
not even, or not equal. *Sian has very irregular teeth.* **irregularly** (adverb).

irrational (adjective)
not sensible, not logical, or unreasonable. *George has an irrational fear of belly buttons.*

irrelevant (adjective)
nothing at all to do with what is being talked about. *Penguins can't drive, but that's irrelevant.*

irresponsible (adjective)
Someone who is **irresponsible** does silly or dangerous things and doesn't think about what might happen. *It was irresponsible of Emma to leave the lion's cage open.* **irresponsibly** (adverb).

irritable (adjective)
easily annoyed. *Hot weather makes Grandma very irritable.*

Islam (noun)
the religion followed by Muslims and based on the teachings of the prophet Mohammed. **Islamic** (adjective).

Islam first began over 1,400 years ago. According to Muslims, the prophet Mohammed was sent by God (known by Muslims as Allah) to teach people about Islam and how to live their lives. It is now the second largest religion in the world. The holy book of Islam is called the Qur'an.

symbol of **Islam**

Its or it's?

Lots of people find it hard to know whether to use "**it's**" or "**its**". Just remember the following:

"**Its**" means "belonging to it".

"**It's**" is short for "it is" or "it has".

island (noun)
an area of land surrounded by water on all sides. *We had to take a boat across the lake to visit the island.*

isolate **isolating isolated** (verb)
to cut someone or something off from everything else. *The farmer isolated the lambs from their mothers.* **isolation** (noun), **isolated** (adjective).

isosceles (adjective)
An **isosceles** triangle has two sides of equal length. See shapes, page 348.

issue (noun)
1 a copy of a newspaper or magazine. *The new issue of the magazine is out next Wednesday.*
2 a subject for discussion. *The main issue is how we'll raise the money for the ball.*
3 a problem or concern. *There's an issue with the balloons for the party.*

IT (noun) (abbreviation)
see information technology.

italics (plural noun)
letters that slope to the right, *like this.*

itch **itches itching itched** (verb)
When your skin **itches**, you want to scratch it. *Oscar's new jumper made him itch.* **itch** (noun), **itchy** (adjective).

item (noun)
a single thing. *Becky chose six items from the shop.*

ivy (noun)
an evergreen plant with pointed leaves that grows on walls, trees, and so on.

a b c d e f g h i j k l m n o p q r s t u v w x y z

Jj

The letter 'j' is special, because it is always followed by a vowel, and never doubled.

jab
jabbing jabbed
1 (verb) to poke someone or something with something sharp. *Sam jabbed me with his pencil to wake me up.*
2 (noun) a friendly word for an injection. *I had my flu jab yesterday.*

jabber **jabbering jabbered** (verb)
to talk in a fast, excited way that is difficult to understand. *Rhys jabbered for hours about the theme park.*

jackal (noun)
a kind of wild dog that hunts and feeds on dead animals.

jacket (noun)
a short coat, which opens at the front and has long sleeves.

Jacuzzi (noun) (trademark)
a large bathtub with jets of water and air which shoot out and massage your body.

jagged (**jag**-ged) (adjective)
sharp and uneven. *The rocks around the beach were very jagged.*

jaguar (noun)
a large wild animal in the cat family, with spotted fur, that is mostly found in South America. *See* **rainforest**.

jail *or* gaol (noun)
a place where people are locked up when they are found guilty of a serious crime. **jail** (verb).

jam (noun)
1 a sweet food made from fruit and sugar that you can spread onto toast, scones, or cakes.
2 If traffic cannot move, it forms a **traffic jam**. *The traffic jam made us late for school this morning.*
3 If you are in a **jam**, you're in a tricky situation.

jam **jamming jammed** (verb)
1 to get stuck. *The kitchen door jammed shut.*
2 If a machine **jams**, it stops working. *The printer keeps jamming.*

January (noun)
the first month of the year.

jar (noun)
a small glass container with a lid that you can screw tightly shut.

javelin (noun)
a long stick with a pointed end, which is thrown in athletics competitions.

jaw (noun)
the bones in your head that your teeth grow out of, and which let you open and close your mouth.

jazz (noun)
a kind of music that usually features woodwind or brass instruments, and in which musicians sometimes make up the tunes as they play. **jazzy** (adjective).

jealous (adjective)
If you are **jealous** of someone, they have something that you would like to have. **jealousy** (noun), **jealously** (adverb).

jeans (noun)
trousers made of a tough material called denim.

Word origin   jeans

The word "jeans" comes from the French word for a city called Genoa, in Italy: "Jennes". Sailors in Genoa wore jeans for working, because they were strong and sturdy.

Jeep (noun) (trademark)
a powerful four-wheel drive car, for driving over rough country.

jelly jellies (noun)
a see-through, sweet, fruity pudding that wobbles.

jellyfish
jellyfish or **jellyfishes** (noun)
a sea animal with a soft body and floating strands called tentacles that drag behind it, and may sting.

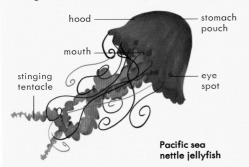

hood — stomach pouch

mouth

stinging tentacle

eye spot

Pacific sea nettle jellyfish

jerk jerking jerked
1 (verb) to pull something suddenly and hard. *Luke jerked on the steering wheel to avoid the branch.* **jerky** (adjective).
2 (noun) a sharp pull. *Mum gave my loose tooth a quick jerk and it came out.*

jet (noun)
1 an aeroplane that has powerful engines and flies very fast.
2 a fast stream of liquid or gas.

jet lag (noun)
a very tired feeling, because you have flown to a country in a different time zone and your body isn't used to it.

Jet Ski (noun) (trademark)
a vehicle for one to three people to sit or stand on, that travels over water.

Jew (noun)
a member of the Hebrew race, who often follows the Jewish religion. **Jewish** (adjective).

jewel (noun)
a precious stone, such as a diamond, ruby, or emerald.

jewellery (noun)
rings, necklaces, bracelets, earrings and other things that people wear to look nice. **jeweller** (noun).

jigsaw (noun)
a picture stuck or printed on card or wood that has been cut up, and has to be put back together to make the picture. Jigsaw is short for "jigsaw puzzle".

job (noun)
1 the work someone does for a living. *Jeff's job is to train racehorses.*
2 a task. *Mum left me a long list of jobs to do around the house.*

jockey (noun)
someone who rides a racehorse.

jog jogging jogged (verb)
1 to run at a steady pace, for exercise. **jogger** (noun), **jogging** (noun).
2 If something **jogs your memory**, it makes you remember something that you had forgotten about.

join joining joined
1 (verb) When you **join** things, you connect them or make them stick, tie or fasten together.
2 (verb) If you **join** a club or group, you become a part of it.
3 (noun) a place or line where two or more things are connected or fastened together.

joint
1 (noun) a place where two of your bones meet, such as your hip joint.
2 (noun) a big piece of meat.
3 (adjective) made by, shared by or belonging to two or more people. *The meal was a joint effort.* **jointly** (adverb).

joke joking joked (verb)
to say funny things that make people laugh. **joke** (noun).

jolly jollier jolliest (adjective)
happy and cheerful. *My Uncle Nick is very jolly.*

jolt jolting jolted
1 (verb) to move in a rough, violent way. *The car jolted us along the bumpy track.*
2 (noun) a sudden, rough movement. *The ship hit an iceberg with a jolt.*

jot jotting jotted (verb)
to write something down quickly.

a b c d e f g h i j k l m n o p q r s t u v w x y z

journal *(noun)*
a diary in which you write about what you have done each day.

journalist *(noun)*
someone who writes articles for newspapers or magazines, or online. **journalism** *(noun)*.

journey *(noun)*
a trip from one place to another. *The journey from Leeds to York takes about 25 minutes.*

joy *(noun)*
great happiness. *There was much joy in our house when the baby was born.* **joyful** *(adjective)*, **joyfully** *(adverb)*.

jubilee *(noun)*
a big celebration to mark the anniversary, especially the twenty-fifth or fiftieth anniversary, of a special event. *The cricket club is holding a tournament to celebrate its jubilee.*

Judaism *(noun)*
the religion that most Jewish people believe and follow, based on a text called the Torah.

Judaism began in the Middle East over 3,500 years ago, and today there are around 14 million Jews around the world. Jews worship in **synagogues**, and their most important day of the week is the **Shabbat**, which starts on Friday evening and ends at sunset on Saturday. During the Shabbat, Jews rest and spend time with their families.

The **Star of David** is a symbol of Judaism.

judge **judging judged** *(verb)*
1 to decide who or what is the best in a competition. *The mayor judged the dog show.* **judge** *(noun)*.
2 to form an opinion about something.
3 to listen to evidence in a court, and decide how a guilty person should be punished. **judge** *(noun)*, **judgement** or **judgment** *(noun)*.

judo *(noun)*
a sport in which two people try to force each other onto the ground using special, controlled movements.

This picture shows two **judokas** (judo competitors) fighting.

belt colour shows level of skill

jug *(noun)*
a container with a handle, which is used for pouring liquids. *Can you pass the milk jug, please?*

juggle **juggling juggled** *(verb)*
1 to keep several objects in the air at the same time, catching each one when it comes down and throwing it up again. **juggler** *(noun)*, **juggling** *(noun)*.
2 to cope with several jobs or things at once. *Roland is struggling to juggle his school work and his karate training.*

juice *(noun)*
1 the liquid that comes out of fruit, vegetables, or cooked meat.
2 a drink made from fruit juice, or sometimes from vegetable juice.

juicy **juicier juiciest** *(adjective)*
containing a lot of juice. *Oranges are juicier than bananas.*

July *(noun)*
the seventh month of the year.

jumble *(noun)*
an untidy pile or collection of things. *My school books are in such a jumble.* **jumbled** *(adjective)*, **jumble** *(verb)*.

jump **jumping jumped** *(verb)*
1 to leap into the air. **jump** *(noun)*.
2 If you **jump at** something, you say "yes" to it. *Carol jumped at the chance to try paragliding.*
3 If you **make someone jump**, you surprise and scare them a little by doing something suddenly. *Wilson made me jump when he appeared at the window.*

jumper (noun)
a warm piece of clothing that you wear on the top half of your body. It has long sleeves and no buttons up the front.

junction (noun)
a place where two or more roads or railway lines meet.

June (noun)
the sixth month of the year.

jungle (noun)
a thick forest, found in places that are hot and where it rains a lot.

Here are some plants and animals that live in **jungles**:

white-lipped viper

matamata turtle

spectacled caiman

bromeliad

white-lipped pit viper

great hornbill

red-eyed tree frog

hanging heliconia

silky sifaka

tarantula

armadillo

junior
1 (adjective) to do with, or designed for, younger children. *This is a Junior Illustrated English Dictionary.*
2 (noun) someone who is younger than someone else or younger than the others in a group. *Could all the juniors sit down, please.*
3 (adjective) Someone who is **junior** is learning a job and has a boss in charge of them. *Brian is a junior manager.*

junk (noun)
1 things that need to be thrown away. *Your room is full of junk!*
2 Junk food is ready-prepared food that doesn't have much goodness in it. *You need to eat less junk food if you want to stay healthy.*
3 Junk mail is letters or emails that you get even though you don't want them.

jury juries (noun)
a group of people who listen to a trial in court and decide whether someone is innocent or guilty of a crime. **juror** (noun).

just
1 (adverb) not long ago, or recently. *Eliza has just left.*
2 (adverb) by a small amount. *I only just managed to eat it all.*
3 (adverb) only, or no more than. *I'm just an ordinary person.*
4 (adjective) fair and right. *We felt that the punishment was just.*

justice (noun)
1 fairness and equal treatment. *Nelson Mandela believed in justice for all.*
2 the use of the law to make sure that people are treated fairly.

justify
justifies justifying justified (verb)
to give a reason why you did something, or explain why you were right to do it. *How can you possibly justify having another ice cream?* **justification** (noun).

jut jutting jutted (verb)
to stick out. *The pier jutted out into the sea.*

a b c d e f g h i j k l m n o p q r s t u v w x y z

Kk

kaleidoscope
(ka-**lie**-do-scope) (noun)
a tube you look through to see beautiful patterns made with mirrors and different coloured shapes.

kangaroo (noun)
a large Australian animal that can jump very far with its big back legs. Females carry their babies in pouches.

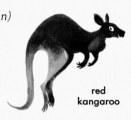

red kangaroo

karaoke (ka-ree-**yoh**-kee) (noun)
When people do **karaoke**, they sing along to popular songs in front of an audience. *I had a karaoke party for my birthday.*

karate (ka-**rah**-tee) (noun)
a martial art from Japan, which involves using kicks, punches, and moves that stop you getting hit.

kayak (**ky**-ak) (noun)
a small, covered boat which you sit in and move using a paddle with two blades. **kayaking** (noun).

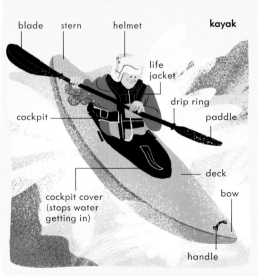

blade stern helmet kayak

life jacket

drip ring

cockpit paddle

cockpit cover (stops water getting in)

deck

bow

handle

Borrowed words

karaoke
karate
kayak
kebab

Lots of words in English are borrowed from other languages. **Karaoke** and **karate** come from Japanese, **kayak** comes from Inuktitut, and **kebab** comes from Turkish.

kebab (noun)
a dish from the Middle East, made with meat that has been grilled or cooked on long skewers.

keen **keener keenest** (adjective)
If you are **keen**, you really want to do something or you are really interested and enthusiastic. *Marco was very keen to be on the basketball team.* **keenly** (adverb), **keenness** (noun).

keep **keeping kept** (verb)
1 to have something forever. *I said Lisa could keep the book, because she liked it so much.*
2 to continue doing something, or to do it again and again. *You keep asking me that question, and I still don't know the answer.*
3 to make something stay the same way. *Max keeps his room very tidy.*
4 to find space for something and leave it there. *I keep my bike in the shed.*
5 to look after an animal. *My aunt keeps chickens.*
6 If you **keep up** with someone, you move at the same speed as they do.

keeper (noun)
a person who looks after something, such as animals in a zoo or items in a museum.

kennel (noun)
a small house for a dog.

kennels (plural noun)
a place where dogs are looked after while their owners go away.

kerb *(noun)*
the edge of a pavement.

ketchup *(noun)*
a thick sauce, eaten cold. *Tomato ketchup.*

kettle *(noun)*
a pot with a handle and lid, used for boiling water.

key
1 *(noun)* a small metal object for opening a lock or starting a vehicle.
2 *(noun)* the part you press on a piano or electronic keyboard to make a sound.
3 *(noun)* a button on a computer keyboard. *Press any key to continue.*
4 *(noun)* The **key** of a map or diagram shows you what the different symbols mean.
5 *(noun)* The **key** of a piece of music tells you which musical scale the piece is based on. *This song is in the key of A major.*
6 *(adjective)* very important. *Violet is one of our key players.*

keyboard *(noun)*
1 the part of a computer used to type letters, numbers, and symbols.
2 the set of keys on a piano.
3 an electronic instrument that is similar to a small piano.

khaki (*kah*-kee) *(noun)*
a light greenish-brown colour, often used in soldiers' uniforms. **khaki** *(adjective)*.

kick kicking kicked *(verb)*
to hit something hard with your foot. *The goalkeeper kicked the ball down the pitch.* **kick** *(noun)*.

kid kidding kidded
1 *(noun)* a friendly word for a child.
2 *(noun)* a young goat.
3 *(verb)* to tell someone something as a joke. *I was just kidding! Of course I didn't see an alien.*

kidnap
kidnapping kidnapped *(verb)*
to take a person from their home or family, often demanding money to give them back. **kidnapping** *(noun)*, **kidnapper** *(noun)*.

kidney *(noun)*
an organ in your body which removes waste from your blood and releases it in your urine.

kill killing killed *(verb)*
to end the life of a person, animal, or plant.

kiln *(noun)*
a special oven in which pottery is baked at a high temperature.

kilo or **kilogram** *(noun)*
a measure of weight. There are 1,000 grams in a kilogram. It is often shortened to "kg".

kilometre *(noun)*
a measure of distance. There are 1,000 metres in a kilometre. It is often shortened to "km".

kilt *(noun)*
a traditional piece of clothing worn by Scottish men, made of wool with a special pattern on it. It is wrapped around the waist like a skirt.

kimono *(noun)*
a traditional Japanese women's dress, made of patterned silk with a wide belt called a sash.

traditional **kimono**

silk material

eri (collar)

obijime (cord)

obi (sash)

sode (sleeve)

zori (sandals)

kind kinder kindest
1 *(noun)* a type or sort. *There are many different kinds of pasta.*
2 *(adjective)* thoughtful and generous. *It's very kind of you to help Mr Jones with his bags.* **kindness** *(noun)*, **kindly** *(adverb)*.

a b c d e f g h i j **k** l m n o p q r s t u v w x y z

king (noun)
1 a man who is the ruler of a country, usually because he comes from a royal family.
2 the most important chesspiece. If your king cannot move out of danger, you lose the game. *See* **chess**.
3 a playing card with a picture of a king on it.

kingdom (noun)
1 a country ruled by a king or queen.
2 a part of the natural world. *The animal kingdom.*

kingfisher (noun)
a small, brightly-coloured bird with a long, sharp, pointed beak.

kiosk (**kee**-osk) (noun)
a small hut or stall where you can buy things, for instance newspapers or tickets.

kiss **kisses kissing kissed** (verb)
to show love or affection, or to greet or say goodbye to someone, by touching them with your lips. **kiss** (noun).

kit (noun)
1 the things that you need to make or do something. *A sewing kit.*
2 the equipment you need for sports or games. *Have you packed your football kit?*

kitchen (noun)
the room in a house or other building where food is prepared and cooked. **kitchen** (adjective).

kite (noun)
a toy made of paper or fabric stretched over a frame attached to strings, which can be flown in the air on windy days.

kitten (noun)
a young cat. *A kitten keeps turning up at our house.*

kiwi (noun)
1 a large bird from New Zealand that cannot fly.
2 a nickname for people from New Zealand.

large body

long beak

kiwi

kiwi fruit (noun)
a fruit with brown, slightly fuzzy skin and juicy green flesh. *See* **fruit**.

knack (noun)
If you **have a knack for** something, you can do it easily. *Jenna has a knack for making people feel comfortable as soon as they arrive.*

knead **kneading kneaded** (verb)
to squash and stretch dough with your hands, before it is baked into bread. *Knead the dough for 10 minutes.*

knee (noun)
the joint in the middle of your leg.

kneel **kneeling knelt** (verb)
to rest with your knees and lower legs on the ground. Sometimes people kneel as a way to show respect, or to pray. *There weren't enough chairs, so some of us had to kneel at the front.*

knickers (plural noun)
underpants worn by girls and women.

knife **knives** (noun)
a tool used for cutting things, such as food, or as a weapon.

types of **kites**

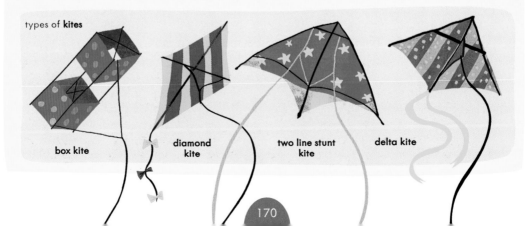

box kite

diamond kite

two line stunt kite

delta kite

Spelling tip

knight   **knit**   **knock**

Lots of words on these pages start with a silent 'k'. It can be tricky to remember, so take the time to learn which words start with a silent 'k'.

knight *(noun)*
1 a soldier in the Middle Ages who fought on horseback, wearing armour, and was expected to behave in a fair and respectful way.

plume (ostrich feathers)
visor
helmet
spike
breastplate
gauntlet (glove)
sword
greave
coat-of-arms

medieval **knight** on horseback

2 a chesspiece with a horse's head on it that always moves three squares at a time in an L-shape. *See* **chess**.

knit **knitting knitted** *(verb)*
to make clothes or other items by looping woollen thread around two large needles. **knitting** *(noun)*.

knob *(noun)*
1 a handle that you can hold or pull with your hand. *I hurt my leg when I walked into the knob on the door.*
2 a control button on a machine. *Turn the knob right to increase the speed.*

knock **knocking knocked** *(verb)*
1 to hit something, especially to hit a door with your fist to tell someone you are there. **knock** *(noun)*.
2 If you **knock something down**, you cause it to fall to the ground.
3 If you **knock someone out**, you hit them so hard they become unconscious.
4 If you **knock someone or something over**, you bump into or hit them, and cause them to fall over.

knot *(noun)*
1 a fastening made by looping string, rope, and so on, around itself tightly. **knot** *(verb)*.

types of **knots**

reef knot   overhand   figure-eight
                  knot   knot

2 a tangle or clump of hair, string, and so on. *Izzie's hair is full of knots.* **knotted** *(adjective)*.

know **knowing knew known** *(verb)*
1 to be certain of something.
2 to have learnt something. *Do you know your times tables?*
3 to have met and remember a person. *Do you know Mrs Macdonald?*

knowledge *(noun)*
all the things that you have learnt. *This quiz tests your knowledge of the Tudors.*

knuckle *(noun)*
one of the joints where your fingers join your hand.

koala *(noun)*
a small Australian animal that lives in trees and carries its young in a pouch. *See* **marsupial**.

Koran *or* **Qur'an** *(noun)*
the holy book of the Islamic religion. Muslims believe that the Koran was revealed to Mohammed by Allah (God), over a period of about 23 years.

kosher *(adjective)*
Food that is **kosher** has been prepared according to Jewish religious laws.

a b c d e f g h i j k l m n o p q r s t u v w x y z

label (noun)

1 a piece of paper, cloth or plastic that gives information about something, such as how much it costs, or who it belongs to.
2 If a picture has **labels**, it has arrows pointing to parts of it and text that explains what they are.

laboratory laboratories (noun)

a room or building where scientists work and do their experiments.

labour (noun)

1 hard work. **labour** (verb).
2 When a woman or female animal is **in labour**, she is giving birth.

lace (noun)

1 **Laces** are cords that you have to tie to fasten some shoes. **lace** (verb).
2 a very fine cloth, with a delicate pattern of holes and stitches. **lacy** (adjective).

lack lacking lacked

1 (verb) If someone or something **lacks** something, that thing is missing.
2 (noun) If there is a **lack of** something, there is not enough of it. *A lack of food.*

ladder (noun)

a wooden or metal frame with steps, which you can climb up and down.

ladle (noun)

a big, deep spoon with a long handle, which is used for serving food.

lady ladies (noun)

a polite word for a woman.

Spelling tip

lady → ladies

Words that end with a consonant and a 'y', such as "lady", remove the 'y' and add '-ies' in the plural: "ladies".

ladybird (noun)

a small, flying beetle, often with spots on its wings.

| eyed ladybird | twenty-two spot ladybird | seven spot ladybird |

three types of **ladybirds**

laid (verb)

the past tense of lay. *We laid flowers on the grave.*

lain (verb)

the past participle of lie. *The treasure had lain at the bottom of the ocean for many years before it was discovered.*

lake (noun)

a large area of fresh water, surrounded by land. *We went rowing on the lake.*

lamb (noun)

1 a young sheep.
2 the meat from a young sheep.

lamp (noun)

a light made of a bulb or flame with a shade or cover around it.

land landing landed

1 (verb) When an aircraft or a bird **lands**, it comes down to the ground from the air. *The aeroplane landed smoothly.*
2 (noun) **Land** is all the parts of the world that are not covered by water. *Reptiles lay their eggs on land.* **land** (adjective).

landing (noun)

1 the area of a house at the top of the stairs that leads to the upstairs rooms. *Please hoover the landing.*
2 arriving back on land from the air. *The landing was very smooth.*

landmark (noun)

an important building or object, that you can see from far away. *The cathedral is a good landmark where we can meet up later.*

A B C D E F G H I J K L M N O P Q R S T U V W X Y Z

landscape

1 *(noun)* what you can see when you look out over the area of land around you. *The landscape in Scotland is very beautiful.*
2 *(adjective)* If a picture is **landscape**, the long edges are on the top and bottom.

landslide *(noun)*

a sudden fall of earth and rocks down the side of a mountain or hill.

lane *(noun)*

1 a small, narrow road. *Our house is at the end of a winding lane.*
2 Roads, racetracks and swimming pools can be divided into different **lanes**. *I'm in lane eight for the 200m final.*

language *(noun)*

1 the set of words and written symbols that people in a country, or particular part of the world, use to communicate with each other. *Japanese is a difficult language for English people to learn.*
2 the way that you speak or express yourself. *I often find Mike's language a bit rude.*

lanky **lankier lankiest** *(adjective)*

very tall and thin. *After his growth spurt, my brother was very lanky.*

lantern *(noun)*

a light with a covering to protect the flame or bulb, and often a handle, so you can carry it or hang it up.

Chinese **lanterns** are hung in the streets at Chinese New Year.

lap

lapping lapped

1 *(noun)* the flat area that you have at the top of your legs when you sit down. *My cat loves sitting on my lap.*
2 *(noun)* the distance once round a race track. *The race is ten laps.*
3 *(verb)* When water **laps** against something, it moves gently against it.
4 *(verb)* When an animal **laps up** a drink, it flicks the liquid up into its mouth with its tongue.

laptop *(noun)*

a computer that doesn't weigh much and folds in half, so that it can be carried and used on your lap.

large **larger largest** *(adjective)*

big. *I have very large feet.*

larva **larvae** *(noun)*

a young insect that is at one of the stages between being an egg and an adult.

lasagna or lasagne *(noun)*

an Italian dish made of layers of pasta and meat or vegetables in a tomato sauce, with a cheese sauce on top. *See* pasta.

laser *(noun)*

1 a machine that makes a beam of light so powerful that it can cut through things, and can be used in some medical operations.
2 A **laser beam** is a strong beam of light, made by a laser.

lasso **lassos or lassoes** *(noun)*

a length of rope with a loop at one end, which can be thrown over an animal to catch it. **lasso** *(verb)*.

last **lasting lasted**

1 *(adjective)* the most recent one. *I bought a new school bag last week.*
2 *(adverb)* after everyone or everything else. *Alexandra always comes last in bike races.*
3 *(verb)* to go on for an amount of time. *The film lasts for two hours.*
4 If something happens **at last**, you have been waiting for it to happen for a long time. *At last our food arrived.*

latch **latches** *(noun)*

a lock or fastening for a door.

late **later latest** *(adjective)*

1 If you're **late**, you don't get somewhere at the time you're meant to. *Joe is always late for school.* **late** *(adverb)*.
2 the second part of a period of time. *We arrived in the late afternoon.*

lately *(adverb)*

not long ago, or recently. *Aunty Dot has been knitting me a lot of scarves lately.*

A B C D E F G H I J K L M N O P Q R S T U V W X Y Z

Latin and English

Over a quarter of English words, as well as our alphabet, come from Latin. Some words have been borrowed directly, such as "via" and "et cetera" (usually shortened to "etc."). Other words have come from Latin but changed over time, such as "pictura"→"picture". Many of our scientific and technological words have also been borrowed from Latin or invented using Latin words, including "apparatus", "data", and "experiment".

Latin *(noun)*
the language of the Ancient Romans.

laugh **laughing laughed** *(verb)*
to make a noise that shows you think something is funny, or that you are happy. **laugh** *(noun)*, **laughter** *(noun)*.

launch
launches launching launched *(verb)*
1 When a ship or a rocket **launches**, it starts off on its journey. **launch** *(noun)*.
2 to start something new. *Mum has launched a new business.*

laundry *(noun)*
clothes, towels, sheets, and so on, that are being washed or about to be washed.

lava *(noun)*
the extremely hot molten rock that comes out of a volcano when it erupts.

lavatory **lavatories** *(noun)*
a polite word for a **toilet**.

lavender *(noun)*
1 a plant with bluish-purple flowers and a nice smell.
2 a light purple colour.
lavender *(adjective)*.

law *(noun)*
1 a rule made by the government of a country that must be obeyed.
2 a general word for the set of laws in a country. *That's against the law.*

lawn *(noun)*
an area of grass, often surrounding a house.

lawyer *(noun)*
someone who advises people about the law, and speaks for them if they are on trial in a court.

lay **laying laid** *(verb)*
1 to put or place something somewhere. *I lay my school uniform out every Sunday night.*
2 Birds, fish and reptiles **lay** eggs.
3 If you **lay the table**, you get it ready for a meal.
4 the past tense of **lie**. *He lay in bed.*

layer *(noun)*
a single thickness of something, often on top of something else. *A layer of paint.*

layout *(noun)*
the way something is arranged.

lazy **lazier laziest** *(adjective)*
If you are **lazy**, you don't like working hard, or doing much at all. *Becca is too lazy to cook.* **lazily** *(adverb)*.

lead **leading led**
1 *(verb)* to be in charge of a group of people. *The conductor leads the orchestra.* **leadership** *(noun)*.
2 *(verb)* to show someone how to get somewhere, often by going first.
3 *(verb)* If you are **leading** a race, you are in front.
4 *(rhymes with "bead")* *(noun)* a long strip of material that you fasten to a dog's collar so that it can't run away.
5 *(rhymes with "bed")* *(noun)* a grey metal that is very heavy.

leader *(noun)*
1 the person in charge of a group of people, an organization, or a country. *The Chinese leader is visiting the UK.*
2 the person at the front of a group of people, especially in a race.

leaf **leaves** *(noun)*
one of the flat parts of a tree or a plant that grows on the end of a twig or stalk. Leaves are usually green.

leaflet (noun)
a printed piece of paper with information about something on it. *I picked up a leaflet about the local athletics club.*

league (noun)
a group of sports clubs that all play each other to see who will get the most points overall.

leak leaking leaked (verb)
1 If a container **leaks**, it lets some of whatever is inside it get out. *My water bottle always leaks.* **leak** (noun), **leaky** (adjective).
2 If a liquid or a gas **leaks**, it gets out of its container. *The apple juice leaked into my school bag.*

lean leaning leaned or leant (verb)
1 When you **lean on** something, you use it as a support. *Grandad leans on his walking stick.*
2 If something **leans**, it is not straight, but over to one side. **leaning** (adjective).

leap leaping leaped or leapt (verb)
to jump up into the air. *Stuart leapt over the fence when he saw the bull coming.*

Leaning Tower of Pisa, Italy

leap year (noun)
a year with 366, instead of the usual 365, days in it. Leap years happen every four years, and the extra day is added in February.

learn learning learned or learnt (verb)
to find out about something, or how to do it. *I learn so much in Mr Rowley's maths lessons.*

leash leashes (noun)
another word for **lead** (4).

least
1 (pronoun) the smallest amount. *I ate the most food, and Matt ate the least.*
2 (determiner) less than all the others. *I'm the least confident singer in the family.*
3 (adverb) less than all others. *Dan played least well.*
4 **at least** not less than, or as a minimum. *You must be at least 1.4m tall to go on the ride.*
5 You say **at least** in an unpleasant situation to suggest that it could have been worse. *Dad lost his wallet, but at least there was no money in it.*

leather (noun)
skin from animals that is specially treated to be made into things such as shoes and bags.

leave leaving left (verb)
1 to go away from somewhere. *We are leaving London in the morning.*
2 If you **leave** someone or something somewhere, you go away and they stay where they are. *I left my handbag in the shop.*
3 If you **leave someone or something behind**, you don't take them with you.
4 If you **leave someone or something out**, you don't include them.

lecture (noun)
1 a talk given to a class or an audience in order to teach them something. **lecturer** (noun), **lecture** (verb).
2 a telling-off that lasts for a long time. *Grandma gave me a lecture about turning the lights off.* **lecture** (verb).

led – lessen

led *(verb)*
the past tense of **lead**. *The waitress led us to our table.*

ledge *(noun)*
a narrow shelf on the outside of a window, or on a mountain.

leek *(noun)*
a long white and green vegetable, which tastes similar to an onion. *See* **vegetable**.

left
1 *(noun)* one of two possible sides, right or left. *Turn to the left.*
2 *(adjective)* on, towards, or to do with the left side of something. This page is on the left-hand side of the book. **left** *(adverb)*.
3 *(verb)* the past tense of **leave**. *We left the shop.*

leg *(noun)*
1 one of the two long parts of your body that start at your hips and end with your feet.
2 The **legs** of something, such as a table or chair, are the parts that rest on the floor and hold it up.

legend *(noun)*
1 an old story that many people know well, but which may not be true.
2 a very famous or well-known person. *Michael Jackson is a legend.* **legendary** *(adjective)*.

leggings *(noun)*
tight, soft trousers made of stretchy material.

lemon *(noun)*
a yellow fruit with thick skin and a sour taste.

lemon

lemonade *(noun)*
a drink made from lemons, sugar, and water, which can be fizzy or still.

lend **lending lent** *(verb)*
If you **lend** something to someone, you let them have it or use it for a while.

length *(noun)*
how long something is, or how long it lasts. *The length of the track is 400m.*

lengthen
lengthening lengthened *(verb)*
to make something longer. *I need to lengthen my trousers.*

lengthways *(adverb)*
in the direction of the longest side. *Fold the paper lengthways.*

lenient *(adjective)*
not very strict.

lens **lenses** *(noun)*
a piece of curved glass that makes light rays bend. Lenses are used in things such as glasses, cameras, and telescopes.

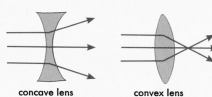

concave lens   convex lens

Different shaped **lenses** make light bend in different ways.

leopard *(noun)*
a large animal in the cat family with a spotty coat. Leopards live in forests and on grasslands in Africa and Asia.

less
1 *(adjective)* not as much. *It'll take less time to get there if we take this short cut.*
2 *(adverb)* not as much. *I like that hat less than this one.*
3 **-less** *(suffix)* without any. *"Flavourless" means "without any flavour".*

lessen **lessening lessened** *(verb)*
to get smaller in size, strength, importance, and so on. *Joe's fear lessened once his parents got home.*

lesson *(noun)*
a period of time in which you are taught something. *I look forward to science lessons.*

let letting let *(verb)*
1 to allow or permit something. *I never let my sister borrow my straighteners.*
2 If you **let** a house or a flat, you rent it to someone else.
3 If you **let go** of someone or something, you stop holding them.
4 If you **let someone down**, you disappoint them in some way.

letter *(noun)*
1 one of the signs in an alphabet, which you use when you write.
2 a written message that you send or receive through the post. *Our cousins always write thank you letters.*

lettuce *(noun)*
a plant with large leaves which are often eaten in salads. *See* vegetable.

level
1 *(adjective)* flat and smooth. *The icing on the cake was perfectly level.*
2 *(noun)* the height a liquid comes up to. *The flood water has reached a very dangerous level.*
3 *(adjective)* equal. *The scores were level at half-time.*
4 *(noun)* a standard. *Gemma has reached the highest level in t'ai chi.*

lever *(noun)*
a handle that you pull to make some machines work. *Don't pull that lever!*

liar *(noun)*
someone who says things that aren't true.

liberal *(adjective)*
1 open to new ideas, and willing to accept behaviour and beliefs that are different from your own.
2 In politics, **liberals** believe in equality and freedom for all.

liberty liberties *(noun)*
freedom. *Nelson Mandela waited 27 years for his liberty.*

librarian *(noun)*
someone who works in a library.

library
libraries *(noun)*
a place where you can borrow or read books, or use computers.

Remember that there are two 'r's in "library".

lick licking licked *(verb)*
to move your tongue over something. *My dog always licks my face in the morning.* **lick** *(noun).*

lice *(plural noun)*
small insects without wings, that can live in the hair or fur of people or animals. The singular of lice is "louse".

lid *(noun)*
the top of a bottle, container, or pen, that you can open or take off. *I've lost the lid of my water bottle.*

lie lying lied
1 *(verb)* to say things that aren't true.
2 *(noun)* something you say which is not true.

lie lying lay lain *(verb)*
1 to spread your body out on a flat surface. *Hannah lay on the floor and screamed.*
2 to be in a place. *Our house lies in a steep valley.*

life lives *(noun)*
the time a person or animal is alive for. *I've never seen a leopard before in all my life.*

Lie or lay?

"Lay" is the past tense of "lie":
"Today I am going to **lie** in bed all day."
"Yesterday I **lay** in bed all day."
"Lay" can also mean "to put or place something somewhere":
"I **lay** my clothes on the bed every night."

A B C D E F G H I J K L M N O P Q R S T U V W X Y Z

life cycle *(noun)*
all the different stages of a plant or an animal's life. *We're learning about the life cycle of a flower. See* **frog**.

lifeguard *(noun)*
someone who is trained to save people if they get into trouble in a swimming pool or the sea.

life jacket *(noun)*
a jacket without arms that is designed to keep you afloat in water.

lifestyle *(noun)*
the way someone lives their life, including the places they go and the things they buy. *Our neighbours' lifestyle is very luxurious.*

lifetime *(noun)*
the length of time a person or animal is alive for. *She achieved many great things in her lifetime.*

lift **lifting lifted**
1 *(verb)* to move something up to a higher place. *Dad lifted Sam onto his shoulders.*
2 *(noun)* a machine similar to a small room that takes people and things between the different floors of a building. *I never use the lift – I take the stairs.*
3 *(noun)* a ride in another person's car. *We gave Alfie a lift to the park.*

light **lighting lit**
1 *(verb)* to set fire to something. *Mum never lets us light the bonfire.*
2 *(verb)* If something **lights up** a place, it makes it brighter. *We'll use this torch to light up our den.*
3 *(noun)* brightness, for example from a lamp or fire. *The light coming from under the door kept me awake.*
4 *(noun)* something, such as a lamp, that creates brightness. *Turn the light on.*

light **lighter lightest** *(adjective)*
1 not very heavy. *This suitcase is so light.*
2 A **light** colour is pale and not dark.
3 A **light** place is not dark. *It's nice and light outside still.*

lighthouse *(noun)*
a building near or in the sea that shows a bright light, to guide ships and to warn of danger.

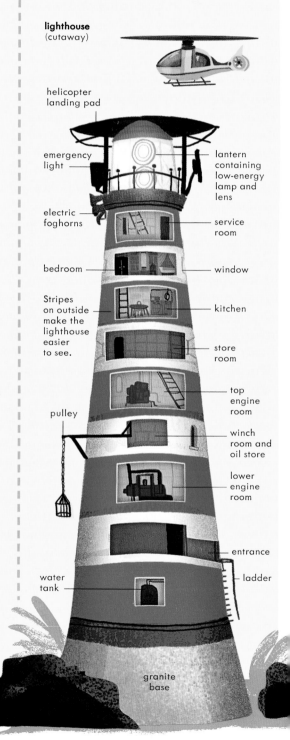

lighthouse (cutaway)

- helicopter landing pad
- emergency light
- electric foghorns
- bedroom
- Stripes on outside make the lighthouse easier to see.
- pulley
- water tank
- lantern containing low-energy lamp and lens
- service room
- window
- kitchen
- store room
- top engine room
- winch room and oil store
- lower engine room
- entrance
- ladder
- granite base

lightning *(noun)*
flashes of bright light in the sky during a thunderstorm.

light year *(noun)*
a unit for measuring distance in space. A light year is the distance that light travels in a year, equal to about 9.5 trillion kilometres (6 trillion miles).

like **liking liked** *(verb)*
If you **like** someone or something, you find them nice, or enjoy being with them.

like
1 *(preposition)* similar to. *Peter is like his brother.*
2 *(adjective)* If you ask what someone or something is **like**, you want a description of them. *What's your new teacher like?*
3 *(preposition)* such as. *I hate big cities, like London.*

likely **likelier likeliest** *(adjective)*
If something is **likely** to happen, it probably will. *I am likely to fall asleep.*

lily **lilies** *(noun)*
a sweet-smelling flower, shaped a little like a trumpet. *See* **flower**.

limb *(noun)*
an arm, a leg, or a branch of a tree.

lime *(noun)*
a small green fruit with a sour taste. *See* **fruit**.

limit **limiting limited**
1 *(noun)* a boundary, end, or edge of something. *There's a limit to my patience.*
2 *(verb)* to stop something going over, or getting higher than, a certain point. *I limit myself to two chocolate biscuits a day.* **limited** *(adjective)*.

limp **limping limped** *(verb)*
to walk unevenly. **limp** *(noun)*.

limp **limper limpest** *(adjective)*
loose and floppy. **limply** *(adverb)*.

line *(noun)*
1 a thin, straight mark, like this —— .
2 a queue of people.
3 If things or people are **in line**, they are all next to one another in a line.

link **linking linked**
1 *(verb)* to join things together. *We all linked arms and sang at the end of the assembly.*
2 *(noun)* something that joins people or things together. *The bridge across the sea is the link between the island and the mainland.*
3 *(noun)* one of the rings that make up a chain. *I broke a link in my necklace.*

lion *(noun)*
a large animal in the cat family. Male lions have lots of fur around their necks, called manes.

— mane

male lion

lioness
lionesses *(noun)*
a female lion.

lip *(noun)*
Your **lips** are the edges of your mouth.

liquid *(noun)*
something that can be poured. *Water is a liquid.* **liquid** *(adjective)*.

lisp *(noun)*
If someone speaks with a **lisp**, they can't say the letter 's' properly.

list *(noun)*
a line of words or numbers, often written one beneath the other. *I'm writing a shopping list for tomorrow.* **list** *(verb)*.

listen **listening listened** *(verb)*
If you **listen** to someone or something, you really concentrate on hearing them. *Jill loves listening to the birds singing in the morning.*

literacy *(noun)*
reading and writing skills.

literate *(adjective)*
able to read and write.

literature *(noun)*
pieces of writing, including novels, plays, and poetry. *My big sister is studying English Literature at university.*

litmus paper *(noun)*
a piece of paper which can be dipped into a liquid to show whether the liquid is an acid or an alkali. If the liquid is an acid, the paper turns red, and if it is an alkali, it turns blue.

litre *(noun)*
a unit for measuring liquid. A litre contains 1,000 millilitres, or around 1.8 pints.

litter *(noun)*
1 rubbish that people leave on the ground, instead of in a bin. *There is far too much litter in town.* **litter** *(verb)*.
2 puppies, kittens, pigs or other animals born at the same time, with the same mother. *Our cat has had her third litter.*

little **littler littlest** *(adjective)*
1 small. *Becky has such little feet.*
2 not much. *We have very little time.*

live **living lived**
1 *(rhymes with "give") (verb)* to be alive. *Some tortoises live for many years.*
2 *(rhymes with "give") (verb)* to have a home somewhere. *We live on a boat.*
3 *(rhymes with "hive") (adjective)* living. *I wish I could see a live dinosaur.*
4 *(rhymes with "hive") (adjective)* now, as it's happening. *I love to see live music.*

lively **livelier liveliest** *(adjective)*
If you are **lively**, you have lots of energy and enthusiasm. *Harpreet is always lively in the mornings.*

liver *(noun)*
one of your organs. Your liver's job is to clean your blood. *See* **organ**.

living
1 *(adjective)* alive now. *He is our greatest living artist.*
2 *(noun)* Your **living** is the money you are paid for working.
3 What you **do for a living** is your job.
4 If you **earn a living**, you make enough money to support yourself.

living room *(noun)*
the room in a house where you sit and relax, and perhaps watch television.

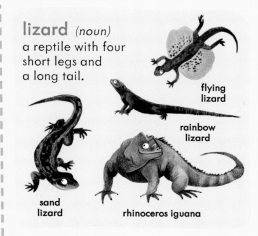

lizard *(noun)*
a reptile with four short legs and a long tail.

flying lizard

rainbow lizard

sand lizard

rhinoceros iguana

some different kinds of **lizards**

llama *(noun)*
an animal in the camel family, which has shaggy hair and lives in South America. Llamas are kept by humans for transporting things, and for their meat.

load **loading loaded**
1 *(noun)* something heavy that is being carried. *All those bags look like too heavy a load for that donkey.*
2 *(verb)* to put things onto or into something. *We loaded the luggage into the boot.*

loaf **loaves** *(noun)*
bread baked into a particular shape.

loan **loaning loaned**
1 *(noun)* an amount of money that you borrow.
2 *(verb)* If you **loan** something, you lend it to someone else. *I loaned Caitlin my umbrella to walk home.*

loathe **loathing loathed** *(verb)*
to hate someone or something very much. *I loathe tidying my room.*

lobster *(noun)*
a sea animal with ten legs and a hard shell, which can be eaten. Lobsters turn red when cooked.

common lobster

local *(adjective)*
near where you live. **locally** *(adverb)*.

location *(noun)*
the place or position of something. *This is a great location for a film.*

locate **locating located** *(verb)*
to find the exact place or position of something. **located** *(adjective)*.

lock **locking locked**
1 *(noun)* the part of a door, case or box that you can only open and close with a key or code.
2 *(verb)* If you **lock** something, it can only be opened with a key, or a code or password.

lodge **lodging lodged** *(verb)*
If you **lodge** with someone, you pay money to live in their house. *We have someone lodging in our spare room for the summer.* **lodger** *(noun)*.

loft *(noun)*
the space under the roof of a house that can be used for storing things or made into a room.

log *(noun)*
a big piece of wood that people often burn on fires.

logic *(noun)*
a sensible, careful way of explaining things, or working things out. **logical** *(adjective)*, **logically** *(adverb)*.

logo *(noun)*
a sign or symbol used by a company to make people remember their product.

lonely **lonelier loneliest** *(adjective)*
If you are **lonely**, you are on your own, and miss being with other people. **loneliness** *(noun)*.

long **longer longest** *(adjective)*
1 lasting for a lot of time. *That was a very long speech.*
2 going on for a great distance. *We went on a long walk yesterday.*
3 from one end to the other. *That cow's tail was nearly a metre long.*

long **longing longed** *(verb)*
If you **long for** something, you want it very much. *Will longs for success.* **longing** *(noun)*.

look **looking looked** *(verb)*
1 to use your eyes to see something. *Look at him go!* **look** *(noun)*.
2 to appear or seem. *You look really tired.* **look** *(noun)*.
3 If you **look after** someone, you care for them.
4 When you **look forward to** something, you can't wait for it to happen. *I am really looking forward to seeing my grandparents this weekend.*

loop *(noun)*
a curve or circle made from something that bends round and crosses over itself. *There were a lot of loops in that roller coaster.* **loop** *(verb)*, **looped** *(adjective)*.

loose **looser loosest** *(adjective)*
1 not tight, but baggy. *These trousers are loose.* **loosely** *(adverb)*, **loosen** *(verb)*.
2 not strong, or not firm. *That knot is loose.* **loosely** *(adverb)*, **loosen** *(verb)*.

lorry **lorries** *(noun)*
a large, powerful truck that can carry heavy loads.

lose **losing lost** *(verb)*
1 If you **lose** something, you can't find it or don't have it any more. *Bill lost most of his hair at 20.*
2 When you **lose** a competition or a match, you are not the winner of it. **loser** *(noun)*.
3 If you **get lost**, you don't know where you are. *We got lost trying to find the shop exit.* **lost** *(adjective)*.

Spelling tip

lose
loose

It's easy to mix up the word "lose" (to be unable to find something) with the word "loose" (the opposite of "tight"). Check your spelling if you are unsure.

loss **losses** *(noun)*
1 something you have lost.
2 If a business **makes a loss**, it doesn't make enough money to cover its costs.

lot *(noun)*
a large amount or number. *Uncle Anthony ate a lot of burgers.*

lottery **lotteries** *(noun)*
a competition in which people buy a numbered ticket, hoping that their numbers will be chosen and they will win a prize.

loud **louder loudest** *(adjective)*
noisy. *That music is far too loud!*

lounge **lounging lounged**
1 *(noun)* a living room, where people relax. *Let's sit in the lounge.*
2 *(verb)* to relax and do very little.

love **loving loved** *(verb)*
If you **love** someone or something, you really care about them. **love** *(noun)*.

lovely **lovelier loveliest** *(adjective)*
1 If someone is **lovely**, they are beautiful to look at or have a very nice personality. **loveliness** *(noun)*.
2 very nice. *This ice cream is lovely.*

low **lower lowest** *(adjective)*
1 not high. *This chair is too low.*
2 deep. *Mr Reid has a very low voice.*
3 **Low tide** is the time when the sea is furthest down the beach.
4 If you are feeling **low**, you are sad or lacking in energy.

lower **lowering lowered** *(verb)*
If you **lower** something, you move it downwards. *We lowered the flag.*

loyal *(adjective)*
If you are **loyal**, you stand by your friends and help them whenever they need you. *Daisy is always loyal, and stands up for me.* **loyalty** *(noun)*, **loyally** *(adverb)*.

luck *(noun)*
things that happen to someone by chance, without any warning. Luck can be good or bad.

lucky **luckier luckiest** *(adjective)*
If you are **lucky**, good things happen to you. **luckily** *(adverb)*.

These are some **lucky** charms, which are believed to bring good luck.

horseshoe **maneki-neko** **four-leaf clover**
(England)   (Japan)   (Ireland)

luggage *(noun)*
suitcases and bags that you take with you on a journey.

lullaby **lullabies** *(noun)*
a song you sing to a baby or small child, to help them fall asleep.

lump *(noun)*
1 a solid piece of something. *A lump of clay.* **lumpy** *(adjective)*.
2 a swollen bump that you may get on a part of your body if you have knocked or hurt it.

lunar *(adjective)*
to do with the Moon.

lunch *(noun)*
the meal you eat in the middle of the day.

lung *(noun)*
one of two bag-like organs inside your chest, which fill with air when you breathe in, and supply oxygen to your body. *See* **organ**.

lurk **lurking lurked** *(verb)*
to hide and wait for someone or something.

luxury **luxuries** *(noun)*
an expensive thing that you don't need, but which is a real treat to have. *These new shoes are a luxury.* **luxurious** *(adjective)*, **luxuriously** *(adverb)*.

lyrics *(plural noun)*
the words of a song.

Mm

machine (noun)
a man-made thing, usually powered by an engine or by electricity, which does a particular job. *Dad has bought himself a new bread-making machine.*

machinery (noun)
machines in general, or a number of machines working together. *Farm machinery.*

mad **madder maddest** (adjective)
1 an unkind way of saying that someone has a mental health problem.
2 crazy or unreasonable. *Rosie's mum said she was mad to go out without a coat.*
3 another word for **angry**, mostly used in the US. *Mr Shaw got really mad at the class.*
4 If you are **mad about** something, you are very keen on it. *Tilly is mad about horses.* **madly** (adverb).

madam (noun)
a very polite and formal way of speaking to a woman. *Excuse me, madam, are you ready to order?*

magazine (noun)
a thin book that is published regularly, which contains articles, photographs, advertisements, and so on. Magazines can also be published online.

maggot (noun)
the small, whitish larva of some flies, such as a housefly.

magic (noun)
1 the power to make impossible and amazing things happen. *Witches and wizards can do magic in stories.* **magical** (adjective), **magically** (adverb).
2 tricks that seem like magic, performed by an entertainer. *I let Rory practise his magic on me.* **magic** (adjective), **magician** (noun).

magnet (noun)
a piece of metal which attracts iron and steel. **magnetic** (adjective).

unlike poles attract

like poles repel

All **magnets** have a north and a south pole.

magnificent (adjective)
wonderful or impressive. *A magnificent performance.* **magnificently** (adverb).

magnify **magnifies magnifying magnified** (verb)
to make something bigger, or make something look bigger.

magnifying glass (noun)
a tool with a handle and a lens that you use to look at something very small, or in close detail.

magpie (noun)
a small bird of the crow family.

European magpie

maid (noun)
a woman whose job is to clean a house or hotel, or a female servant.

mail (noun)
1 letters and parcels, or anything sent in the post. *We get our mail at 8.30 a.m.*
2 another word for **email**.

main (adjective)
most important. *The main ingredient in toffee is sugar.*

mainland (noun)
the largest part of a country, not including any islands around it.

mainly (adverb)
1 most importantly. *I mainly like cricket.*
2 most often, or usually. *Rob mainly wears jeans.*
3 almost completely. *I liked the start of the film, but it was mainly rubbish.*

maintain
maintaining maintained *(verb)*
1 to look after something and keep it working well. *Steve maintains my computer for me.* **maintenance** *(noun)*.
2 to claim something. *Yasmin maintains she saw Tom leaving later that evening.*

maize *(noun)*
a tall plant, originally from Mexico, which produces sweetcorn.

majesty *(noun)*
You say **Your Majesty** when you are talking to a king or queen.

major *(adjective)*
1 very important or serious. *Finishing this painting will be a major task.*
2 Music that is in a **major key** sounds cheerful and positive. *This song is in G major.*

majority **majorities** *(noun)*
the biggest part or greatest number. *The majority of children on the school trip behaved very well.*

make **making made**
1 *(verb)* to create or do something. *Jan has made you a birthday cake. Stefan made a rude comment about my drawing.*
2 *(verb)* to cause something to happen or develop. *Going past the dentist made Alpesh nervous.*
3 *(verb)* to force someone or something to do something. *You can't make me like broccoli.*
4 *(noun)* a brand or product name. *How many different makes of car can you spot?*
5 If you **make do**, you manage with what is available.
6 If you **make something up**, such as an excuse or a story, you invent it using your imagination.

make-up *(noun)*
coloured liquids and powders people put on their face, to look nice or to change their appearance in plays and films.

traditional Japanese theatre **make-up**

male *(noun)*
a man, boy, or masculine animal. **male** *(adjective)*.

malicious *(mal-**ish**-us) (adjective)*
Something that is **malicious** is unkind and meant to do harm. *There is too much malicious gossip in this school.* **malice** *(noun)*, **maliciously** *(adverb)*.

mall *(noun)*
a collection of shops in a single large building. This word is more commonly used in the US.

mammal *(noun)*
a type of animal. Most female mammals give birth to live babies, and they all feed them with their own milk.

Cats are **mammals** and give birth to kittens.

mammoth
1 *(noun)* a very large animal that lived long ago. It was similar to an elephant but covered in fur, with long, curved tusks. *See **Ice age**.*
2 *(adjective)* enormous. *That is a mammoth burger.*

man **men** *(noun)*
1 a grown-up male human.
2 **Man** is sometimes used to mean all of mankind or humankind.

manage
managing managed *(verb)*
1 to be in charge of a business, a group of people, or something that is happening. *I will manage the next project.* **management** *(noun)*.
2 to be able to do something without help. *Can you manage that heavy bag?*

manager *(noun)*
someone who is in charge of other people. *A football manager.*

mane *(noun)*
the thick hair on a horse's or a male lion's head and neck. *See **lion**.*

manga *(noun)*
a popular cartoon style from Japan.

mangle mangling mangled (verb)
to crush and twist something.
mangled (adjective).

mango mangos or **mangoes** (noun)
a tropical fruit with sweet orange flesh
and a big, flat stone inside. *See* fruit.

manhole (noun)
an opening in the surface of a road
that allows access to drains, pipes
or cables below.

maniac (**may**-nee-ak) (noun)
someone whose behaviour is very wild,
violent, and dangerous. *That man was
driving like a maniac.*

manipulate
manipulating manipulated (verb)
1 to handle something complicated
with skill and care.
2 to persuade people to do what you
want, or make things turn out well for
yourself. **manipulative** (adjective).

mankind (noun)
see humankind.

manner
1 (noun) a way or style. *The car rattled
in a worrying manner.*
2 (noun) a way of behaving. *Alfie has
a pleasant, friendly manner.*
3 manners (plural noun) the way you
behave, especially when talking to
people or eating. *It's bad manners
to talk with your mouth full.*

manor (noun)
a large, old country house surrounded
by land.

mansion (noun)
a very large, impressive house.

mantelpiece (noun)
the shelf above a fireplace.

manual
1 (adjective) worked or done by hand.
*We have to use the manual controls
on the side of the television. Manual
labour.* **manually** (adverb).
2 (noun) a handbook which tells you
how to make or work something.

manufacture
manufacturing manufactured (verb)
to make something using machinery,
usually in a factory. **manufacturer**
(noun), **manufacturing** (noun).

many more most (adjective)
a large number of people or things.
Many of the guests brought presents.

Maori Maori or **Maoris** (noun)
one of the native people of New
Zealand (which they call Aotearoa),
who have lived there since before the
Europeans arrived. **Maori** (adjective).

map (noun)
a detailed plan of an area, with symbols
to show things such as roads and
buildings. Maps help you to find
your way around.

marathon (noun)
a long-distance race run over 26.2 miles
or 46.2 kilometres.

Word origin   marathon

The word "marathon" comes from the
Ancient Greek story of Pheidippides.
Pheidippides was a messenger who
ran over 26 miles from Marathon to
Athens, in Greece, to tell people that
the Greek army had won the Battle
of Marathon against the Persians.

marble (noun)
1 a type of hard white or coloured
stone, often used for sculptures or
for decoration in buildings.
2 a small, coloured glass ball, used
for playing games.

march
marches marching marched (verb)
1 to walk with regular, rhythmic steps,
like soldiers.
2 to walk along roads in a large group
to protest against something. *Teachers
are marching against pay cuts.*

a b c d e f g h i j k l m n o p q r s t u v w x y z

Word origin — March

The word "March" comes from the Latin "Martius". It was named after Mars, the Roman god of war. His month marked the beginning of the season for warfare in Roman times.

March *(noun)*
the third month of the year.

mare *(noun)*
a grown-up female horse.

margarine *(noun)*
a spread made from vegetable oils that you can use instead of butter.

margin *(noun)*
the blank space at the side of a page, around the text. *The teacher told me off for doodling in the margin of my work.*

marine *(adjective)*
to do with the sea. *Marine biology is the study of animals and plants that live in the sea.*

mark marking marked
1 *(verb)* to make a sign on something. *Sam marked all his favourite footballers in the magazine.*
2 *(verb)* to check and comment on a piece of school work or homework, or an exam. **mark** *(noun)*.
3 *(noun)* a piece of dirt or a stain on something. *There's a mark on my jeans.*

market *(noun)*
a place where you can buy things such as food, clothes or gifts from stalls. *We bought lots of fresh fruit at the market.*

marmalade *(noun)*
a food similar to jam, made from oranges or other citrus fruits.

maroon *(noun)*
a dark purplish-red colour.
maroon *(adjective)*.

marquee *(mar-**kee**) (noun)*
a very large tent used for big events such as weddings or parties.

marriage *(noun)*
1 a ceremony where two people make an official promise to be partners for life.
2 the state of being married. *Mum and Dad will celebrate 25 years of marriage next week.*

married *(adjective)*
Someone who is **married** has a husband or wife.

marrow *(noun)*
1 a large green vegetable with a long, rounded shape.
2 the soft substance found inside bones.

marry
marries marrying married *(verb)*
1 If you **marry** or **get married**, you become someone's husband or wife in a special ceremony. *Jon and Chris got married last weekend.*
2 to perform the marriage ceremony for a couple.

marsh marshes *(noun)*
an area of land that is always swampy and wet.

marsupial
*(mar-**soo**-pee-al)*
(noun)
an animal such as a koala that carries its babies in a pouch on the front of its body.

koala and baby

marvellous *(adjective)*
amazing or wonderful. *The decorations at the party were marvellous.*

mascara *(noun)*
make-up used to make eyelashes look longer, darker, and thicker.

mascot *(noun)*
something that is supposed to bring good luck. *Our team's mascot is a teddy bear called Bruno.*

masculine *(adjective)*
male, or having a style or features that are supposed to be typical of men. *Nia said I have very masculine handwriting.*

mask (noun)
something you can wear over your face to hide, disguise or protect it. *People wear decorated masks during the Carnival of Venice.*

Venetian mask

mass **masses**
1 (noun) a large number of people or things together. *A mass of old papers.*
2 Mass (noun) the service of Communion in the Catholic church.
3 mass-produced (adjective) If something is **mass-produced**, it is made in large numbers, usually by machines.

massage (*mass*-arj)
massaging massaged (verb)
to rub someone's body to loosen their muscles and get rid of pain, or to help them relax. **massage** (noun).

massive (adjective)
huge and bulky. *That is a massive truck.*
massively (adverb).

mast (noun)
1 the upright pole on a boat that supports its sails.
2 a tall metal structure used to send out radio, television or phone signals.

masterpiece (noun)
a brilliant work of art, such as a book, film, painting, or piece of music.

mat (noun)
1 a small carpet or rug.
2 a piece of wood, plastic or cloth which protects a table from stains or burns.

match **matches matching matched**
1 (noun) a thin stick of wood with chemicals on one end, which catches fire when you rub it against the side of a matchbox. *Light a match.*
2 (noun) a contest between two people or teams in sports such as football, cricket, or boxing.
3 (verb) to look exactly the same, or be the same colour or pattern.
4 (verb) to group together things which look the same or belong together.

mate (noun)
1 An animal's **mate** is the partner it has babies with.
2 a friendly word for a friend.

material (noun)
1 another word for **fabric**. *Maddie's dress was made from a light, silky material.*
2 the things you need to make or do something, such as art materials. *Alfie is collecting material for a presentation on his home town.*

materialistic (adjective)
If someone is **materialistic**, they care most about money and possessions.

maternal (adjective)
to do with mothers, or acting or feeling like a mother. *Sarah is very maternal towards her new baby brother.*

maternity (adjective)
to do with having a baby. *Aunt Laura has had to buy maternity clothes to fit over her tummy.* **maternity** (noun).

mathematics or **maths** (noun)
the study of numbers, measurement, and shapes. *I'm slowly improving at maths.* **mathematical** (adjective).

matinée or **matinee** (noun)
an afternoon performance of a play or show.

matt (adjective)
not shiny. *Matt paint.*

matter **mattering mattered**
1 (verb) to be important. *It doesn't matter if we're a little bit late.*
2 (noun) something important, or something that needs to be dealt with. *Family matters.*
3 If you ask someone, **"What's the matter?"** you want to know what's wrong.

mattress **mattresses** (noun)
a soft, thick rectangular pad that you sleep on, usually on a bed.

mature (adjective)
fully grown-up or ripe. *Ethan is very mature for his age.* **mature** (verb).

a b c d e f g h i j k l m n o p q r s t u v w x y z

Spelling tip

maximize
maximise

Some words, like "maximize", can be spelt '-ise' or '-ize'. When you are writing, make sure that you stick to the same ending rather than switching between the two.

maximize or **maximise**
maximizing maximized *(verb)*
1 to make something as big as possible. *To maximize our chances of getting in, we need to arrive early.*
2 to make a window take up the full space of a computer screen.

maximum *(noun)*
the most possible. *The maximum I'll pay for my new school bag is £20.*
maximum *(adjective).*

may *(verb)*
1 If something **may** happen, it is possible, but not certain. *Claire may go to the concert, but she isn't sure.*
2 a polite way of asking if you can do or have something. *May I have some more pasta?*
3 a way of saying that someone is allowed to do something. *You may leave the room now.*

May *(noun)*
the fifth month of the year.

maybe *(adverb)*
possibly, or perhaps. *"Do you think they'll win?" "Maybe."*

mayhem *(noun)*
a situation of extreme confusion or mess. *There was mayhem at the zoo when the elephant escaped.*

mayonnaise *(noun)*
a cold, creamy sauce made with eggs, vinegar, and oil.

mayor *(noun)*
the most important person on a town or city council.

maze *(noun)*
a puzzle in which you have to find the right route along twisted or branching paths. A maze can be on paper, on a screen, or made of hedges or walls.

a hedge **maze** seen from above

MB *(abbreviation)*
see megabyte.

meadow *(noun)*
a field full of grass and wild flowers, where animals are often kept.

meal *(noun)*
food that is eaten at a particular time of day. *People say that breakfast is the most important meal of the day.*

mean meaning meant *(verb)*
1 to be a way of saying something, in different words or a foreign language. *"École" means "school" in French.*
2 to intend or to want something to happen. *Kamil meant to call his granny, but he dialled the wrong number.*
3 to be serious when you say something. *When Dad says it's bedtime, he really means it.*

mean meaner meanest *(adjective)*
unkind, unfair, or not generous.

mean *(noun)*
the average of a group of numbers, that you can work out by adding them together and then dividing the total by how many numbers there are. *The mean of 6, 7 and 11 is 8.*

meaning *(noun)*
what something means, or its sense. *Some English words, like "tear", have more than one meaning.*

meantime *(noun)*
the time in between. *Lily waited for her mum to get back, and did her homework in the meantime.*

meanwhile *(adverb)*
at the same time. *Ben went out to play football; meanwhile, his brother cooked dinner.*

measles *(noun)*
an infectious disease which causes a fever and a rash.

measure
measuring measured *(verb)*
to find the size, volume or speed of something. **measure** *(noun),* **measurement** *(noun).*

meat *(noun)*
the flesh of an animal, when it is used for food. *Poppy doesn't eat meat.* **meaty** *(adjective).*

mechanic *(noun)*
someone whose job is to look after and repair machines, especially engines.

mechanical *(adjective)*
worked by a machine or by moving parts, such as clockwork.

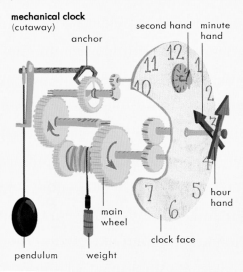

mechanical clock
(cutaway)
anchor
second hand   minute hand
main wheel
clock face
pendulum   weight
hour hand

medal *(noun)*
a small piece of metal given as a prize, or as a reward for doing something very brave. *A gold medal.*

media *(plural noun)*
all the ways of communicating news and opinions, such as newspapers, radio, television, and websites.

mediaeval *(adjective)*
see **medieval**.

median *(noun)*
the number or amount that is found in the middle of a range. *The median of the numbers 1 to 5 is 3.*

medical
1 *(adjective)* to do with medicine and health. *Medical advice.*
2 *(noun)* a thorough health check.

medicine *(noun)*
1 something that you take to help you recover from an illness, especially a liquid that you drink. **medicinal** *(adjective).*
2 the science that deals with preventing, curing and treating diseases and injuries.

medieval *or* **mediaeval** *(adjective)*
to do with the Middle Ages, the period between AD1000 and AD1500.

mediocre *(adjective)*
of only average or poor quality, or not good enough. **mediocrity** *(noun).*

meditate
meditating meditated *(verb)*
to spend time thinking quietly and deeply, especially as a way of being calm and relaxed, or as a religious exercise. **meditation** *(noun).*

medium
1 *(adjective)* in the middle, not too little or too much. *I am medium height.*
2 *(noun)* a way of expressing or communicating something. *The medium of television.*

meek meeker meekest *(adjective)*
quiet and obedient. **meekness** *(noun).*

a b c d e f g h i j k l **m** n o p q r s t u v w x y z

Spelling tip

meat
meet

Be careful not to mix up the word "meat", meaning "animal flesh that you eat", with the word "meet", meaning "to get together". Remember that "m**eat**" is what you "**eat**".

meet **meeting met** *(verb)*
1 to get to know someone for the first time. *George's parents met at university.*
2 to see someone by chance. *I met Milly coming back from the supermarket.*
3 to see someone because you have arranged to see them. *Let's meet at six.*
4 to come together. *The two roads meet at the top of the hill.*

meeting *(noun)*
a time when people come together to talk about something, especially at work.

megabyte *(noun)*
a measurement of data, for example to show how large a computer file is. It is often shortened to "MB".

mellow
mellower mellowest *(adjective)*
gentle, mild, or relaxed. *This tea has a mellow taste.* **mellow** *(verb)*.

melody **melodies** *(noun)*
a tune, or the main tune in a piece of music. *The melody is very simple.* **melodious** *(adjective)*.

melon *(noun)*
a large fruit with sweet, juicy flesh and lots of seeds. See **fruit**.

melt **melting melted** *(verb)*
When something **melts**, it turns from a solid to a liquid because it has been heated. *Has the ice melted?*

member *(noun)*
someone who belongs to a group, club, or family. *I am a member of a hockey team.* **membership** *(noun)*.

Member of Parliament
or **MP** *(noun)*
someone who is chosen to represent the people in an area of a country in a government.

memorable *(adjective)*
easily remembered, or worth remembering. **memorably** *(adverb)*.

memorize or **memorise**
memorizing memorized *(verb)*
to learn something by heart.

memory **memories** *(noun)*
1 the ability to remember things, or the part of your mind that stores the things you remember. *My gran's memory is getting worse, so she has to write things down.*
2 something that you remember. *Huw doesn't have many memories of the house where he was born.*
3 the part of a computer that stores information.
4 memory stick *(noun)* a small device that can be plugged into a computer, on which files and documents can be saved.

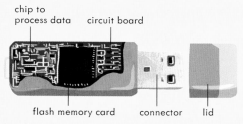

chip to process data   circuit board

flash memory card   connector   lid

inside a **memory stick**

menace *(noun)*
a serious threat or danger. *Global warming is a menace to our planet.* **menacing** *(adjective)*.

mend **mending mended** *(verb)*
to repair something.

mental *(adjective)*
1 to do with the mind. **mentally** *(adverb)*.
2 done in your head, not written down. *Mental maths.*
3 a friendly way of saying crazy or very angry. *Mum went mental when we got home two hours late.*

mention

mentioning mentioned *(verb)*
When you **mention** something, you talk about it, but only for a short time. *Pam mentioned her new car.* **mention** *(noun)*.

menu *(noun)*

1 a list of the dishes and drinks available at a café or restaurant.
2 a list of choices in a computer program.

mercury *(noun)*

a silvery, liquid metal that is poisonous.

mercy *(noun)*

If you show **mercy**, you decide not to punish or harm someone. **merciful** *(adjective)*, **mercifully** *(adverb)*.

merely *(adverb)*

only. *I merely asked whether Ali had finished yet.*

merit *(noun)*

If something has **merit**, it is good or deserves praise. **merit** *(verb)*.

mermaid *(noun)*

a creature from stories, with a woman's head and body and a fish's tail.

merry **merrier merriest** *(adjective)*

very cheerful and friendly.

mess **messing messed**

1 *(noun)* a dirty or untidy thing or state. *The kitchen is a mess.* **messy** *(adjective)*, **messily** *(adverb)*.
2 *(verb)* If you **mess about** or **mess around**, you are not serious and behave in a silly way.
3 mess up *(verb)* to make a mistake.

message **messaging messaged**

1 *(noun)* a way of communicating with someone when you can't speak to them in person. *Arthur left a message to say he'd gone home early.*
2 *(verb)* to send someone a message on a computer or mobile phone using a program or app. *I'll message you when I'm ready to leave.*

messenger *(noun)*

a person, computer program or app that delivers a message.

metal *(noun)*

a substance that is usually hard and can be worked into different shapes. Most metals are mined from the ground. Gold, silver, copper, iron, lead and tin are all metals.

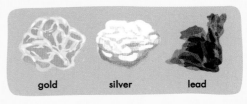

gold   silver   lead

three **metals** in their natural forms

metaphor *(noun)*

a way of describing something by saying that it is something else, for example, "You are my sunshine". **metaphorical** *(adjective)*, **metaphorically** *(adverb)*.

meteor *(noun)*

a piece of metal or rock in space, which burns up if it passes through the Earth's atmosphere.

meteorite *(noun)*

a piece of metal or rock from space which has passed through the Earth's atmosphere without burning up, and landed on the Earth's surface.

meter *(noun)*

1 a device which counts or measures something. *An electricity meter shows how much electricity you use at home.*
2 the US spelling of **metre**.

method *(noun)*

a way of doing something. *Rajesh taught me a very useful method for adding fractions.*

methodical *(adjective)*

careful, logical, and well-organized. **methodically** *(adverb)*.

metre *(noun)*

a measurement of length. There are 100 centimetres in a metre and 1,000 metres in a kilometre.

metric *(adjective)*

The **metric system** of measuring is based on metres, litres, and kilograms.

The prefix 'micro-'

microchip

microscope

microscopic

When you see the prefix 'micro-' before a word, that word will often have something to do with being very small. It comes from the Greek word "mikros", meaning "small".

microchip *(noun)*
a small piece of silicon with electronic circuits on it, used in computers and for identification, such as for pets, and on passports and credit cards.

microphone *(noun)*
an electronic device that picks up sound, either to record it or to make it louder. *Cara's microphone wasn't working, so no-one could hear her singing.*

microscope *(noun)*
a scientific instrument that makes tiny objects look much bigger.

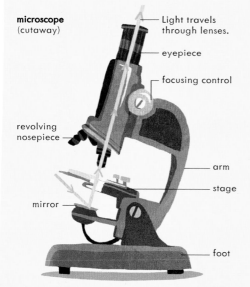

microscope (cutaway)

Light travels through lenses.

eyepiece

focusing control

revolving nosepiece

arm

stage

mirror

foot

microscopic *(adjective)*
so small that it can only be seen through a microscope.

microwave *(noun)*
a small oven that cooks food quickly. **microwave** *(verb)*.

midday *(noun)*
twelve o'clock in the middle of the day. Also called "noon". **midday** *(adjective)*.

middle *(noun)*
the centre, or near the centre of an area, a range, or a group. **middle** *(adjective)*.

middle-aged *(adjective)*
If someone is **middle-aged**, they are between about 40 and 60 years old.

Middle Ages *(noun)*
the period of European history between about AD1000 and AD1500.

Middle East *(noun)*
the part of western Asia between the Mediterranean Sea and India, including most Arabic-speaking countries and Israel. **Middle Eastern** *(adjective)*.

midnight *(noun)*
twelve o'clock in the middle of the night. **midnight** *(adjective)*.

midwife **midwives** *(noun)*
a nurse who is specially trained to help women have their babies.

might *(verb)*
If something **might** happen, it's possible that it will happen.

migraine *(noun)*
a very bad headache which can make you feel sick.

migrate **migrating migrated** *(verb)*
1 to move from one place to another during a certain season. *Swallows migrate to Europe from Africa every summer.* **migration** *(noun)*.
2 to move to another place to live. **migration** *(noun)*.

mild **milder mildest** *(adjective)*
not strong or severe. *A mild flavour.* **mildness** *(noun)*, **mildly** *(adverb)*.

mile *(noun)*
a measure of distance, equal to about 1.6 kilometres.

military *(adjective)*
to do with soldiers and the armed forces.
military *(noun)*.

milk milking milked
1 *(noun)* a white drink that comes
from cows, goats, or sheep.
2 *(noun)* the liquid that female mammals
feed to their young.
3 *(verb)* to get milk from cows, sheep,
or goats.

mill *(noun)*
1 a piece of machinery used for grinding
things. *A pepper mill.*
2 a building that contains or contained
a mill. *This house was once a flour mill.*

millennium millennia *(noun)*
1 a thousand years.
2 the calendar date of AD2000.

millimetre *(noun)*
a very small unit of measurement, equal
to 0.1 centimetre. There are 1,000
millimetres in a metre.

million *(noun)*
a thousand thousand, or 1,000,000.

millionaire *(noun)*
a very rich person.

mime miming mimed *(verb)*
to say or show something using only
gestures and movement. **mime** *(noun)*.

mimic mimicking mimicked *(verb)*
to imitate a noise or a person's way
of speaking or behaving. *The parrot
mimicked the sound of the doorbell.*

minaret *(noun)*
the tall, pointed tower of a mosque,
from which the call to prayer is made
or broadcast.

mince mincing minced *(verb)*
to chop meat or vegetables into very
small pieces, often using a machine
called a mincer. **mince** *(noun)*.

mincemeat *(noun)*
a sticky, spiced mixture of dried fruit
that is used in baking, especially
around Christmas.

mind minding minded
1 *(verb)* to be concerned or unhappy
about something. *Do you mind sharing
a bathroom with your brother?*
2 *(verb)* to look after something.
Danny is minding my bike for me.
3 *(verb)* to watch out for something.
Mind the step.
4 *(noun)* the part of you that thinks,
and feels emotions. *I can see the
place in my mind but I can't remember
its name.*
5 If you have or keep someone or
something **in mind**, you remember and
think about them. *It's important to keep
in mind the other people on the slope
when you are skiing.*
6 If you **make up your mind**, you decide.
*I couldn't make up my mind about what
to have for dinner.*
7 If you tell someone to **mind out** for
something, you are warning them to be
careful of it. *Mind out for ice on the roads.*
8 Something that **takes your mind off**
something else distracts you from it.
*I sang a song to take my mind off the
pain in my stomach.*

mine mining mined
1 *(verb)* to take coal, metals, precious
stones or other substances out of the
ground. *I am worried about the effect
that mining for copper will have on
the environment here.* **mine** *(noun)*,
miner *(noun)*, **mining** *(noun)*.
2 *(pronoun)* belonging to me.
That book is mine.
3 *(noun)* a bomb that is hidden just
below the ground or underwater, and
explodes when something touches it.

mineral
1 *(noun)* a substance which is taken out of
the ground in a mine. **mineral** *(adjective)*.

malachite   copper   sulphur
three types of **minerals**

2 mineral water *(noun)* bottled water
which comes from an underground spring.

miniature (*min-it-cher*) (adjective)
very small, or a very small copy of
something. *A miniature garden.*

minibeast (noun)
an insect or other very small animal,
such as a spider or centipede.

minibus minibuses (noun)
a small bus, usually carrying eight
to sixteen passengers.

minimize or **minimise**
minimizing minimized (verb)
1 to make something as small
or as unimportant as possible.
*The train company promised to
minimize delays.*
2 to keep a program window open
on a computer, but hidden from the
main desktop.

minimum (adjective)
smallest or lowest. *The minimum number
of players is three.* **minimum** (noun).

minister (noun)
1 a priest in charge of a church.
2 someone who is responsible for
a government department, such as
education or health.

minor (adjective)
1 not very important. *Minor details.*
2 Music that is in a **minor key** usually
sounds sad.

minority minorities (noun)
1 the smaller number out of a group.
A minority of the guests are vegetarian.
minority (adjective).
2 a group of people who are a different
race, or have a different language or
religion from most of the people in
the population.

Spelling tip

minority   minorities

Words that end with a consonant and
then a 'y' **remove the 'y'** and add '**-ies**'
to become plural.

mint (noun)
1 a green, leafy herb
with a strong, fresh
taste. **mint** (adjective),
minty (adjective).
2 a mint-flavoured sweet.

mint

minus (preposition)
1 taking away, especially in sums.
Ten minus six is four.
2 **Minus numbers** are negative, or below
zero. *The temperature is minus five.*

minute
1 (*min-it*) (noun) a unit of time. There
are 60 seconds in a minute and 60
minutes in an hour.
2 (*my-newt*) (adjective) very small or
tiny. *Ben took a minute amount of salad.*

miracle (*mir-ak-ul*) (noun)
an extraordinary event that seems
impossible. *By some miracle, he survived
the shipwreck.* **miraculous** (adjective),
miraculously (adverb).

mirage (*mir-arj*) (noun)
something you see in the distance which
is not really there.

mirror (noun)
a piece of glass with a layer of silver
on the back, which reflects the image
of what is in front of it.

misbehave
misbehaving misbehaved (verb)
to behave badly or be naughty.
misbehaviour (noun).

mischief (noun)
cheeky or naughty behaviour. *Ethan
is a good boy really, but he's full of
mischief.* **mischievous** (adjective),
mischievously (adverb).

miserable (adjective)
1 Someone who is **miserable** is very
unhappy. *I was miserable when my team
lost.* **misery** (noun), **miserably** (adverb).
2 Something that is **miserable** makes you
feel unhappy. *The weather is miserable.*

misfortune (noun)
bad luck, or a piece of bad luck.

The prefix 'mis-'

misbehave
mislay
mislead
misprint

Words that begin with the prefix 'mis-' usually have the meaning of something not being right, or going wrong.

For example, to "**misbehave**" is to behave badly, and a "**misprint**" is a mistake in something that is printed.

mislead misleading misled *(verb)*
to deliberately give someone wrong information, or make them think something is true when it isn't.

misprint *(noun)*
a small mistake in something that has been printed or typed.

Miss *(noun)*
a word used when talking to a young or unmarried woman, or the title which is used before the surname of an unmarried woman. *Our teacher is called Miss Martin.*

miss misses missing missed *(verb)*
1 to aim at something and fail to hit it. *The batsman missed the ball. My shot missed the goal.* **miss** *(noun)*.
2 to fail to catch, do, see or notice something. *Meg tried to catch the ball, but she missed it. I wanted to see Paul this morning, but I missed him.*
3 If you **miss** a bus, flight, train, and so on, you arrive too late to get on it. *We missed the train by two minutes.*
4 to not see, not hear, or not be present for something. *Beth missed the swimming class today.*
5 to be unhappy because you are not with a person, or in a place. *Finn misses his dad very much.*

missile *(noun)*
a weapon which is thrown or fired at a target.

missing *(adjective)*
If someone or something is **missing**, they are lost or not in their place.

misspell misspelling misspelled
or **misspelt** *(verb)*
to spell something wrongly.

mist *(noun)*
a thin cloud of water droplets in the air.
misty *(adjective)*.

mistake
mistaking mistook mistaken
1 *(noun)* something that is wrong or incorrect.
2 *(verb)* to be wrong about something, or to think that someone is someone else. *I mistook Daisy for her sister.*
mistaken *(adjective)*.

mistletoe *(noun)*
an evergreen plant with white berries, which people often use as a Christmas decoration. Mistletoe grows on other trees.

berries

mistletoe

mistreat mistreating
mistreated *(verb)*
to treat someone or something roughly or badly.

misunderstanding *(noun)*
When there is a **misunderstanding**, someone has understood a situation wrongly, which may lead to a problem or a disagreement. *There was a misunderstanding about who was supposed to buy the food.*

misuse *(miss-**yooz**)*
misusing misused *(verb)*
to use something wrongly, or not in the way it is meant to be used.
misuse *(miss-**yuce**) (noun)*.

mix mixes mixing mixed *(verb)*
to put two or more things together and combine them, often by stirring. *I mixed red and yellow paints to make orange.*
mixture *(noun)*, **mixed** *(adjective)*.

mixer *(noun)*
an electrical machine for mixing things.

a b c d e f g h i j k l m n o p q r s t u v w x y z

moan moaning moaned *(verb)*
1 to make a low, unhappy sound.
Barry moaned in pain.
2 to complain. *Maisie wouldn't stop moaning about the food.*

moat *(noun)*
a channel filled with water around a castle, designed to keep enemies out.

mobile
1 *(adjective)* able to move or be moved from place to place. *A mobile home.*
mobility *(noun).*
2 *(noun)* a hanging decoration.
3 *(noun)* see **mobile phone**.

mobile phone *or* **mobile** *(noun)*
a small telephone that you can carry around with you.

mock mocking mocked
1 *(verb)* to make fun of someone or something in an unkind way.
mockery *(noun).*
2 *(adjective)* pretend. *There will be a mock battle at the county fair.*
3 *(noun)* a practice examination.

mode *(noun)*
the number that appears most often in a group of numbers. *In the group of numbers 1, 2, 5, 5, 6, the mode is 5.*

model
1 *(noun)* a small copy of something larger. *Arthur built a model of the castle with his dad.* **model** *(adjective).*
2 *(noun)* someone who wears designer clothes in fashion shows, advertisements, and magazines. **model** *(verb).*
3 *(noun)* someone who poses for an artist or photographer. **model** *(verb).*
4 *(adjective)* an ideal or perfect example of something. *Poppy is a model student.*

moderate *(adjective)*
average, or not extreme or excessive. *Warm the oil in a large pan over a moderate heat.* **moderation** *(noun),*
moderately *(adverb).*

modern *(adjective)*
up-to-date and new, not old-fashioned.

modernize *or* **modernise**
modernizing modernized *(verb)*
to make something modern and up-to-date. *They're going to modernize the IT room at my school.* **modernization** *(noun).*

modest *(adjective)*
Someone who is **modest** doesn't boast or show off. *Ella is brilliant at maths, but she's very modest about it.*
modesty *(noun),* **modestly** *(adverb).*

modify
modifies modifying modified *(verb)*
to change or alter something slightly.
Daniel modified his design to make the table less wobbly. **modification** *(noun).*

Mohammed *or* **Muhammad** *(noun)*
Mohammed is the main prophet in the religion of Islam and he is believed to have started the religion. Mohammed is so important to Muslims that after they say his name, they always add "peace be upon him".

moist *(adjective)*
slightly damp. *You need to plant the seed in moist soil for it to grow.*
moisture *(noun),* **moisten** *(verb).*

mole *(noun)*
1 a small, brown mark on your skin.
2 a small, furry animal that digs tunnels and lives underground.

European mole

molten *(adjective)*
Metals and rock that are **molten** are so hot that they have melted into a liquid.

moment *(noun)*
1 a very short period of time. *Can you wait a moment, please?*
2 at the moment right now. *At the moment, Erin is on her way home.*

monarch *(noun)*
a king or queen. **monarchy** *(noun).*

monastery **monasteries** *(noun)*
the building or buildings where a group of monks live and work.

Monday *(noun)*
the first day of the week, after Sunday and before Tuesday.

money *(noun)*
coins and notes used to buy things.

mongrel *(noun)*
a dog that is a mixture of breeds.

monitor **monitoring monitored**
1 *(verb)* to watch a situation and see how it changes.
2 *(noun)* the screen of a computer.

monk *(noun)*
a man who has promised to devote his life to serving God, and lives in a religious community.

monkey *(noun)*
a small animal, usually with a long tail. Most monkeys live in trees in hot countries.

black squirrel monkey

monsoon *(noun)*
the name for the season in India and Southeast Asia when it rains a lot.

monster *(noun)*
1 a frightening creature in stories, films, and so on. *I used to be scared that there was a monster under my bed.*
2 someone who behaves very cruelly.
monstrous *(adjective)*.

month *(noun)*
a period of 28 to 31 days. There are 12 months in a year. **monthly** *(adjective)*, **monthly** *(adverb)*.

monument *(noun)*
a statue or structure built to remind people of an event or person. *In my village there is a monument to First World War soldiers.*

mood *(noun)*
the way you are feeling. *Oscar is in a good mood today.*

Spelling tip

moody moodier moodiest

When adding the endings '**–ier**' and '**–iest**' to a word which ends with a consonant and then a '**y**', remember to **take the 'y' away** first.

moody
moodier moodiest *(adjective)*
If you are **moody**, you are often grumpy, or your mood changes often.
moodily *(adverb)*.

moon *(noun)*
1 The **Moon** is the large, round lump of rock which goes around the Earth and reflects light from the Sun.
2 any large piece of rock that goes around a planet. *Mars has two moons.*

new Moon (invisible) crescent Moon (waxing) half-Moon gibbous Moon (waxing)

full Moon gibbous Moon (waning) half-Moon crescent Moon (old Moon)

phases of the **Moon**

moonlight *(noun)*
the light that comes from the Moon.
moonlit *(adjective)*.

moor **mooring moored**
1 *(verb)* If you **moor** a boat, you tie it onto something so it doesn't float away.
mooring *(noun)*.
2 *(noun)* an open area of land often covered with grass and heather, and with very few trees or bushes.

moose **moose** *(noun)*
a type of large deer. The males have wide, flat, branching antlers.

a b c d e f g h i j k l **m** n o p q r s t u v w x y z

Spelling tip

mop   mopping   mopped

One-syllable words that have a single vowel then a consonant at the end **double the final consonant** before the endings '**-ing**' or '**-ed**' are added. Other words that follow this pattern are "beg", "dig", and "stop".

mop mopping mopped
1 *(noun)* a tool with a long handle and a head made of sponge or cloth that you use to clean floors.
2 *(verb)* to clean something with a mop.

mope moping moped *(verb)*
to be moody and lacking in energy. *Stop moping around the house and go outside to play.* **mopey** *(adjective).*

moral
1 *(adjective)* to do with what is right and wrong. *Moral standards.*
morality *(noun),* **morally** *(adverb).*
2 *(adjective)* A **moral** person acts in a good way, and tries to get other people to act in this way.
3 *(noun)* the lesson you can learn from a story. *The moral of this story is, "Slow and steady wins the race".*

morale *(mor-**ahl**)* *(noun)*
how hopeful, confident, happy or sad someone or a group of people is feeling. *Morale was low after we lost the game.*

more most
1 *(determiner)* greater in number, size, amount, and so on. *My big brother eats more food than I do.*
2 *(pronoun)* a greater number or amount of something that has already been mentioned. *I have two guinea pigs, but I'd like more.*
3 *(adverb)* a word used to make the comparative form of some adjectives and adverbs. *Ben is more handsome than Chris.*

morning *(noun)*
the part of the day between sunrise and noon. *I'm going to go horse riding tomorrow morning.*

Morse code *(noun)*
a code which represents letters of the alphabet using a mixture of long and short sounds or flashes of light.

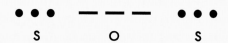

S   O   S

Dots show short sounds or flashes, and dashes show long ones. This picture shows how to signal SOS in **Morse code**.

mortar *(noun)*
a mixture of sand, water and cement used in building to stick bricks or stones together, which hardens as it dries.

mortgage *(noun)*
a loan from a bank to buy a home, which is paid back over a number of years.

mosaic *(moh-**zay**-ik)* *(noun)*
a picture or pattern made of small pieces of coloured stone, glass, and so on. *We saw some Roman mosaics on holiday.*

Moslem *(noun)*
see **Muslim**.

mosque *(mosk)* *(noun)*
a building where Muslims come together to worship.

mosquito
*(moss-**kee**-toe)*
mosquitoes or
mosquitos *(noun)*
a small fly with long legs. Most species of mosquito feed on the

mosquito

blood of humans or animals, which can sometimes lead to diseases being spread.

moss mosses *(noun)*
a type of spongy plant which often grows on wood, rocks, and damp ground.

mostly *(adverb)*
usually, mainly, or most often. *Aaron mostly has school dinners, but sometimes he takes a packed lunch.*

moth *(noun)*
an insect similar to a butterfly. Most types of moths only come out at night.

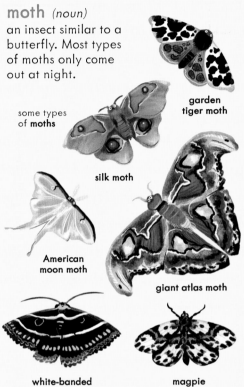

some types of **moths**

garden tiger moth

silk moth

American moon moth

giant atlas moth

white-banded noctuid moth

magpie moth

mother *(noun)*
a woman who has a child or children. *My mother is very kind.*

motherhood *(noun)*
the state of being a mother.

motion *(noun)*
movement.

motionless *(adjective)*
not moving at all. *The deer was motionless in the middle of the road.*

motivate
motivating motivated *(verb)*
to give someone a reason to do something, or to encourage and inspire them to do something. *Our football coach is really good at motivating us.*
motivation *(noun)*, **motivated** *(adjective)* .

motor *(noun)*
part of a machine or vehicle which uses electricity to make the machine work. *The motor was very loud.*

motorbike *(noun)*
a large, heavy bicycle powered by an engine, that can carry one or two people. *The best bit of the film was when the hero drove a motorbike through a market.*

motorcycle *(noun)*
another word for **motorbike**.

motorway *(noun)*
a large road with several lanes, designed for fast-moving traffic. *We drove for two hours on the motorway.*

motto mottos *or* **mottoes** *(noun)*
a short sentence or phrase that sums up the beliefs or aims of a person, family, organization, and so on. *Our school motto is "Progress through teamwork".*

mould moulding moulded
1 *(verb)* to make something into a shape. *I moulded the dough into a loaf shape.*
2 *(noun)* an object or container you can use to shape something. *A jelly mould.*
3 *(noun)* a fungus that grows on food that has gone bad, such as bread, or on walls. **mouldy** *(adjective)*.

moult *(malt)*
moulting moulted *(verb)*
When an animal **moults**, some of its fur or feathers fall out. *Our dog is moulting all over the house.*

mound *(noun)*
a heap, or a small hill. *There is a mound of dirty socks in my room.*

mount mounting mounted *(verb)*
to get onto a horse or a bicycle.

mountain *(noun)*
a very high hill, often with steep sides. *Mount Everest is the tallest mountain in the world.* **mountainous** *(adjective)*.

a b c d e f g h i j k l m n o p q r s t u v w x y z

mountain bike – mow

mountain bike — labels: seat, seat post, rear reflector, mud guard, reflector, seat stay, cassette (gears), rim, tyre tread, rear derailleur, chain stay, chain, seat tube, crank, pedal, top tube, handlebar, stem, brake, brake cable, head tube, front forks, down tube, spoke, hub, tyre

mountain bike *(noun)*
a strong bicycle with gears, for riding on rough roads and tracks. **mountain biking** *(noun)*.

mountaineer *(noun)*
someone who climbs mountains.

mourn mourning mourned *(verb)*
to be very sad because someone has died. **mourner** *(noun)*, **mourning** *(noun)*.

mouse mice *(noun)*
1 a small, furry animal with a long tail.
2 a small device which is connected to a computer and used to move and place the cursor and select items on the computer screen.

harvest mouse

mousse *(moose) (noun)*
1 a smooth, light, foamy food, which can be sweet or savoury. *Chocolate mousse.*
2 a foamy substance that is used for styling hair.

moustache *(noun)*
the hair that grows on someone's top lip. *My brother is growing a moustache.*

mouth *(noun)*
1 the part of your face that you use for eating and speaking.
2 the opening of a cave or tunnel.
3 the place where a river meets the sea.

move moving moved
1 *(verb)* to go from one place to another. *We moved from the kitchen to the garden.*
2 *(verb)* to carry or take something from one place to another. *We need to move these rocks.*
3 *(verb)* to go to live in a different place. *We're moving to Canada.*
4 *(noun)* a turn in a game such as chess.
5 *(noun)* a step or action in a dance.

movement *(noun)*
an action that you can see. *The cat made a sudden movement.*

movie *(noun)*
a film. *That movie was so funny.*

moving *(adjective)*
Something that is **moving** makes you feel strong emotions.

mow mowing mowed mown *(verb)*
to cut grass. **mower** *(noun)*.

MP (abbreviation)
see Member of Parliament.

mp3
1 (noun) a type of digital sound file. Music that you download from the internet is usually in mp3 format.
2 mp3 player (noun) a small, portable device that plays mp3s.

mph (abbreviation)
a short way of writing "miles per hour", a measure of speed.

Mr (**miss**-ter)
a man's title, used before his surname. *Mr Smith.*

Mrs (**miss**-iz)
a married woman's title, used before her surname. *Mrs Smith.*

Ms (mizz)
a title used by women who may prefer people not to know whether they are married or not. *Ms Smith.*

much
1 (adverb) a lot. *It's much too expensive.*
2 (adjective) a large amount of something. *I don't have much money.*
3 (pronoun) a large amount of something that has already been mentioned. *Could I borrow some sugar please? I don't have much.*

Much

The word "much" is usually used in these three ways:

*How **much** food is left?*

1. In questions.

2. In negative phrases.

*Not **much** at all!*

3. With words such as "too", "very" and "so": "That's far **too much** mashed potato for me."

Otherwise, you use "a lot of": "I have **a lot of** homework".

muck (noun)
dirt or mess. **mucky** (adjective).

mucus (**mew**-kuss) (noun)
the thick liquid inside your nose and lungs.

mud (noun)
a sticky mixture of soil and water. **muddy** (adjective).

muddle muddling muddled (verb)
to mix up or confuse. **muddle** (noun), **muddled** (adjective).

muesli (**mewz**-lee) (noun)
a breakfast food made of oats, dried fruit, and nuts.

muffin (noun)
1 a small, round, flat bread roll.
2 a small cake with a rounded top.

muffle muffling muffled (verb)
to make a sound quieter. **muffled** (adjective).

mug (noun)
a large cup with a handle.

Muhammad
see Mohammed.

multicultural (adjective)
to do with the cultures and traditions of different races and religions.

multiple
1 (adjective) many, or numerous.
2 (noun) a number that can be divided by another number without a remainder. *20 is a multiple of four.*

multiply multiplies multiplying multiplied (verb)
1 When you **multiply** a number, you make it a number of times bigger. *Eight multiplied by four is 32.* **multiplication** (noun).
2 to grow in number. *The weeds in the garden have multiplied.*

multiracial (adjective)
to do with people of many different races.

multistorey (adjective)
having several storeys or levels. *We parked in a multistorey car park.*

mum – mussel

mum *(noun)*
short for **mummy** (1).

mumble mumbling mumbled *(verb)*
to say something very quietly, or without making your words clear.

mummy mummies *(noun)*
1 a friendly word for **mother**.
2 a dead body which has been specially preserved and wrapped in cloth.

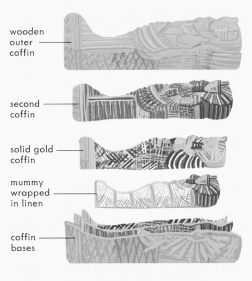

wooden outer coffin

second coffin

solid gold coffin

mummy wrapped in linen

coffin bases

the **mummy** and coffins of the Ancient Egyptian Pharaoh, Tutankhamun

mumps *(noun)*
an illness which causes a fever, a sore throat, and a swollen face.

munch
munches munching munched *(verb)*
to chew or crunch something.

mural *(noun)*
a wall painting.

murder murdering murdered *(verb)*
to kill someone on purpose.
murder *(noun)*, **murderer** *(noun)*.

murky murkier murkiest *(adjective)*
dark, muddy, and gloomy. *The water in the river is very murky.*

murmur
murmuring murmured *(verb)*
to speak quietly or make a quiet sound.

muscle *(noun)*
a body part that stretches and tightens to allow you to move. Muscles help you to breathe, swallow, and move your arms and legs, for example.
muscular *(adjective)*.

museum *(noun)*
a building that contains a collection of interesting things that people can look at. *We went to a science museum.*

mushroom *(noun)*
a type of fungus which usually has a short stem and a rounded top. Some mushrooms can be eaten. *See* **fungus**.

music *(noun)*
1 sounds that are put together in a way that is nice to listen to.
2 written or printed musical notes on a page.

musical
1 *(adjective)* to do with music, or having a pleasant sound. **musically** *(adverb)*.
2 *(adjective)* Someone who is **musical** can sing or play music well.
3 *(noun)* a show or film that includes lots of singing and dancing.

musician *(noun)*
someone who sings or plays music at an event, or as a job.

Muslim *or* **Moslem** *(noun)*
someone who follows the religion of Islam.

mussel *(noun)*
a kind of shellfish with a dark blue oval shell.

water sucked in

water pushed out

foot

blue mussel

must *(verb)*
1 If you **must** do something, you have to do it, or feel that you need to do it. *You must remember to clean your teeth before you go to bed.*
2 You use **must** to say that you believe something to be true. *You must be hungry – have something to eat.*

mustard *(noun)*
a spicy yellow-brown paste that is usually eaten with meat.

a jar of **mustard**

musty mustier mustiest *(adjective)*
smelling mouldy and stale. *A musty attic.*

mutter muttering muttered *(verb)*
to say something very quietly. *"I wish he'd be quiet," Ellen muttered.*

muzzle *(noun)*
1 an animal's nose and mouth.
2 a guard put around a dog's mouth, to stop it from biting.

my *(determiner)*
belonging to me.

myself *(pronoun)*
me and nobody else. *I hurt myself. I cooked dinner myself.*

mystery mysteries *(noun)*
1 something strange which cannot be explained or solved. *Where he went is a mystery.* **mysterious** *(adjective)*, **mysteriously** *(adverb)*.
2 a type of story in which strange and puzzling things happen.

myth *(noun)*
1 a traditional story about gods and heroes, or about how things were created. **mythical** *(adjective)*.
2 something which lots of people believe is true, but isn't. *It's a myth that eating carrots helps you see in the dark.*

mythology mythologies *(noun)*
a collection of ancient stories about gods and heroes. *Greek mythology.* **mythological** *(adjective)*.

These are some creatures from Ancient Greek **mythology**.

eagle's wings

lion's tail

griffin

human torso

horse's body

centaur

snake's head

goat's head

lion's head

chimera

wings

human head

lion's body

sphinx

Nn

nag nagging nagged (verb)
If you **nag** someone, you keep telling them to do something. *Mum's always nagging me to tidy my room.*

nail (noun)
1 one of the hard parts at the ends of your fingers and toes. *I'm trying to stop biting my nails.*
2 a small, spiked piece of metal that you hammer into something. **nail** (verb).

nail varnish (noun)
a brightly-coloured, shiny paint that you can wear on your nails.

naked (adjective)
If you are **naked**, you haven't got any clothes on. **nakedness** (noun).

name naming named
1 (noun) what someone or something is called. *My dog's name is Coco.*
2 (verb) to give something a name. *I named my new goldfish Pickles.*
3 (noun) a reputation. *Hope wants to make a name for herself in the world of women's football.*
4 (noun) a person who is famous for something. *He's a big name in cycling.*

nanny nannies (noun)
someone who is paid to look after children in their own home while their parents are busy or working.

nap napping napped (verb)
to sleep for a short time, especially during the day. *The baby naps between 3 p.m. and 4 p.m.* **nap** (noun).

nappy nappies (noun)
a piece of thick, soft material or paper, that you fasten around a baby's bottom.

narrative (noun)
a story or an account of something that has happened.

Word origin narrative narrator
These words come from the Latin word "narrare", which means "to tell or explain".

narrator (noun)
A **narrator** tells a story, often out loud. *The narrator in the book is a girl called Scout.* **narrate** (verb), **narration** (noun).

narrow
narrower narrowest (adjective)
thin, or not wide. *This path is very narrow.* **narrowness** (noun).

narrow-minded (adjective)
A **narrow-minded** person won't accept that they might be wrong, or listen to other people's opinions.

nasty nastier nastiest (adjective)
1 horrible or unpleasant. *This drink has a nasty taste.*
2 unkind or mean. *Helen is always nasty to Sarah.* **nastiness** (noun), **nastily** (adverb).

nation (noun)
a country, and all the people in it, who share the same laws and often speak the same language. **national** (adjective), **nationally** (adverb).

nationality nationalities (noun)
Your **nationality** is the nation or country you come from. *Hubert's nationality is French.*

native
1 (noun) someone who was born in a particular country. *Hubert is a native of France.* **native** (adjective).
2 Your **native country** is the country where you were born.

Nativity
1 (noun) the birth of Jesus Christ.
2 Nativity play (noun) a play telling the story of the birth of Jesus Christ. *I was a shepherd in the Nativity play.*

A B C D E F G H I J K L M N O P Q R S T U V W X Y Z

natural

1 *(adjective)* to do with nature, including all the animals and plants in it.
2 *(adjective)* normal, or to be expected. *It's natural to cry when you hurt yourself.* **naturally** *(adverb)*.
3 *(noun)* If you are **a natural** at something, you are good at it without having to try very hard.

nature *(noun)*

1 everything in the world that has not been made by humans, including all plants and animals, and the weather.
2 Your **nature** is your personality and the way you behave.

naughty

naughtier naughtiest *(adjective)* badly-behaved. *Millie is such a naughty child.* **naughtiness** *(noun)*, **naughtily** *(adverb)*.

navel *(noun)*

the small, round dip in your tummy, often called your belly button.

navigate

navigating navigated *(verb)* to work out the direction that a ship, plane, or other vehicle should travel in, using maps and sometimes compasses and other instruments.

navy navies

1 *(noun)* the part of a country's armed forces that fights at sea. **naval** *(adjective)*.
2 navy blue *(noun)* a very dark blue colour. **navy blue** *(adjective)*.

near nearing neared

1 *(preposition)* not far from, or close to. *I live near the swimming pool.*
2 *(verb)* to approach.

nearby *(adjective)*

not far away. *We went to the nearby park.* **nearby** *(adverb)*.

nearly *(adverb)*

almost. *I nearly lost my temper when Brian turned up late.*

neat neater neatest *(adjective)*

tidy and well-organized. *This garden is very neat.* **neatly** *(adverb)*.

necessary *(adjective)*

If something is **necessary**, you must do it or have it. **necessity** *(noun)*, **necessarily** *(adverb)*.

neck *(noun)*

the part of your body between your head and your shoulders.

necklace *(noun)*

a piece of jewellery that you wear around your neck.

nectar *(noun)*

the sweet liquid in flowers, which bees collect and make into honey.

need needing needed *(verb)*

1 If you **need** something, you must have it. *I need a drink.* **need** *(noun)*.
2 If you **need** to do something, it's important that you do it. *We need to visit Gran more often.*

needle *(noun)*

1 a thin, pointed stick of metal. Different kinds of needles are used for sewing, knitting, or for giving injections.
2 a long, thin leaf of an evergreen tree.

Spelling tip　needle

The 'ul' sound at the end of a word is often spelt 'le', as in "need**le**", and also in "ab**le**", "app**le**" and "cand**le**".

It can also be spelt '-al', such as in "natur**al**" and "loc**al**". This ending tends to be seen more in adjectives, but there are exceptions, such as "anim**al**" and "hospit**al**".

The 'ul' sound can also be spelt '-el', for example in "trav**el**" and "tunn**el**".

negative *(adjective)*

1 A **negative** sentence is one that has the word "no" or "not" in it, for example, "He is not my friend."
2 If a person is **negative**, they tend to see the bad side of everything and everyone. **negativity** *(noun)*.
3 A **negative** number is less than 0.

a b c d e f g h i j k l m **n** o p q r s t u v w x y z

neglect **neglecting neglected** (verb)
If you **neglect** someone or something, you don't look after them. **neglect** (noun), **neglectful** (adjective).

negotiate
negotiating negotiated (verb)
to discuss something with everyone involved until you find a solution that everyone agrees on. **negotiation** (noun).

neighbour (noun)
someone who lives next door to you, or near you. *Our neighbour helped us move our sofa.*

neighbourhood (noun)
the area around where you live. *Our neighbourhood was badly flooded last year.* **neighbourhood** (adjective).

neither
1 (determiner) not one or the other. *Neither team has got enough players.*
2 (pronoun) not one or the other of two things or people already mentioned. *Do you want milk or sugar, or neither?*

neither/nor, either/or

neither/nor
Neither/nor has the meaning "not either of the two things or people": "I like **neither** tea **nor** coffee."

either/or
Either/or is used in sentences when you are talking about a comparison or choice between two things: "You can **either** have tea **or** coffee."

If you have used the word "**not**" in a sentence, it should be followed by "either/or", not "neither/nor": "I **do not** like **either** tea **or** coffee."

If you are agreeing with a negative sentence, you can use "not either" or "neither": "I don't like coffee." "Me neither."/"I don't either."

nephew (noun)
Someone's **nephew** is their brother's or sister's son.

nerve (noun)
1 very thin threads inside your body that send messages between your brain and other parts of your body, so that you can feel and move.
2 courage. *You've got to have nerve to go skydiving.*
3 If someone or something **gets on your nerves**, they annoy you. *That beeping sound is starting to get on my nerves.*

nervous (adjective)
worried or scared. *David gets nervous before exams.* **nervousness** (noun), **nervously** (adverb).

chewed-up wood mixed with saliva

nest (noun)
a home that birds and other animals build to lay their eggs in, and bring up their babies. **nest** (verb).

wasp nest

net (noun)
1 a short word for **internet**. *Kay sells her old clothes on the net.*
2 material with lots of small holes between the threads.
3 something made from material with holes in, for example for catching fish.

netball (noun)
a game in which two teams of seven players try to throw a ball through a net on top of a pole.

nettle (noun)
a plant that stings you if you touch it.

network (noun)
a group of things or people that are all connected to each other, such as railway lines or computers.

common stinging nettle

never *(adverb)*
not at any time. *I never eat broccoli.*

nevertheless *(adverb)*
even though, or in spite of that. *Kirsty was tired and hungry. Nevertheless, she carried on walking.*

new newer newest *(adjective)*
just started, made, or bought. *New shoes.*

news *(noun)*
information about things that have happened recently.

newsagent *(noun)*
a shop that sells newspapers and magazines, as well as some food and other everyday things.

newspaper *(noun)*
a set of sheets of paper or pages on a website that contain information about what is happening in the world.

newt *(noun)*
a small animal with a long tail, that lives on land but lays its eggs in water.

next *(adjective)*
1 coming after something else. *We need to get off the bus at the next stop.* **next** *(adverb).*
2 Next to means alongside, or nearest. *Billy's bike is next to mine.*
3 Next door means the house or building next to this one. *Annie lives next door.*

nibble nibbling nibbled *(verb)*
to eat something by taking lots of very small bites out of it.

nice nicer nicest *(adjective)*
1 pleasant and kind. *It was so nice of Mary to give me a lift home.*
2 pretty and attractive. *That's a really nice dress.*

nickname *(noun)*
the friendly or jokey name someone's friends and family sometimes call them. *Rebecca's nickname is Bex.*

niece *(noun)*
Someone's **niece** is their brother's or sister's daughter.

night *(noun)*
the time between when the Sun sets and when it rises, when the sky is dark. *You should have lights on your bike if you ride it at night.* **night** *(adjective).*

nightie *(noun)*
a short word for "nightdress", the loose dress some girls and women wear in bed.

nightmare *(noun)*
1 a scary dream.
2 a scary situation. *Our holiday was a nightmare.* **nightmarish** *(adjective).*

nil *(noun)*
nothing, or zero. *The score was nil-nil at half-time.*

nimble nimbler nimblest *(adjective)*
moving quickly and lightly. *My gerbil is very nimble.* **nimbly** *(adverb).*

nipple *(noun)*
one of the round, reddish bumps on a person or animal's chest. Babies suck milk through their mothers' nipples.

nits *(plural noun)*
the eggs laid by insects called lice, in someone's hair.

no
1 *(interjection)* You say **no** when you don't want something, or don't agree with something. *"Would you like some tea?" "No, thank you."*
2 *(determiner)* not any. *There are no biscuits in the biscuit tin.*
3 *(determiner)* not. *Please arrive no later than 7 p.m.*

nobody *(pronoun)*
not a single person. *Mr Owen held extra maths lessons, but nobody came.*

nocturnal *(adjective)*
Nocturnal animals, such as badgers, only come out at night.

Badgers are **nocturnal.**

noise *(noun)*
a sound, usually one that you don't want to hear. *The noise from the party was terrible.*

noisy noisier noisiest *(adjective)*
making a lot of noise. *Our washing machine is very noisy.* **noisiness** *(noun)*, **noisily** *(adverb)*.

nominate
nominating nominated *(verb)*
If you **nominate** someone for a job or task, you say that you think they are the right person to do it. *I nominated Lola to be our team captain.* **nomination** *(noun)*.

nonfiction *(noun)*
writing that gives information about real things, people, or events, instead of made-up stories. **nonfiction** *(adjective)*.

nonsense *(noun)*
something silly, without any meaning. *Pete talks nonsense most of the time.*

nonstop *(adjective)*
without any pauses or breaks. *This is a nonstop flight.* **nonstop** *(adverb)*.

no-one or **no one** *(pronoun)*
nobody at all. *No-one likes to be last.*

normal *(adjective)*
ordinary, or usual. *Our normal school day ends at 3.15 p.m.* **normally** *(adverb)*.

north
1 *(noun)* one of the four points of the compass. *See* **compass.**
2 *(adjective)* in or towards the north of a place. *North London.* **north** *(noun)*, **northern** *(adjective)*.
3 *(adjective)* from the north. *North wind.*
4 The **North Pole** is the point right at the top of the Earth that is always covered with ice and snow.

nose *(noun)*
the part of your face above your mouth, which you use to breathe and smell.

nostril *(noun)*
one of the two holes in your nose, through which you breathe and smell.

nosy nosier nosiest *(adjective)*
A **nosy** person is too interested in finding out all about everything and everyone. *My Aunt Mabel is very nosy, and wants to know all about my friends.* **nosily** *(adverb)*.

not *(adverb)*
a word used to talk about the opposite or absence of something. *I'm not feeling well today. Jack is not at home.*

note *(noun)*
1 a short letter or message. *Mandy sent a note to say thank you for the flowers.*
2 a piece of paper money. *Have you got change for a ten pound note?*
3 a single sound in music. *Rupert's singing was mostly good, but he didn't quite get the last note.*
4 a symbol that stands for a sound in written music.

treble clef   C D E F G A B C D E F

bass clef   E F G A B C D E F G A

Each musical **note** has its own position on the five-line stave.

nothing *(pronoun)*
not anything at all. *I've had nothing to eat all day.*

notice noticing noticed
1 *(verb)* to spot someone or something. *I didn't notice that my pen was leaking until it was too late.*
2 *(noun)* a poster or letter giving information about something. *There's a notice at the park that says dogs must be kept on leads.*

nought *(noun)*
the number 0, or zero.

Nouns

There are three main kinds of **nouns**:

Common nouns

Common nouns name types of things, for example, "metal", "girl", and "submarine". A type of common noun called an **abstract noun** names things that you can't touch, such as "anger" and "kindness".

Proper nouns

Proper nouns name people, places, or specific things, and always start with a capital letter, for example, "Paris", "Russia", and "Caroline Young".

Collective nouns

Collective nouns name a group of things, such as "a choir of singers".

noun *(noun)*
a word that names a person or a thing.

novel *(noun)*
a book that tells a story. **novelist** *(noun)*.

now
1 *(adverb)* at this time, or immediately. *"Come here now!" Mum yelled.*
2 *(conjunction)* because of the fact that. *Baking is easier now I have a mixer.*

nowhere *(adverb)*
no place. *There was nowhere left for the robbers to hide.*

nuclear power *(noun)*
energy that is made by splitting atoms (the tiny things that make up everything in the world).

nude *(adjective)*
without any clothes on. **nudity** *(noun)*.

nudge **nudging** **nudged** *(verb)*
to give someone or something a small push or poke, often with your elbow. **nudge** *(noun)*.

nuisance *(noun)*
someone or something that annoys you or causes problems.

numb *(num)*
number **numbest** *(adjective)*
unable to feel anything. *My fingers are numb.* **numbness** *(noun)*, **numb** *(verb)*.

number *(noun)*
a word or symbol used for counting and doing maths. All numbers are combinations of 0 1 2 3 4 5 6 7 8 and 9. **numbered** *(adjective)*.

numeracy *(noun)*
the ability to understand and work with numbers.

numerator *(noun)*
In fractions, the **numerator** is the number above the line. In the fraction ¾, 3 is the numerator. (4 is the denominator.)

numerical *(adjective)*
to do with numbers. *Arrange the pages in numerical order.* **numerically** *(adverb)*.

nun *(noun)*
a woman who dedicates her life to serving God, and lives with other nuns.

nurse *(noun)*
someone who looks after people who are ill, often in a hospital. **nurse** *(verb)*, **nursing** *(noun)*.

nursery **nurseries** *(noun)*
1 a place where little children are cared for while their parents work.
2 a place where plants are grown.
3 Nursery school is where children can go between the ages of around three and five.

nut *(noun)*
a hard fruit that grows on some trees and plants. Some types of nuts can be eaten. **nutty** *(adjective)*.

pistachio (in shell)

hazelnut

edible nuts

Brazil nut

nutrition *(noun)*
the goodness that food provides, which helps you to grow and stay healthy. **nutritious** *(adjective)*.

a b c d e f g h i j k l m n o p q r s t u v w x y z

Oo

oak (noun)
a kind of big tree that loses its leaves in winter, and has seeds called acorns.

oak tree

oar (noun)
a pole, often made of wood, with one wide, flat end, which you use for rowing a small boat.

oasis oases (noun)
a place in a desert where there is some water, so plants and trees grow.

obedient (adjective)
If you are **obedient**, you do what you're told. *Our new puppy isn't very obedient.* **obedience** (noun), **obediently** (adverb).

obese (adjective)
Someone who is **obese** weighs much more than is healthy. **obesity** (noun).

obey obeying obeyed (verb)
to do what someone tells you to, or to follow orders. *Soldiers must obey their officers.*

object objecting objected
1 (**ob**-jekt) (noun) a thing, that you can see and touch, but that is not alive. *We could see a strange black object in the water.*
2 (**ob**-jekt) (noun) the aim or the thing that you are trying to achieve. *The object of this experiment is to see what effect fizzy drinks have on teeth.*
3 (**ob**-jekt) (noun) The **object** of a verb is the thing that the verb acts upon. It usually comes after the verb. For example, in the sentence, "I am brushing my hair", "my hair" is the object.
4 (ob-**jekt**) (verb) If you **object** to something, you dislike it or disagree with it. *I object to the amount of homework we get.*

objective
1 (noun) the thing that you are trying to achieve. *Our objective is to raise enough money to build a new playground this summer.*
2 (adjective) based on facts, not on feelings or opinions. *Your written projects on the war must be objective.* **objectively** (adverb).

obligatory (adjective)
If something is **obligatory**, you must do or have it. *It's obligatory to take off your shoes before entering a mosque.* **obligation** (noun).

oblong (noun)
a shape with four straight sides and four right-angled corners, which has two sides that are longer than the other two. **oblong** (adjective). *See* **quadrilateral**.

oboe (noun)
a long musical instrument that you blow into to make sounds, with metal keys that you press to change the note. **oboist** (noun).

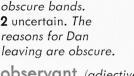

reed —

keys —

oboe

— bell

obscure (adjective)
1 not well-known. *My brother likes obscure bands.*
2 uncertain. *The reasons for Dan leaving are obscure.*

observant (adjective)
good at noticing things.

observation (noun)
1 looking at or watching someone or something very closely and carefully. *Leah was taken to hospital for observation.*
2 something you say or write based on something that you have noticed. *Mark made an observation about my socks.*

observatory observatories (noun)
a building containing telescopes and other scientific instruments for studying the sky and the stars.

A B C D E F G H I J K L M N O P Q R S T U V W X Y Z

observe **observing observed** *(verb)*
1 If you **observe** someone or something, you watch them very carefully. *Elin likes to observe the birds in the garden.*
2 to notice something. *I observed that all the chairs were taken.*
3 to make a remark about something you have noticed. *"Your hair's grown since I last saw you," Meg observed.*

obsess
obsesses obsessing obsessed *(verb)*
to think about someone or something all the time. *Tim obsesses about football.*
obsession *(noun)*, **obsessed** *(adjective)*, **obsessive** *(adjective)*, **obsessively** *(adverb)*.

obstacle *(noun)*
something that gets in the way. *There was an obstacle in the road.*

obstruct
obstructing obstructed *(verb)*
to block something, such as a road or a view. *A railing obstructed my view of the stage.* **obstruction** *(noun)*.

obtain **obtaining obtained** *(verb)*
to get something.

obvious *(adjective)*
If something is **obvious**, it's very clear to see or understand. *It's obvious that she loves him.* **obviously** *(adverb)*.

occasion *(noun)*
1 an important event, or a celebration. *A special family occasion.*
2 a time when something happens. *We've been there on several occasions.*

occasionally *(adverb)*
If something happens **occasionally**, it doesn't happen often.
occasional *(adjective)*.

occupy
occupies occupying occupied
1 *(verb)* to live or work in a place. *Who occupies the first floor?*
2 *(verb)* If something **occupies** you, it keeps you busy. *The new game occupied the children for ages.*
3 *(adjective)* If a toilet is **occupied**, someone is already in it.

Spelling tip

occur occurring occurred

It can be hard to remember how to spell "occur" and all the words that are related to it. Remember that they all have a double 'c' in the middle. "Occur" only has one 'r', but when you add an ending that starts with a vowel to it, you need to double the 'r': "occurring", "occurred", "occurrence".

occur **occurring occurred** *(verb)*
to happen. *The accident occurred last Tuesday.* **occurrence** *(noun)*.

ocean (**oh**-shun) *(noun)*
one of the five large areas of salt water on Earth.

Arctic Ocean
Atlantic Ocean
Pacific Ocean
Indian Ocean
Southern Ocean

This map shows the Earth's five **oceans**.

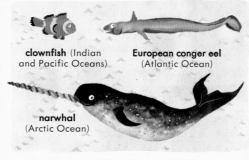

clownfish (Indian and Pacific Oceans)
European conger eel (Atlantic Ocean)
narwhal (Arctic Ocean)

These are some animals that live in the **oceans**.

o'clock *(adverb)*
a word used to say what time it is. *It's one o'clock.*

Word family

octagon	These words all come from the Latin word for "eight", "octo". An "octagon" has eight sides, an "octave" has eight notes, "October" was the eighth month of the Roman calendar, and an "octopus" has eight arms.
octave	
October	
octopus	

octagon *(noun)*
a shape with eight straight sides.
octagonal *(adjective)*. See **shapes**,
page 348.

octave *(noun)*
the eight-note gap in a musical scale
between a note and the note of the same
name above or below it.

October *(noun)*
the tenth month of the year.

octopus octopuses *(noun)*
a sea animal with a soft body and eight
long arms with suckers on them.

Giant Pacific octopus

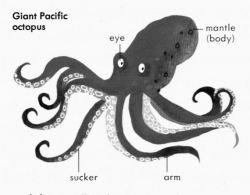

eye — mantle (body)

sucker — arm

odd odder oddest *(adjective)*
1 strange or unusual. *Maureen wears
some very odd hats.* **oddly** *(adverb)*.
2 not matching. *There are lots of odd
socks in my drawer.*
3 An **odd** number can't be divided by
two. Odd numbers include 7, 37 and 55.

odour *(noun)*
a smell, usually a bad one.

off
1 *(preposition)* away from a place
or thing. *We got off the bus.*
2 *(adjective)* When a machine is **off**,
it's not switched on.
3 *(adverb)* not in work or school.
I'm taking next Friday off.
4 *(adverb)* at a smaller price. *The red
coat had £10 off.*
5 *(adjective)* cancelled. *The party is off.*
6 *(adjective)* If food is **off**, it has gone
bad. *I think this milk is off.*

offence *(noun)*
1 a crime. *A driving offence.*
2 If you **cause offence**, you upset
someone. *The cartoon caused offence.*
3 If you **take offence**, you are upset
or annoyed by something.
4 You say "**no offence**" to show that
you don't want what you're saying
to upset anyone.

offend offending offended *(verb)*
1 If you **offend** someone, you say or do
something that upsets or annoys them.
2 to commit a crime. **offender** *(noun)*.

offensive *(adjective)*
rude or upsetting. **offensively** *(adverb)*.

offer offering offered *(verb)*
1 to ask someone if they would like
something. **offer** *(noun)*.
2 to say you are willing to do
something. *I offered to sit in the back.*

office *(noun)*
a room or building where people work,
usually at desks. **office** *(adjective)*.

officer *(noun)*
a person who is in charge of other
people, especially in the army, navy,
air force or police force.

official
1 *(adjective)* approved by someone
in charge. *The official list of guests.*
officially *(adverb)*.
2 *(noun)* someone in an important
position. *A race official.*

offline *(adjective)*
not connected to the internet, or not done on the internet. **offline** *(adverb)*.

off-putting *(adjective)*
Something that is **off-putting** is unpleasant or makes you feel uncomfortable. *The soup tastes all right, but the smell is off-putting.*

offspring *(noun)*
an animal's young, or someone's child or children. *A cow's offspring is called a calf.*

often *(adverb)*
lots of times, or regularly. *We often have fruit for dessert.*

ogre (**oh**-ger) *(noun)*
a cruel giant in a fairy story.

oil *(noun)*
a thick, slippery liquid. Different kinds of oil are used as fuel for vehicles, to make machines run smoothly, and for cooking and heating. **oily** *(adjective)*.

oil platform *(noun)*
a large platform used as a base for drilling for oil under the sea or under the ground.

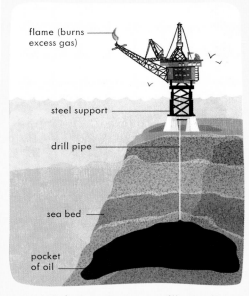

flame (burns excess gas)

steel support

drill pipe

sea bed

pocket of oil

Oil platforms are used to get **oil** from under the sea. The oil is often used as a fuel.

old older oldest *(adjective)*
1 Someone **old** has lived for a long time.
2 Something that is **old** has existed for a long time. *That's a very old church.*
3 a word used to say the age of someone or something. *I am eight years old.*
4 a word used to describe something that you had before you got a new one. *My old phone broke.*

old-fashioned *(adjective)*
in a style that is no longer popular. *The café was a bit old-fashioned.*

"Old-fashioned" is a **compound adjective**, made up of two words joined together by a hyphen.

omit omitting omitted *(verb)*
to leave something out. *Polly omitted the part about the werewolf from her story.* **omission** *(noun)*.

on
1 *(preposition)* touching, and supported by. *The cat is sleeping on the chair. Put your cup on the table.*
2 *(preposition)* travelling in. *We were on the bus by 9 p.m.*
3 *(adjective)* working. *The television is on all day in their house.*
4 *(adverb)* about. *I want to watch this programme on the Vikings.*
5 *(adverb)* using or playing a machine or instrument. *Jim is on the computer.*
6 *(adverb)* If you have a piece of clothing **on**, you are wearing it. *I'm going to get my coat on. What have you got on?*

once *(adverb)*
1 one single time. *Sarah only wore her purple glittery shoes once.*
2 at a time in the past. *This town was once full of little shops.*
3 If you do something **at once**, you do it immediately.

one-way *(adjective)*
in one direction only. *You can't drive down there, it's a one-way street. A one-way ticket lets you travel to a place but not back again.*

onion *(noun)*
a round vegetable that grows in the ground, with a strong taste and smell. Onions can make your eyes water when you chop them. *See* **vegetable**.

online
1 *(adjective)* connected to the internet.
2 *(adverb)* on the internet. *I'm going to do some shopping online.*

only
1 *(adverb)* not more than. *I only played video games for ten minutes today.*
2 *(adverb)* and no-one or nothing else. *I only eat porridge for breakfast.*
3 *(adjective)* with no others. *This is her only successful film.*
4 *(conjunction)* but. *Iain should have won, only Diana cheated.*
5 An **only child** has no brothers or sisters.

onomatopoeia *(noun)*
using words which sound like their meaning. **onomatopoeic** *(adjective)*.

sizzle

Some examples of onomatopoeia are:

> **hiss   pop   sizzle**
> **crash   purr   bang**

onward *or* onwards *(adverb)*
1 from that point or time. *Babies eat solid food from about six months onwards.*
2 ahead, or in a forward direction. *We walked onward towards the hill despite the rain.*

ooze **oozing oozed** *(verb)*
to flow slowly. *The jam oozed out of my doughnut when I bit into it.*

opaque *(adjective)*
If something is **opaque**, you can't see through it or make sense of it. *Stella always wears opaque tights.*

open **opening opened**
1 *(adjective)* not shut. *The door was open, so I came in.* **open** *(verb)*.
2 *(verb)* to take off the cover, lid, or fastening of a container, so that you can get what is inside it. *Can you open this jar for me? Open your bag, please.*
3 *(verb)* to unfold something, or spread it out. *Open your books.* **open** *(adjective)*.
4 *(adjective)* uncovered, or not protected. *Open sea.*
5 *(adjective)* If you are **open** about something, you are honest about it. *Sam was open about his mistake.* **openly** *(adverb)*.

opening *(noun)*
1 the beginning. *The opening of the film is very scary.* **open** *(verb)*, **opening** *(adjective)*.
2 a gap or hole. *Our new tent has an opening at both ends.*

opera *(noun)*
a play in which the words are sung, not spoken. **operatic** *(adjective)*.

operation *(noun)*
1 When doctors perform an **operation**, they cut open someone's body, usually to repair something, or to take out something harmful. *I'm having an operation to remove my tonsils.* **operate** *(verb)*.
2 a large event that is carefully planned and organized. *The operation to collect all the litter on the beaches went well.* **operational** *(adjective)*.

opinion *(noun)*
1 Your **opinion** is the ideas and beliefs you have about something. *They have strong opinions about hunting.*
2 You say "**in my opinion**" to introduce your ideas about something. *In my opinion, nobody should take any notice of Nigel.*

opponent *(noun)*
the person against you in a game, argument, or fight. *Jack's opponent was much bigger than him.*

opportunity **opportunities** *(noun)*
a chance to do something.

oppose **opposing opposed** *(verb)*
If you **oppose** something, you say that
you are against it and try to stop it from
happening. *I oppose the new uniform.*

opposite
1 *(preposition)* If someone or something
is **opposite** you, they are facing you.
opposite *(adjective)*.
2 *(adjective)* completely different.
*When the teacher came, we ran in
the opposite direction.* **opposite** *(noun)*.

opposition *(noun)*
1 the person or team against you
in a game, argument, or fight.
2 If there is **opposition** to something,
lots of people say that they don't think
it is a good idea. *There was a lot of
opposition to the new road.*

optical *(adjective)*
to do with eyes, and seeing. *Look at this
optical illusion.*

optician *(noun)*
a person who tests your eyesight, and
fits glasses and contact lenses.

optimistic *(adjective)*
If you are **optimistic**, you are positive,
and believe that good things will
happen. **optimist** *(noun)*.

option *(noun)*
a choice. *There were three sandwich
options: ham, chicken, or egg.*

optional *(adjective)*
If something is **optional**, you can choose
whether or not to do it, or have it.

orange *(noun)*
1 a round fruit with thick skin and
sweet, juicy flesh. *See* fruit.
2 the colour of an orange, which can
be made by mixing yellow and red.
orange *(adjective)*.

orbit *(noun)*
the invisible, often oval-shaped path
that something follows when it is going
around a planet or a star in space.
*The Earth's orbit of the Sun
takes 365 days.*
orbit *(verb)*.

This picture
shows the
Moon's **orbit**
around the
Earth.

Moon

Earth

orchard *(noun)*
a place where fruit trees grow.

orchestra *(noun)*
a large group of musicians who
play their instruments together.
orchestral *(adjective)*.

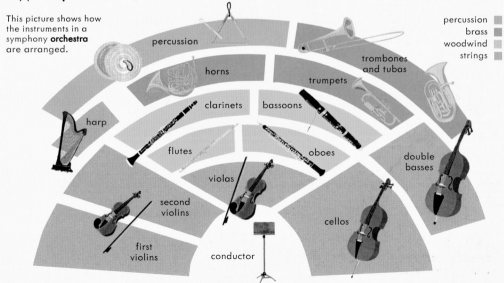

This picture shows how
the instruments in a
symphony **orchestra**
are arranged.

percussion
brass
woodwind
strings

percussion

horns

trombones
and tubas

trumpets

clarinets

bassoons

harp

flutes

oboes

double
basses

violas

second
violins

cellos

first
violins

conductor

ordeal *(noun)*

a very difficult thing to go through.

order ordering ordered *(verb)*

1 to tell someone that they must do something. *Mum ordered me to clean my room.* **order** *(noun).*
2 to ask for something in a café, restaurant, and so on. **order** *(noun).*
3 If you put things **in order**, you arrange or organize them. *In alphabetical order.*

ordinary *(adjective)*

normal, or not different or special. *Today was an ordinary day.* **ordinarily** *(adverb).*

organ *(noun)*

1 part of your body that has a special job. *Your lungs are the organs you use for breathing.*

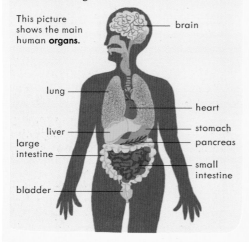

This picture shows the main human **organs**.

brain
lung
heart
liver
stomach
large intestine
pancreas
small intestine
bladder

2 a musical instrument that looks similar to a piano, but which may have several keyboards, and has lots of pipes where the sound comes out. **organist** *(noun).*

organic *(adjective)*

Fruit and vegetables that are **organic** are grown using only natural products to help them grow, or to kill pests.

organization or organisation *(noun)*

1 a big group or company, made up of people working together.
2 the job of running something. *The organization of the trip was left to me.*

organize or organise
organizing organized *(verb)*

1 to plan and arrange something. *Nathan organized the party himself.*
2 to put things in order. *Liz organizes her DVDs alphabetically.* **organizer** *(noun).*

organized or organised *(adjective)*

Someone who is **organized** is good at planning things and being in the right place at the right time, with all the things they need. *I'm much more organized than I used to be.*

origami *(noun)*

the Japanese art of paper folding.

origin *(noun)*

where something begins, or began. *What's the origin of the word "daisy"?*

original

1 *(adjective)* first, or earliest. **originally** *(adverb).*
2 *(adjective)* new, clever, and interesting. *Matt is full of original ideas.*
3 *(noun)* the actual thing, not a copy. *The original painting was lost, so we could only see a copy.*

ornament *(noun)*

a small object that is put in a room to look nice.

orphan *(noun)*

a child whose parents are both dead. **orphaned** *(adjective).*

orphanage *(noun)*

a place where orphans live and are cared for.

orthodontist *(noun)*

a special kind of dentist who fits braces and helps people get straighter teeth.

ostrich
ostriches *(noun)*

a very large bird with long legs that lives in parts of Africa, and cannot fly.

male **ostrich**

other

1 *(adjective)* different people or things. *I love sprouts, but other people in my family don't.*
2 *(adjective)* more of the same kind of thing. *Babies enjoy being with other babies.*
3 *(pronoun)* a different person or thing that has already been mentioned. *Half of the group are here, but where are the others?*
4 Every other means one out of every two. *We eat meat every other day, on Monday, Wednesday, and Friday.*

otherwise

1 *(conjunction)* if not. *I need to drink a lot of water throughout the day, otherwise I feel ill.*
2 *(adverb)* apart from that. *I'm a bit nervous, but otherwise I'm fine.*

otter *(noun)*

a furry animal that lives near water and catches fish to eat.

European otter

ought *(ort) (verb)*

If you **ought** to do something, you should do it. *We ought to eat more fresh fruit.*

our *(adjective)*

belonging to or linked to us. *Our school is going to be on television tonight.*

out

1 *(adjective)* not at home. *My sister was out all evening.*
2 *(adverb)* away from a place. *The parrot flew out of its cage.*
3 *(adverb)* not lit or burning any more. *The candles on the cake went out.*
4 *(adjective)* no longer playing in a game. *When we play cricket, Dad is always out first.*

outburst *(noun)*

a sudden release of strong emotion. *The Prime Minister's angry outburst surprised everyone.*

Out of

The words "out of" can be used to mean many different things, including:

1. from the inside to the outside of: We got **out of** the car.

2. not part of, or beyond: I was **out of** my comfort zone. The plane flew **out of** sight.

3. from a source or thing: This table is made **out of** wood.

4. with the reason of: Paul acted **out of** a desire to help.

5. without, or no longer having: We're **out of** milk.

6. a fraction or part of a group: Only two **out of** every ten thousand people will get this disease.

outdo **outdoes outdoing outdid outdone** *(verb)*

If you **outdo** someone, you do something better than they did. *Karen's saxophone solo was good, but Justin outdid her.*

outdoor *(adjective)*

happening outside. *Outdoor activities.*

outdoors *(adverb)*

in the open air, or outside. *I prefer being outdoors.*

outer *(adjective)*

on the outside, or furthest from the inside or middle. *The outer layer of the cake is chocolate cream.*

outfit *(noun)*

clothes that all go together. *Aunt Jean wore a pink outfit to the wedding.*

outgoing *(adjective)*

confident and friendly. *Reuben is very outgoing, and loves meeting people.*

outgrow

outgrowing outgrew outgrown *(verb)*
to become too big for something.

A B C D E F G H I J K L M N O P Q R S T U V W X Y Z

outing (noun)
a short trip for enjoyment.

outline (noun)
a line which shows the shape of
something. **outline** (verb).

outnumber
outnumbering outnumbered (verb)
to be larger in number than another
group. *Children outnumber adults in
this family.* **outnumbered** (adjective).

outside
1 (adverb) in the open air, not in a
building. *Let's go and play outside.*
outside (adjective).
2 (preposition) out in the open, not
in a building or under shelter. *Fatima
is outside my house.*
3 (noun) the part of a thing which
surrounds the rest of it. *The outside
of the chocolate bar was nice, but the
inside was horrible.*

outstanding (adjective)
very good indeed. *An outstanding
school report.* **outstandingly** (adverb).

oval (noun)
a shape that looks similar
to a picture of an egg.
oval (adjective).

This egg is an
oval shape.

oven (noun)
the part of a cooker
that you put things
inside to bake or roast.

over
1 (preposition) above, or on top of
something. *The picture over the sofa.*
2 (preposition) across. *Lucy stepped
over the line.*
3 (preposition) more than. *Billy ate over
20 biscuits in one day.*
4 (preposition) during or through a
period of time. *We went to my uncle's
house over Christmas.*
5 (adjective) finished. *The party's over.*
6 (preposition) about. *They were
arguing over the results.*
7 (adjective) If you are **over** something,
you have recovered from it or stopped
worrying about it. *I'm over losing my bag.*

The prefix 'over-'

- overdue
- overflow
- overgrown
- oversleep

The prefix **'over-'** often
means "too much" or
"to excess". It usually
doesn't need a hyphen
when you add it before
a word, for example:
"I hardly got to do any
swimming, because the
pool was overcrowded."

overall
1 (adverb) in general, or on the whole.
Overall, I think the fête was a success.
2 (adjective) including everything.
*The overall cost was a bit higher
than expected.*

overarm (adverb)
If you throw or hit something **overarm**,
you do it with your arm above your
shoulder. **overarm** (adjective).

overboard (adverb)
off a boat and into the water.
The pirate fell overboard.

**overcome overcoming
overcame overcome** (verb)
to beat or conquer something. *I
overcame my nerves and sang a solo.*

overcrowded (adjective)
If a place is **overcrowded**, there are
too many people there. *The beach
was overcrowded.*

overdose (noun)
too much of a medicine or drug.
overdose (verb).

overdue (adjective)
late. *My library books are overdue.*

overflow
overflowing overflowed (verb)
If something **overflows**, it spills out over
the edge of its container. *The bath
water overflowed when I left the taps on.*

overgrown (adjective)
If an area is **overgrown**, it's full of weeds and not well cared for.

overhead (adverb)
above you. **overhead** (adjective).

overhear
overhearing overheard (verb)
to hear what someone else is saying without them knowing that you're listening. *I overheard their plan.*

overjoyed (adjective)
extremely happy.

overlap
overlapping overlapped (verb)
If two things **overlap**, one of them is partly covered by the other.

overnight (adverb)
1 for the night. **overnight** (adjective).
2 very suddenly. *Tom got a new job and his mood changed overnight.*

overpower
overpowering overpowered (verb)
to defeat someone because you are stronger than they are.

overrated (adjective)
Something that is **overrated** is not as good as many people say it is.

overseas (adjective)
from, to, or to do with another country or other countries. *Mum's business has overseas customers.* **overseas** (adverb).

oversleep
oversleeping overslept (verb)
to sleep for longer than you should have done, or meant to. *I overslept again.*

overtake
overtaking overtook overtaken (verb)
If you **overtake** someone or something, such as a car, you go past it to get in front of it.

overweight (adjective)
heavier than it's healthy to be.

overwhelming (adjective)
very great in amount, or very strong. *An overwhelming emotion.* **overwhelmed** (adjective).

owe owing owed (verb)
1 If you **owe** someone money, they have lent it to you, and you haven't paid it back yet.
2 If you **owe** someone something, you feel that you should give it to them or do it for them. *I owe you an apology.*
3 **owing to** because of. *Owing to the snow, the roads are closed.*

owl (noun)
a bird which hunts small animals at night. Owls have large eyes, flat faces, and a sharp, hooked beak.

snowy owl

own
owning owned
1 (verb) to possess or have something. *I own lots of books.* **owner** (noun), **ownership** (noun).
2 (adjective) belonging to you. *I have my own room at last.*
3 If you are **on your own**, you are by yourself. *Ian lives on his own.*
4 If you **own up** to doing something wrong, you tell someone you've done it.

ox oxen (noun)
a large animal with horns, used for pulling things in some parts of the world.

oxygen (noun)
a gas found in the air, that you can't see or smell, but that people and animals need to breathe to stay alive.

oyster (noun)
a flat shellfish that you can eat, and that sometimes creates a valuable little ball in its shell, called a pearl.

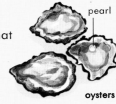
pearl
oysters

ozone (noun)
1 a poisonous, strong-smelling gas.
2 The **ozone layer** is a layer of ozone gas high above the Earth, which stops some of the Sun's harmful rays from reaching the Earth and damaging living things.

a b c d e f g h i j k l m n o p q r s t u v w x y z

Pp

pace **pacing paced**
1 (noun) the speed at which someone or something moves. *We walked at a fast pace so we wouldn't get too wet in the rain.*
2 (noun) a step, or a stride. *The pool was only 20 paces from our hotel room.*
3 (verb) If you **pace**, you walk around a small space again and again, usually because you are sad or worried. *The lion paced around his cage.*

pack **packing packed**
1 (verb) to put things into a bag or case, ready to go somewhere. **packing** (noun).
2 (noun) a collection or set of things. *I always buy a pack of three pairs of socks. A pack of cards.*
3 (verb) to make something very full. *The crowd packed into the concert hall.* **packed** (adjective).
4 (noun) a group of wild animals. *Wolves usually hunt for food in packs.*

package (noun)
a parcel. *A package has come for you.*

packaging (noun)
the wrapping or box that something is sent or sold in. *You must remove the packaging before cooking the pizza.*

packet (noun)
a small box or bag that you buy or get things in. *A packet of crisps.*

pact (noun)
a serious promise that is made between two people, organizations, or countries. *Rhys and I made a pact to keep in touch when he moved to Belgium.*

pad (noun)
1 lots of sheets of paper, all fastened together at one end.
2 a piece of thick, soft material. *I put a cool pad on Oliver's sore knee.* **padding** (noun), **padded** (adjective).

paddle **paddling paddled**
1 (verb) to walk and splash in shallow water. *We paddled in the sea.*
2 (noun) a short, wide oar, used to make canoes and other small boats move.
3 (verb) to make a canoe or other small boat move through water, using a paddle.

paddock (noun)
a small field where horses are kept or exercised.

paddy field (noun)
a field where rice is grown, which is often kept flooded with water.

paddy field and rice farmers

padlock (noun)
a lock with a curved metal bar you can fix onto things. **padlocked** (adjective).

page (noun)
1 one side of a piece of paper in a book, newspaper, or magazine.
2 text and images that you can see on your computer screen.

pain (noun)
1 the feeling in a part of your body when something hurts.
2 great suffering or sadness.

painful (adjective)
If something is **painful**, it hurts you. *My new shoes were so painful, I had to take them off.* **painfully** (adverb).

Spelling tip

painful → painfully

When '-ful' is added to the end of a word to mean "full of", it only ever has one 'l': "painful". When you add '-fully' to a word, it has two 'l's.

painkiller (noun)
a type of medicine that you take to stop pain.

paint painting painted
1 (noun) a coloured liquid that you put onto a surface. *A pot of paint.*
2 (verb) to put paint onto a surface, either to make it look nicer or to make a picture. *We painted the walls of my bedroom bright yellow.* **painter** (noun), **painting** (noun).

pair (noun)
1 two things or people that match or go together. *A pair of socks. A pair of twins.*
2 Some things are **a pair** because they have two similar parts that are joined together, for example a pair of trousers, or a pair of scissors.

palace (noun)
a very grand building, usually the home of a king, queen, or very important person. *Buckingham Palace.*

pale paler palest (adjective)
light, or not bright. *I have pale skin.*

palindrome (noun)
a word or phrase that is spelt the same forwards and backwards. The word "racecar" and the name "Hannah" are palindromes.

palm (noun)
1 the flat area on the inside of your hand, between your wrist and fingers.
2 a tall tree that grows in hot countries, with large leaves that grow out of its trunk.

pamper
pampering pampered (verb)
to treat yourself or someone else to something luxurious. *I pamper my dog with dog treats.* **pampered** (adjective).

pamphlet (noun)
a small, thin booklet. *Our school gave us a pamphlet about bullying.*

pan (noun)
a metal container with a handle, in which you cook food.

pancake (noun)
a thin, flat, round cake made from eggs, flour and milk and cooked in a pan.

pancreas pancreases (noun)
one of your organs, which makes chemicals that help break down the food you eat. *See* **organ**.

panda (noun)
a large black and white bear that lives in forests of bamboo trees in parts of China.

giant panda

pane (noun)
a sheet of glass in a window or a door.

panel (noun)
1 a board with controls on it. *The control panel inside the space centre is enormous.*
2 a group of people who discuss or judge something. *The panel couldn't decide on a winner.*
3 a flat sheet of wood or metal.

panic
1 (noun) a feeling of worry or of not knowing what to do. *Charlotte was in a panic because she couldn't find her phone.* **panic** (verb), **panicky** (adjective).
2 (adjective) If you are **panic-stricken**, you are overcome with fear.

pansy pansies (noun)
a type of small, brightly-coloured flower often grown in gardens. *See* **flower**.

pant panting panted (verb)
to breathe with short, quick breaths. *The dog pants after she's been running.*

panther (noun)
a black leopard or jaguar.

pantomime (noun)
a play usually put on at Christmas, which is often based on a fairy tale and has lots of songs and silly jokes in it.

pants (plural noun)
underwear that you wear under your clothes on the bottom half of your body.

a b c d e f g h i j k l m n o p q r s t u v w x y z

Word origin — paparazzi

This word has been borrowed from Italian. It comes from the surname of a photographer character in a famous film called "La Dolce Vita".

Other Italian words that we use in English are "zero" and "volcano"; lots of words related to food, such as "pasta", "broccoli", and "pizza", and words to do with music, such as "duet", "opera", and "piano".

paparazzi *(plural noun)*
photographers who follow famous people around to take photographs of them. *The paparazzi waited outside the star's hotel all night.*

paper *(noun)*
1 thin material used for writing or printing on, made from tiny pieces of wood. *I wrote my shopping list on a piece of paper.*
2 a newspaper. *I never have time to read the paper.*

paperback *(noun)*
a book with a cover made of thick paper, not hard board.

papier-mâché
(*pap*-ee-ay *mash*-ay) *(noun)*
a mixture of ripped-up paper and glue, which goes hard when it dries and is used for making models, masks, and so on. **papier-mâché** *(adjective)*.

parable *(noun)*
a story that has a lesson about how you should behave. *The parable of the Good Samaritan teaches us to be kind to strangers.*

parachute *(noun)*
a large piece of cloth fastened to thin ropes, which is used to drop people and things slowly and safely out of aeroplanes to the ground.

parade *(noun)*
lots of people, and sometimes decorated trucks, moving slowly along a road on a special day, while people watch.

paradise *(noun)*
a wonderful place, or heaven.

paragraph *(noun)*
a section in a long piece of writing that starts on a new line.

parallel *(adjective)*
Parallel lines go in the same direction and stay the same distance away from each other.

paralysed *(adjective)*
Someone who is **paralysed** has lost movement and feeling in part of their body, usually because of an accident or illness. **paralysis** *(noun)*, **paralyse** *(verb)*.

parasite *(noun)*
an animal or plant that gets its food by living on or inside another animal or plant. **parasitic** *(adjective)*.

parasol *(noun)*
a large umbrella that protects you from the sun.

parcel *(noun)*
something that has been wrapped in paper or put in a box, usually so that it can be sent by post.

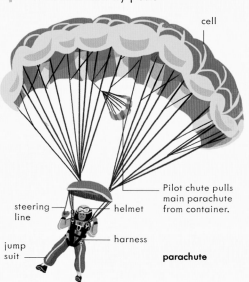

cell

steering line

helmet

Pilot chute pulls main parachute from container.

jump suit

harness

parachute

pardon **pardoning pardoned**
1 *(interjection)* You say **pardon** as a polite way of asking someone to repeat what they have just said.
2 *(interjection)* You say **pardon** after you have done something rude, such as burping, to say sorry.
3 *(verb)* If you **pardon** someone, you forgive or excuse them, or don't punish them.

parent *(noun)*
a mother or father. **parental** *(adjective)*, **parenthood** *(noun)*.

parish **parishes** *(noun)*
an area that has its own church.

park **parking parked**
1 *(noun)* a public area of land, often with grass and trees for people to use for walking, relaxing, playing, and so on.
2 *(verb)* When someone **parks** a vehicle, they leave it somewhere until they need it again. *We park our car on the street.*

parliament *(noun)*
the group of people who have been elected to make the laws of a country.

parrot *(noun)*
a bird with a curved beak and often with bright feathers.

Indian ring-necked parrot

parsnip *(noun)*
a pale yellow, sweet-tasting vegetable that grows underground. *See* **vegetable**.

part **parting parted**
1 *(noun)* a bit, a piece, or a section of something. *I've cleaned that part of the kitchen.*
2 *(noun)* a role in a play or a film.
3 *(verb)* When two people or things **part**, they separate. *We parted outside the cinema.* **parting** *(noun)*.
4 *(verb)* If you **part** two things, you separate them. *Part the curtains.*
5 If you **take part** in something, you do it. *We all took part in the school talent show.*

participate
participating participated *(verb)*
If you **participate** in something, you are involved in it or take part in it. *The whole village participated in the carnival.* **participant** *(noun)*, **participation** *(noun)*.

Participles

In English, there are two kinds of participles: the **present participle** and the **past participle**.

In the sentence, "I am eating", "eating" is the **present participle**.

In the sentence, "I have eaten", "eaten" is the **past participle**.

Some participles can be used as adjectives, for example: "confusing", "broken", and "worried".

participle *(noun)*
a form of a verb. (See box above.)

particular *(adjective)*
1 special or specific people or things. *Grandad only wants particular people to come to his birthday party.*
2 fussy. *Noah is very particular about what he eats.*

parting *(noun)*
1 the line in your hair where it's combed in two different directions. *Lily usually has a centre parting.*
2 a separation, or saying goodbye. *Our parting was very sad.*

partly *(adverb)*
not completely, or a little. *It was partly my fault, and partly hers.*

partner *(noun)*
1 the person you do something with. *Tom is my dance partner for the competition.* **partnership** *(noun)*.
2 someone's husband, wife, or the person they live with.

A B C D E F G H I J K L M N O P Q R S T U V W X Y Z

part of speech
parts of speech *(noun)*
a word, such as "noun", "verb", "adverb", and so on, that describes a word's type and job. *See* **word classes**, *page 3.*

part-time *(adjective)*
A **part-time** job or course is one that you only do for a few hours a day, or a few days a week.

party **parties** *(noun)*
1 an occasion organized for people to get together and have fun. *Grandma's having a party for her 80th birthday.*
2 A **political party** is an organization of people who all believe in similar things, and try to win elections.

pass **passes passing passed** *(verb)*
1 to go past someone or something. *If you pass the school, you've gone too far.*
2 to give someone something. *Please pass me the ketchup.*
3 to spend some time. *We passed the day bird-watching.*
4 to kick, throw or hit a ball to someone else in your team. **pass** *(noun)*.
5 to succeed in an exam or test. *I passed my grade four flute exam.* **pass** *(noun)*.
6 pass away to die.
7 pass out to faint.

passage *(noun)*
1 a narrow corridor or space linking two places.
2 a short part from a book, article, or piece of music. *The passage we studied was tricky to understand.*

passenger *(noun)*
someone travelling in a vehicle, who is not the driver.

passer-by **passers-by** *(noun)*
a person who happens to be walking past when something happens. *When the man shouted, passers-by stared.*

passion *(noun)*
a very strong feeling, often of love, desire, or enthusiasm. *Jerry's passion for cheese is amazing.* **passionate** *(adjective)*, **passionately** *(adverb)*.

Passover *(noun)*
a Jewish festival held in the spring, in memory of how Moses led the Jews out of slavery in Egypt.

passport *(noun)*
a special booklet with information about you, which you need to travel between different countries.

password *(noun)*
a secret word or set of numbers that you need to get into many computers, phones, online accounts, and so on.

past
1 *(noun)* the time before now, the present. *In the past, there were dinosaurs on Earth.* **past** *(adjective).*
2 *(preposition)* after, or on the other side of. *The church is past the housing estate.*
3 *(preposition)* When you are telling the time, you use **past** to say how many minutes after the hour it is. *It's ten past three.*
4 You use the **past tense** to talk about things that happened before now.

pasta *(noun)*
a kind of food made from flour, eggs and water, which is made into different shapes.

conchiglie

macaroni   spaghetti

lasagna or lasagne   penne

fusilli   tagliatelle   farfalle

Pasta shapes have Italian names.

paste **pasting pasted**
1 (noun) a soft, sticky mixture that you can spread, such as toothpaste.
2 (verb) to stick with glue.

pasteurized or pasteurised (adjective)
Drinks, such as milk, that are **pasteurized** have been heated to kill germs.

pastry **pastries** (noun)
1 dough made from flour, fat and water that is rolled flat and made into pies, tarts, and so on.
2 a small, sweet cake.

Danish pastry

palmier

two kinds of **pastries**

pasty **pasties** (noun)
a small pie, made from meat and vegetables wrapped in pastry.

pat **patting patted** (verb)
to tap something gently with the flat part of your hand. *Joe patted the dog.*

patch **patches**
1 (noun) a small, uneven area. *Dad has a bald patch on his head.*
2 (noun) a small piece of fabric, sewn or stuck onto something to hide a hole. **patch** (verb).
3 If you **patch something up**, you fix it quickly, but not very well.

pâté (noun)
a soft paste, usually made of meat or fish, that you spread on toast or crackers.

paternal (adjective)
to do with fathers, or being a father. *Paternal feelings.* **paternity** (noun).

path (noun)
a track that people can walk along.

pathetic (adjective)
weak, or useless. **pathetically** (adverb).

patient
1 (adjective) able to wait calmly for things for a long time, or to keep doing something for a long time without giving up. **patiently** (adverb), **patience** (noun).
2 (noun) someone who is being treated by a doctor, nurse, and so on.

patio (noun)
a paved-over area just outside a house, where people can sit and relax.

patrol (noun)
a group of people, such as the police, who walk or drive around an area to keep it safe. **patrol** (verb).

pattern (noun)
1 the way that colours and shapes are arranged to form a design. **patterned** (adjective).
2 a model or design you can copy, or use as a guide, especially in sewing and other crafts.

pause **pausing paused** (verb)
1 to stop what you are doing or saying for a while. *We paused for a rest, then carried on running.* **pause** (noun).
2 to stop a video or song for a while.

pavement (noun)
the raised path people walk along at the side of a street.

paw (noun)
the foot of an animal, such as a cat or a dog.

pay **paying paid**
1 (verb) to give someone money for something. *Dad paid me to wash the car.* **payment** (noun).
2 (noun) money you get for doing a job. *My pay was very low this month.*

PC (noun) (abbreviation)
the initials of the words "**P**ersonal **C**omputer". *I'd like to get a new PC.*

PE (noun) (abbreviation)
the initials of the words "**P**hysical **E**ducation". PE is the lesson at school in which you do some kind of sport or exercise.

Acronyms

Words like **PC** and **PE**, which are made up of the initials or first few letters of two or more words, are called **acronyms**.

pea *(noun)*
a small, round, green seed which grows in a row inside a pod, and is eaten as a vegetable. *See* pod.

peace *(noun)*
1 a time without war or conflict. *After the First World War, there was peace for 21 years.* **peacetime** *(noun).*
2 calm and quiet. *"I never get any peace!" Dad groaned.*
peaceful *(adjective),* **peacefully** *(adverb).*

peach peaches *(noun)*
a soft, juicy fruit with a slightly furry, pink and yellowish skin and a rough, hard stone in the middle. *See* fruit.

peacock *(noun)*
a blue and green male bird with tail feathers that can spread out into a huge fan shape.

peacock

peak *(noun)*
1 the top of something, such as a mountain. *We took lots of photos when we reached the peak.*
2 the highest or best point of something. *She is at the peak of her sporting success.* **peak** *(verb).*

pear *(noun)*
a juicy, rounded fruit that is narrower at the top than at the bottom. *See* fruit.

pearl *(noun)*
a small, hard, often white ball that grows inside the shells of some oysters and mussels, and can be very valuable. *Dad bought Mum pearl earrings for her birthday. See* oyster.

pebble *(noun)*
a small, round stone, often found on beaches.

peck pecking pecked *(verb)*
When a bird **pecks** something, it taps it again and again with its beak.

peculiar *(adjective)*
odd or unusual. *Tom's T-shirt is a very peculiar colour.* **peculiarly** *(adverb).*

pedal *(noun)*
a lever that is connected to something, such as a bicycle or piano, which you push with your foot to move or control it. **pedal** *(verb).*

pedestrian *(noun)*
1 a person who is walking, usually in a town.
2 pedestrian crossing a special place where cars have to stop to let pedestrians cross the road.

peel peeling peeled
1 *(noun)* the skin of a fruit or vegetable. *Our pigs love eating potato peel.*
2 *(verb)* to take the skin off a fruit or vegetable. *Mum always gets me to peel the potatoes for dinner.*
3 *(verb)* When something **peels**, parts of its outer layer come off. *The paint on the walls is peeling. I got sunburnt and now my skin is peeling.*

peep peeping peeped *(verb)*
1 to take a quick look, often in secret. *I peeped into the bag.* **peep** *(noun).*
2 If you **take a peep**, you have a quick look.

peer peering peered *(verb)*
to look very closely at something. *Mark peered into the cloudy water.*

peg *(noun)*
1 a plastic, metal or wooden clip used to hold things in place, for example tents, or clothes on a washing line. **peg** *(verb).*
2 a hook for hanging things on. *We all have our own pegs in the changing room.*

pelican *(noun)*
a large bird with a pouch under its beak which it uses to scoop up fish.

pen *(noun)*
1 a thin tool which has ink inside it, and is used for writing.
2 a small, enclosed area where farm animals such as sheep and pigs are kept.

penalty **penalties** *(noun)*
1 a punishment for breaking a rule. *The penalty for parking here without a ticket is a £60 fine.*
2 In sport, a **penalty** is a punishment for doing something wrong, which often means that the other team get an extra chance to score.

pence *(plural noun)*
a plural of penny. *That cake cost 75 pence from the bakery.*

pencil *(noun)*
a long, thin, wooden stick with a core of dark grey material called graphite inside it, used for drawing and writing. *I got some new sketching pencils for my birthday.*

penguin *(noun)*
a black and white bird that cannot fly but can swim well. Penguins mostly live in the Antarctic. *See* swim.

penny **pence** or **pennies** *(noun)*
a small coin, which has a value of one hundredth of a pound. The short way of writing and saying "penny" is 'p'. *Those sweets cost 20p.*

pension *(noun)*
money that is paid regularly to people who have retired. **pensioner** *(noun)*.

people *(plural noun)*
human beings. *People can be so kind. There were hundreds of people at the beach today.*

pepper *(noun)*
1 small, spicy seeds which are often ground up and used to flavour food.
2 a hollow, crunchy vegetable which can be red, green, orange, or yellow. *See* vegetable.

per
1 *(preposition)* in each, or for each. *We can have three pancakes per person.*
2 **per cent** *(noun)* one in every hundred, shown by the symbol (**%**). 5% means "5 in every 100". **percentage** *(noun)*.

perch **perches perching perched**
1 *(verb)* to sit on the edge of something.
2 *(noun)* a place where a bird rests when it's not flying.

percussion *(noun)*
musical instruments which you play by hitting or shaking them. **percussion** *(adjective)*.

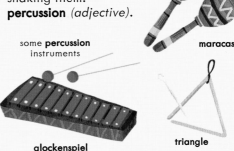

some **percussion** instruments

maracas

glockenspiel

triangle

bongos

cymbals

perfect **perfecting perfected**
1 *(**per**-fect)* *(adjective)* without any faults at all. *The food was perfect.* **perfectly** *(adverb)*, **perfection** *(noun)*.
2 *(per-**fect**)* *(verb)* to make something completely free from faults.

perform
performing performed *(verb)*
to put on a show for other people. **performance** *(noun)*.

perfume *(noun)*
a nice-smelling liquid that you put on your skin. **perfumed** *(adjective)*.

perhaps *(adverb)*
1 a word used to say that something might happen, but you're not sure.
2 a word used when you are suggesting something. *Perhaps we should go home.*

perimeter *(noun)*
the distance all around a shape or area. *The perimeter of this field is 800m.*

period *(noun)*
a length of time. *The school day is divided into five periods.*

perk
1 *(noun)* an advantage or benefit. *One of the perks of living here is that it's only five minutes from the shops.*
2 If you **perk up**, you feel better and livelier than you did before. *Kevin was feeling ill, but he's perked up now.*

permanent *(adjective)*
lasting forever, or there all the time. *The top of the mountain is so high that there is permanent snow up there.* **permanently** *(adverb)*, **permanence** *(noun)*.

permission *(noun)*
If you **give permission** for something, you say that it can happen. *Mum gave us permission to go to the park.*

permit **permitting permitted**
1 *(per-**mit**) (verb)* to allow something. *Swimming is not permitted in the lake.*
2 *(**per**-mit) (noun)* a document giving permission to do something. *You need a permit to park on the street outside Grandad's house.*

Word family

permission (noun)

permit (noun)   permit (verb)

These words are all related. The noun "permission" is formed by removing the final 't' of the verb "permit", and then adding '-ssion'.

Remember that the noun "permission" has the general meaning of allowing someone to do something, whereas the noun "permit" refers to a written document.

---

persevere
persevering persevered *(verb)*
to keep going, or keep trying, even when things are difficult. **perseverance** *(noun)*.

persist **persisting persisted** *(verb)*
to keep doing something, even when people have asked you to stop, or when it's difficult. *Jacqueline's little sister persisted in annoying us.* **persistence** *(noun)*, **persistent** *(adjective)*.

person **people** *(noun)*
a single human being.

personal *(adjective)*
private, or to do with only one person, not everyone. *My texts are personal.* **personally** *(adverb)*.

personality **personalities** *(noun)*
what kind of person you are. *Martin has a cheerful and kind personality.*

perspective *(noun)*
1 the way that things which are nearer to you look bigger than things that are far away.
2 Things **in perspective** are drawn so they look the right height, depth, width, and distance away from each other.
3 an attitude or a way of looking at something. *If you think about it from my perspective, it wasn't very helpful.*

persuade
persuading persuaded *(verb)*
to try to get someone to do something by telling them reasons why they should. *The shop assistant persuaded me to buy the speakers.* **persuasion** *(noun)*, **persuasive** *(adjective)*.

pessimist *(noun)*
a person who focuses on the bad things that happen, and expects bad things to happen to them. **pessimism** *(noun)*, **pessimistic** *(adjective)*.

pest *(noun)*
1 an insect or small animal that damages crops or plants.
2 a nuisance, or a really annoying person. *My little brother is a pest.*

pester **pestering pestered** *(verb)*
to keep asking for something over and over again. *Leah pestered her mum until she got a new phone.*

pet *(noun)*
an animal that you keep at home, for enjoyment and company.

petal *(noun)*
one of the parts of a flower, which is usually brightly coloured. *See* **plant**.

petition *(noun)*
a request to someone in power to do or change something, which is usually signed by many people.

petrol *(noun)*
liquid fuel used in cars, motorbikes, and some other vehicles.

phantom *(noun)*
a ghost or spirit.

jewellery from **Pharaoh** Tutankhamun's tomb

Pharaoh
(**fair**-oh) *(noun)*
one of the kings of Ancient Egypt. *Tutankhamun was a famous Pharaoh. See* **mummy**.

pharmacist *(noun)*
an expert in medicines and how they are used. **pharmacy** *(noun)*.

phase *(noun)*
a period or stage in a process. *Peter is going through a moody phase.*

pheasant *(noun)*
a long-tailed bird. The males of the most common type of pheasant are reddish-brown with a white stripe around their necks.

philosophy
(fill-**oss**-off-ee) *(noun)*
1 the study of what we know and believe about ourselves and the world. **philosopher** *(noun)*, **philosophical** *(adjective)*.
2 a set of beliefs or ideas that guide how a person behaves.

phobia *(noun)*
an extreme fear of something. *Tanya has a phobia of spiders.*

phone **phoning phoned**
1 *(noun)* short for **telephone**.
2 *(verb)* to call someone using a telephone. *Dad had to phone the school when I was ill.*

phonics *(plural noun)*
a way of teaching people to read and write English by teaching them about the different sounds that letters represent when they are written down.

photo *(noun)* *(abbreviation)*
short for **photograph**.

photocopy
photocopying photocopied *(verb)*
to use a machine to make a copy of a page of writing or a picture. **photocopier** *(noun)*, **photocopy** *(noun)*.

photograph *(noun)*
a picture taken by a camera. **photography** *(noun)*, **photographer** *(noun)*, **photographic** *(adjective)*.

phrase *(noun)*
a group of words that have a meaning, but do not form a sentence.

physical *(adjective)*
to do with our bodies, or done with the body. *Running and swimming are physical activities.* **physically** *(adverb)*.

physics *(noun)*
the science that studies energy, movement, heat, sound, and light. **physicist** *(noun)*.

piano *(noun)*
a large musical instrument with black and white keys that you press with your fingers to make a sound. **pianist** *(noun)*.

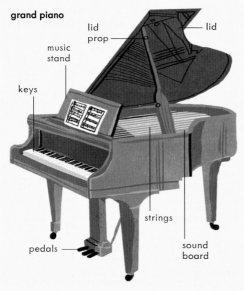

grand piano

lid prop

lid

music stand

keys

strings

pedals

sound board

pick **picking picked** *(verb)*
1 to choose. *Ms Shepherd picked me for the netball team.*
2 to take a fruit, vegetable or flower off its plant or stalk. *We picked strawberries all afternoon.*
3 If you **pick on someone**, you treat them unfairly and unkindly.
4 If you **pick something up**, you lift it.
5 If you **pick someone or something up**, you collect them. *Dad picks me up after school.*

pickle **pickling pickled**
1 *(verb)* to put food in vinegar or salty water so that it doesn't go off. **pickled** *(adjective)*.
2 *(noun)* a mixture of chopped, cooked vegetables and spices, often eaten with cold meats or cheese.

pickpocket *(noun)*
a thief who takes things out of people's pockets and bags when they aren't looking.

picky **pickier pickiest** *(adjective)*
fussy, or hard to please. *Patrick is very picky about what he eats.*

picnic *(noun)*
a meal that you pack up and eat outdoors. **picnic** *(verb)*.

picture *(noun)*
1 a drawing, painting, or photograph.
2 If you **take a picture**, you take a photograph of someone or something.

pie *(noun)*
a dish of meat, vegetables, or fruit, usually with pastry underneath and on top, which is baked in an oven.

piece *(noun)*
1 a bit or part of something, not all of it. *A piece of birthday cake.*
2 something that has been written, or made. *That piece of music is amazing.*

pier *(noun)*
a platform of metal and wood that sticks out over the sea, and often has different entertainments on it.

pierce **piercing pierced** *(verb)*
to make a hole in something. *My cousin has had her ears pierced.*

piercing
1 *(adjective)* very loud and shrill. *Mrs Jones has such a piercing voice.*
2 *(noun)* a small hole made in part of someone's body so that they can wear jewellery in it.

pig *(noun)*
an animal with a short, flat nose and a curly tail, which is kept for its meat called pork. **piggy** *(adjective)*.

Hampshire pig

pigeon *(noun)*
a common bird that often lives in cities.

piggy-back *(noun)*
If someone gives you a **piggy-back**, you ride on their back, with your arms round their neck and legs round their waist.

piglet *(noun)*
a baby pig. See **baby**.

pile *(noun)*
a heap or mound of things all on top of each other. *What a big pile of junk!*

pill (noun)
a small, solid tablet that contains medicine, which you swallow.

pillar (noun)
a thick post made of wood, concrete, metal or stone, which holds up part of a building.

pillow (noun)
a large, soft cushion which you rest your head on while you sleep. *I like to sleep with three pillows.*

pilot (noun)
1 someone who flies an aircraft. *My great-grandfather was a pilot in the Second World War.* **pilot** *(verb)*.
2 someone who guides a ship in and out of port.

pin **pinning pinned**
1 *(noun)* a small, thin, pointed piece of metal, used to fix things together. *I use pins to hold the fabric while I sew.*
2 *(verb)* to fasten or fix something with a pin. *Belle pinned her poster on the notice board.*
3 Pins and needles is the name for the tingling, burning feeling you can get in part of your body if you have been in the same position for a long time.

PIN (noun) (abbreviation)
a shorter way of saying "**P**ersonal **I**dentification **N**umber", which is the four-digit number people use at a cashpoint, or when using a bank card, for security reasons.

pinch **pinches pinching pinched**
1 *(verb)* to squeeze something between your thumb and first finger. *The smell was so bad, I had to pinch my nostrils.*
2 *(noun)* a tiny amount of something. *These chips need a pinch of salt.*

pine (noun)
a tree that has cones and sharp, thin leaves called needles, which don't drop off in the winter. *See* cone.

pineapple (noun)
a fruit with juicy yellow flesh and a thick, prickly skin. *See* fruit.

ping pong (noun)
see table tennis.

pip (noun)
a small, hard seed inside a fruit.

pipe **piping piped**
1 *(noun)* a tube used to carry liquids or gases. *The water pipe burst.*
2 *(verb)* If you **pipe** something, you send it through tubes. *Mum piped icing onto the cake.*
3 *(noun)* a tube-like musical instrument with holes, which you blow into to make a sound.

pirate **pirating pirated**
1 *(noun)* someone who attacks ships at sea. **piracy** *(noun)*.
2 *(verb)* to copy DVDs, computer games, and so on, and sell them without permission. **piracy** *(noun)*, **pirated** *(adjective)*.

pistol (noun)
a small gun that is held in one hand.

pit (noun)
1 a hole in the ground or a dip in something. *We dug a pit in the sand.*
2 a coal mine.

pitch **pitches pitching pitched**
1 *(noun)* a piece of ground where sports such as football and cricket are played.
2 *(noun)* The **pitch** of a note or sound is how high or low it is.
3 *(verb)* When you **pitch** a tent, you put it up.

pitiful (adjective)
1 If someone or something is **pitiful**, they make you feel sorry for them.
2 useless or worthless. **pitifully** *(adverb)*.

pity **pities pitying pitied**
1 *(verb)* If you **pity** someone, you feel sorry for them. *I pity the person who has to clean that mess up.*
2 *(noun)* If you say that something is a **pity**, you mean it's a shame or unfortunate. *It's a pity Mike isn't coming.*

pizza (noun)
a flat, round piece of dough covered with toppings which usually include a tomato sauce and cheese.

place – plaque

This picture shows the order of the **planets** in our Solar System (not to scale).

Sun

Mercury **Venus** **Earth** **Mars** **Jupiter** **Saturn** **Uranus** **Neptune**

rings

place **placing placed**
1 *(noun)* a position, a building, or an area. *This place is really beautiful.*
2 *(verb)* to put something somewhere carefully. *He placed the crown carefully on her head.*
3 *(noun)* the position that you come in a competition or race. *I got fourth place.*
4 If something is **in place**, it's in its proper position. *Everything was in place.*

plague *(noun)*
a serious disease that spreads quickly from one person to another.

plain **plainer plainest**
1 *(adjective)* not decorated, or not fancy. *Lisa's wedding dress was very plain.*
2 *(adjective)* simple and straightforward.
3 *(adjective)* **Plain** foods don't have much flavour. *This soup is a bit plain.*
4 *(noun)* a large, flat area of land. *The plains of Africa.*

plait *(plat)* *(noun)*
To make a **plait**, you divide hair, string, dough, and so on, into sections, and then twist them over each other. **plait** *(verb)*.

plan **planning planned**
1 *(verb)* to work out how you are going to do something. **plan** *(noun)*.
2 *(verb)* If you **plan** to do something, you mean to do it. *We plan to go on holiday next month.*
3 *(noun)* a picture showing what something looks like from above, such as a building or an area. *The plans for the new house are finished.*

plane *(noun)*
a short word for "aeroplane", a machine with wings and a powerful engine that can fly. *See* **aeroplane**.

planet *(noun)*
a large, round object that moves around a star. Earth is one of eight planets that orbit the Sun.

plank *(noun)*
a long, flat strip of wood used in building, for example for floors.

plankton *(noun)*
very tiny animals and plants which live in water and are eaten by many larger animals, including some kinds of whales.

plant
planting planted
1 *(noun)* a living thing that is often green and has stems, roots, and leaves.
2 *(verb)* If you **plant** something, you put it in soil to grow.
3 *(noun)* a factory or power station.

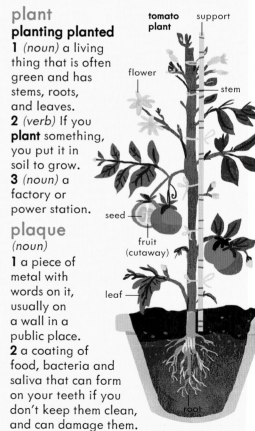

tomato plant   support

flower

stem

seed

fruit (cutaway)

leaf

root

plaque *(noun)*
1 a piece of metal with words on it, usually on a wall in a public place.
2 a coating of food, bacteria and saliva that can form on your teeth if you don't keep them clean, and can damage them.

plaster (noun)
1 a small, sticky bandage that you put on a part of your body that you have cut or grazed.
2 a paste that is spread onto walls and ceilings to make them smooth, and dries hard. **plaster** (verb), **plasterer** (noun).
3 If a part of your body is **in plaster**, it has a very hard kind of bandage around it to keep it still and protected while a broken bone heals.

plastic (noun)
a material made from chemicals that is used for making lots of different things, such as toys, cups, bags, and chairs. **plastic** (adjective).

plastic surgery (noun)
an operation to change someone's appearance or repair damage.

plate (noun)
a flat dish that you serve food on.

platform (noun)
1 a flat, raised area that people can stand on.
2 the part of a railway station where people can get on and off trains.

platypus (noun)
an Australian mammal with a furry body, a wide tail and bill, and webbed feet similar to a duck's.

play playing played
1 (verb) to have fun, often with toys and friends. *We play outside most evenings.*
2 (verb) to take part in a game or sport.
3 (verb) to be able to make a musical instrument make music. *Sam plays the piano.*
4 (noun) a story acted on a stage or television by actors, for an audience.
5 (verb) to act a part in a play, television show, and so on. *Jill played the Wicked Stepmother.*

playground (noun)
an area next to a school, in a park, and so on, where children can go to play.

playgroup (noun)
a place where young children go to play and learn together.

plead pleading pleaded (verb)
1 to beg someone to do something. *I pleaded with Mum to buy me a new pair of trainers.*
2 to say whether you are guilty or not guilty in a court case. *He pleaded not guilty.*

pleasant (adjective)
If someone or something is **pleasant**, they are nice and easy to like. *Mr Smith is a pleasant man.* **pleasantly** (adverb).

please pleasing pleased
1 (interjection) You say **please** to ask for something politely.
2 (verb) to make someone happy. *It pleased me very much to see Ashleigh again.* **pleased** (adjective).

pleasure (noun)
a feeling of enjoyment or happiness. *Eating chocolate gives me great pleasure.* **pleasurable** (adjective).

pleated (adjective)
A **pleated** piece of clothing or fabric has lots of regular folds in it.

plenty (noun)
lots, or at least as much as you need. *We always have plenty of food in the fridge.* **plentiful** (adjective).

plot (noun)
1 a secret plan. *The burglar's plot went wrong.* **plot** (verb).
2 the story of a book, film, or play. *I found the plot a bit confusing.*

plough (rhymes with "cow") (noun)
a piece of equipment that farmers use to get the ground ready for planting seeds. **plough** (verb). See **farm**.

Spelling tip — plough
Watch out for the silent 'gh' at the end of "plough". There is also a silent 'gh' in "night" and "high". The letters 'gh' can also make a 'ff' sound, as in "cough" and "rough", or they can make a hard 'g' sound, as in "ghost" and "ghastly".

a b c d e f g h i j k l m n o p q r s t u v w x y z

pluck **plucking plucked** (verb)
1 to play notes on a stringed instrument by pulling on the strings.
2 to pull feathers out of a dead bird so that you can eat it.
3 to pick fruit or flowers.

plug (noun)
1 the stopper you put in the hole in a sink or bath to keep the water in.
2 a small plastic box with metal prongs that fit into a socket in a wall. A wire connects it to electrical equipment such as a fridge, so that it can get the electricity it needs to work.

plum (noun)
a small, soft fruit, which can have purple, red or yellow skin, and has a hard seed in the middle called a stone. See **fruit**.

plumber (**plum**-er) (noun)
someone who fits and mends water pipes, taps, and heating systems.
plumb (verb), **plumbing** (noun).

plump **plumper plumpest** (adjective)
having a full, rounded shape. *Ricky is getting a bit plump. Plump pillows.*

plunge **plunging plunged** (verb)
to dive or jump into water, or to push something into water.

plural (noun)
the form of a word you need to use for more than one of something. *The plural of "dictionary" is "dictionaries". See **plurals**, page 350.*

plus (preposition)
in maths, plus means add. The plus sign looks like this: **+**.

p.m. (abbreviation)
the time between noon and midnight. *We usually eat dinner at 6 p.m.*

pocket (noun)
a part of your clothes that's similar to a small bag that you can keep things in. *I think my bus pass fell out of my pocket.*

pocket money (noun)
a sum of money that you get regularly, usually from a parent or carer, to buy things with.

pod (noun)
1 a part of a plant that contains seeds. *Peas grow in a pod.*

garden peas and **pea pod**

2 a small cabin or container, often in a spacecraft or other vehicle.

podcast (noun)
a digital recording similar to a radio programme which you can download from the internet.

poem (noun)
a piece of writing in lines which often have a rhythm, and which sometimes rhyme. **poetry** (noun), **poetic** (adjective).

poet (noun)
someone who writes poems.

point **pointing pointed**
1 (verb) to show where something is, usually with your finger. *Siobhan pointed at the bird on the windowsill.*
2 (noun) the sharp end of something. *The point of my pencil has broken off.*
3 (noun) the purpose or reason for something. *The point of the lesson was to learn about the Egyptians.*
4 (noun) Many games and sports involve scoring **points**. *I got four points, but Steph got eight.*
5 (noun) a particular place or time. *We got to the hotel at 7 p.m., by which point we were all very tired.*
6 (verb) If you **point something out**, you make other people notice it. *Abdul pointed out that we had forgotten to buy snacks.*

pointless (adjective)
If something is **pointless**, there's no good reason for doing it. **pointlessly** (adverb).

poison (noun)
a substance which can make you ill and may even kill you.
poisonous (adjective), **poison** (verb).

poke **poking poked** (verb)
to jab someone or something hard,
usually with your finger. *I poked Ian
in the ribs when he started snoring.*
poke (noun).

polar bear (noun)
a very large,
white bear
that lives
in the
Arctic and
usually
eats seals.

polar bear

pole (noun)
1 a long, round,
smooth piece of wood, metal, or
plastic. *The tent pole snapped in two.*
2 The **North Pole** and the **South Pole**
are at the top and bottom of the Earth.
polar (adjective).

pole vault (noun)
an athletic event where people jump
over a very high bar using a bendy
pole to help them. **pole-vault** (verb).

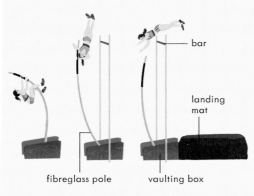

bar

landing
mat

fibreglass pole   vaulting box

stages of a **pole vault**

police (plural noun)
the people whose job is to make sure
nobody breaks the law, and to catch
criminals. **police officer** (noun).

policy **policies** (noun)
a general plan of action, suggested by
a person or organization. *The school
changed its uniform policy, so now we
have to wear ties.*

Spelling tip   polish

Sometimes, capital letters can make
a big difference. A "pole" is a stick,
but a "Pole" is a person from Poland.
To "polish" something is to make it
shiny, but "Polish" means either
"coming from or to do with Poland",
or "the language spoken in Poland".
Also, be careful not to mix up the
words "poll" and "pole", as they sound
the same.

polish **polishes polishing polished**
1 (verb) to rub something until it shines.
I always forget to polish my shoes.
2 (noun) a spray or cream that helps
make things shiny.

polite **politer politest** (adjective)
If you are **polite**, you are not rude
and have good manners. *It's polite
to hold the door open for people.*
politeness (noun), **politely** (adverb).

politician (noun)
someone who is a member of a country's
government, and is involved in how that
country is run.

politics (noun)
all the activities involved in running a
country, especially discussions between
politicians and political parties.
political (adjective), **politically** (adverb).

poll (noun)
1 a count of votes in an election.
2 a survey about what people think or
believe. *A poll found that 65 per cent of
students like the food in the cafeteria.*

pollen (noun)
the powder, usually yellow, found inside
flowers. It is carried from one flower to
another by insects or the wind so that
the flower can produce seeds.

pollution (noun)
damage caused to the environment
by things people do, such as burning
fuels and dumping waste. **pollute** (verb).

a b c d e f g h i j k l m n o p q r s t u v w x y z

pond *(noun)*
a small pool of fresh water, often found in a garden or park.

pony ponies *(noun)*
a small horse.

poo *(noun)*
the solid waste that comes out of your body when you go to the toilet.

pool *(noun)*
1 a small area of water or liquid.
2 an area of water for swimming.
3 a game in which you hit coloured balls into pockets on a table, with a long stick called a cue.

poor poorer poorest *(adjective)*
1 If you are **poor**, you don't have much money.
2 not very good. *Bill is a poor singer.*
3 a word you use if you feel sorry for someone. *That poor boy is hungry.*

poorly
1 *(adverb)* badly. *A poorly cooked steak.*
2 *(adjective)* unwell or ill. *I feel poorly.*

pop popping popped
1 *(verb)* to burst with a bang.
2 *(noun)* modern, popular music, with a strong and often fast beat.
3 *(verb)* to go somewhere quickly and not stay there for long. *Mum popped to the shops.*

Pope *(noun)*
the head of the Roman Catholic Church.

poppy poppies *(noun)*
a colourful flower with big petals and a hairy stem.

In some countries, including the UK, red paper **poppies** are worn to remember people who have died in wars. The tradition was inspired by a poem called "In Flanders Fields" by the First World War soldier John McCrae. Many battles took place at Flanders, in Belgium, and many soldiers died there. The poem mentions the poppies that grew on their graves.

popular *(adjective)*
If someone or something is **popular**, lots of people like them. **popularity** *(noun)*.

population *(noun)*
1 the people who live in a place.
2 the number of people who live in a place. *The population of Paris is around 2.2 million.*

porch porches *(noun)*
a sheltered area outside the front door of a building.

porcupine *(noun)*
an animal with lots of stiff, sharp spikes called quills on its back.

Cape porcupine

pore *(noun)*
one of the tiny holes in your skin that sweat comes out of.

pork *(noun)*
meat which comes from a pig.

porridge *(noun)*
a thick, sticky food made from oats and milk or water, often eaten for breakfast.

port *(noun)*
1 a place where boats can be loaded and unloaded.
2 a town which has a harbour.
3 If you are facing the front of a ship, **port** is the left side.

portable *(adjective)*
able to be carried easily.

portion *(noun)*
a part, serving, or piece of something.

portrait *(noun)*
a drawing, painting or photograph of someone. *Jack painted my portrait.*

pose posing posed *(verb)*
1 to keep your body in a certain position, often for a photo. **pose** *(noun)*.
2 to pretend to be someone else.

posh posher poshest *(adjective)*
a friendly word for people or things that are thought to be high-class and worth a lot of money.

Spelling tip — position

Sometimes it can be tricky to know whether a word ends '**-tion**' or '**-sion**'.

If the ending sounds like '**shun**', it will usually be spelt '**-tion**', as in "posi**tion**" and also in "addi**tion**" and "solu**tion**".

If it sounds like '**zhun**', it will usually be spelt '**-sion**', as in "confu**sion**" and "explo**sion**".

position positioning positioned
1 *(noun)* where someone or something is. *They have managed to work out the ship's position.*
2 *(noun)* the way someone is sitting, lying, or standing. *Is that position comfortable for you?*
3 *(noun)* a job. *Ms Hill left because she found a new position in Dubai.*
4 *(verb)* to put something somewhere. *Lindsay positioned the hat on my head.*
5 *(noun)* where you come in a race. *Dad got third position in the sack race.*
6 *(noun)* a situation. *Tim is in a rather tricky position.*

positive *(adjective)*
1 giving the answer "yes". *A positive response.* **positively** *(adverb)*.
2 confident or certain. *I'm positive we'll win the tournament.* **positively** *(adverb)*.
3 hopeful and cheerful. *Victoria is such a positive person.* **positively** *(adverb)*.

possession *(noun)*
something that belongs to someone. **possess** *(verb)*.

possessive *(noun)*
the form of a noun or pronoun that shows that something belongs to it. In "This ball is mine" and "Tom's bat", "mine" and "Tom's" are possessives.

possible *(adjective)*
If something is **possible**, it might happen, or might be true. *Is it possible for people to read minds?* **possibility** *(noun)*, **possibly** *(adverb)*.

post posting posted
1 *(verb)* to send a letter or parcel to someone. *I posted Russell's birthday card today.*
2 *(noun)* a long, thick piece of wood, metal or concrete that is stuck in the ground to support something or show where something is.
3 *(noun)* a job. *The post of head teacher has become available.*
4 the post *(noun)* the letters and parcels that are delivered each day.

postcard *(noun)*
a card you send, often with a picture of where you are on holiday on the front.

postcode *(noun)*
the set of letters and numbers at the end of your address.

poster *(noun)*
a large picture or notice that you put on a wall. *I have a poster of a dog in my bedroom.*

postman postmen or postwoman postwomen *(noun)*
someone who delivers the post.

post office *(noun)*
a place where you go to buy stamps and to post letters and parcels.

postpone
postponing postponed *(verb)*
to make something happen later than it was going to.

pot *(noun)*
a deep, round container. Some pots are used for cooking and storing food; others are used for growing plants.

potato potatoes *(noun)*
a roundish vegetable that grows under the ground, and can be cooked in lots of different ways. *See* **vegetable**.

jacket potato   chips   mashed potato

three ways of cooking **potatoes**

potential *(noun)*

1 Your **potential** is the things that you are capable of achieving in the future.
2 If an idea, place, and so on **has potential**, you think that it can be developed into something better.

pottery **potteries** *(noun)*

1 a place where things are made out of clay, and baked hard. **potter** *(noun)*.
2 making things out of clay. *Auntie Em enjoys pottery and painting.*

potty **potties** *(noun)*

a seat with a bowl that young children use before they are able to use the toilet.

pouch **pouches** *(noun)*

a soft bag for holding things.
See **kangaroo** and **marsupial**.

poultry
(noun)

farm birds that are kept for their eggs and meat. Chickens, ducks and geese are all types of poultry.

Geese are a type of **poultry**.

pounce
pouncing pounced *(verb)*

to jump on something suddenly and grab it. *The tiger pounced on the deer.*

pound **pounding pounded**

1 *(noun)* the main unit of money in the UK and some other countries. A pound is equal to 100 pence.
2 *(noun)* a unit of weight, equal to about 450g.
3 *(verb)* to keep hitting something very hard. *The rain pounded on the roof.*

pour **pouring poured** *(verb)*

1 If you **pour** a liquid, you make it flow out of something, such as a jug. *Could you pour me a glass of water, please?*
2 to rain very hard.

pout **pouting pouted** *(verb)*

to stick your lips out, sometimes because you are upset or cross. *Elijah pouted when his mum told him he couldn't have a new toy.*

poverty *(noun)*

the state of being very poor. *Too many people in the world still live in poverty.*

powder *(noun)*

lots of tiny grains. **powdery** *(adjective)*.

power *(noun)*

1 control over people and things. **powerful** *(adjective)*.
2 great force or strength. **powerful** *(adjective)*.
3 a kind of energy, such as electricity or nuclear power.
4 When there is a **power cut**, the electricity supply stops for a while.

practical *(adjective)*

1 to do with actually doing, making or using something, rather than having ideas about it.
2 A **practical** person is good at making and doing things with their hands.
3 sensible or useful. *That's not a very practical way to spend the money.*

practically *(adverb)*

1 almost. *It's practically impossible to wake Matt up in the morning.*
2 in a sensible way. *Abby handled the problem very practically.*

practice *(noun)*

something that you do again and again, so that you get good at it. *Ella does her clarinet practice every evening.*

practise **practising practised** *(verb)*

1 to do something lots of times, so that you'll be able to do it well. *I practise singing every day.*
2 If someone **practises** a religion, they follow its teachings and go to services or celebrations.

Spelling tip
practice
practise

Be careful when you are spelling these words.

"Practice", with a 'c', is a noun.
"Practise", with an 's', is a verb.

praise praising praised (verb)
1 to say that someone has done well, or that you like something. *The teacher praised my drawing.* **praise** (noun).
2 to thank and worship God or a god. **praise** (noun).

pram (noun)
a small carriage that you can push a baby around in.

prank (noun)
a joke or trick that you play on someone.

prawn (noun)
a small shellfish that you can cook and eat. Prawns turn pink when you cook them.

pray praying prayed (verb)
When you **pray**, you talk to the god you believe in, and ask for help or guidance. **prayer** (noun).

precaution (noun)
something that you do to prevent something dangerous or unpleasant from happening. *Let's take an umbrella as a precaution.*

precious (**presh**-uss) (adjective)
very valuable. *That necklace is precious.*

precise (adjective)
exact and accurate. *You have to be precise when you weigh the ingredients.* **precisely** (adverb).

predator (noun)
an animal that hunts and kills other animals. **predatory** (adjective).

"Predator" comes from the Latin "praedari", meaning "to rob".

predicament (noun)
a tricky or awkward situation.

predict predicting predicted (verb)
to say what you think will happen in the future. *I predict that the sun will come out this afternoon.* **prediction** (noun).

prefer preferring preferred (verb)
If you **prefer** something, you like it better than another thing. *I prefer butter to margarine.* **preference** (noun).

Prefixes

Some examples of prefixes are:

un- Dad was **un**happy about all the mess we'd made.

re- I had to **re**do my hair after I went out in the rain.

prefix prefixes (noun)
a group of letters that are added to the front of a word to change its meaning. *See* prefixes, *page 351.*

pregnant (adjective)
A **pregnant** woman or animal has a baby growing inside her. **pregnancy** (noun).

prehistoric (adjective)
from the time before things were written down to create the history we can read about. **prehistory** (noun).

Elasmosaurus was a **prehistoric** animal.

prejudice (noun)
an unfair or unreasonable opinion about someone or something. **prejudiced** (adjective).

prepare preparing prepared (verb)
to get ready. **preparation** (noun).

preposition (noun)
a word showing the position of things or people in relation to each other. *See* prepositions, *page 351.*

preschool or **pre-school** (adjective)
to do with children who are too young to go to school. **pre-school** (noun).

prescription (noun)
a note from a doctor to take to a chemist, so you can get the medicine you need.

a b c d e f g h i j k l m n o p q r s t u v w x y z

A B C D E F G H I J K L M N O P Q R S T U V W X Y Z

present **presenting presented**
1 (*prez-ent*) (*noun*) a gift. *Mum always gives me a lovely birthday present.*
2 (*prez-ent*) (*noun*) now, not the past or the future.
3 (*prez-ent*) (*adjective*) in the place you are meant to be. *Is everybody present?*
4 (*priz-ent*) (*verb*) to talk, introduce guests, and so on, on a radio or television programme. **presenter** (*noun*).
5 (*priz-ent*) (*verb*) to give something to someone. *Present your ticket at the door.*

presentation (*noun*)
1 the way something looks. *The food was nice, but the presentation was bad.*
2 a special ceremony, where a gift is given. *There was a presentation when Mr Jones left.*

preserve
preserving preserved (*verb*)
1 If you **preserve** something, you look after it, so that it doesn't get spoilt. **preservation** (*noun*).
2 to treat food so that it doesn't go bad.

president (*noun*)
the person people elect to lead a country which doesn't have a king or a queen. **presidency** (*noun*).

press **presses pressing pressed**
1 (*verb*) to push firmly.
2 the press (*noun*) the general name for people who find news and write news reports.

pressure (*noun*)
1 stress, or things that people expect you to do. *There is too much pressure to pass exams at this school.*
2 the force made when one thing pushes on another.

presume
presuming presumed (*verb*)
to think that something is true, because it seems quite likely. *I presume that you're looking forward to the weekend?*

pretend
pretending pretended (*verb*)
to act as if something is true, even when it's not. *Tara pretended to be my friend.*

pretty **prettier prettiest**
1 (*adjective*) nice to look at.
2 (*adverb*) quite. *This app is pretty good.*

prevent
preventing prevented (*verb*)
If you **prevent** something, you stop it from happening. **prevention** (*noun*).

preview (*noun*)
a chance to see something, such as a film or a play, before most people can.

previous (*adjective*)
the one before. *I liked our previous teacher better.* **previously** (*adverb*).

prey (*pray*) (*noun*)
an animal that is hunted by other animals. *Mice are often the prey of owls.*

Spelling tip

prey
pray

Be careful not to confuse the words "pray" and "prey". They sound the same, but have different meanings.

---

price (*noun*)
what you pay for something.

priceless (*adjective*)
worth more than any amount of money. *My cats are priceless to me.*

prick **pricking pricked** (*verb*)
to make a small hole in something with a sharp point, such as a needle. **prick** (*noun*).

prickly (*adjective*)
covered in spines, spikes, or thorns. *Hedgehogs are very prickly.*

pride (*noun*)
1 a feeling of happiness and being pleased with yourself, because you have done something well.
2 If you **take pride in** something, you are proud of it. *She takes pride in her work.*
3 a group of lions.

priest (*noun*)
someone who leads religious services.

primary (adjective)

1 first, or most important. *The primary problem is cost.*
2 Primary school is where most children go from the age of around four to eleven.
3 Primary colours are ones that can't be made by mixing other colours. They are red, yellow, and blue. Other colours are mixtures of these three.

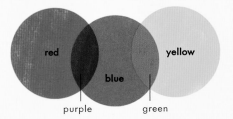

red
yellow
blue
purple
green

This picture shows how mixing the three **primary colours** creates new colours.

prime

1 (adjective) the best, or most important. *Prime beef.*
2 (noun) A **prime number** is a number that you can only divide by itself. 7, 13 and 29 are prime numbers.

prince (noun)

the son of a king or queen, or the husband of a princess.

princess princesses (noun)

the daughter of a king or queen, or the wife of a prince.

print printing printed (verb)

to use a machine to produce copies of a document, book, newspaper, or magazine. **printer** (noun).

print-out (noun)

a printed copy of a computer document.

priority priorities (noun)

something that is more important than anything else.

prison (noun)

a building or set of buildings where people are kept as a punishment for breaking the law. **prisoner** (noun).

private (adjective)

If something is **private**, you don't want everyone to know about it, see it, or use it. **privacy** (noun), **privately** (adverb).

Spelling tip   prize

Some words which end '-ize' can also be spelt '-ise', such as "real**ize**"/"real**ise**" and "organ**ize**"/"organ**ise**". However, "pri**ze**" (when it means a reward) must always be spelt with a 'z'.

prize (noun)

a reward for winning something. *The prize is a trip to a theme park.*

pro- (prefix)

Pro- means "for" or "in favour of" when added to a word, for example, "pro-hunting".

probably (adverb)

likely, but not certainly. *The bus will probably be late.* **probable** (adjective).

problem (noun)

1 a tricky or difficult situation that you need to sort out. **problematic** (adjective).
2 a puzzle or question to be solved. *A maths problem.*

process processes (noun)

a series of things that have to be done one after another for something to happen. *The process of making bread.*

procession (noun)

lots of people walking or driving together through the streets. *A carnival procession.*

prod prodding prodded (verb)

to poke someone or something, usually with your finger. *We prodded Dad to wake him up.* **prod** (noun).

produce producing produced

1 (prod-**yuce**) (verb) to make or create something. *Our garden produces lots of vegetables.*
2 (prod-**yuce**) (verb) to bring out or show. *The magician produced a rabbit from under his hat.*
3 (**prod**-yuce) (noun) things that are grown or made for eating. *We try to buy only organic produce.*

a b c d e f g h i j k l m n o p q r s t u v w x y z

A B C D E F G H I J K L M N O P Q R S T U V W X Y Z

product (noun)
1 something that is made or manufactured. *There are so many hair products in the shops.*
2 what you get when you multiply two numbers together. *The product of 3 and 6 is 18.*

production (noun)
1 the process of making a product.
2 a play, show, opera, and so on.

professional (adjective)
paid to do something. *A professional footballer.* **professional** (noun), **professionally** (adverb), **profession** (noun).

profile (noun)
1 basic information about something, or about someone's life.
2 the view of your face from the side.

profit (noun)
the money you make when you sell something, after you've taken away the cost of making or buying it. **profitable** (adjective), **profit** (verb).

program (noun)
instructions for a computer to follow, written in a special code. **programmer** (noun), **program** (verb).

programme (noun)
1 a show on the television or radio.
2 a leaflet you get at an event, which tells you about it.

progress
progresses progressing progressed
1 (verb) to get better at something. *Erin is progressing well at school.* **progress** (noun), **progression** (noun).
2 If you **make progress**, you are getting better, or moving forward.

project (noun)
1 a plan, or idea. *Making a pond is a project for the whole school.*
2 a piece of work which takes time and research. *A project on the Romans.*

promise **promising promised** (verb)
to say that you'll definitely do something. *I promise I'll come.* **promise** (noun).

Pronouns

Here are the names of some of the most common types of pronouns you will see, and examples of how they are used:

personal pronouns
he/she/it; him/her.
Jake kicked the ball. → **He** kicked it.

possessive pronouns
his; hers; theirs
That's Jake's ball. → That's **his** ball.

relative pronouns
who; which; that
The boy **who** kicked the ball is here.

pronoun (noun)
a word that replaces a noun (a thing) in a sentence. *See* word classes, *page 3 and* pronouns, *page 351.*

pronounce
pronouncing pronounced (verb)
The way you **pronounce** a word is the way that you say it. *Different people pronounce the word "grass" with a short 'a' or a long 'a'.* **pronunciation** (noun).

proof (noun)
something that shows that a thing is true. *Do you have any proof that she took your phone?*

prop **propping propped**
1 (verb) If you **prop** something somewhere, you lean it there so that it doesn't fall over.
2 (verb) If you **prop something up**, you support it with something.
3 (noun) a movable object that is used in a play or film. *There was panic when we thought we'd lost one of the props.*

propeller (noun)
a set of blades that spin around to make a plane or a ship move. *See* helicopter.

proper *(adjective)*
1 correct or right. *Did you put your sports clothes in the proper place?* **properly** *(adverb)*.
2 real or suitable. *Why don't you wear a proper coat when it's raining?*

proper noun *(noun)*
the name of a person, place, time, or organization, such as "Faye", "Oxford", and "December". Proper nouns always start with a capital letter.

property **properties** *(noun)*
1 the things you own. *Please don't take my property without asking.*
2 a building and the land around it. *This house is a very valuable property.*

prophet *(noun)*
In some religions, a **prophet** is someone who is believed to have been contacted by God and then passed on his message to people on Earth.

propose **proposing proposed** *(verb)*
1 to suggest something. *I propose we go home now.* **proposition** *(noun)*.
2 to ask someone to marry you. *John proposed to Eleanor on top of a mountain.* **proposal** *(noun)*.

prosecute
prosecuting prosecuted *(verb)*
to accuse someone in a court of committing a crime. **prosecution** *(noun)*.

protect **protecting protected** *(verb)*
to look after someone or something, or guard them. **protection** *(noun)*.

protein *(noun)*
a substance that you get from food, especially foods such as meat and beans, which your body needs to grow and repair itself.

seeds

egg

meat

yogurt

These foods are all sources of **protein**.

protest **protesting protested** *(verb)*
to say that you disagree with something, often in public. *Lots of people have been protesting about the plans to knock down the gallery.* **protest** *(noun)*, **protester** *(noun)*.

Protestant *(noun)*
a Christian who is not a Roman Catholic.

protractor *(noun)*
a plastic tool shaped like a semicircle that you use to measure angles in maths.

protractor

proud **prouder proudest** *(adjective)*
1 If you are **proud**, you are pleased about what you or someone else has done. *I'm proud of my brother for winning the gymnastics competition.* **proudly** *(adverb)*.
2 **Proud** people don't accept help from others easily, because they want to be independent.

prove **proving proved** *(verb)*
to show that something is true. *Please get your parents to sign the letter to prove that they have seen it.*

provide **providing provided**
1 *(verb)* to bring or give something that is needed. *Mum provided the drinks at half-time.* **provision** *(noun)*.
2 **provided** *(conjunction)* as long as, or if. *I will go, provided you do too.*

province *(noun)*
an area of a country. *Dad is on a work trip to the Sichuan province of China.*

prowl **prowling prowled** *(verb)*
to move very quietly and secretly. *The fox prowled around the farm.*

prune **pruning pruned**
1 *(verb)* to trim a tree or bush to make it grow back more strongly.
2 *(noun)* a dried plum.

PS or **ps** *(abbreviation)*
You write **PS** to introduce a short note added to the end of a letter or email, after you have written your name.

Spelling tip psychiatrist

There is a silent 'p' at the beginning of "psychiatrist". Not many words have a silent 'p', but some others you may see are "pterodactyl" (a kind of extinct flying reptile) and "pneumonia" (an illness that affects the lungs).

psychiatrist (sy-**ky**-uh-trist) (noun)
a doctor who helps people who have mental illnesses.

pub (noun)
a place where people, usually adults, can go to meet, drink, and sometimes eat together.

puberty (**pew**-ber-tee) (noun)
the time when your body changes from being a child to an adult.

public
1 the public (noun) people in general.
2 (adjective) for everyone. Public transport is great in London.
3 If something happens **in public**, everyone can see it.

publish
publishes publishing published (verb)
to produce and and sell books, magazines, newspapers, and so on.

pudding (noun)
a sweet food that is served after the main course in a meal.

puddle (noun)
a pool of liquid, such as rainwater.

puff puffing puffed (verb)
1 to breathe or blow something, such as air or smoke, in short bursts. **puff** (noun).
2 If something **puffs up**, it swells. My eyes puff up with hay fever.

pull pulling pulled (verb)
1 to hold something and move it towards you. **pull** (noun).
2 If you **pull out** of something, you stop doing it. Adam pulled out of the race.

pulse (noun)
a steady beat, especially the pumping of your blood around your body by your heart, which you can feel in your neck and in your wrist.

pump pumping pumped
1 (noun) a machine that forces liquid, air or gas from one place to another.
2 (verb) to force liquid, air or gas into or out of something. They pumped the flood water into the river.

pumpkin (noun)
a big, round, orange fruit that people often think is a vegetable.

pun (noun)
a joke based on a word that has more than one meaning, or words that sound similar.

A Jack-o'-lantern is a Halloween decoration made in some countries by carving a **pumpkin**.

An example of a pun is: "When a clock is hungry it goes back four seconds."

punch punches punching punched
1 (verb) to hit someone with your fist. **punch** (noun).
2 (noun) a tool for making holes, especially in paper or leather.
3 (noun) a drink made from fruit juices, spices, and usually alcohol.

punctual (adjective)
If you are **punctual**, you are not early or late, but arrive at the right time. My New Year's resolution is to be more punctual. **punctually** (adverb), **punctuality** (noun).

punctuation (noun)
marks that you use when you write to make your meaning clear. Punctuation marks include full stops, commas, and colons. See punctuation, page 349.

puncture (noun)
a hole in something that is filled with air, such as a ball or a tyre. I had to walk home because my bike tyre got a puncture. **puncture** (verb).

punish
punishes punishing punished (verb)
If you **punish** someone, you make them suffer in some way for doing something wrong. *My parents punished me for lying by taking away my phone for a week.* **punishment** (noun).

pupil (noun)
1 someone who is learning from a teacher. *How many pupils are in your class?*
2 the round, black part of your eye.

puppet (noun)
a small doll that you control by putting your hand inside it, or by pulling strings.

puppy **puppies** (noun)
a young dog. *We called the puppy Tess.*

purchase
purchasing purchased (verb)
to buy something. **purchase** (noun).

pure **purer purest** (adjective)
clean, or not mixed with anything else. *Pure orange juice.* **purity** (noun).

purple (noun)
the colour that is made when you mix red and blue together. **purple** (adjective).

purpose (noun)
1 a reason. *The purpose of this trip is to study the castle.*
2 If you do something **on purpose**, you do it deliberately. *Lucas tripped me up on purpose.* **purposely** (adverb).

purr **purring purred** (verb)
1 When a cat **purrs**, it makes a low sound in its throat to show that it is happy. *Our cat always purrs loudly.*
2 to make a low sound, like a cat.

purse (noun)
a small bag that you carry money in.

pursue **pursuing pursued** (verb)
to follow or chase someone or something. **pursuit** (noun).

push **pushes pushing pushed** (verb)
1 to move something away from you, often using your hand. **push** (noun).
2 to move yourself forward.

put **putting put** (verb)
1 When you **put** something somewhere, you move it so that it is in that place. *I put my book on the bedside table.*
2 When you **put something down**, you stop carrying it.
3 When you **put something off**, you decide to do it later rather than now.
4 If something **puts someone off**, it makes them not want to do something. *I was put off getting food by the long queue.*

puzzle (noun)
1 a game or activity which you have to think about to solve. *A crossword puzzle.*
2 something that's tricky to understand.

pyjamas (plural noun)
a loose top and trousers that you can wear in bed.

pylon (noun)
a tall, tower-like structure that is used for carrying electricity cables high above the ground.

pyramid (noun)
1 a solid shape with triangular sides that meet at the top. *See shapes, page 348.*
2 a huge, pyramid-shaped stone tomb that an Egyptian Pharaoh was buried in.

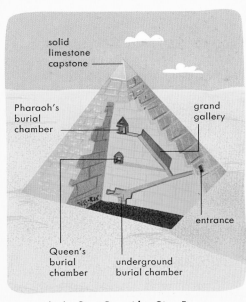

solid limestone capstone

Pharaoh's burial chamber

grand gallery

entrance

Queen's burial chamber

underground burial chamber

inside the **Great Pyramid** at Giza, Egypt

a b c d e f g h i j k l m n o p q r s t u v w x y z

Qq

quack *(noun)*
the loud, harsh noise that a duck makes.
quack *(verb)*.

The prefix 'quad-'

quadrilateral

quadruple

quadruplets

The prefix 'quad-' means "four". It comes from the Latin word for four, "quattor". "**Quad**ruplets" are four babies born at the same time, and "**quad**ruple" means "four times as many".

quad bike *(noun)*
a small motor vehicle with four large wheels and no roof, which is often used for driving over rough land.

quadrilateral *(noun)*
a flat shape with four straight sides.

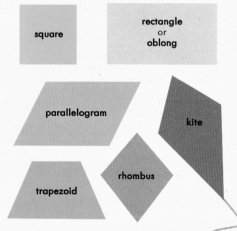

All these shapes are **quadrilaterals**.

quadruple *(adjective)*
four times as big, or four times as many.
quadruple *(verb)*.

quadruplet *(noun)*
one of four babies born at the same time to the same mother.

quaint
quainter quaintest *(adjective)*
charming, unusual, or old-fashioned.
We had lunch in a quaint little village.

quake **quaking quaked**
1 *(verb)* to shake or tremble, especially with fear.
2 *(noun)* an **earthquake**.

qualification *(noun)*
something which proves that you have reached a certain standard or passed a test. *What qualifications do you need to be a teacher?*

qualify
qualifies qualifying qualified *(verb)*
1 to complete a course and pass tests which allow you to work in certain jobs.
2 to reach the level needed to enter a competition.

quality **qualities** *(noun)*
1 how good or bad something is.
2 a feature or characteristic of someone or something. *Liv has many good qualities.*

quantity **quantities** *(noun)*
an amount or number of something. *Check the quantity of butter you need.*

quarantine *(noun)*
When a person or animal is in **quarantine**, they are kept away from others in case they have a disease. **quarantine** *(verb)*.

quarrel
quarrelling quarrelled *(verb)*
to have an argument or an angry discussion. **quarrel** *(noun)*.

quarry **quarries** *(noun)*
a place where stone is dug from the ground, often for building. **quarry** *(verb)*.

quarter *(noun)*
1 one of four equal parts of something.
2 When you are telling the time, **quarter past** means 15 minutes past the hour, and **quarter to** means 15 minutes before the hour.

A B C D E F G H I J K L M N O P Q R S T U V W X Y Z

quay *(key)* *(noun)*
a place where boats and ships can stop to be loaded or unloaded.

queasy
queasier queasiest *(adjective)*
If you are **queasy**, you feel as though you are going to be sick.

queen *(noun)*
1 a female ruler of a country, or the wife of a king.
2 a chesspiece that can move in any direction. *See* chess.
3 a playing card with a picture of a queen on it.

queer queerer queerest *(adjective)*
odd or strange. *I had a queer feeling that we were being watched.*

quench
quenches quenching quenched *(verb)*
1 to put out a fire with water.
2 to get rid of your thirst with a drink.

query *(kweer-ee)* **queries** *(noun)*
a question, especially one you ask because you are doubtful or want information. **query** *(verb)*.

quest *(noun)*
a difficult journey with a challenge or reward at the end of it. **quest** *(verb)*.

question *(noun)*
1 a sentence that asks something.
2 a problem, or something that is being discussed. *The question of time travel.*

question mark *(noun)*
the punctuation mark (**?**) used to show that a question is being asked.

questionnaire *(noun)*
a set of questions used to find out people's opinions about something.

queue *(kyoo)* *(noun)*
a line of people waiting for something. **queue** *(verb)*.

quick quicker quickest *(adjective)*
1 fast, or not taking very long. **quick** *(adverb)*, **quickly** *(adverb)*.
2 clever, or able to learn things without difficulty.

quiet quieter quietest *(adjective)*
1 not making much or any noise. *Martha's voice is very quiet.* **quietly** *(adverb)*.
2 calm, still, and peaceful.

quilt *(noun)*
a thick, padded bedcover.

quit quitting quit *or* **quitted** *(verb)*
1 to leave a place or a job, or to stop doing something.
2 to exit a program or application on a computer.

quite *(adverb)*
1 rather, or fairly. *I am quite hungry.*
2 completely. *We haven't quite finished our dinner yet.*

quiver quivering quivered *(verb)*
to tremble or shake very slightly. **quivering** *(adjective)*.

quiz quizzes *(noun)*
a set of questions that tests your knowledge of something. *We have a history quiz tomorrow.* **quiz** *(verb)*.

quotation *(noun)*
words from a book, play, speech, and so on, repeated or written down by someone else.

quotation mark *(noun)*
the punctuation mark (**'**) or (**"**) that you write before and after words to show a quotation, or that someone is speaking.

quote quoting quoted *(verb)*
to repeat words that were spoken or written by someone else. **quote** *(noun)*.

Qur'an *or* **Koran** *(noun)*
the holy book of Islam.

Spelling tip

quote → quoting → quoted

When you add the ending '–ing' or '–ed' to a word that ends with a silent 'e', remember to remove the silent 'e' first.

a b c d e f g h i j k l m n o p q r s t u v w x y z

Rr

rabbi (*rab-eye*) (noun)
a priest in the Jewish religion.

rabbit (noun)
a small, furry animal
with long ears.

lop-eared
rabbit

race

racing raced
1 (verb) to go very fast.
We raced to get the train.
2 (noun) a competition to see
who is the fastest at something.
race (verb).
3 (noun) a group of people who
originally come from the same area
of the world, and have similar features
such as skin and hair colour.

racial (adjective)
to do with race. *Racial abuse.*

racist (adjective)
1 Someone who is **racist** does not
believe that all people are equal, and
treats people from some races unfairly.
racism (noun), **racist** (noun).
2 Something that is **racist** is offensive
to people of certain races.

rack (noun)
a shelf with spaces to put things on
or in. *Put your shoes on the rack.*

racket or **racquet** (noun)
1 an oval frame with strings stretched
across and a handle, which you use
to play sports such as tennis, squash,
or badminton.
2 a friendly word for lots of loud noise.
Stop making such a racket!

radar (noun)
a system that planes and ships use
to find the position of things in the
air or at sea. Radar stands for "**Ra**dio
Detecting **A**nd **R**anging".

radiator (noun)
a metal heater full of hot liquid, which
keeps a room warm.

radio (noun)
a machine that picks up electrical
waves in the air and turns them into
sound, so that you can listen to music,
programmes, news, and so on.

radish radishes (noun)
a small vegetable, usually
with a red skin and a
white inside, that is
often eaten in salads.

radish

radius radiuses or **radii** (noun)
the distance from the centre of a circle
or sphere to the outside. *See* circle.

raffle (noun)
a way of raising money by selling
tickets, some of which win prizes.

raft (noun)
a small, flat boat made of things,
usually logs, tied together. *See* boat.

rag (noun)
a piece of old cloth, or old clothing.

rage raging raged
1 (verb) to be violent or noisy. *The fire
raged all night.*
2 If you are **raging**, or **in a rage**,
you are very angry.

ragged (*rag-id*) (adjective)
torn and scruffy. *Joe's clothes were
very ragged.*

raid raiding raided (verb)
to attack a place secretly and suddenly.
We raided the fridge. **raid** (noun).

rail (noun)
1 one of the metal bars that trains
run on.
2 If you travel **by rail**, you go somewhere
on a train.
3 a bar that you can hold onto. *Hold
the rail when you come down the stairs.*

railway (noun)
1 the long metal bars that trains travel on.
2 a network of train routes.

rain raining rained (verb)
When it **rains**, water falls from clouds
in the sky. **rain** (noun), **rainy** (adjective).

rainbow *(noun)*
an arch of different colours in the sky, caused by the sun shining through raindrops.

The colours of the **rainbow** are: red, orange, yellow, green, blue, indigo, and violet.

raindrop *(noun)*
a drop of rain.

rainfall *(noun)*
the amount of rain that falls in a certain place over a certain time.

rainforest *(noun)*
a very thick forest in a hot country where it rains a lot, which is home to lots of different animals and insects.

These are some animals that live in **rainforests**.

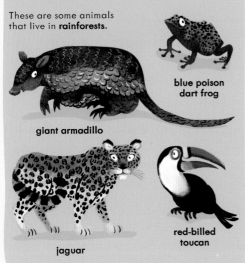

giant armadillo

blue poison dart frog

jaguar

red-billed toucan

raise **raising raised** *(verb)*
1 to lift something up so that it's higher.
2 If you **raise a child**, you support and teach them until they are old enough to get by on their own.
3 If you **raise money**, you collect it, often for a charity or for another good cause.

raisin *(noun)*
a dried grape.

rake *(noun)*
a gardening tool with metal teeth, used for breaking up lumps of soil and collecting grass and leaves. **rake** *(verb)*.

ram **ramming rammed**
1 *(verb)* to crash into something on purpose.
2 *(verb)* to push something into a space.
3 *(noun)* a male sheep.

RAM *(noun)* *(abbreviation)*
the part of a computer's memory that is lost when you turn the computer off. RAM stands for "**R**andom **A**ccess **M**emory".

Ramadan *(noun)*
the ninth month of the Islamic year, when many Muslims don't eat between sunrise and sunset.

ramble **rambling rambled** *(verb)*
1 to speak for a long time in a way that is not easy to understand.
2 to go on a long walk in the countryside for fun. **ramble** *(noun)*.

ramp *(noun)*
a slope that connects two levels.

ran *(verb)*
the past tense of **run**.

ranch **ranches** *(noun)*
a large cattle farm.

random *(adjective)*
1 without any plan or particular order. *Random numbers.* **randomly** *(adverb)*.
2 If you do something **at random**, you do it without any plan or purpose.
3 a friendly word for unusual, or unexpected. *That film's a bit random.*

range **ranging ranged**
1 *(noun)* a selection or collection of things. *There's a huge range of food on the menu.*
2 *(noun)* a long row of mountains.
3 *(noun)* how far something can go or travel. *These walkie-talkies have a range of one kilometre.*
4 *(verb)* to be between two points. *The guests' ages ranged from 9 to 99.*

a b c d e f g h i j k l m n o p q r s t u v w x y z

rank *(noun)*
the job someone does, and how important they are, in an organization. *Dad's rank is sergeant.*

ransom *(noun)*
money that has to be paid before someone is set free. *The kidnappers demanded a ransom.*

rant **ranting ranted** *(verb)*
to talk or shout about something in an angry way. *Freya wouldn't stop ranting about the price of popcorn at the cinema.* **rant** *(noun)*.

rap **rapping rapped**
1 *(noun)* a kind of music in which the words are spoken, not sung. **rap** *(verb)*, **rapper** *(noun)*.
2 *(verb)* to hit something hard and fast. *Liam rapped on the door.*

rapid *(adjective)*
happening quickly, or in a short time. **rapidly** *(adverb)*.

rare **rarer rarest** *(adjective)*
1 unusual, or not seen very often. *Pandas are very rare in the wild.* **rarely** *(adverb)*.
2 Rare meat is hardly cooked at all.

rash **rashes** *(noun)*
spots or red patches that appear on your skin when you are ill or allergic to something.

raspberry **raspberries** *(noun)*
a small, dark pink fruit with lots of seeds. *See* berry.

rat *(noun)*
an animal similar to a large mouse, with a long tail.

black rat

rate **rating rated**
1 *(noun)* how quickly something happens. *Cars pass this point at the rate of two a minute.*
2 *(noun)* a fee. *What's your rate for this kind of work?*
3 *(verb)* to value someone or something, or say what you think of it. *Lots of people really rate this new album.*

rather *(adverb)*
1 quite, or fairly. *It's rather cold today.*
2 If you would **rather** do or have one thing than another, you'd prefer it.
3 rather than and not, or instead of. *He's shy rather than unfriendly.*

ratio *(noun)*
how many of one thing there are compared to another, shown in the smallest numbers possible. For example, in a class of five boys and 15 girls, the ratio of boys to girls is one to three or 1:3.

rattle **rattling rattled** *(verb)*
to make a knocking noise. *That window rattles when the wind blows.*

raw *(adjective)*
not cooked. *I can't stand raw carrots.*

ray *(noun)*
1 a beam of strong light.
2 a large fish with a flat body, fins similar to wings, and a long tail.

fin

tail

manta ray   eye

razor *(noun)*
a sharp blade that people use to shave off unwanted hair.

reach
reaches reaching reached *(verb)*
1 to be able to touch something. *I can't reach the door handle.*
2 to stretch out with your hand. *Iona reached for the top shelf.*
3 to arrive in a place. *We reached the platform just as the train was leaving.*
4 to go as far as a certain point. *Dan's hair reaches his shoulders.*

react **reacting reacted** *(verb)*
The way that you **react** to something is what you do or say, or how you behave when it happens. *Tara reacted quickly when she saw the car coming.* **reaction** *(noun)*.

read reading read (verb)
to look at, and be able to understand, written or printed words. **reading** (noun).

ready (adjective)
1 If you are **ready**, you are prepared to do something and can start right away. *I'll be ready to leave in two minutes.*
2 If something is **ready**, you can have it. *Breakfast is ready.*

ready meal (noun)
a meal that has already been made, so you just have to heat it up.

real (adjective)
Something **real** actually exists, and is not made-up, fake, or imagined. *We saw a real lion on safari.*

realistic (adjective)
1 very similar to the real thing. *That portrait is very realistic.*
2 A **realistic** person is sensible and views things as they really are. *We need to be realistic about how far we're able to walk.*

reality realities (noun)
the way things are, rather than the way we might imagine or like them to be.

realize or **realise**
realizing realized (verb)
to become aware of something. *I only realized I was wearing odd shoes when I got to school.* **realization** (noun).

really (adverb)
1 very. *Lucy is really good at karate.*
2 genuinely or truly. *Are you really going to eat all that food?*

reappear
reappearing reappeared (verb)
to come back to somewhere where you can be seen again. *Mark vanished, then reappeared.*

rear (noun)
the back of something. *The rear of the car hit the wall.* **rear** (adjective).

rearrange
rearranging rearranged (verb)
to organize or arrange something in a different way. *I've rearranged the furniture in my bedroom.*

reason (noun)
why someone did something, or why something happened. *The reason I didn't catch the ball was because I wasn't wearing my glasses.*

reasonable (adjective)
fair and right. **reasonably** (adverb).

reassure
reassuring reassured (verb)
to make someone feel better about something that's worrying them. **reassuring** (adjective), **reassurance** (noun).

rebel (**reh**-bul) (noun)
someone who fights against people in charge, or refuses to obey rules. **rebel** (re-**bell**) (verb), **rebellious** (adjective), **rebellion** (noun).

receipt (re-**seet**) (noun)
the slip of paper you get when you buy something, to prove you've paid for it.

receive receiving received (verb)
to get or accept something. *I received lots of birthday cards.*

Spelling tip

receipt   receive

These words follow the spelling guideline: 'i' before 'e' except after 'c', when the letters make an 'ee' sound.

recent (adjective)
happening a short time ago. *I got a dog for my recent birthday.* **recently** (adverb).

reception (noun)
1 If your phone has good **reception**, you can send texts and make calls easily.
2 the way something is received. *The crowd gave the band a warm reception.*
3 the entrance area of a hotel, office, or other building.
4 a big party, such as that held after a wedding.

a b c d e f g h i j k l m n o p q r s t u v w x y z

recipe *(noun)*
instructions for how to make a particular dish. *This is my Gran's recipe for scones.*

recite reciting recited *(verb)*
to say something aloud that you have learnt by heart.

reckon reckoning reckoned *(verb)*
1 to think or have an opinion about something. *I reckon Tim will come back.*
2 to work out that. *I reckon it'll take five minutes to fix your bike.*

recognize or **recognise**
recognizing recognized *(verb)*
1 to see someone and know who they are. **recognition** *(noun).*
2 to see something and know you have seen it before. *I recognize that jumper.*

recommend
recommending recommended *(verb)*
to tell someone that something is good. *The waiter recommended the fish.* **recommendation** *(noun).*

reconsider
reconsidering reconsidered *(verb)*
to think about something again, especially when there is a chance you might change your mind about it.

record recording recorded
1 *(verb)* to write something down or enter it into a computer. **record** *(noun).*
2 *(verb)* to change music or other sounds into a form that can be stored, for example on a disc, computer, or phone. **recording** *(noun).*
3 *(noun)* an achievement which nobody has done better before. *He holds the world record for the long jump.*

recorder *(noun)*
a musical instrument, shaped like a pipe with holes in it, that you blow into to make sounds.

mouthpiece

barrel

foot joint

finger hole

descant recorder

recover
recovering recovered *(verb)*
to get better after an illness or a tough time. **recovery** *(noun).*

rectangle *(noun)*
a shape with four straight sides and four right angles. **rectangular** *(adjective). See* quadrilateral.

recycle recycling recycled *(verb)*
to collect waste so it can be used again, instead of throwing it away.

red *(noun)*
the colour of a ripe strawberry, or of blood. **red** *(adjective).*

reduce reducing reduced *(verb)*
to make smaller in number or amount. *We must reduce our waste.* **reduction** *(noun).*

reed *(noun)*
1 a plant with a thin, hollow stem that grows near water.
2 part of the mouthpiece of some instruments, such as a clarinet, which vibrates when air passes over it to make a sound.

reef *(noun)*
a line of rocks or coral in the sea.

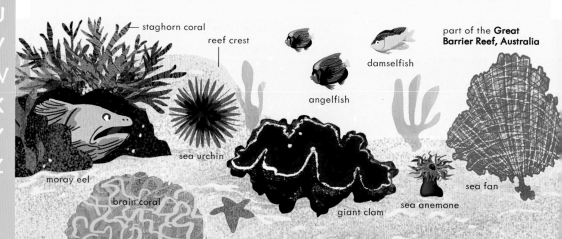

staghorn coral

reef crest

damselfish

angelfish

part of the **Great Barrier Reef, Australia**

moray eel

sea urchin

brain coral

giant clam

sea anemone

sea fan

reek **reeking reeked** *(verb)*
to smell very strongly, usually of something bad. *The fridge reeks of sour milk.*

ref *(noun) (abbreviation)*
short for **referee**.

refer **referring referred** *(verb)*
1 to mention someone or something. *Neil referred to his dog seven times over lunch.*
2 to look at something for information. *Let me refer to my diary.*

referee *(noun)*
the person who supervises a sports match to make sure players obey the rules. This word is sometimes shortened to "ref". *The referee called half-time.*

reference *(noun)*
1 a mention of something, either in speech or in writing. *In his speech, Grandad made a reference to the time I lost my shoes.*
2 a report about your achievements, skills, and abilities.

reference book *(noun)*
a book that you use to find information.

referendum *(noun)*
a vote made by the people of a country about an important question.

refill **refilling refilled** *(verb)*
to fill something up again. *I'm going to refill my glass.* **refill** *(noun)*.

reflect **reflecting reflected** *(verb)*
1 Some shiny surfaces **reflect** whatever is in front of them, so that you can see it on that surface. *Diane was reflected in the mirror.* **reflection** *(noun)*.
2 to think deeply about something. *The play made me reflect on love.*

reflex **reflexes** *(noun)*
something that you do without thinking, as an automatic response to something. *Blinking and sneezing are reflexes.* **reflex** *(adjective)*.

reform **reforming reformed** *(verb)*
to improve something or make it better. *The government needs to reform the law.*

refrain **refraining refrained** *(verb)*
to stop yourself from doing something. *Please refrain from putting your feet on the seats.*

refreshing *(adjective)*
Something **refreshing** makes you feel less tired, and full of energy. *My home-made lemonade is very refreshing.* **refreshed** *(adjective)*.

refreshments *(plural noun)*
food and drink often offered at an event, such as a party or a fête.

refrigerator *(noun)*
a cabinet used to keep food and drink cold, often shortened to "fridge".

refugee *(noun)*
someone who has been forced to leave their home because of war, lack of food, or other troubles.

refund **refunding refunded** *(verb)*
to give money back to someone, usually because the thing they bought isn't right, or because an event has been cancelled. **refund** *(noun)*.

refuse **refusing refused** *(verb)*
to say that you will not do or accept something. *Mum refused to clear up the mess.* **refusal** *(noun)*.

regal *(adjective)*
to do with kings and queens, or fit for a king or queen. *We saw some of Queen Victoria's regal gowns at the museum.*

region *(noun)*
an area of a country. *The Basque region is in northern Spain.* **regional** *(adjective)*.

register
registering registered
1 *(noun)* a list of names. *Our class register has 26 names on it.*
2 *(verb)* to enter your name and details on a list. *You need to register to use this website.*

regret **regretting regretted** *(verb)*
If you **regret** something, you wish it hadn't happened. *I regret being mean to Tess.* **regret** *(noun)*.

a b c d e f g h i j k l m n o p q **r** s t u v w x y z

regular *(adjective)*

1 Something **regular** happens at the same time, every time. *The trains are regular, and come once an hour.*
2 A **regular** pattern stays the same and doesn't change.
3 normal or medium-sized. *I only want a regular burger, not a large one.*
4 A **regular** shape has sides and angles that are all equal.
5 A **regular** verb follows a normal pattern when its different forms are made.

regularly *(adverb)*

often. *My uncle visits us regularly.*

rehearse

rehearsing rehearsed *(verb)*
to practise something you are going to perform. *We rehearsed the play all weekend.* **rehearsal** *(noun)*.

reign **reigning reigned** *(verb)*

When a king or queen **reigns**, they rule a country. **reign** *(noun)*, **reigning** *(adjective)*.

rein *(noun)*

one of two long, thin straps that is used to control a horse.

> The word "reign" sounds exactly like "rain" and "rein", so try not to mix them up.

reindeer

reindeer *(noun)*
a type of deer which lives in cold countries and can have large horns called antlers.

antlers

reindeer

reject **rejecting rejected**

1 *(re-jekt) (verb)* to say you don't want something, or that it is not good enough. *I rejected Tom's plan.* **rejection** *(noun)*.
2 *(ree-jekt) (noun)* a failure, or something that's not good enough.

related *(adjective)*

1 If you are **related** to someone, you are in the same family. **relation** *(noun)*.
2 If two things are **related**, they have something to do with each other, or are connected in some way. *Our problems are related to our lack of time.*

relationship *(noun)*

1 the way people are connected, or how they feel about each other and treat each other. *Our relationship is good.*
2 the way in which things are connected. *The relationship between money and happiness isn't as simple as people think.*
3 If you are **in a relationship** with someone, you spend a lot of time together and have an emotional connection.

relative *(noun)*

someone in your family.

relatively *(adverb)*

compared with others. *My bike was relatively cheap.*

relax

relaxes relaxing relaxed *(verb)*
1 to rest and stop worrying about things. *I have a bath when I need to relax.* **relaxation** *(noun)*.
2 When you **relax** your muscles, you let them go loose.

relay *(noun)*

a race in which members of a team take it in turns to run, swim, and so on.

release **releasing released** *(verb)*

1 to free or let go of someone or something. **release** *(noun)*.
2 When a song, film, and so on, is **released**, you can get it or see it.

relevant *(adjective)*

If something is **relevant**, it has something to do with whatever is happening or being discussed. *That television programme is not relevant to our conversation.* **relevance** *(noun)*.

reliable *(adjective)*

Someone or something that is **reliable** can be trusted and doesn't let people down. **reliability** *(noun)*, **reliably** *(adverb)*.

relief (noun)
1 a feeling of happiness, because something bad or upsetting is over. **relieved** (adjective).
2 money and other supplies given to people who are in great need. *The government is sending famine relief.*

religion (noun)
belief in God or gods, and the different ways of worshipping them, including services and festivals. **religious** (adjective).

reluctant (adjective)
If you are **reluctant** to do something, you don't really want to do it. *Greg was reluctant to go out in the rain.* **reluctantly** (adverb).

rely **relies relying relied** (verb)
If you **rely on** someone, you trust them and need them. *Mrs Finn relies on us to help her do her shopping.* **reliant** (adjective).

remain **remaining remained** (verb)
to stay or be left behind, or left over. *Only one child remained in the classroom.*

remainder (noun)
1 the rest, or what's left over. *Six people went home and the remainder stayed.*
2 what's left if one number can't be divided exactly by another one. *If you divide ten by three, the remainder is one.*

remark **remarking remarked** (verb)
to say something about someone or something else. *Everyone remarked on my new coat.* **remark** (noun).

remarkable (adjective)
extraordinary, or surprising. *It's remarkable that they survived the avalanche.* **remarkably** (adverb).

remember
remembering remembered (verb)
1 If you **remember** something, you haven't forgotten it. *I remember my first day at school.*
2 to do something you meant to do. *Ayaz remembered to buy his mum some flowers.*
3 to be able to think of something again. *Can you remember which way to go?*

remind **reminding reminded** (verb)
to help someone remember something. *Dad reminded Harry to take his PE kit.* **reminder** (noun).

remote **remoter remotest** (adjective)
far away from everywhere else. *We landed on a remote island.*

remote control (noun)
a small device with buttons on that you hold in your hand and use to control machines, such as televisions, without touching them.

television
remote control

remove
removing removed (verb)
If you **remove** something, you take it away. **removal** (noun).

renew **renewing renewed** (verb)
to replace something old with something new. **renewable** (adjective).

renewable energy (noun)
power that comes from sources that can never be used up, such as the Sun, wind, and waves. See **energy**.

rent (noun)
money that you pay to live in a house or flat that belongs to someone else. **rent** (verb).

repair **repairing repaired** (verb)
to mend or fix something that has been broken or damaged. **repair** (noun).

repay **repaying repaid** (verb)
to pay someone back. *I repaid the money Kate lent me.* **repayment** (noun).

repeat **repeating repeated** (verb)
to say, show or do something again. *Mr Patel repeated the question.* **repeatedly** (adverb).

repel **repelling repelled** (verb)
1 to keep or send someone or something away. *This spray repels mosquitoes.*
2 to disgust someone. *The smell of goats repels me.* **repellent** (adjective).

repetition (noun)
the repeating of words or actions.

a b c d e f g h i j k l m n o p q **r** s t u v w x y z

The prefix 're-'

replace
replay
reread

Words that begin with 're-' often have the meaning of something being repeated, or doing something again.

For example, to "replay" means "to play again", and to "reread" something is to read it again.

replace **replacing replaced** *(verb)*
1 to change something for something else, often a new version of something broken or faulty. *The shop replaced my broken camera.* **replacement** *(noun)*.
2 to put something in place of something else. *Mum replaced the picture in the frame with one of my paintings.*

replay *(noun)*
1 a second sports match, held when the first one ended in a draw. **replay** *(verb)*.
2 a second showing of a piece of video, so that people can see what happened again. *When you see the replay it's obvious he was fouled.* **replay** *(verb)*.

replica *(noun)*
an exact copy or model of something, especially one that is smaller than the original. *I bought a replica of the Eiffel Tower as a souvenir.*

reply **replies replying replied** *(verb)*
to answer. *Why won't she reply to my email?* **reply** *(noun)*.

report *(noun)*
1 an account, written by teachers, of the progress of each child in a school.
2 a piece that someone writes or says about something that is happening or has happened. *A news report.*
report *(verb)*.

reporter *(noun)*
someone who researches and writes stories about things that are going on in the world for websites, newspapers, magazines, television, and so on.

represent
representing represented *(verb)*
1 to stand for something, or mean something. *On a map, this symbol represents a church.*
2 If you **represent** someone or something, you do something for them or instead of them. *I have represented the county in cricket.* **representative** *(noun)*.

reproduce
reproducing reproduced *(verb)*
When people or animals **reproduce**, they have babies. **reproduction** *(noun)*.

reptile *(noun)*
an animal that lays eggs and has cold blood and scaly skin, such as lizards and snakes.

three kinds of **reptiles**

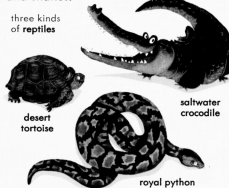

desert tortoise

saltwater crocodile

royal python

republic *(noun)*
a country which chooses a president to be in charge, not a king or a queen.

repulsive *(adjective)*
really disgusting. *That smell is repulsive.*

reputation *(noun)*
what other people think about you. *Lee has a reputation for hard work.*

request
requesting requested *(verb)*
to ask for something politely. *Emma requested a drink.* **request** *(noun)*.

require **requiring required** *(verb)*
If you **require** something, you need it. **requirement** *(noun)*.

reread **rereading reread** *(verb)*
to read something again. *I liked the book so much I reread it.*

rescue rescuing rescued (verb)
to save someone or something from
something dangerous or horrible.
rescue (noun), **rescuer** (noun).

**research researches
researching researched** (verb)
to study something and find out
more about it. **research** (noun),
researcher (noun).

**resemble
resembling resembled** (verb)
to look like someone or something
else. *Josh really resembles his dad.*
resemblance (noun).

resent resenting resented (verb)
If you **resent** something, you are annoyed
about it. *I resent my brother having a
bigger room than me.* **resentment** (noun).

reserve reserving reserved
1 (verb) to save something for yourself
or for someone else. *We need to
reserve a table.* **reserved** (adjective),
reservation (noun).
2 (noun) an extra member of a team,
who plays if another player is injured
or can't play.
3 (noun) a place where animals can
live in safety. *A nature reserve.*

reservoir (**rez**-er-vwar) (noun)
a big lake, built for storing water.

resident (noun)
someone who lives in a place. *The
residents of the village are angry
about all the mess.*

resign resigning resigned (verb)
to give up a job. **resignation** (noun).

resist resisting resisted (verb)
to fight against something. *I resisted
the temptation to finish the pudding.*
resistance (noun).

resort (noun)
1 a place where people go on holiday.
2 If something is a **last resort**, you do it
because nothing else has worked.

resource (noun)
a thing that people need and use. *The
school does not have enough resources.*

respect respecting respected (verb)
If you **respect** someone, you think
a lot of them and value their opinion.
respect (noun), **respectful** (adjective).

respiration (noun)
the action of breathing. **respire** (verb).

**respond
responding responded** (verb)
to reply or react to something. *I'll respond
to Amy's text later.* **response** (noun).

**responsibility
responsibilities** (noun)
1 a duty, or something you are in
charge of. *Cleaning the fish tank
is my responsibility.*
2 If you **take responsibility** for something
that went wrong, you admit that it was
your fault.

responsible (adjective)
1 If you are **responsible** for a task, you
have control over it and must make sure
that it gets done.
2 If you are **responsible** for something,
it is your fault that it happened. *Who
is responsible for breaking the window?*
3 If you are a **responsible** person,
you are sensible and can be trusted.
responsibly (adverb).

rest resting rested
1 (verb) to relax for a while. *I need to
rest after that game of table tennis.*
2 (noun) the others, or what is left. *The
dog ate the rest of my chips. I'm going
inside, where are the rest of you going?*
3 If you **have or take a rest**, you stop
doing something for a while and relax.

restaurant (noun)
a place where people pay to sit and
eat meals.

Word origin   restaurant

This word originally comes from the
French word "restaurer", which means
"to restore or refresh", because having
food can make you feel more lively.

restless – rhinoceros

restless *(adjective)*
If you are **restless**, you can't stay still or focus on what you need to do. *Geography lessons make me restless.* **restlessness** *(noun)*.

restore **restoring restored** *(verb)*
to repair something old or broken, and make it as it used to be. **restoration** *(noun)*.

restrict **restricting restricted** *(verb)*
to limit something. *We have to restrict the number of people who can go on the trip.* **restriction** *(noun)*.

result *(noun)*
1 something that happens because of something else. *There was flooding as a result of all the rain.*
2 the final score. *What was the result of the Wales versus Scotland match?*

retire **retiring retired** *(verb)*
to stop working, usually because you have reached a certain age. **retirement** *(noun)*.

retreat **retreating retreated** *(verb)*
to go back, away from difficulties or a tricky situation. *The army lost the battle and retreated.* **retreat** *(noun)*.

retro *(adjective)*
a friendly word for something that is old, and has been out of fashion, but is now in fashion again. *Katie wears a lot of retro clothes.*

return **returning returned** *(verb)*
1 to go back to somewhere you've been before.
2 to send something back. *I often return things I buy online.*
3 A **return ticket** is one you can use to travel to a place, and then come back again.

reunite **reuniting reunited** *(verb)*
If you are **reunited** with someone, you see them again after a long time. **reunion** *(noun)*.

reusable *(adjective)*
Something **reusable** can be used more than once. *Remember to take your reusable bags to the shops.*

revenge *(noun)*
something that you do to someone because they were nasty or unfair to you or one of your friends.

> The letter 'v' is always followed by a vowel or a 'y'.

reverse **reversing reversed** *(verb)*
1 to move backwards, especially in a car, truck, or other vehicle.
2 to turn something in the opposite direction. *The school reversed its policy.*

review *(noun)*
A **review** of a film, book, play, and so on, is a piece of writing that tells other people what you thought of it. **reviewer** *(noun)*, **review** *(verb)*.

revise **revising revised** *(verb)*
to look again at something you have already studied, to make sure you know it for a test or exam. **revision** *(noun)*.

revolting *(adjective)*
Something **revolting** is disgusting and makes you feel sick. *Revolting soup.*

revolution *(noun)*
1 a time when the people in a country try to overthrow their government.
2 a massive change. *The industrial revolution. The digital revolution.*
3 one turn of something, such as a wheel.

revolve **revolving revolved** *(verb)*
to turn round and round in a circle. **revolving** *(adjective)*.

reward *(noun)*
something nice that you get because you did something good, or useful. **reward** *(verb)*.

rhinoceros **rhinoceroses** *(noun)*
a large animal with thick skin and two horns on its nose. These endangered animals are often called "rhinos" for short.

horns

white rhinoceros

rhubarb *(noun)*

a plant with long red or green stalks that can be cooked and eaten, usually in sweet dishes.

rhubarb

rhyme **rhyming rhymed**

1 *(verb)* If a word **rhymes** with another word, it ends with the same sound as it. For example, "fun" rhymes with "sun".
2 *(noun)* a short poem that lots of people know, such as a nursery rhyme.

rhythm *(noun)*

a regular beat in a poem, piece of music, or dance. **rhythmic** *(adjective)*.

rib *(noun)*

one of the curved bones that form a cage around your lungs and heart. *See skeleton.*

rice *(noun)*

very small white or brown grains from a plant, which can be cooked and eaten. *See paddy field.*

rich **richer richest** *(adjective)*

1 If you are **rich**, you have lots of money.
2 If food is **rich**, it probably has a lot of fat or sugar in it, and you can't eat much of it before you feel a little bit sick. *Chocolate mousse is very rich.*

rid **ridding rid** *(verb)*

1 to make someone or something free of something. *The cat rid the barn of mice.*
2 If you **get rid of** something, you throw it away or free yourself of it.

riddle *(noun)*

a question which seems to make no sense, but which has a clever, unexpected answer.

ride **riding rode ridden**

1 *(verb)* to sit on something, such as a bike or a horse, and move along. *Olive rides her bike everywhere.*
ride *(noun)*, **rider** *(noun)*.
2 *(noun)* something that you sit on while it moves, for a fun experience at a fairground or theme park.

ridiculous *(adjective)*

very silly. *That hat is ridiculous.*

rigging *(noun)*

the ropes on a boat or ship which support and control the sails.

right

1 *(adjective)* the side that is opposite to "left". These words are on the right-hand side of this page.
2 *(adjective)* correct. *Danny got all the answers right.* **right** *(adverb)*.
3 *(adjective)* good, or fair. *It's not right to steal.*
4 *(adverb)* exactly, or directly. *We stayed right at the edge of the town.*

right angle *(noun)*

an angle of 90°.

The corners in a square are **right angles**.

rigid *(adjective)*

stiff and difficult to bend. *Rigid plastic.*
rigidity *(noun)*.

rim *(noun)*

the edge or top of something. *The rim of my glass is chipped.*

rind *(noun)*

the outer layer on cheese, bacon, and some fruits, such as lemons.

ring **ringing rang rung**

1 *(noun)* a circle.
2 *(noun)* a band you wear around your finger as jewellery. *A wedding ring.*
3 *(verb)* what a bell does when you press or hit it, or pull its rope.
4 *(verb)* to call someone on the phone. *I rang Dad on Father's Day.*

ringtone *(noun)*

the sound a mobile phone makes to let you know that someone is calling you.

rink *(noun)*

a big area for roller-skating or ice-skating.

rinse **rinsing rinsed** *(verb)*

to wash something in clean water until the water runs clear. *Rinse your hair to get the shampoo out.* **rinse** *(noun)*.

A
B
C
D
E
F
G
H
I
J
K
L
M
N
O
P
Q
R
S
T
U
V
W
X
Y
Z

riot *(noun)*
a group of people behaving in
a noisy, violent way. **riot** *(verb)*.

rip **ripping ripped**
1 *(verb)* to tear something, such as
a piece of paper. **rip** *(noun)*.
2 **rip-off** *(noun)* a friendly word for
something that costs more than it's
worth. *That coat's such a rip-off!*

ripe **riper ripest** *(adjective)*
ready to be picked or eaten.
*The strawberries in the garden
were ripe, so we picked them.*

ripple *(noun)*
a very small wave on the surface of
a pond, lake, and so on. **ripple** *(verb)*.

rise **rising rose risen** *(verb)*
to move upwards. *The Sun rises in the
east every morning.*

rival *(noun)*
someone you are competing against.
Cameron is my rival. **rival** *(adjective)*.

river *(noun)*
a large stream of fresh water that
flows into the sea, or into a lake.

road *(noun)*
a flat, wide path with a smooth surface
that vehicles can drive on.

roadworks *(plural noun)*
repairs being done to a road.

roam **roaming roamed** *(verb)*
to wander without any special place
to go. *We roamed around the fields.*

roar **roaring roared** *(verb)*
to make a loud, fierce sound, like
a lion. **roar** *(noun)*.

roast **roasting roasted** *(verb)*
to cook something with fat in a hot oven.
roast *(noun)*, **roast** *(adjective)*.

rob **robbing robbed** *(verb)*
to steal from someone. **robber** *(noun)*.

robin *(noun)*
a small, wild bird
with a red breast.

robot *(noun)*
a machine that can
do things that a
human usually does.
robotic *(adjective)*.

toy
robot

rock **rocking rocked**
1 *(noun)* a large stone.
2 *(verb)* to move gently backwards
and forwards, or from side to side.
3 *(noun)* a kind of music that usually
involves loud guitars and drums, and
has a very strong beat.

the stages
of a **river**

source
of river

mountains
and hills

gorge (deep river valley
cut through rock)

tributary (river
joining larger river)

rapids (fast-
moving water)

meander
(curve of a river)

waterfall   pool

river bank

oxbow lake (formed
when a meander gets
cut off from a river)

mouth
of river

marshland

rocket (noun)
1 a firework that shoots up into the sky and explodes.
2 a machine shaped like a long tube, which can travel into space.

space **rocket** launching

rodent (noun)
one of a group of animals that have long front teeth. Rats, mice, squirrels and hamsters are rodents.

role (noun)
1 a part in a play. *Jenny has the lead role in the school play.*
2 a job, or what you have to do as part of a team. *Mrs Chen's role is to help new children settle in.*

roll **rolling rolled**
1 (verb) to move by turning over and over. *I dropped some of my marbles and they rolled into the drain.*
2 (verb) to move on wheels. *The car rolled down the hill.*
3 (noun) a small loaf of bread, for one person.
4 (noun) A **roll** of something is in the shape of a tube. *A roll of wrapping paper.*

roller coaster (noun)
a ride where you sit in carriages that move along a track that rises, falls, twists, and loops.

roller skates
(plural noun)
boots with small wheels fixed to them, that carry you along.
roller-skate (verb), **roller-skating** (noun).

a pair of **roller skates**

ROM (noun) (abbreviation)
one of the types of memory on a computer, which cannot be changed. ROM stands for "**R**ead-**O**nly **M**emory".

romance (noun)
a time when two people are in love, or a story about this. *Georgie is always daydreaming of romance.*

Roman numerals (plural noun)
letters used by the Ancient Romans as a way of writing numbers.

I	II	III	IV	V	VI	VII	VIII	IX	X
1	2	3	4	5	6	7	8	9	10

numbers 1 to 10 in **Roman numerals**

romantic (adjective)
like a love story, or expressing love.

roof (noun)
the covering over a building.

room (noun)
1 one of the parts of a house or building, with its own door and walls.
2 space. *Is there room for me?*

roost (noun)
a place where birds rest or build their nests. **roost** (verb).

roots (plural noun)
1 the parts of a plant or tree that grow underground. **root** (verb). See **plant**.
2 where you come from, or spent a lot of time growing up. *My roots are in Devon.*

rope (noun)
a long piece of thick, strong string.

rose (noun)
a flower with a thorny stem and, often, a nice smell. Roses grow on bushes.

Rosh Hashanah (noun)
the Jewish New Year, which usually happens in early autumn and involves a two day celebration.

rot **rotting rotted** (verb)
When something such as food or wood **rots**, it goes bad. **rotten** (adjective).

rotate **rotating rotated** (verb)
to move round and round like a wheel. **rotation** (noun).

rough (ruff)
rougher roughest (adjective)
1 not smooth. *Cats have rough tongues.*
2 not gentle or caring. *Don't be too rough with the gerbils.*
3 not exact. *I've done a rough sketch.*
roughly (adverb).

round – ruin

round **rounder roundest**
1 *(adjective)* shaped like a circle or a ball. *A round window.*
2 *(preposition)* surrounding. *Our garden has a wall round it.*
3 *(preposition)* moving in a circle. *We drove round the town three times.*
4 *(noun)* a stage in a competition. *France went out in the first round.*

roundabout *(noun)*
1 a road layout that makes drivers go round in a circle to join the road they need.
2 a machine children can ride on, that goes round and round.

rounders *(noun)*
a game that involves hitting a ball and then running between posts to score points.

route *(noun)*
a way of getting somewhere.

> Don't mix up the words "route" and "root".

routine
1 *(noun)* a regular way of doing things. *Chloe has a morning routine.*
2 *(noun)* a set of dance steps.
3 *(adjective)* not unusual. *Isaac has a routine appointment with the dentist.*

row **rowing rowed**
1 *(rhymes with "low")* *(noun)* a line of things or people. *A row of parked cars.*
2 *(rhymes with "low")* *(verb)* to make a boat move by using oars.
3 *(rhymes with "cow")* *(noun)* an argument. *I had a row with Laura.*
4 *(rhymes with "cow")* *(noun)* a terrible noise. *"What a row!"*

royal *(adjective)*
to do with a king, queen, or a member of their family. **royalty** *(noun)*.

rub **rubbing rubbed** *(verb)*
1 If you **rub** something, you move your hand or a cloth backwards and forwards over it.
2 If you **rub something out** that you've written, you use a rubber to make it disappear.

rubber *(noun)*
1 a tough, bendy substance made from a liquid called latex, used for making things such as tyres. **rubbery** *(adjective)*.
2 a small piece of rubber used for removing pencil marks from paper.

trunk of rubber tree
bark removed here
diagonal cut
latex
cup

Latex is collected from the trunks of **rubber** trees.

rubbish *(noun)*
1 things you throw away because you don't need or want them any more.
2 If something you say or write is **rubbish**, it makes no sense.

ruby **rubies** *(noun)*
a precious red jewel. *See* **gem**.

rucksack *(noun)*
a big bag that you can carry on your back. *This rucksack is so heavy.*

rudder *(noun)*
a piece of metal or wood at the back of a boat or plane that helps steer it. *See* **boat**.

rude **ruder rudest** *(adjective)*
If you are **rude**, you are not polite and have bad manners. **rudeness** *(noun)*, **rudely** *(adverb)*.

rug *(noun)*
1 a thick mat.
2 a blanket you can spread on the ground when you have a picnic.

rugby *(noun)*
a game which two teams play by throwing, kicking and running with an oval-shaped ball.

rugby ball

ruin **ruining ruined**
1 *(verb)* to spoil something.
2 *(noun)* a building that is badly damaged, or almost destroyed.

rule **ruling ruled**

1 (noun) an instruction that tells you what you must and must not do, or how you have to behave. *The school rules are very strict.*
2 (verb) to be in charge of a country. *The king ruled for 45 years.* **rule** (noun).

ruler (noun)

1 someone who is in charge of a country. *She was an excellent ruler.*
2 a long, straight piece of plastic, wood or metal that you use to measure things, or for drawing straight lines.

rumble **rumbling rumbled** (verb)

to make a low, rolling sound, like the sound of thunder. *The truck's engine rumbled.* **rumble** (noun).

rumour (noun)

something that people say, but that may not be true. *There's a rumour that our head teacher is leaving.*

run **running ran run**

1 (verb) to move quickly by putting one leg in front of the other. *I ran all the way home.* **run** (noun), **runner** (noun).
2 (verb) to be in charge of something. *The year six students run the school magazine themselves.*
3 (verb) to take someone somewhere in a car. *Shall I run you home?*
4 (noun) one point in a game of cricket.
5 (noun) a small, enclosed, outdoor area for an animal such as a rabbit.
6 (verb) If you **run away**, you try to escape from someone or something.
7 (verb) The fuel a machine **runs on** is what it uses to work. *Our car runs on diesel.*
8 (verb) If you **run out** of something, you haven't got any more of it.

run-down (adjective)

1 If a place is **run-down**, it looks shabby. *The town centre is so run-down.*
2 If a person is **run-down**, they don't have much energy and feel a little ill.

rung

1 (noun) one of the steps on a ladder.
2 (verb) the past participle of **ring**.

Spelling tip

runner-up → runners-up

Notice that if you want to make the word "runner-up" plural, you add an 's' to "runner": "runners-up".

runner-up **runners-up** (noun)

the person or team that comes second in a race or competition.

runny **runnier runniest** (adjective)

1 Something **runny** flows like liquid.
2 If you have a **runny nose**, liquid keeps leaking out of it, usually because you are ill or allergic to something.

runway (noun)

the strip of land that aircraft use for taking off and for landing.

rural (adjective)

in the countryside, or to do with the countryside. *My uncle loves his rural life.*

rush **rushes rushing rushed**

1 (verb) to go somewhere in a hurry. *Guy rushed downstairs.* **rush** (noun).
2 **Rush hour** is one of the two busiest times on the road or on public transport, when lots of people are going to or coming home from work.

rust (noun)

the orangey-red substance that appears on iron or steel when they have been in wet conditions for some time. **rust** (verb), **rusty** (adjective).

rustle **rustling rustled** (verb)

1 When leaves, papers, and so on **rustle**, they make a soft, crackling sound as they move together gently. **rustling** (noun).
2 If you **rustle up** something, you make or provide it quickly. *Anya rustled up some dinner.*

ruthless (adjective)

Someone who is **ruthless** is cruel and has no pity. **ruthlessness** (noun).

Ss

Sabbath (noun)
the weekly day of rest in some religions. The Jewish Sabbath is Saturday, and the Christian Sabbath is Sunday.

sack (noun)
1 a large bag made of strong cloth or plastic, used for carrying heavy things such as coal, potatoes, flour, and so on.
2 If you **get the sack** from your job, you no longer have that job and must leave. *Mike got the sack because he kept coming into work late.* **sack** (verb).

sacred (**say**-krid) (adjective)
special and holy to followers of a religion. *On our trip to India we visited a sacred Hindu temple.*

sacrifice sacrificing sacrificed
1 (noun) killing an animal or person as an offering to a god. **sacrifice** (verb), **sacrificial** (adjective).
2 (verb) to give up something important or enjoyable, for a good reason. *Amy sacrificed her Saturday afternoon to clear out the garage.* **sacrifice** (noun).

sad sadder saddest (adjective)
1 If you are **sad**, you are unhappy. *The ending of the book made me sad.* **sadness** (noun), **sadden** (verb), **sadly** (adverb).
2 Something **sad** makes you feel unhappy. *Have you heard the sad news?*

saddle (noun)
1 the seat of a bicycle. *This saddle is not very comfortable.*
2 a kind of seat that allows a rider to sit on a horse or other animal. **saddle** (verb).

safari (noun)
a holiday that you go on to see large, wild animals, especially in Africa. *We saw giraffes, hippos, elephants and lions on safari.*

safe safer safest
1 (adjective) not in danger of being damaged, hurt, or stolen. *Put the money in the drawer where it will be safe.* **safety** (noun).
2 (adjective) not dangerous, or not risky. *Is this ladder safe?* **safely** (adverb).
3 (noun) a strong box where you can lock away money or valuable things.

sag sagging sagged (verb)
to hang or sink down loosely. *The sofa sagged in the middle.*

sail sailing sailed
1 (noun) a large piece of cloth that can be stretched out to make a boat move when the wind catches it.
2 (verb) to travel in a boat or ship. *Ellen MacArthur sailed around the world solo.*

sailor (noun)
a person who sails a boat, or who works on a boat or ship.

saint (noun)
a person who Christians recognize for having lived a very holy life. Saint is sometimes shortened to "St".

sake (noun)
If you do something **for the sake of** someone or something, you do it to help or please them. *We moved to the countryside for the sake of my mum's health.*

salad (noun)
1 a mixture of raw vegetables, such as lettuce and tomatoes.
2 a mixture of cold foods. *Potato salad.*

salary salaries (noun)
the money someone is paid regularly for the work they do.

Word origin   salary
This word comes from the Latin word "sal", meaning "salt". Roman soldiers were given money so that they could buy salt, which was considered to be very important at the time.

sale *(noun)*
1 the act of giving someone something in exchange for money.
2 a time when things are sold at lower prices than usual. *These shoes were half price in the sale.*
3 for sale available for people to buy.
4 on sale available for people to buy, or available at less than the usual price.

salesman **salesmen** *or*
saleswoman **saleswomen** *or*
salesperson **salespeople** *(noun)*
someone who sells you something.

saliva *(noun)*
the liquid in your mouth that keeps it moist, and helps you swallow food.

salmon
salmon *(noun)*
a large fish with a silvery skin and pink flesh, which can be eaten.

Atlantic salmon

salt *(noun)*
1 white flakes or powder that adds a savoury flavour to foods.
2 If you **take something with a pinch of salt**, you don't believe that it is really true.

salute **saluting saluted** *(verb)*
When soldiers **salute**, they stand straight and raise their hand to their forehead to show respect. **salute** *(noun)*.

same *(adjective)*
1 exactly like something else. *Sophie was wearing the same top as her friend.*
2 shared or not different. *The children all go to the same school.*

sample *(noun)*
a small amount of something that shows what the whole of it is like. *I got a free perfume sample from the shop.*
sample *(verb)*.

samurai **samurai** *(noun)*
a Japanese warrior in the past, who was highly skilled and lived according to strict rules.

sand *(noun)*
lots of tiny bits of rock found on beaches and in deserts. **sandy** *(adjective)*.

sandal *(noun)*
a light, open shoe with straps that go over your foot.

sandwich **sandwiches** *(noun)*
two pieces of bread with meat, cheese or other food in between them.

sang *(verb)*
the past tense of **sing**.

sank *(verb)*
the past tense of **sink**.

sap *(noun)*
the sticky liquid in the stems of plants.

sapphire (**saf**-*fire*) *(noun)*
a bright blue precious stone. *See* **gem**.

sarcastic *(adjective)*
If you are **sarcastic**, you say the opposite of what you really mean in a mocking way, often to make someone look silly. *A sarcastic comment.* **sarcasm** *(noun)*.

sardine *(noun)*
a small sea fish, often sold in tins as food.

sari (**sah**-*ree*) *(noun)*
a long piece of material that is wrapped around the body as a dress. Saris are mainly worn by women in South Asia.

satellite *(noun)*
1 a moon or other natural object that travels around a planet.
2 a machine that travels around the Earth to collect information about space or the weather, or to send signals.

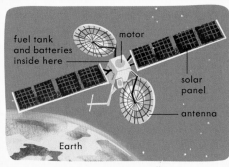

fuel tank and batteries inside here
motor
solar panel
antenna
Earth

communications satellite

a b c d e f g h i j k l m n o p q r **s** t u v w x y z

satellite dish (noun)
a dish-shaped object for receiving television signals that are sent by satellite.

satellite television (noun)
television programmes that are sent by satellite.

satisfaction (noun)
a feeling of happiness and pride because you have done something that you wanted to do, or you have done something well.

satisfactory (adjective)
good enough. *The service at the hotel wasn't great, but it was satisfactory.*

satisfy
satisfies satisfying satisfied (verb)
to please someone by doing what they wanted or hoped for you to do. **satisfied** (adjective).

sat nav (noun) (abbreviation)
a piece of equipment that uses information from satellites to find directions and plan routes. It's short for "satellite navigation".

Saturday (noun)
the first day of the weekend, which comes after Friday.

sauce (noun)
a thick liquid that is served with food and can be savoury or sweet.

saucepan (noun)
a metal cooking pot with a long handle.

saucer (noun)
a small, curved plate that you put under a cup.

sauna (**sor**-nah) (noun)
a room where you sit in hot air or steam to relax, or as a health treatment.

sausage (noun)
minced meat inside a thin skin.

Cumberland sausage

savage (adjective)
wild and vicious.
A savage attack.

save saving saved (verb)
1 to rescue someone or something from danger. *Carys saved her hamster from the neighbour's cat.*
2 to keep something that may be useful later. *Ben saved the magazine for his mum to read.*
3 to keep money to use in the future rather than spending it now.
4 to use less of something. *We can save electricity by switching our computers off at night.*
5 to stop a ball from going into a goal in sport. **save** (noun).
6 to keep a file in your computer's memory so that you can look at it or work on it later.

savings (plural noun)
money that you have saved.

savoury (adjective)
Savoury food doesn't taste sweet.

soup   sandwich   pork pie

some **savoury** foods

saw sawing sawed sawn
1 (noun) a tool with a thin, zigzag blade used for cutting wood.
2 (verb) to cut wood with a saw.
3 (verb) the past tense of **see**.

sawdust (noun)
the powder that you get when you saw wood.

saxophone (noun)
a curved musical instrument that you blow into to make a sound, which is usually made of brass and often played in jazz music. It's often shortened to "sax".

say saying said (verb)
1 to speak or tell someone something. *What did you say?*
2 to give information or show something. *What does that sign say?*
3 If you **have your say**, you have a chance to give your view or your opinion.

saying *(noun)*
a well-known phrase that people use.

scab *(noun)*
the hard, rough covering that forms over a wound while it is healing.

scaffolding *(noun)*
metal poles and wooden boards that are put up when something is being built or repaired, to let workers reach the higher parts.

scald **scalding scalded** *(verb)*
to burn yourself with very hot liquid or steam. **scald** *(noun)*.

Spelling tip

scald   scold

Be careful not to get the word "scald" confused with the word "scold", meaning "to tell someone off". They only have one letter different, and sound very similar.

scale
1 *(noun)* one of the small, hard pieces of skin that cover the bodies of fish, and reptiles such as snakes. **scaly** *(adjective)*.
2 *(noun)* a series of musical notes going up or down in order.
3 *(noun)* the relationship between the measurements on a map or model and the real measurements. *The scale of this map is 1cm to 1km.*
4 scales *(plural noun)* an instrument used for weighing things or people.

scalp *(noun)*
the skin on the top of your head, where your hair grows.

scalpel *(noun)*
a small, sharp knife used by surgeons, or for art and craft projects.

scamper
scampering scampered *(verb)*
to run with short, quick steps.
We scampered away when the light in the creepy old house came on.

scan **scanning scanned** *(verb)*
1 to look quickly through a book or piece of writing because you are searching for a particular part.
2 to look carefully along something. *The captain scanned the horizon for ships.*
3 to make a digital image of something using a scanner, so that you can look at it on a computer screen. *I scanned some photos to put on the website.* **scan** *(noun)*.
4 When a machine **scans** something, it reads numbers or a barcode to get information about it.
5 to take pictures of the inside of a person's body using a special machine, so that doctors can see if there is anything wrong. **scan** *(noun)*.

scandal *(noun)*
something shocking, which is bad for the reputation of a person or organization. *The Mayor lost her job because of the voting scandal.* **scandalous** *(adjective)*.

scanner *(noun)*
1 a machine that makes digital images of documents or pictures, so that they can be viewed and stored on a computer.
2 a machine which can see inside human bodies or inside luggage.

scar *(noun)*
a mark left on your skin by an old cut or wound. **scar** *(verb)*.

scarce *(adjective)*
rare and not easily found. *Tigers are very scarce in the wild these days.*

scarcely *(adverb)*
hardly. *I've scarcely seen Susie today.*

scare **scaring scared** *(verb)*
to frighten a person or an animal. *We accidentally scared the deer, and it ran away.* **scare** *(noun)*, **scared** *(adjective)*, **scary** *(adjective)*, **scarily** *(adverb)*.

scarecrow *(noun)*
a model of a person put in a field to frighten birds away.

scarf **scarfs** or **scarves** *(noun)*
a piece of material worn round your neck or on your head to keep you warm.

scatter scattering scattered *(verb)*
1 to throw things over a wide area.
2 to go off in different directions. *When the police arrived, the gang scattered.*

scene *(noun)*
1 a view, or a picture. *A mountain scene.*
2 a part of a play or film where the events all happen in the same place.
3 the place where something happens, or has happened. *The scene of the accident.*

scenery *(noun)*
1 the natural features in an area, such as trees, hills, mountains, and lakes.
2 the painted backgrounds used on stage in plays, operas, and ballets.

scent *(noun)*
1 a pleasant smell. **scented** *(adjective).*
2 an animal's smell.

sceptical *(**skep**-tic-ul) (adjective)*
If you are **sceptical** about something, you doubt whether it is really true.
sceptic *(noun)*, **scepticism** *(noun).*

schedule *(**shed**-yool)*
scheduling scheduled
1 *(noun)* a plan, programme, or timetable. *Did you check the train schedule?*
2 *(verb)* If you **schedule** an event, you plan it for a particular time.

scheme *(skeem)*
scheming schemed *(noun)*
1 *(noun)* a plan or arrangement. *A new healthy eating scheme.*
2 *(verb)* to plot or plan, often in a secret or dishonest way. **scheming** *(adjective).*

school *(noun)*
1 a place where people go to be taught.
2 a group of fish or other sea animals. *A school of porpoises.*

science *(noun)*
the study of nature and all the physical things in the world, through observing, testing, measuring, and experimenting.
scientist *(noun)*, **scientific** *(adjective).*

science fiction *or* **sci-fi** *(noun)*
fantasy stories set in the future or in different worlds.

scissors *(plural noun)*
a tool with two sharp blades, used for cutting paper, fabric, and so on.

scold scolding scolded *(verb)*
an old-fashioned way of saying to tell someone off.

scoop scooping scooped
1 *(verb)* to pick something up using your cupped hands, a spoon, or a shovel. *We scooped up the sand to build a sand castle.*
2 *(noun)* a ball of ice cream or other food made by a rounded spoon.

scooter *(noun)*
1 a flat board with wheels and a pole with handles at the top. You stand on the board with one foot, and push yourself forward with the other.
2 a type of small motorbike, used especially in towns and cities.

scooter

score scoring scored
1 *(verb)* to get a goal or win a point in a game.
2 *(noun)* the number of points or goals that each person or team wins in a game.

scorpion *(noun)*
a small animal with eight legs, two pincers at the front of its body, and a sting at the end of its tail.

sting

giant hairy scorpion

Scouts *(noun)*
a friendly name for the Scout Association, an organization for young people that encourages outdoor activities and learning new skills.
scout *(noun).*

scowl scowling scowled *(verb)*
to make an angry or bad-tempered face. **scowl** *(noun).*

scramble
scrambling scrambled *(verb)*
1 to climb up something quickly, using your hands and feet.
2 to rush somewhere or hurry to get something. *We scrambled for the last chocolate in the box.* **scramble** *(noun)*.

scrap **scrapping scrapped**
1 *(noun)* a small piece of something, such as paper or food, that is left over.
2 *(noun)* metal from old cars or machines.
3 *(verb)* to get rid of something. *We had to scrap the old design because it didn't work.*

scrapbook *(noun)*
a book in which you stick pictures, photos, tickets, and other things that you want to remember.

scrape **scraping scraped** *(verb)*
to clean, peel or scratch something with a sharp object.

scratch
scratches scratching scratched *(verb)*
1 to make a mark or a slight cut in something using something sharp, such as claws. *My cat just scratched me!* **scratch** *(noun)*.
2 to rub a part of you that itches.
3 If you do something **from scratch**, you start from the beginning.

scrawl **scrawling scrawled** *(verb)*
to write in a quick, careless way. **scrawl** *(noun)*.

scream **screaming screamed** *(verb)*
to cry out loudly in fear, anger, or excitement. **scream** *(noun)*.

screech
screeches screeching screeched *(verb)*
to make a high, unpleasant sound. *The car's brakes screeched.* **screech** *(noun)*.

screen *(noun)*
1 the front of a television or computer monitor, where the images are shown.
2 the white surface that films are shown on in a cinema. *A six-screen cinema.*
3 a barrier that can be put up and taken down. **screen** *(verb)*.

screw **screwing screwed**
1 *(noun)* a pointed piece of metal with a spiral groove in it, used for fixing things together.
2 *(verb)* to fasten something with screws.
3 *(verb)* If you **screw on** a lid, you turn or twist it so it is tight.
4 *(verb)* If you **screw up** paper, foil, or another material, you make it into a ball, ready to be thrown away.

screwdriver *(noun)*
a tool with a flat or cross-pattern tip that you fit into the top of a screw to turn it.

scribble **scribbling scribbled** *(verb)*
1 to write carelessly or quickly. *Marcus scribbled a note to his brother.* **scribble** *(noun)*.
2 to make meaningless marks with a pencil, pen, or crayon. *Lola scribbled all over the paper.* **scribble** *(noun)*.

script *(noun)*
the written version of what an actor or television presenter says.

scroll **scrolling scrolled**
1 *(noun)* a rolled-up piece of paper or parchment with writing on it.
2 *(verb)* to move the text and pictures on a screen up or down, so that you can see them. *Scroll down the page.*

scrub **scrubbing scrubbed** *(verb)*
to clean something by rubbing it hard with a brush.

scruffy
scruffier scruffiest *(adjective)*
untidy and in poor condition. *Dad wears scruffy clothes for gardening.*

Spelling tip

scruffy scruffier scruffiest

When adding the endings '–er' and '–est' to a word which ends with a consonant and then a 'y', remember to change the 'y' to an 'i' first.

a b c d e f g h i j k l m n o p q r **s** t u v w x y z

scuba diving (noun)
swimming underwater while breathing air from a tank on your back through a tube. **scuba diver** (noun). See **dive**.

sculpture (noun)
1 a work of art that is carved or shaped out of wood, stone, metal, and so on.
2 the art or work of making sculptures. **sculptor** (noun), **sculpt** (verb).

sea (noun)
1 a large, open area of salt water. *We went swimming in the sea.*
2 the general word for the salt water that covers most of the Earth.

seafood (noun)
fish or shellfish that you can eat.

seagull (noun)
a large grey or white bird that lives near the sea.

sea horse (noun)
a type of fish with a head shaped like a horse's head and a long, curling tail.

long-snouted sea horse

seal
sealing sealed
1 (noun) an animal that spends a lot of its life in water, but can also live on land. Seals have a rounded head, short, thick fur, flippers, and a tail.
2 (verb) to close something tightly or securely. *Seal the packet to keep the biscuits fresh.* **seal** (noun).

sea lion (noun)
a type of large seal that has flaps over its ears and long flippers.

California sea lion — whiskers

tail — flippers

seam (noun)
a line of sewing that joins two pieces of fabric together.

Word family

seafood
seagull
sea horse
sea lion

These are all compound words, based on the root word "sea". As you can see, some compound words are all one word, but others have a space in between.

seaplane (noun)
an aircraft that can take off and land on water.

search
searches searching searched (verb)
to look for something closely and thoroughly. *Gabby searched the room for her pencil case.* **search** (noun).

search engine (noun)
a program or website which helps you to search for information online.

searchlight (noun)
a large, powerful light that can be aimed in different directions.

seasick (adjective)
If you are **seasick**, you feel ill because of the rocking movement of a boat or ship. **seasickness** (noun).

seaside (noun)
a place by the sea where people go for days out or holidays. *We had a day at the seaside.* **seaside** (adjective).

season seasoning seasoned
1 (noun) one of the four parts into which the year is divided. The four seasons are spring, summer, autumn, and winter. **seasonal** (adjective).
2 (noun) the time of year when it is normal or allowed to do a particular activity. *The football season starts in August.*
3 (verb) to add flavour to food using salt, spices, and so on. **seasoning** (noun).
4 If a food is **in season**, it is easily available and fresh.

seat seating seated
1 *(noun)* a piece of furniture or a place where you can sit.
2 *(verb)* to have room for people to sit down. *This table seats six.*

seat belt *(noun)*
a strap in a vehicle that goes across your body to keep you safe.

seaweed *(noun)*
a plant that grows in sea water.

second
1 *(adjective)* after the first, or next. **second** *(adverb)*, **secondly** *(adverb)*.
2 *(noun)* a sixtieth of a minute.
3 *(noun)* a very short period of time. *Hold on a second.*

secondary *(adjective)*
1 to do with the second stage of something. *Secondary education.*
2 less important than something else.

secondary school *(noun)*
a school for pupils aged 11 upwards.

second-hand *(adjective)*
If something is **second-hand**, it has belonged to another person first. *James got a good deal on a second-hand car.*

secret *(noun)*
1 a mystery, or something that not many people know. *Mary made me promise to keep her secret.* **secrecy** *(noun)*, **secret** *(adjective)*, **secretly** *(adverb)*.
2 If you do something **in secret**, you do it privately, without anyone else knowing. *We lit the candles on George's birthday cake in secret.*

secret agent *(noun)*
a spy, or someone who finds out secret information.

secretary secretaries *(noun)*
someone whose job is to type letters and emails, answer the telephone, and do other office work. **secretarial** *(adjective)*.

section *(noun)*
a particular part or piece of something. *The first section of the book is about the author's childhood.*

secure *(adjective)*
1 safe, firmly closed or fastened, or well-protected. *Is your helmet secure?* **secure** *(verb)*, **securely** *(adverb)*.
2 If you feel **secure**, you feel safe and confident.

security *(noun)*
1 a feeling of being safe and cared for.
2 things that are done to keep someone or something safe.
3 people whose job it is to keep someone or something safe.

see seeing saw seen *(verb)*
1 to look at or notice someone or something. *Priya saw her friend outside.*
2 to understand, or to recognize something. *I see what you mean.*
3 to meet someone. *I'm going to see Will on Sunday.*
4 If you **see about** something, you deal with it or think it over.
5 If you **see through** someone or something, you are not tricked by them.

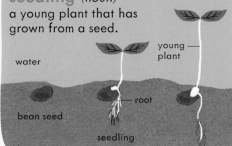

seed *(noun)*
a small, hard object that comes from a plant, and can grow into a new plant.

seedling *(noun)*
a young plant that has grown from a seed.

young plant

water

root

bean seed

seedling

This picture shows how a **seed** becomes a **seedling**.

seek seeking sought *(verb)*
an old-fashioned way of saying to look for something, or to try to do something. *The knights were seeking an evil monster.*

seem seeming seemed *(verb)*
to appear to be, or to give the impression of being. *Rory seemed calm, but inside he was furious.*

a b c d e f g h i j k l m n o p q r s t u v w x y z

A B C D E F G H I J K L M N O P Q R **S** T U V W X Y Z

seep **seeping seeped** (verb)
to flow or trickle slowly.

seesaw (noun)
a playground toy made of a long board with seats that rock up and down.

segment (noun)
a piece of something. See circle.

seize (seez) **seizing seized** (verb)
1 to take something quickly or with force.
2 If something **seizes up**, it jams or stops working.

select **selecting selected** (verb)
1 to pick or choose. **selection** (noun).
2 to use a mouse to choose something on a computer screen.

selective (adjective)
choosing carefully, or only choosing the best people or things available.

self **selves** (noun)
your individual personality or identity.

self-catering (adjective)
If you go on a **self-catering** holiday, you do your own cooking while you're there.

self-centred (adjective)
thinking only about yourself.

self-confident (adjective)
If you are **self-confident**, you feel good about yourself and what you can do.
self-confidence (noun).

self-conscious (adjective)
If you are **self-conscious**, you worry that people are looking at you, and you worry about what they think of you.
self-consciously (adverb).

self-control (noun)
being in control of your feelings, or being able to say no to things that you know are not good for you.
self-controlled (adjective).

selfie (noun)
a photo that you have taken of yourself.

selfish (adjective)
putting the things you want and your own feelings first. **selfishly** (adverb), **selfishness** (noun).

self-service (adjective)
In a **self-service** shop or restaurant, you help yourself to what you want and then pay for it.

sell **selling sold** (verb)
to give someone something in exchange for money. I sold my old computer.

Sellotape (noun) (trademark)
clear, sticky tape that you use to fasten things together.

semicircle (noun)
half a circle. **semicircular** (adjective). See circle.

semicolon (noun)
the punctuation mark (;), used to separate parts of a sentence or list, or to show a pause in a sentence.

semi-detached (adjective)
A **semi-detached** house is joined to another house on one side.

semifinal (noun)
a match to decide which of two teams or people will play in the final.
semifinalist (noun).

The prefix 'semi-'

semicircle   semi-detached

When the prefix 'semi-' is added to a word, it usually gives that word the meaning "half" or "partly". For example, a "semicircle" is half a circle, and a "semi-detached" house is only joined to another house on one side.

semicolons

You use **semicolons** to show a pause that is longer than a comma, but not as long as a full stop. It can be useful when you are separating things in a complicated list, which may already contain commas, for example:
On our tour of Europe we visited Paris, France; Madrid, Spain; Rome, Italy and Warsaw, Poland.

send sending sent (verb)
1 to make someone or something go somewhere. *I sent Tammy to the shop. I sent an email to Joshua.*
2 send off to make a player leave the sports field as a punishment.

senior (adjective)
Someone who is **senior** to you is older or more important than you.

senior citizen (noun)
an older person, especially someone who has stopped working.

sensation (noun)
1 a feeling. *Kelly had a tingling sensation in her toes.*
2 something that causes a lot of excitement and interest. *The new musical is a sensation.* **sensational** (adjective).

sense (noun)
1 Your five **senses** are sight, hearing, touch, taste, and smell.
2 the ability to feel or be aware of something. *Amanda has a good sense of direction.*
3 good judgement or understanding. *Andy should have the sense not to run into the road.*
4 If something **makes sense**, it has a meaning or is sensible. *That sentence doesn't make sense.*

senseless (adjective)
1 pointless, or without meaning. *It was a senseless attack.*
2 unconscious. *Jim fell down senseless.*

sensible (adjective)
If you are **sensible**, you think carefully and don't do silly or dangerous things. *Anam is usually very sensible, so I was surprised when she wore shorts out in the snow.* **sensibly** (adverb).

sensitive (adjective)
1 aware of other people's feelings. *Thank you for your sensitive message.* **sensitivity** (noun), **sensitively** (adverb).
2 easily upset. *Billy is sensitive about his freckles.* **sensitivity** (noun).
3 easily irritated, or likely to react. *Hannah has very sensitive skin.*

Word family

sensation	These words, which all begin with 'sens-', are to do with feeling, noticing, or being aware of something. They come from the Latin word "sentire", meaning "to feel, know, or perceive".
sense	
senseless	
sensible	
sensor	

sensor (noun)
an instrument that can detect changes in temperature, movement, pressure, and so on. *The security light has a sensor that detects movement.*

sentence (noun)
1 a group of words that contains a verb and makes sense. A sentence starts with a capital letter and ends with a full stop.
2 a punishment given to a criminal in court. *A prison sentence.* **sentence** (verb).

separate separating separated
1 (*sep-er-ate*) (verb) to part or divide people or things. *Separate the egg yolks from the whites.* **separation** (noun).
2 (*sep-er-rut*) (adjective) different, individual, or not together. *We have separate bedrooms.* **separately** (adverb).
3 (*sep-er-ate*) (verb) If a married couple **separate**, they stop living together, often before a divorce. **separation** (noun).

September (noun)
the ninth month of the year.

sequel (**see**-kwell) (noun)
a book or film that continues the story from one that came before.

sequence (**see**-kwence) (noun)
a series of things that follow one another in order. *Find the next number in this sequence: 1, 4, 7, 10...*

serene (adjective)
calm and peaceful. **serenity** (noun), **serenely** (adverb).

a b c d e f g h i j k l m n o p q r s t u v w x y z

A B C D E F G H I J K L M N O P Q R **S** T U V W X Y Z

serial (noun)
a story that is told in several parts. *A television serial.* **serial** (adjective).

series series (noun)
1 a group of related or connected things that follow one another in order. *This book is the first in a series of six.*
2 a number of television or radio programmes that are often linked by their story or theme. *A comedy series.*

serious (adjective)
1 thoughtful, and not light-hearted or silly. *Chen is a quiet, serious boy.*
2 telling the truth, or not joking. *Jane is serious about buying a dog.* **seriously** (adverb).
3 very bad, or worrying. *A serious illness.* **seriously** (adverb).

sermon (noun)
a speech given by a priest in church, which is meant to teach or explain something.

servant (noun)
someone who is paid to work in another person's home, doing housework, cooking, and so on.

serve serving served (verb)
1 to work or do things for someone.
2 to give people food or drinks in a café, restaurant, and so on, or to help someone in a shop.
3 to begin play in games such as tennis, by hitting the ball. **serve** (noun).

service
1 (noun) a system or group of people that provides something that people need. *A bus service. The police service.*
2 (noun) the way that you are looked after in a shop or restaurant. *People often give waiters a tip for good service.*
3 (noun) a religious ceremony or meeting.
4 services (plural noun) an area next to a big road where you can eat, rest, and fill up your vehicle with fuel.

serviette (noun)
a square piece of cloth or paper that you can use to wipe your hands and your mouth at meals.

Spelling tip session

When you see the letters 'ss' in the middle of a word, they often make a 'sh' sound, such as in "session".

However, they can also make an 's' sound, such as in "across" and "happiness".

session (noun)
a period of time used for doing an activity. *An athletics training session.*

set setting set
1 (noun) a group of things that go together. *A chess set.*
2 (noun) the scenery for a play or film.
3 (adjective) fixed. *We eat dinner at a set time every day.*
4 (adjective) ready. *Are we all set to go?*
5 (adjective) taking place. *The story is set in Ancient Egypt.*
6 (verb) to put, fix or arrange something. *Set the alarm for 6 a.m.*
7 (verb) If a liquid **sets**, it becomes solid.
8 (verb) When the Sun **sets**, it goes down below the horizon in the evening.
9 If you **set someone or something free**, you release them from where they are trapped.
10 If you **set off** on a journey, you start travelling. *We set off for the coast.*
11 If you **set something up**, you get it ready to be used, or arrange it.

setting (noun)
the background place and time of a story, play, or event. *The setting of this story is northern Spain.*

settle settling settled (verb)
1 to sort out, decide or agree on something. *We settled the argument.* **settled** (adjective).
2 to sink slowly and become still. *The fog settled over the village.*
3 to make yourself comfortable. *Philip settled on the sofa.* **settled** (adjective).
4 If you **settle in**, you get used to a new place, such as a house or school.

several *(adjective)*
a small number of people or things. *We have several fish.* **several** *(pronoun)*.

severe severer severest *(adjective)*
1 strict or harsh.
2 very bad. *My cousin has severe asthma.* **severity** *(noun)*.

sew *(so)* **sewing sewed sewn** *(verb)*
to use a needle and thread or a sewing machine to join, fasten or repair fabric. **sewing** *(noun)*.

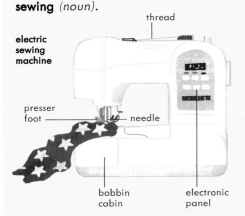

electric sewing machine

thread

presser foot — needle

bobbin cabin

electronic panel

sewage *(noun)*
liquid and solid waste that is carried away from buildings in sewers and drains.

sewer *(noun)*
an underground pipe that is part of a network that carries liquid and solid waste away from buildings.

sex sexes *(noun)*
one of the two groups, either male or female, that people and animals belong to.

sexist *(adjective)*
Someone who is **sexist** thinks that people of different sexes aren't equal, and treats members of one sex unfairly. *It is sexist to say that women don't understand football.* **sexist** *(noun)*, **sexism** *(noun)*.

shabby
shabbier shabbiest *(adjective)*
Something **shabby** is in a bad condition because it's old or hasn't been taken care of. *I cleared out my shabby clothes.* **shabbiness** *(noun)*.

shack *(noun)*
a small, roughly built hut or house.

shade shading shaded
1 *(verb)* to protect something from the light. *The hat shaded Rose's face.*
2 *(noun)* an area that is sheltered from the light. *Come and sit in the shade.* **shady** *(adjective)*.
3 *(noun)* a lighter or darker version of a colour. *Shades of blue.*
4 *(verb)* to make part of a drawing darker than the rest. **shading** *(noun)*.

shadow *(noun)*
a dark shape made by something blocking out light. **shadowy** *(adjective)*.

shake shaking shook shaken *(verb)*
1 to tremble or quiver.
2 to take hold of something and move it quickly up and down or from side to side. *Shake the bottle.*

shaky shakier shakiest *(adjective)*
1 unsteady and wobbly. *Shaky legs.*
2 not very good, or not very strong. *My spelling is a bit shaky.*

shall should *(verb)*
1 "I **shall**" means "I will".
2 a word you can use to make suggestions about the future. *Shall we meet on the corner at half past five?*

shallow
shallower shallowest *(adjective)*
not deep. *Shallow water.*

shame *(noun)*
1 a feeling of guilt and sadness about something bad that you have done. **shameful** *(adjective)*, **shamefully** *(adverb)*.
2 When you say something is **a shame**, you mean it's a pity or a sad thing.

shampoo *(noun)*
a soapy liquid used for washing hair, carpets, and so on. **shampoo** *(verb)*.

shape *(noun)*
1 the form or outline of something. See shapes, page 348.
2 If someone is **out of shape**, they are not fit and healthy. *Dad has got out of shape since his knee operation.*

a b c d e f g h i j k l m n o p q r s t u v w x y z

share **sharing shared**

1 *(verb)* to divide what you have between two or more people.
2 *(verb)* to have something in common, or to use something together. *We have to share a classroom with another class.*
3 *(noun)* the portion of something that you have or are given.

shark *(noun)*

a sea fish with a long body and a fin on its back.

two types of **sharks**

hammerhead shark

fin

strong, sharp teeth

great white shark

sharp **sharper sharpest** *(adjective)*

1 having an edge or point that is able to pierce or cut things. **sharpen** *(verb)*.
2 sudden. *Look out for the sharp bend.* **sharply** *(adverb).*
3 slightly sour. *Lemon juice tastes sharp.*
4 clear, or clearly outlined. *The picture on the television isn't very sharp.*
5 cross and critical. *Mum called me in a sharp voice.* **sharply** *(adverb).*
6 quick-witted or clever. *A sharp mind.*

shatter **shattering shattered** *(verb)*

to break into tiny pieces. *The vase fell to the ground and shattered.*

shattered *(adjective)*

1 broken into tiny pieces.
2 a friendly word for exhausted.
3 shocked and upset.

shave **shaving shaved** *(verb)*

to remove hair on your head, face or body with a razor.

shawl *(noun)*

a piece of soft material, worn by women over their shoulders and sometimes their heads, or wrapped around a baby.

she *(pronoun)*

You use **she** to talk about a girl, a woman, or a female animal. *She has red hair.*

shear

shearing sheared shorn *(verb)*
to cut the wool off a sheep.

shears *(plural noun)*

a cutting tool with two blades, used for trimming hedges, grass, and so on.

shed **shedding shed**

1 *(noun)* a small hut you can use for storing things.
2 *(verb)* to let something fall or drop off. *Some trees shed their leaves in the winter. Dad's trying to shed five kilos.*

sheep **sheep** *(noun)*

a farm animal that eats grass and is kept for its wool and meat.

Wensleydale sheep

sheer *(adjective)*

1 extremely steep, or vertical. *There was a sheer drop near the edge of the path.*
2 total and complete. *Sheer delight.*

sheet *(noun)*

1 a large, rectangular piece of thin cloth used to cover a bed.
2 a thin, flat piece of paper, glass, metal, and so on. *A sheet of paper.*

shelf **shelves** *(noun)*

a flat board on a wall or in a cupboard, used for storing or displaying things.

shell *(noun)*

a protective outer case. *Nuts, shellfish and eggs all have shells.*

shell

Walnuts have a **shell**.

Spelling tip

sheep   shellfish

The singular and plural forms of these words are exactly the same. Other words that follow this pattern include "series", "deer", and "salmon".

shellfish shellfish (noun)
an animal that lives in water and has a hard shell, such as a crab or a mussel.

shelter (noun)
a place where you can keep dry in wet weather, or stay safe from danger. **shelter** (verb), **sheltered** (adjective).

shepherd (noun)
someone whose job is to look after sheep.

sheriff (noun)
the person who is in charge of making sure people obey the law in a particular county in America.

shield shielding shielded
1 (noun) a piece of armour that soldiers or police officers carry to protect their bodies from attack.
2 (verb) to protect someone or something from danger, or from something horrible.

shift shifting shifted
1 (verb) to move something, especially something heavy.
2 (noun) a period of nonstop work.

shimmer
shimmering shimmered (verb)
to shine with a gently flickering light.

shin (noun)
the front part of your leg, between your knee and ankle.

shine shining shone (verb)
to give off a steady, bright light.
shiny (adjective).

ship shipping shipped
1 (noun) a large boat used for sea travel.
2 (verb) to transport things or people, especially by ship. **shipping** (noun).

shipwreck (noun)
1 a disaster that causes a ship to sink or be stranded.
2 the broken remains of a ship.

shirt (noun)
a piece of clothing that you wear on the top half of your body. Shirts usually have a collar, sleeves, and buttons. *I tore my school shirt on the fence.*

shiver shivering shivered (verb)
to shake with cold or fear. *Alice was shivering despite her coat.*
shiver (noun), **shivery** (adjective).

shoal (noun)
a large group of fish swimming together.

shock shocking shocked
1 (noun) a sudden, violent fright. *The loud bang gave me a shock.*
2 (verb) to horrify or disgust someone. *The news of the crash shocked us all.*
shocking (adjective), **shocked** (adjective).
3 (noun) If someone gets an **electric shock**, electricity goes through their body and can injure or even kill them.

shoe (noun)
something that you wear on your foot to protect it and keep it warm and dry.

shone (verb)
the past tense of **shine**.

shook (verb)
the past tense of **shake**. *The wind shook the house.*

shoot shooting shot
1 (verb) to fire a gun. **shot** (noun).
2 (verb) to take photographs, or make a film. **shoot** (noun).
3 (verb) to move very fast. *The cat shot up the tree.*
4 (verb) to aim at the goal in football, basketball, or other sports. **shot** (noun).
5 (noun) a young plant that has just appeared above the surface of the soil, or a new part of a plant that is just beginning to grow.

shooting star (noun)
a piece of rock from space, which burns up and leaves a bright trail as it enters the Earth's atmosphere.

Spelling tip

shop   shopping   shopped

Remember that one-syllable words that end with a vowel then a consonant **double the consonant** before '**-ing**' or '**-ed**' are added. Other words that follow this pattern are "stop" and "sob".

shop shopping shopped
1 *(noun)* a place where you go to choose and buy things.
2 *(verb)* to go to the shops, or online, to buy things. **shopper** *(noun)*, **shop** *(noun)*.

shopkeeper *(noun)*
someone who owns or runs a small shop.

shoplifter *(noun)*
someone who takes things from a shop without paying for them. **shoplifting** *(noun)*, **shoplift** *(verb)*.

shopping *(noun)*
1 the activity of going to shops or online to buy things. *Marc loves shopping.*
2 all the things that someone has bought in a shop. *Put the shopping in the car.*

shore *(noun)*
the edge of the land, where it meets the sea, a river, or a lake.

short shorter shortest *(adjective)*
1 not tall or long. *A short book.* **shorten** *(verb)*.
2 not lasting a long time. **shorten** *(verb)*.
3 If something is **short for** something, it is a shorter way of saying or writing it. *Sat nav is short for satellite navigation.*
4 If you are **short of** something, you have less of it than you need. *Henry is very short of money.*

shortage *(noun)*
When there is a **shortage** of something, there is not enough of it. *A food shortage.*

shortly *(adverb)*
soon, or any minute. *Get ready, they'll be arriving shortly.*

shorts *(plural noun)*
short trousers that cover the top part of your legs.

short-tempered *(adjective)*
Someone who is **short-tempered** becomes angry very quickly and easily.

shot
1 *(noun)* the firing of a gun.
2 *(noun)* kicking or hitting a ball in a particular direction. *Tina took a shot at the goal.*
3 *(noun)* a photograph. *A good shot.*
4 *(noun)* an injection. *A tetanus shot.*
5 *(verb)* the past tense of **shoot**.

should *(verb)*
1 If you **should** do something, you ought to do it or you are supposed to do it. *I should wait for my mum.*
2 If something **should** happen, it's what you would expect. *The potatoes should be cooked by now.*

shoulder *(noun)*
the part of your body at the top of your arm. *Shari has very wide shoulders.*

shout shouting shouted *(verb)*
to call out loudly. **shout** *(noun)*.

shove *(shuv)* **shoving shoved** *(verb)*
to push someone or something roughly. *Angus shoved me!* **shove** *(noun)*.

shovel *(noun)*
a type of spade with raised sides, used for moving soil, coal, snow, and so on. **shovel** *(verb)*.

show showing showed shown
1 *(verb)* to display or let something be seen. *Show me the picture.*
2 *(verb)* to explain or demonstrate something. *Show me how to do that.*
3 *(verb)* to guide or lead someone. *Let me show you to your seat.*
4 *(verb)* to be visible. *That stain won't show.*
5 *(noun)* a performance, television programme, or exhibition.
6 If you **show off**, you try to impress people by showing them how well you can do something, or by telling them how much you know. **show-off** *(noun)*.

show business *(noun)*
the world of theatre, films, television, and entertainment. It is sometimes shortened to "showbiz".

shower **showering showered**
1 *(noun)* a short, light fall of rain.
2 *(noun)* a machine that lets out a fine spray of water for washing your body.
3 *(verb)* to go in a shower and wash yourself. *I'll shower in the morning.*
4 *(verb)* to give or throw large amounts of something. *The guests showered the bride and groom with confetti.*

shrank *(verb)*
the past tense of shrink.

shred *(noun)*
a small piece of cloth or paper.
shred *(verb)*.

shriek *(noun)*
a shrill, piercing cry. **shriek** *(verb)*.

shrill **shriller shrillest** *(adjective)*
high-pitched and piercing. *Mum's voice is shrill when she's angry.*

shrimp *(noun)*
a small shellfish, which is pink when cooked and can be eaten.

shrine *(noun)*
a place or building dedicated to a god or a saint.

Itsukushima shrine, Japan

shrink
shrinking shrank shrunk *(verb)*
to become smaller. *My jumper shrank after it got wet.*

shrivel **shrivelling shrivelled** *(verb)*
If something such as a plant **shrivels**, it dries out and becomes smaller. **shrivelled** *(adjective)*.

shrub *(noun)*
a small plant or bush with woody stems.

shrug **shrugging shrugged** *(verb)*
to raise your shoulders to show that you don't know or aren't interested.

shrunk *(verb)*
the past participle of shrink.

shudder
shuddering shuddered *(verb)*
to shake suddenly from cold, fear, or disgust. **shudder** *(noun)*.

shuffle **shuffling shuffled** *(verb)*
1 to walk slowly, hardly raising your feet from the floor.
2 to mix together playing cards, papers, and so on. **shuffle** *(noun)*.

shut **shutting shut** *(verb)*
1 to close something that has a door, lid, cover, and so on. *Shut the door behind you.* **shut** *(adjective)*.
2 to close to the public. *The shop shuts at six.* **shut** *(adjective)*.
3 shut down to stop something from working. *Shut down your computer.*
4 shut down to close something forever. *The local factory has shut down.*
5 You say "**shut up!**" as a rude way of telling tell someone to stop speaking or making a noise.

shutter *(noun)*
a cover that protects the outside of a window and keeps out the light.

shuttle *(noun)*
a bus or other form of transport that travels frequently between two places.

shy **shyer shyest** *(adjective)*
If someone is **shy**, they are nervous of speaking out or meeting new people. **shyness** *(noun)*, **shyly** *(adjective)*.

sibling *(noun)*
a brother or sister.

a b c d e f g h i j k l m n o p q r s t u v w x y z

sick sicker sickest (adjective)
1 unwell. *I feel sick.* **sickness** (noun).
2 If you are **sick**, you bring up your food. **sick** (noun).
3 If you are **sick of** something, you have had enough of it. *I'm sick of finding cat hairs all over the house.*

sicken sickening sickened (verb)
to make someone feel shocked and disgusted. *Violence sickens me.*

sickly sicklier sickliest (adjective)
1 weak and often ill.
2 making you feel ill, usually because something is too rich, too sweet, or not pleasant to look at. *A sickly pudding.*

side (noun)
1 the edge of a shape or object. *A hexagon has six sides.*
2 the part to the left or the right of something. *The bikes are round the side of the house.*
3 the front or back part of something flat. *Write on both sides of the paper.*
4 the area at or around the edge of something. *The side of the road.*
5 a team. *Which side are you going to support?*
6 If you **side with** someone or **take someone's side**, you support them in an argument.

sideways (adverb)
moving or facing towards one side. *I had to go through the gap sideways.* **sideways** (adjective).

sieve (siv) (noun)
a container with lots of very small holes in it, used for separating liquids from solids or powder from lumps. **sieve** (verb).

sigh sighing sighed (verb)
to breathe out deeply, often to show that you are sad, frustrated, relieved, or pleased. **sigh** (noun).

sight (noun)
1 the ability to see.
2 a view or a scene. *A marvellous sight.*

sightseeing (noun)
going to visit tourist attractions.
sightseeing (adjective), **sightseer** (noun).

sign signing signed
1 (noun) a symbol that stands for something. *A plus sign.*
2 (noun) a public notice giving information. *The sign says no smoking.*
3 (noun) a way of telling someone something without speaking. *Jon gave a sign that he was ready to leave.*
4 (verb) to write your name in your own way. *Please sign here.*
5 sign language (noun) a way of communicating by using your hands to make signs and gestures. Sign language is used especially by deaf people.

signal (noun)
1 a type of communication that does not use speech. *Don't move until I give you the signal.* **signal** (verb).
2 a set of lights which tells road and rail traffic whether to stop or go. *Wait until the signal says to go.*

signature (noun)
the individual way that you write your name.

Sikh (seek) (noun)
a member of the Indian religion of Sikhism. Male Sikhs wear turbans and do not cut their hair.
Sikh (adjective).

Sikhism was started in the 16th century by Guru Nanak, and there are now 20 million Sikhs in the world, mostly living in northern India. Sikhs believe that there is only one God, that everyone is equal before God, and that in order to serve God we must live good lives and help other people.

Sikh symbol

silent (adjective)
making no noise, or completely quiet.
silence (noun), **silently** (adverb).

silhouette (sil-oo-**ett**) (noun)
a dark shape seen against a light background, so that you can just see its outline. **silhouetted** (adjective).

silk (noun)
a very light, soft fabric.

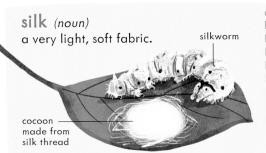

silkworm

cocoon made from silk thread

Silk is made from the cocoons of silkworms and other caterpillars.

silky (adjective)
smooth, soft, and pleasant to touch. *The cat's fur is so silky.*

silly sillier silliest (adjective)
foolish, not serious, or not sensible. *It's silly to spend all your pocket money on sweets.* **silliness** (noun).

silver (noun)
1 a precious, shiny, grey metal used in jewellery, coins, and so on.
2 coins or cutlery made from silver or silver-coloured metal.
3 the colour of silver. **silver** (adjective), **silvery** (adjective).

SIM card (noun)
a small piece of plastic inside a mobile phone, with an electronic chip that connects the user to a network.

similar (adjective)
alike, or of the same type. *Archie and his sister are very similar.* **similarly** (adverb), **similarity** (noun).

simile (**sim**-i-lee) (noun)
a way of describing something by comparing it with something else, for example, "Her eyes are as bright as stars and her lips are like roses".

simple simpler simplest (adjective)
1 easy to understand or do. *A simple question.* **simplicity** (noun).
2 plain and not fussy. *A simple meal.* **simplicity** (noun).

simplify simplifies simplifying simplified (verb)
to make something easier or less complicated. **simplification** (noun).

simply (adverb)
1 in a simple way.
2 absolutely. *Our school trip was simply brilliant.*

sin sin or sins (noun)
bad behaviour that goes against moral and religious rules. *The Bible says that stealing is a sin.* **sinful** (adjective).

since
1 (preposition) from the time that. *I've lived here since I was three.*
2 (conjunction) because. *You can have a treat since you've been so helpful.*

sincere (sin-**seer**)
sincerer sincerest (adjective)
If you are **sincere**, you are honest and truthful, or you really mean what you are saying. *Chandni gave a sincere apology for breaking my tennis racket.* **sincerity** (noun), **sincerely** (adverb).

sing singing sang sung (verb)
to make music with your voice. **singer** (noun), **singing** (noun).

singe singeing singed (verb)
to burn something slightly on its surface or tip. *Dad singed his hair on the candle!*

single
1 (adjective) individual or only one. *Twelve tulips and a single rose.*
2 (adjective) not married or in a relationship. *Is Mr Harte single?*
3 (adjective) one-way. *A single ticket.*
4 (adjective) just for one. *There are only four single rooms in this hotel.*
5 (noun) a song that you can buy separately from an album.

singular (adjective)
to do with one thing or one person. *"Child" is the singular form of "children".*

sink sinking sank sunk
1 (verb) to go down slowly, especially below the surface of water.
2 (verb) to make a boat or ship sink. *Nathan deliberately sank my toy boat.*
3 (noun) a large bowl with taps and a plughole, used for washing.

a
b
c
d
e
f
g
h
i
j
k
l
m
n
o
p
q
r
s
t
u
v
w
x
y
z

sip sipping sipped *(verb)*
to drink slowly, in small amounts. *Mark sipped his milkshake to make it last longer.* **sip** *(noun)*.

sir *(noun)*
1 a polite and formal way of talking to a man. *Excuse me, sir.*
2 the formal title of a knight. *Sir Lancelot searched for the Holy Grail.*

siren *(noun)*
a machine that makes a loud noise to get people's attention. *We pulled over when we heard the ambulance siren.*

sister *(noun)*
Your **sister** is a girl or woman who has the same parents as you.

sit sitting sat *(verb)*
1 to rest on your bottom. *We had to sit on the floor for an hour.*
2 If you **sit an exam**, you try to answer the questions in it.

site *(noun)*
1 the place where something is found or built, or where something has happened. *The site of the battle.*
2 short for **website**.

situation *(noun)*
the state of something or the things that are happening at a particular time. *What's the situation on the roads?*

size *(noun)*
the measurement of how large or small something is.

sizzle sizzling sizzled *(verb)*
to make a hissing noise, like something being fried in oil.

skate skating skated
1 *(noun)* a boot with a blade on the bottom, used for moving across ice.
2 *(noun)* a boot with a set of wheels on the bottom. *See roller skates.*
3 *(verb)* to move smoothly across ice or across the ground, wearing skates. **skater** *(noun)*, **skating** *(noun)*.

skateboard *(noun)*
a small board with four wheels underneath, that you stand on and ride.

skeleton *(noun)*
all the bones in a person or an animal's body, which are connected and support their body and protect their organs.

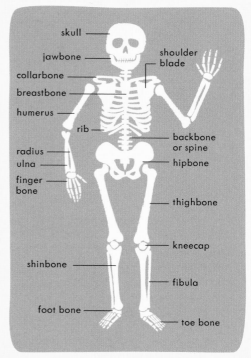

human skeleton

sketch sketches *(noun)*
a quick, rough drawing of something. **sketch** *(verb)*.

ski *(noun)*
one of a pair of long, narrow boards which you fasten to special boots and use for travelling over snow. **ski** *(verb)*, **skier** *(noun)*, **skiing** *(noun)*.

skid skidding skidded *(verb)*
to slide out of control on a slippery surface. *The car skidded on the icy road.*

skill *(noun)*
the ability to do something well. *I want to improve my art skills.* **skilful** *(adjective)*, **skilled** *(adjective)*, **skilfully** *(adverb)*.

skim skimming skimmed *(verb)*
1 to take something off the top of a liquid.
2 to glide quickly and smoothly across a surface or through the air.
3 to read something quickly, to see what it is about.
4 **Skimmed milk** is milk that has had all its fat removed.

skin *(noun)*
1 the outer covering on the bodies of humans and animals.
2 the outer layer of a fruit or vegetable.

skinny skinnier skinniest *(adjective)*
very thin. *Naomi has really skinny legs.*

skip skipping skipped
1 *(verb)* to jump over a turning rope.
2 *(verb)* to move along with little hops on each foot in turn.
3 *(verb)* to leave something out or not do something on purpose. *Can we skip the adverts?*
4 *(noun)* a very large open container for rubbish.

skirt *(noun)*
a piece of clothing worn by women and girls, which hangs from the waist.

skive skiving skived *(verb)*
a friendly word for staying away from school or avoiding work. **skiver** *(noun)*.

skull *(noun)*
the big, round bone inside your head that protects your brain. *See* skeleton.

sky skies *(noun)*
the space high above the Earth which you can see when you look up.

skyscraper *(noun)*
a very tall building with lots of floors.

slab *(noun)*
a large, flat block of stone, wood, or other heavy material.

slack slacker slackest *(adjective)*
loose, or not tight. *The rope is slack.*

slam slamming slammed *(verb)*
to hit or close something quickly and loudly. *Jessica slammed the book shut.*

slang *(noun)*
words and expressions used in friendly speech by particular groups of people. *Jamaican slang.* **slang** *(adjective)*.

slant slanting slanted *(verb)*
to slope or be at an angle. *My writing slants to the right.* **slant** *(noun)*.

slap slapping slapped *(verb)*
to hit someone or something hard with the palm of your hand. **slap** *(noun)*.

slash slashes slashing slashed *(verb)*
to make a quick, sweeping cut in something. **slash** *(noun)*.

slate *(noun)*
1 a blue-grey rock that can be split into thin pieces, and is often used in building.
2 a roof tile made from slate.

slave *(noun)*
someone who is owned by someone else, and has to work for them without being paid. **slavery** *(noun)*.

slay slaying slayed *or* **slew slain** *(verb)*
an old-fashioned word for killing a person or animal in a violent way.

sledge *or* **sled** *(noun)*
a vehicle with long pieces of wood or metal underneath, used for carrying people or things over snow and ice.

husky sledge   husky dog   sledge

sleep sleeping slept *(verb)*
to close your eyes and let your body and mind rest completely, usually at night. **sleep** *(noun)*.

sleeping bag *(noun)*
a long, padded fabric bag that you can sleep in when camping or staying somewhere for a short time.

a b c d e f g h i j k l m n o p q r **s** t u v w x y z

sleepy **sleepier sleepiest** *(adjective)*
1 tired and wanting to go to sleep.
sleepily *(adverb)*, **sleepiness** *(noun)*.
2 quiet and not busy. *A sleepy village.*

sleet *(noun)*
a mixture of falling snow and rain.

sleeve *(noun)*
the part of a piece of clothing that covers your arm.

sleigh *(slay) (noun)*
a high-sided sledge that carries people and is pulled by horses or other animals.

slender
slenderer slenderest *(adjective)*
slim or thin. *A slender waist.*

slept *(verb)*
the past tense of **sleep**.

slice *(noun)*
a thin piece of food that is cut from a larger piece. *Would you like a slice of cake?* **slice** *(verb)*.

slide **sliding slid**
1 *(verb)* to move smoothly over a surface. *Jon slid across the floor.*
2 *(noun)* a big playground toy with a steep slope, that you sit on and slide down.
3 *(noun)* a clip that you can wear in your hair to keep it tidy.

slight **slighter slightest** *(adjective)*
small or not very important. *A slight delay.* **slightly** *(adverb)*.

slim **slimmer slimmest** *(adjective)*
1 thin or narrow.
2 very small. *The chances of us getting there in time are slim.*

slime *(noun)*
a slippery, sticky substance. *Snails leave a trail of slime.* **slimy** *(adjective)*.

sling **slinging slung**
1 *(noun)* a piece of fabric which hangs from your neck and supports your arm when you've hurt it.
2 *(verb)* to throw something carelessly. *Martha slung her bag across the floor when she got in.*

slip **slipping slipped**
1 *(verb)* to lose your balance on a slippery surface. *Pippa slipped on the ice.*
2 *(verb)* to move quickly and easily, or without being noticed. *Greg slipped out.*
3 *(verb)* to put something somewhere quickly, or without anyone noticing. *Leah slipped a note under the door.*
4 *(noun)* a small mistake. *I made a couple of slips in my music exam.*
5 *(noun)* a small piece of printed paper.

slipper *(noun)*
a soft, light shoe that you wear indoors.

slippery *(adjective)*
smooth, oily, or wet, and very hard to grip or stand on.

slit *(noun)*
a long, narrow cut in something.
slit *(verb)*.

slither **slithering slithered** *(verb)*
to slide along like a snake.

slogan *(noun)*
a word or phrase used in an advertisement, that is easy to remember.

Word origin   slogan

The word "slogan" has an unusual origin. It comes from the Gaelic word "sluagh-ghairm", which means "battle cry". Just as each tribe had its own special battle cry, now many companies and products have a word or phrase that helps you recognize them.

slope **sloping sloped** *(verb)*
If a surface **slopes**, it is at an angle and not level. *The floor slopes down at one side.* **slope** *(noun)*, **sloping** *(adjective)*.

sloppy **sloppier sloppiest** *(adjective)*
1 wet or slushy. *A sloppy mixture.*
2 a friendly word for careless and untidy. *Sloppy work.*

slot *(noun)*
a small, narrow space or gap where you can put something, especially a coin.

**pygmy three-
toed sloth**

**brown-throated
sloth and baby**

sloth *(slowth)* *(noun)*
a very slow-moving animal with long
claws that lives in trees in South America.

slouch
slouches slouching slouched *(verb)*
to sit, stand or walk in a lazy way, with
your shoulders and head drooping. *It's
not good to slouch at your desk.*

slow **slower slowest** *(adjective)*
1 not fast, or moving at a low speed.
slowness *(noun)*, **slowly** *(adverb)*.
2 behind the right time. *That clock is
five minutes slow.*
3 If you **slow something down**, you make
it move or happen at a lower speed.

slow motion *(noun)*
a way of showing film or video so that
things happen much more slowly than in
real life, to show extra detail or to make
it seem more dramatic.

sludge *(noun)*
soft, thick mud or other solid matter that
sinks to the bottom of a liquid.

slug *(noun)*
a soft, slimy animal, similar to a snail
but without a shell.

garden slug

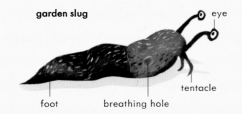

eye

tentacle

foot   breathing hole

slum *(noun)*
an area of poor, dirty and overcrowded
housing in a town or city.

slump **slumping slumped** *(verb)*
to fall in a heavy or uncontrolled way.
Patrick slumped to the ground.

slur **slurring slurred** *(verb)*
to speak in a way that is hard to
understand, by running words into
one another.

slush *(noun)*
snow or ice that has partly melted.
slushy *(adjective)*.

sly **slyer slyest** *(adjective)*
crafty, cunning, and secretive. *Millie
gave me a sly smile.* **slyly** *(adverb)*.

smack **smacking smacked** *(verb)*
1 to hit someone with the palm of your
hand. **smack** *(noun)*.
2 to hit something suddenly and hard.
The waves smacked against the wall.

small **smaller smallest** *(adjective)*
1 little. *A small child.*
2 not very important. *A small mistake.*

smart **smarter smartest** *(adjective)*
1 neat, clean, or well-dressed. *You look
very smart in your suit.* **smartly** *(adverb)*.
2 a word for clever or quick-thinking,
used especially in the US.

smash
smashes smashing smashed *(verb)*
1 to break into lots of pieces. *The cup
smashed when it hit the floor.*
2 to break something into pieces by
hitting it hard or dropping it.
3 to hit a ball fast and hard.
smash *(noun)*.

smell **smelling smelled** *or* **smelt**
1 *(verb)* to sense through your nose.
I can smell coffee.
2 *(verb)* to give off a smell, especially
an unpleasant one. *Your trainers smell
horrible!* **smelly** *(adjective)*.
3 *(noun)* an odour or a scent. *I love the
smell of fresh bread.*

smile **smiling smiled** *(verb)*
When you **smile**, your mouth turns up
at the corners to show that you are
happy or amused, or that you are being
friendly. **smile** *(noun)*.

smirk **smirking smirked** *(verb)*
to smile in a mean or unpleasant way.
smirk *(noun)*.

A B C D E F G H I J K L M N O P Q R **S** T U V W X Y Z

smog *(noun)*
a mixture of fog and smoke pollution that sometimes hangs in the air over cities and areas with lots of factories.

smoke smoking smoked
1 *(noun)* the greyish mixture of gas and tiny particles that is given off when something burns. **smoky** *(adjective)*, **smoke** *(verb)*.
2 *(verb)* to breathe in smoke from a cigarette or cigar held in the mouth. **smoker** *(noun)*, **smoking** *(noun)*.

smooth
smoother smoothest *(adjective)*
1 even and flat, not rough or bumpy. **smoothness** *(noun)*.
2 happening easily, with no problems or difficulties. **smoothly** *(adverb)*.

smoothie *(noun)*
a cold drink made from squashed-up fruit mixed with milk, yogurt, or ice cream.

smother *(smuth-er)*
smothering smothered *(verb)*
1 to cover someone's nose and mouth so that they can't breathe.
2 to cover something completely.

SMS *(noun)* *(abbreviation)*
a way of sending short text messages from one mobile phone to another, or a message sent using this system. SMS stands for "**S**hort **M**essage **S**ervice".

smudge smudging smudged *(verb)*
to make a messy mark by rubbing ink, paint, and so on. **smudge** *(noun)*.

smug smugger smuggest *(adjective)*
If you are **smug**, you are pleased with yourself in an annoying way. **smugness** *(noun)*, **smugly** *(adverb)*.

smuggle
smuggling smuggled *(verb)*
1 to take people or things into a country illegally. **smuggler** *(noun)*, **smuggling** *(noun)*.
2 to take something into or out of a place secretly. *I smuggled crisps into the cinema.*

snack *(noun)*
a small, light meal.

snag *(noun)*
a small problem or difficulty. *There was a snag in our plan.*

snail *(noun)*
a small animal with a soft, slimy body and a shell on its back.

snake *(noun)*
a long, thin animal that has no legs and moves along the ground.

Different **snakes** have different markings.

grass snake

rainbow boa   Indian cobra

snap snapping snapped
1 *(verb)* to break with a sudden, loud noise. *The branch that Luke was hanging from snapped.* **snap** *(noun)*.
2 *(verb)* to try to bite someone. *The dog snapped at me.*
3 *(verb)* to speak sharply and angrily to someone. *"Don't touch my necklace!"* Caitlin snapped.
4 *(noun)* a game where you have to match pairs of cards and shout "snap!".
5 *(noun)* a friendly word for a photograph. *Holiday snaps.*

snarl snarling snarled *(verb)*
If an animal **snarls**, it shows its teeth and growls.

snatch
snatches snatching snatched *(verb)*
to take or grab something quickly and roughly. *Ella snatched her diary out of her brother's hands.*

sneak sneaking sneaked *(verb)*
1 to move quietly and secretly. *Melissa sneaked up on me from behind and made me jump.*
2 to take something secretly into or out of a place. *Ronan sneaked his pet mouse into school.*

sneer sneering sneered *(verb)*
to smile or speak in an unpleasant, mocking way. *Jamal sneered at my rusty old bike.* **sneer** *(noun).*

sneeze sneezing sneezed *(verb)*
to make a sudden noise and push air through your mouth and nose, for instance when you have breathed in dust, or when you have a cold or hay fever. **sneeze** *(noun).*

sniff sniffing sniffed *(verb)*
1 to breathe in noisily through your nose, often because you have a cold. *Lawrence's sniffing kept me awake all night.* **sniff** *(noun).*
2 to smell something. *The dog sniffed the lamppost.*

sniffle sniffling sniffled *(verb)*
to breathe noisily through your nose, usually because you have a cold or you're crying. *There were lots of people in the audience sniffling.* **sniffle** *(noun),* **sniffly** *(adjective).*

snigger
sniggering sniggered *(verb)*
to laugh quietly and unkindly. *The girls sniggered at his torn trousers.*

snip snipping snipped *(verb)*
to cut little pieces off something with scissors. *Snip the strips of paper into squares.*

snivel snivelling snivelled *(verb)*
to cry or complain in a whining way. *"It's not fair!" Samantha snivelled.*

snob *(noun)*
someone who looks down on people who are not rich, clever, or upper class. **snobbish** *(adjective).*

snooker *(noun)*
a game in which players use long sticks called cues to knock coloured balls across a large table and into pockets around the edges to score points.

snoop snooping snooped *(verb)*
a friendly way of saying to look around somewhere secretly. *I caught my brother snooping around my bedroom.*

snooze
snoozing snoozed *(verb)*
to sleep lightly for a short time, usually during the day. *Our cat is always snoozing.* **snooze** *(noun).*

snore snoring snored *(verb)*
to breathe noisily through your nose and mouth while you are asleep. *I couldn't get to sleep because Sophia was snoring.* **snore** *(noun).*

snorkel *(noun)*
a tube that you can breathe through when you swim underwater.

mouthpiece

mask and **snorkel**

snort snorting snorted *(verb)*
to breathe out noisily through your nose like a horse, especially when you are angry or laughing. **snort** *(noun).*

snout *(noun)*
the nose and mouth of an animal such as a pig.

snow *(noun)*
small, light flakes of ice that sometimes fall from the sky when it is very cold. *I love playing in the snow.* **snow** *(verb),* **snowy** *(adjective).*

snowball *(noun)*
snow that has been pressed together into a ball that you can throw.

snowboard *(noun)*
a board that you can stand on to slide downhill over snow. **snowboarding** *(noun),* **snowboarder** *(noun).*

snowflake *(noun)*
a single piece of snow that falls from the sky.

snowman *(noun)*
snow that has been made into the shape of a person and decorated.

Every **snowflake** has a different pattern.

a b c d e f g h i j k l m n o p q r s t u v w x y z

snowplough (noun)
a large vehicle with a big blade on the front used to push snow off a road.

snug snugger snuggest (adjective)
small, cosy, and comfortable.

snuggle snuggling snuggled (verb)
to sit or lie close to someone or something, so that you are warm and comfortable.

so
1 (conjunction) for this reason. *Mila was tired, so she went to bed early.*
2 (adverb) very much, or enough for something to happen. *James was so hungry, he ate the whole pizza.*
3 (adverb) also, or as well. *You're from Manchester? So am I!*
4 You say or write **and so on** to mean "and other, similar things".

soak soaking soaked (verb)
1 to make something wet through, or to keep something in water.
soak (noun), **soaking** (adjective).
2 When something **soaks up** liquid, it absorbs it or takes it in.

soap (noun)
a substance that you rub on your skin with water to wash yourself.
soapy (adjective).

soar soaring soared (verb)
to fly very high in the air.

sob sobbing sobbed (verb)
to cry loudly because you are very upset.

soccer (noun)
another word for football, used especially in the US.

sociable (adjective)
Someone who is **sociable** enjoys talking to people and spending time with them.

social (adjective)
1 to do with the way that people live together. *Unemployment is a big social problem in our area.*
2 to do with activities that you do with other people in your spare time. *Guy has a busy social life. Social networking.*
socially (adverb).

Word family

sociable
social
society

These words all come from the Latin word "socialis", which means "to do with companions and living together", so when you see a word that begins with 'soc', it often has something to do with people doing things together.

social worker (noun)
someone whose job is to work with people or families who have problems or need help.

society societies (noun)
1 all the people who live in a country or area and share the same way of life and traditions. *We are learning about Ancient Roman society.*
2 an organization for people who share the same interests. *A chess society.*

sock (noun)
a piece of clothing that you wear on your foot, inside your shoe. *Holly never wears matching socks.*

socket (noun)
a hole or set of holes into which you fit an electrical plug or a bulb.

sofa (noun)
a long, comfortable seat with arms and a back, and room for two or more people.

soft softer softest
1 (adjective) not stiff or hard, but easy to press or bend into a different shape. *I like soft pillows on my bed.*
soften (verb), **softness** (noun).
2 (adjective) smooth and pleasant to touch. *My cat has very soft fur.*
3 (adjective) quiet and gentle. *Soft music.* **softly** (adverb).
4 soft drink (noun) a cold drink that does not contain alcohol.

software *(noun)*
a general name for computer programs.

soggy soggier soggiest *(adjective)*
very damp or wet. *The pitch is too soggy to play on.*

soil *(noun)*
ground or earth in which plants can grow.

solar *(adjective)*
to do with the Sun.

solar energy *or*
solar power *(noun)*
energy from the Sun that can be used for heating, lighting, and so on.

Solar System *(noun)*
the Sun and the planets that move around it. *See* planet.

sold *(verb)*
the past tense of sell.

soldier *(noun)*
someone who is in the army. *A Roman soldier.*

sole *(noun)*
the bottom part of your foot.

solid
1 *(noun)* not a liquid or a gas, but something that is hard. Wood, plastic, glass and stone are all solids. **solid** *(adjective).*
2 *(adjective)* hard and firm. *The water in the pond had frozen solid.*
3 *(adjective)* not hollow. *A solid chocolate egg.*

solitary *(adjective)*
1 If someone is **solitary**, they spend a lot of time alone.
2 single. *Not one solitary person came.*

solo *(noun)*
a piece of music that is played or sung by one person. *I'm doing a flute solo in the school concert.* **soloist** *(noun).*

helmet

body armour

tunic

shield

sandals

Roman soldier

solution *(noun)*
the answer to a problem or difficulty. *The solution to the puzzle is on the next page.*

solve solving solved *(verb)*
to find the answer to a problem. *Can you solve the mystery?*

some
1 *(adjective)* a number of people or things, or an amount of something. *There were some children in the park. Would you like some cake?*
2 *(determiner)* a certain number of people or things, but not all. *Some of us had seen the film already.*
3 *(pronoun)* a certain number of people or things that have been mentioned, but not all of them. *"Are the guests here yet?" "Only some."*

somebody *or* **someone** *(pronoun)*
a person. *Somebody tried to call you a minute ago.*

somehow *(adverb)*
in some way, without knowing exactly how. *We need to get rid of all this rubbish somehow.*

somersault *(noun)*
When you do a **somersault**, you tuck your head into your chest and roll over forwards, on the ground or in the air. **somersault** *(verb).*

something *(pronoun)*
a thing. *Are you looking for something?*

sometimes *(adverb)*
at times, but not always. *Sometimes I see Layla on the bus.*

somewhere *(adverb)*
in some place, without knowing exactly where. *Ryan left his sports bag somewhere at school.*

son *(noun)*
Someone's **son** is their male child.

song *(noun)*
1 a piece of music with words that are sung.
2 the musical sounds made by a bird.

a b c d e f g h i j k l m n o p q r s t u v w x y z

A B C D E F G H I J K L M N O P Q R **S** T U V W X Y Z

soon sooner soonest *(adverb)*
in a short time. *I'll come back soon.*

soot *(noun)*
black powder that is made when you
burn things such as coal or wood.
sooty *(adjective).*

sore sorer sorest
1 *(adjective)* painful, or hurting.
My knee is really sore.
2 *(noun)* an area of infected, painful
skin. *I've got a cold sore.*

sorrow *(noun)*
great sadness. **sorrowful** *(adjective),*
sorrowfully *(adverb).*

sorry
1 *(interjection)* a word that you say
when you feel bad because you have
done something wrong or because
someone is suffering.
2 If you **feel sorry for** someone, you feel
sad that something bad has happened
to them or that they are upset.

sort sorting sorted
1 *(noun)* a type or kind. *What sort
of soup is that?*
2 *(verb)* to arrange things into groups.
I've sorted all my computer games.
3 *(verb)* If you **sort something out**, you
deal with it or arrange it. *We need
to sort out a lift to karate practice.*

sought *(verb)*
the past tense of **seek**.

soul *(noun)*
Some people believe that your **soul** is
a part of you which cannot be seen, but
which makes you the person you are,
and goes on living when your body dies.

sound sounding sounded
1 *(noun)* something that you hear.
2 *(verb)* If a horn, bell, and so on
sounds, it makes a noise.
3 *(verb)* to seem to be, or to make
people think that. *Your new school
sounds brilliant.*

sound effects *(plural noun)*
noises that go with the action in a play
or film and make it seem more realistic.

soundtrack *(noun)*
the recorded sound for a film or
television show. *The soundtrack
is fantastic.*

soup *(noun)*
a liquid food
made by cooking
vegetables, and
sometimes meat
or fish, with water
and flavourings.

vegetable soup

sour *(adjective)*
1 having a sharp or bitter taste.
Lemons taste sour. **sourness** *(noun).*
2 not fresh, or tasting bad. *The milk
has turned sour.*

source *(noun)*
1 the place, person or thing that
something comes from. *The source
of the rumour.*
2 the place where a stream or river
starts. *The source of the River Thames.*

south
1 *(noun)* one of the four points of
the compass. See **compass**.
2 *(adjective)* in or towards the south of
a place. *South London.* **south** *(noun),*
southern *(adjective).*
3 *(adjective)* from the south.
There is a south wind today.
4 The **South Pole** is the point right at
the bottom of the Earth that is always
covered with ice and snow.

souvenir *(soo-ven-**ear**) (noun)*
something that you keep to remind you
of a place, event, and so on. *I bought
a fridge magnet as a souvenir of our
trip to the zoo.*

Word origin souvenir

"Souvenir" is the French word for
"to remember". A souvenir helps you
to remember somewhere you have been,
or something you have done.

sow **sowing sowed sown** *or* **sowed**
1 *(rhymes with "go")* *(verb)* to put seeds in the soil to grow.
2 *(rhymes with "how")* *(noun)* a female pig.

space *(noun)*
1 an empty or clear area. *They've made a space in the park for the new skate ramp. There's no space for another chair.* **spacious** *(adjective)*.
2 the universe beyond the Earth's atmosphere, where all the stars and planets are.
3 a gap, especially between written or printed words.

spacecraft *or* **spaceship** *(noun)*
a vehicle that travels in space.

spacesuit *(noun)*
the protective clothes and helmet that an astronaut wears in space when outside a spacecraft.

spade
1 *(noun)* a tool with a flat blade and a long handle, used for digging.
2 **spades** *(plural noun)* one of the four suits in a pack of cards, with a black symbol like an upside-down heart with a stalk at the bottom. *See* card.

spaghetti *(noun)*
long, thin strings of pasta. *See* pasta.

spam *(noun)*
unwanted emails or letters, often containing advertisements, that are sent to lots of people at the same time.

span *(noun)*
1 the length or width of something from one end to the other. *Elephants have a life span of up to 70 years.* **span** *(verb)*.
2 Your **span** is the distance between your little finger and thumb when your hand is outstretched.

spanner *(noun)*
a tool that is used for tightening and loosening nuts.

spare *(adjective)*
free or extra. *We've got some spare time this afternoon. We need a spare tyre.*

spark *(noun)*
1 a small flash of electricity. **spark** *(verb)*.
2 a small piece of burning material from a fire. *We moved away from the bonfire to avoid the sparks.*

sparkle **sparkling sparkled** *(verb)*
to give off small flashes of light. *The frost on the cobweb sparkled in the sunlight.* **sparkling** *(adjective)*.

sparrow *(noun)*
a small brown
bird, which
you may
see in towns
or the countryside.

house sparrow

spawn *(noun)*
the mass of eggs laid by fish and amphibians, such as frogs. *See* frog.

speak **speaking spoke spoken** *(verb)*
to talk, or to say words. *I haven't spoken to Laura for a long time.*

speaker *(noun)*
1 someone who gives a speech in public.
2 the part of a television, radio, music player, and so on, that sounds come out of. Speaker is short for "loudspeaker".

spear *(noun)*
a long, pointed weapon. **spear** *(verb)*.

special *(adjective)*
1 different and important. *Today is a special day: it's my birthday.*
2 particular. *There's a special key for this door.*

speciality **specialities** *(noun)*
something that you are particularly good at. *My speciality is the 200m sprint.*

species (**spee**-sheez) **species** *(noun)*
one of the groups into which living things are divided, according to the things about them that are the same or similar. *The whale is a species of mammal.*

specific *(adjective)*
particular or definite. *I'm looking for a specific song.* **specifically** *(adverb)*.

speck *(noun)*
a very small piece of something, such as dust or dirt.

spectacles *(plural noun)*
an old-fashioned word for glasses.

spectacular *(adjective)*
amazing and dramatic to look at. **spectacularly** *(adverb)*.

spectator *(noun)*
someone who watches an event.

speech **speeches** *(noun)*
1 the ability to speak.
2 a talk given to a group of people.
3 a set piece in a play, spoken by one of the characters.

speech bubble *(noun)*
a shape in a picture that is drawn next to a person to show the words they are saying.

speechless *(adjective)*
unable to speak, especially when you are surprised or shocked.

speech marks *(plural noun)*
the punctuation marks (' ') or (" ") that you use in writing to show when a person is thinking or saying something, for example: "We must get out of here quickly," warned the wizard. They are also called "quotation marks". *See* punctuation, *page 349.*

speed **speeding sped** *or* **speeded**
1 *(noun)* how fast or slow something moves. *Faster than the speed of light.*
2 *(verb)* to travel very fast, or to travel faster than the speed limit allows.
3 *(noun)* quickness of movement.
4 If you **speed something up**, you make it move or happen faster.

speed camera *(noun)*
a roadside camera that records how fast the vehicles that go past it are moving.

speed limit *(noun)*
the highest speed at which you are allowed to travel in a particular area. *The speed limit near the school is 20mph.*

spell **spelling spelled** *or* **spelt**
1 *(verb)* to write or say the letters of a word in the correct order. *Can you spell "because"?* **spelling** *(noun)*.
2 *(noun)* words that are supposed to have magical powers. *The wicked fairy cast a spell.*
3 *(noun)* a short period of time. *A spell of fine weather.*

spellcheck *(noun)*
When you do a **spellcheck** on a computer, you tell the computer to check that all the words you have typed are spelt correctly. **spellcheck** *(verb)*.

spend **spending spent** *(verb)*
1 to use money to buy things.
2 If you **spend** time or energy, you use it. *I spent three hours on my homework.*

sphere *(sfear) (noun)*
the shape of a ball. **spherical** *(adjective)*.

spice *(noun)*
a dried part of a plant with a strong taste, that is used to flavour foods. **spicy** *(adjective)*.

spider *(noun)*
a small animal with eight legs and no wings. Some spiders make webs to trap insects to eat. *See* cobweb.

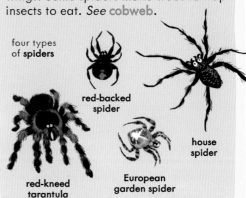

four types of **spiders**

red-backed spider

house spider

red-kneed tarantula

European garden spider

spike *(noun)*
a sharp point. **spiky** *(adjective)*.

spill **spilling spilled** *or* **spilt** *(verb)*
If you **spill** something, such as a drink, you let it fall out of its container by accident.

spin spinning spun (verb)
1 to turn round and round quickly. **spin** (noun).
2 to make something turn round quickly. *In this game you spin a wheel instead of rolling dice.*

spinach (noun)
a green, leafy vegetable, which can be eaten raw or cooked.

spine (noun)
1 all the bones in your back that support the top part of your body. *See skeleton.*
2 a hard, sharp point on an animal or plant. **spiny** (adjective).

spiral (noun)
a line that goes round and round in circles from a central point, with each circle getting slightly bigger. **spiral** (adjective).

This nautilus shell has a **spiral** shape.

spire (noun)
a tall, narrow point on top of some buildings.

spit spitting spat or spit (verb)
1 to force saliva out of your mouth. **spit** (noun), **spittle** (noun).
2 If you **spit out** food or drink, you force it out of your mouth. *When I realized the milk was off, I spat it out.*

spite (noun)
1 deliberate nastiness. *Lydia didn't wish me a happy birthday out of spite.* **spiteful** (adjective), **spitefully** (adverb).
2 **in spite of** without taking notice of, or even though something is happening. *Yusef went jogging in spite of the rain.*

splash
splashes splashing splashed (verb)
to hit water so that it flies up and out in different directions. *The car splashed water over me.* **splash** (noun).

splinter (noun)
a thin, sharp piece of wood, glass, metal, and so on. **splinter** (verb).

split splitting split
1 (verb) to tear or break open. *My shorts split at school today.*
2 (verb) to break or share something into separate pieces. *Let's split the prize.*
3 (noun) a crack or tear.
4 (verb) If a couple **splits up**, they stop going out together or living together.

splutter
spluttering spluttered (verb)
1 to speak or breathe with difficulty, such as when your mouth is full of water.
2 to make choking and spitting noises.

spoil spoiling spoiled or spoilt (verb)
1 to damage or ruin something. *Jordan's little sister spoilt my painting.*
2 If parents **spoil** their children, they let them get what they want too often. **spoilt** (adjective).

spoke (verb)
the past tense of speak.

spoken (verb)
the past participle of speak.

sponge (noun)
1 a soft pad filled with holes, which can be used for washing and cleaning. **spongy** (adjective).
2 a type of light cake.

Victoria sponge

sponsor sponsoring sponsored (verb)
1 to give money to people who are raising money for charity.
2 to support someone or something with money. *My mum's company sponsored the exhibition.*

spooky
spookier spookiest (adjective)
ghostly or creepy. *A spooky tale.*

spoon (noun)
a piece of cutlery with a handle and a bowl-shaped part on the end, used for eating desserts, soups, and so on.

sport or sports (noun)
a general name for games that you play to get exercise.

a b c d e f g h i j k l m n o p q r s t u v w x y z

spot spotting spotted
1 (noun) a small, round mark.
spotted (adjective).
2 (noun) a small, sore, red area on someone's skin. **spotty** (adjective).
3 (noun) a place. *This is a good spot for a picnic.*
4 (verb) to notice something.

spotless (adjective)
completely clean. **spotlessly** (adverb).

spotlight (noun)
a very powerful light used to light up a small area.

spout (noun)
a tube through which you pour liquid. *The spout of a kettle.*

sprain spraining sprained (verb)
to injure a joint by twisting it. *Liz sprained her ankle.*

sprang (verb)
the past tense of spring.

spray spraying sprayed (verb)
to make liquid shoot over a wide area in very small drops. **spray** (noun).

spread spreading spread (verb)
1 to unfold something or to stretch something out. *Joel spread his arms.*
2 to cover a surface with something. *Spread butter on the bread.*
3 to let other people know about something. *Don't spread gossip.*
4 to reach more people or a wider area. *The disease is spreading quickly.*

spring springing sprang sprung
1 (noun) the season between winter and summer, when it becomes warmer and leaves start to grow on the trees.
2 (verb) to jump suddenly. *The lion sprang on the antelope's back.*
3 (noun) a coil of metal which goes back to its original shape after being pushed down or stretched.
4 (noun) a place where water comes up from underground.

sprinkle sprinkling sprinkled (verb)
to spread something around in small amounts. *Sprinkle cheese on the pasta.*

sprint sprinting sprinted (verb)
to run, swim or cycle quickly over a short distance. **sprint** (noun), **sprinter** (noun).

sprout sprouting sprouted
1 (verb) When a plant **sprouts**, it starts to grow and produce shoots or buds.
2 Brussels sprout (noun) a round, green vegetable.

Brussels sprout plant

— sprout

sprung (verb)
the past participle of spring.

spun (verb)
the past tense of spin.

spurt spurting spurted
1 (verb) When liquid **spurts**, it flows or gushes suddenly. **spurt** (noun).
2 (noun) a sudden burst of energy, growth, or speed.

spy spies spying spied
1 (verb) If you **spy on** someone, you watch them closely from a hidden place.
2 (noun) someone who secretly collects information about someone or something for another country, company, person, and so on. **spy** (verb).

squabble (noun)
a small argument about something that is not important. **squabble** (verb).

squad (noun)
a group of people involved in the same activity, such as soldiers.

square squaring squared
1 (noun) a shape with four equal sides and four right angles. **square** (adjective). *See right angle. See shapes, page 348.*
2 (noun) an open space surrounded by houses or other buildings. *Trafalgar Square.*
3 (verb) to multiply a number by itself. *4 squared is 16.*
4 square root (noun) the number that, when multiplied by itself, gives a certain number. *The square root of 25 is 5.*

squash
squashes squashing squashed
1 *(verb)* to crush or flatten something. *Someone squashed my banana!*
2 *(noun)* a fruit drink that you add water to before you drink it. *Orange squash.*
3 *(noun)* a type of vegetable with a hard skin and lots of seeds. *Pumpkins are a type of squash. See* vegetable.
4 *(noun)* a game played between two people with rackets and a ball, in a room called a squash court.

squat **squatting squatted** *(verb)*
to crouch down with your knees bent. *We squatted behind the fence waiting to surprise Dad.*

squawk
squawking squawked *(verb)*
to make a loud, harsh cry, like a parrot. **squawk** *(noun).*

squeak **squeaking squeaked** *(verb)*
to make a short, high-pitched sound. *That door always squeaks.* **squeak** *(noun),* **squeaky** *(adjective).*

squeal **squealing squealed** *(verb)*
to make a high-pitched sound, usually because you are frightened, excited, or in pain. *James squealed when he saw the spider.* **squeal** *(noun).*

squeeze **squeezing squeezed** *(verb)*
1 to press something firmly from opposite sides. *Squeeze the tube to get the toothpaste out.* **squeeze** *(noun).*
2 to force something into or through a small space. *We only just squeezed onto the bus.* **squeeze** *(noun).*

squid *(noun)*
a sea animal with a long, soft body, eight arms, and two tentacles. *See* ink.

squint **squinting squinted** *(verb)*
If you **squint** at something, you almost close your eyes in order to see it more clearly. *George squinted at the sign.*

squirm **squirming squirmed** *(verb)*
to wriggle about, usually because you are bored or uncomfortable. *Omar squirmed all through the long speech.*

squirrel *(noun)*
a small animal with a thick, bushy tail, which climbs trees and mostly eats nuts and seeds.

grey squirrel   American red squirrel

two types of **squirrels**

squirt **squirting squirted** *(verb)*
to send out a stream of liquid. *Ruby squirted her brother with a water pistol.* **squirt** *(noun).*

stab **stabbing stabbed** *(verb)*
to hurt someone by piercing their body with a knife or other sharp object. **stabbing** *(noun).*

stable
1 *(noun)* a building or a part of a building where a horse is kept.
2 *(adjective)* firm and not wobbly. *Check that the ladder is stable.*

stack **stacking stacked** *(verb)*
to pile things up, one on top of another. *Could you stack those plates, please?* **stack** *(noun).*

stadium **stadiums** or **stadia** *(noun)*
a sports ground surrounded by rows of seats.

staff *(plural noun)*
the people who work in a place such as a school, office, or shop. *Ask a member of staff.*

stag *(noun)*
an adult male deer.

stage *(noun)*
1 a particular part or time during a process. *The plans are at an early stage.*
2 a raised area where people perform. *I'm too shy to go on stage.*

stagger **staggering staggered** *(verb)*
to walk or stand in a wobbly way. *Tilly finally staggered over the finish line.*

a b c d e f g h i j k l m n o p q r **s** t u v w x y z

A B C D E F G H I J K L M N O P Q R S T U V W X Y Z

stain (noun)
a mark on something that is hard to remove. *My T-shirt has food stains on it from my lunch.* **stain** (verb).

stairs (plural noun)
steps that lead from one level of a building to another. *I'll use the stairs.*

stale (adjective)
no longer fresh.

stalk (stork) **stalking stalked**
1 (noun) the long, main part of a plant, from which the leaves, flowers and fruit grow. *See* plant.
2 (verb) to follow a person or animal slowly and quietly. *The leopard stalked the antelope.*

stall **stalling stalled**
1 (noun) a table from which things are sold in a market or fair.
2 (verb) to stop suddenly. *The car's engine stalled.*
3 (plural noun) In a theatre, the **stalls** are the seats on the ground floor. *We had a good view from the stalls.*

stallion (noun)
an adult male horse.

stammer
stammering stammered (verb)
If you **stammer** when you speak, you repeat sounds or words, or struggle to say some words. **stammer** (noun).

stamp **stamping stamped**
1 (noun) a small piece of paper that you stick on a letter or parcel to show that you have paid to send it by post.

2 (noun) an object used to print a mark on paper. *We made stamps using potatoes.* **stamp** (verb).

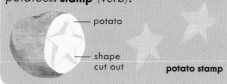

potato

shape cut out

potato stamp

3 (verb) to bang your foot down. *Greg stamped his feet in rage. Don't stamp on those flowers!*

stand **standing stood**
1 (verb) to be on your feet with your body upright.
2 (noun) a covered area for spectators at a sports ground.
3 (noun) an object designed to hold something or display it. *Dad has a stand for his tablet in the kitchen.*
4 (verb) to put something down somewhere. *Stand the vase over there.*
5 (verb) If you **can't stand** something, you hate it or can't bear it.
6 (verb) If a letter **stands for** a word, it is a shortened version of that word. *US stands for United States.*
7 (verb) If something **stands out**, it is noticeable.
8 (verb) When you **stand up**, you go from a sitting to a standing position.

standard
1 (adjective) usual or average.
2 (noun) a way of judging or measuring how good or bad something is. *The standard of the food was very high.*

stand-by (noun)
If someone or something is **on stand-by**, they are ready to be used or ready for action if needed.

stank (verb)
the past tense of stink.

staple (noun)
a small piece of wire which is pushed through sheets of paper to hold them together. **staple** (verb), **stapler** (noun).

star **starring starred**
1 (noun) a ball of burning gases in space, some of which can be seen from the Earth as a tiny point of light in the sky at night. **starry** (adjective).
2 (noun) a shape with several points, usually five or six. *See* shapes, *page 348.*
3 (noun) a very popular actor or entertainer. *Jenna wants to be a star.*
4 (verb) to take the main part in a film, play, or television programme. *Ryan will star in the next episode.*

starboard (noun)
If you are facing the front of a ship, **starboard** is the right side.

starch starches (noun)
a substance in foods such as potatoes, bread and rice which gives you energy. **starchy** (adjective).

stare staring stared (verb)
to look at someone or something for a long time, without moving your eyes. **stare** (noun).

starfish starfish (noun)
a sea animal that has a flat body and five or more arms.

cushion star

arm

start starting started (verb)
1 to begin doing something that you weren't doing before. **start** (noun).
2 If you **start** a machine or car, you use the controls to make it work. **start** (noun).

startle startling startled (verb)
to surprise someone and make them jump. *The noise from my alarm clock startled me.* **startled** (adjective), **startling** (adjective).

starve starving starved (verb)
to suffer or die because you have no food. **starvation** (noun).

starving (adjective)
1 suffering or dying because you don't have enough food.
2 very hungry. *I'm starving: when will dinner be ready?*

state stating stated
1 (verb) to say something, often a fact. *Please state your name.*
2 (noun) the way that someone or something is. *My room is in a bad state.*
3 (noun) another word for a country, or a part of a country. *Florida is sometimes called "The Sunshine State".*
4 (noun) the government of a country. *Most schools here are run by the state.*

statement (noun)
something, such as an announcement or speech, that gives facts.

station (noun)
1 a place where trains or buses stop.
2 a building used as a base by a police force or fire brigade.

Spelling tip

stationary stationery

The words "stationary" and "stationery" are easy to mix up, as they only have one letter different.
To help you use the right word, try remembering that "stationery" with an 'e' includes envelopes.

stationary (adjective)
not moving. *The doors will not open until the train is stationary.*

stationery (noun)
writing materials, such as paper, envelopes, and pens.

statue (noun)
a model of a person or animal made from stone, metal, and so on.

Great Sphinx statue, Egypt

stave (noun)
the set of five lines on which musical notes can be written.

stay staying stayed (verb)
1 to not move, or to remain where you are. *Stay here while I get the car.*
2 to spend time somewhere. *We didn't stay very long at the party.*
3 to visit a place for a period of time, often for a holiday. *We stayed at the seaside for a week.* **stay** (noun).

steady steadier steadiest (adjective)
1 not shaking, or not moving about.
2 quite slow, but continuous. *We're making steady progress.* **steadily** (adverb).

steak (noun)
a thick slice of meat or fish.

steal stealing stole stolen (verb)
to take and keep something that does not belong to you. **stolen** (adjective).

a b c d e f g h i j k l m n o p q r **s** t u v w x y z

steam steaming steamed
1 *(noun)* the hot gas that is made when water boils. **steam** *(verb)*, **steaming** *(adjective)*.
2 *(verb)* When glass **steams up**, it gets covered with tiny drops of water, which makes it hard to see through. *My glasses have steamed up.* **steamy** *(adjective)*.

steel *(noun)*
a hard, strong metal which is made mainly from iron.

steep steeper steepest *(adjective)*
sharply sloping up or down. *A steep hill.* **steeply** *(adverb)*.

steer steering steered *(verb)*
to make a vehicle go in the direction you want. *Owen sat at the back and steered the boat.*

stem *(noun)*
the long, main part of a plant, from which the leaves, flowers and fruit grow. *See* plant.

stencil *(noun)*
1 a piece of card, plastic or metal with a picture cut out of it, which can be painted or coloured over to transfer the picture onto a surface. **stencil** *(verb)*.
2 a picture made using a stencil.

sun stencil

step stepping stepped
1 *(verb)* to move your foot forward and put it down. *I accidentally stepped on a snail.* **step** *(noun)*.
2 *(noun)* the sound of someone walking. *I can hear steps in the street.*
3 *(noun)* one of the flat surfaces on a set of stairs.
4 *(noun)* a dance move.
5 *(noun)* a stage in a process. *The next step is to put all the parts together.*

stepbrother *(noun)*
your stepfather or stepmother's son.

stepfather *(noun)*
a man who is married to your mother, but is not your father.

stepmother *(noun)*
a woman who is married to your father, but is not your mother.

stepsister *(noun)*
your stepfather or stepmother's daughter.

stereo *(noun)*
sound that comes from two or more different speakers at once. **stereo** *(adjective)*.

stereotype *(noun)*
a simplified idea of a person or thing. **stereotypical** *(adjective)*.

sterling *(noun)*
the money used in Great Britain.

stern sterner sternest
1 *(adjective)* serious and strict. *Paula gave me a stern look.* **sternly** *(adverb)*.
2 *(noun)* the back of a boat or ship.

stew *(noun)*
meat, fish or vegetables cooked slowly in liquid. **stew** *(verb)*.

steward *(noun)*
1 a man who looks after passengers on a plane or a ship.
2 someone who helps to direct people at a public event, such as a concert or sports event.

stewardess *(noun)*
a woman who looks after passengers on a plane or a ship.

stick sticking stuck
1 *(noun)* a long, thin branch from a tree or a long, thin piece of wood.
2 *(noun)* a long, thin piece of something.
3 *(noun)* a long, thin piece of metal or wood that helps you to stand or walk.
4 *(verb)* to glue or fasten.
5 *(verb)* to push something pointed into something else.
6 If someone or something is **stuck**, they are unable to move. *We were stuck in traffic for hours.*
7 If something **sticks out**, it is very noticeable.
8 If you **stick up for** someone, you defend them from someone who is being mean or unfair.

sticker *(noun)*
a paper or plastic shape with
a sticky back.

sticky **stickier stickiest** *(adjective)*
1 made to stick to other things.
A sticky label. **stickiness** *(noun)*.
2 covered in something that makes it
stick to other things. *Milo's fingers are
all sticky.* **stickiness** *(noun)*.

stiff **stiffer stiffest** *(adjective)*
1 firm and difficult to bend or move.
stiffness *(noun)*.
2 If you feel **stiff**,
your muscles hurt.
stiffly *(adverb)*.

stile *(noun)*
steps or a short
ladder that you
use to climb over
a wall or fence.

wooden stile

still
1 *(adjective)* not moving. *We need to
stay still so we don't scare the animals.*
2 *(adverb)* even now. *Are you still here?*
3 *(adjective)* not fizzy. *Still water.*
4 *(adverb)* nevertheless, or all the same.
It's wet, but I'd still like to go for a walk.

sting **stinging stung** *(verb)*
1 If a plant or an insect **stings** you, it
touches or pierces your skin and hurts
you. **sting** *(noun)*.
2 to hurt with a sharp pain. *My eyes
are stinging.*

stink **stinking stank stunk** *(verb)*
to have a strong, unpleasant smell.
stink *(noun)*, **stinky** *(adjective)*.

stir **stirring stirred** *(verb)*
1 to mix a liquid by moving a spoon
or stick round and round in it.
2 to move slightly.

stitch **stitches stitching stitched**
1 *(verb)* to sew. **stitch** *(noun)*.
2 *(noun)* a sharp pain in your side,
caused by exercise.

stole *(verb)*
the past tense of **steal**.

stolen
1 *(verb)* the past participle of **steal**.
2 *(adjective)* Something that is **stolen**
has been taken from its owner.

stomach *(noun)*
1 the part of your body that holds
your food after you have swallowed it.
See **organ**.
2 the front part of your body, just below
your waist.

stone *(noun)*
1 a small piece of rock. **stony** *(adjective)*.
2 a hard material used for building,
making sculptures, and so on.
3 a hard seed found in the middle
of some fruits. *See* **avocado**.
4 a unit of weight equal to 14 pounds,
or just over six kilograms.

stood *(verb)*
the past tense of **stand**.

stool *(noun)*
a seat without a back.

stoop **stooping stooped** *(verb)*
1 to bend down low.
2 to have your head and shoulders bent
forwards, often because of old age.
stoop *(noun)*.

stop **stopping stopped**
1 *(verb)* When something **stops**, it comes
to an end. *Sit down when the music stops.*
2 *(verb)* If you **stop** something, you put
an end to it or don't do it any more.
3 *(verb)* to no longer move or work.
My watch has stopped.
4 *(noun)* one of the places where a
bus or train picks people up.

Spelling tip

stoop $\longrightarrow$ stooping

stop $\longrightarrow$ stopping

Remember that if a word has one syllable
and only one vowel before the final
consonant, you double the final consonant
before adding '–ing' or '–ed'. If there
are two vowels, you don't.

a b c d e f g h i j k l m n o p q r s t u v w x y z

stopwatch stopwatches (noun)
a watch that you can start and stop, often used for timing races.

store storing stored
1 (verb) to put things away until they are needed. **store** (noun), **storage** (noun).
2 (noun) a large shop. We spent an hour in the department store.

storey (noun)
one layer or floor of a building.

storm (noun)
a time of bad weather with strong wind and rain, and sometimes thunder and lightning. **stormy** (adjective).

story stories (noun)
something that you tell or write about things that have happened. Stories can be about something real or made-up. I love hearing ghost stories.

Spelling tip

storey
story

The words "storey" and "story" sound exactly the same, but have different meanings, so be careful to write the right word.
To make "storey" plural, you just add an '-s', but to make "story" plural you drop the 'y' and add '-ies': "stories".

---

stove (noun)
a piece of equipment used for cooking or for heating a room.

straight straighter straightest
1 (adjective) not bent or curved. A straight line. **straighten** (verb).
2 (adjective) level or neat. Put your hat straight. **straighten** (verb).
3 (adverb) immediately or directly. After our lunch we'll go straight to the park.
4 **straight away** or **straightaway** (adverb) at once, or immediately. We need to get going straight away.
5 If you go **straight on**, you go ahead and don't turn left or right.

straightforward (adjective)
1 not difficult or complicated. This game is pretty straightforward.
2 honest or to the point. Please give me a straightforward answer.

strain straining strained
1 (noun) stress or tension. Our friendship is under a lot of strain.
2 (verb) If you **strain** to do something, you try very hard or you need to stretch your body to do it.
3 (verb) If you **strain** a muscle in your body, you damage it by pulling it or overusing it.
4 (verb) If you **strain** a mixture, you pour it through a filter or a sieve to separate the solids from the liquid. Strain the vegetables before serving.

strand (noun)
1 a single thread or hair.
2 one of the threads or wires that are twisted together to form a rope.

stranded (adjective)
If you are **stranded** somewhere, you are stuck there and cannot get away. We were stranded on the island.

strange
stranger strangest (adjective)
1 odd or unexpected. Tom said something strange today. **strangeness** (noun), **strangely** (adverb).
2 new or unfamiliar. I noticed a strange car in the driveway.

stranger (noun)
1 someone you don't know.
2 someone who is new to a place.

strangle strangling strangled (verb)
to kill someone by squeezing their throat so that they can't breathe.

strap (noun)
a strip of leather, plastic, canvas, and so on, used to fasten things or for carrying something. **strap** (verb).

straw (noun)
1 dried stalks of corn, wheat, and so on.
2 a thin, hollow tube that you can drink through.

strawberry— stroke

strawberry
strawberries *(noun)*
a soft, red summer fruit.

strawberry

stray **straying strayed**
1 *(verb)* to wander away
or get lost. *Don't stray from the path.*
2 *(noun)* a lost cat or dog.

streak *(noun)*
a long mark or stripe of colour.
Streaks of paint. **streaky** *(adjective).*

stream *(noun)*
1 a small river.
2 a large line of moving people, cars,
and so on. **stream** *(verb).*
3 a group of schoolchildren who are
at the same level in their work.

streamlined *(adjective)*
made to be able to move through air
or water very quickly and easily.

streamlined car

street *(noun)*
a road in a village, town or city with
houses or other buildings along it.
Milo lives on the same street as me.

strength *(noun)*
1 how strong someone or something is.
The boxer's strength is very impressive.
strengthen *(verb).*
2 Someone's **strengths** are their good
points, or the things they can do well.

stress *(noun)*
worry or pressure. *Mum is under
a lot of stress.* **stressful** *(adjective),*
stressed *(adjective).*

stretch
stretches stretching stretched *(verb)*
1 to make something bigger or longer.
Stretch the dough. **stretchy** *(adjective).*
2 to hold out a part of your body as
far as you can. **stretch** *(noun).*
3 to spread out or cover an area. *The
forest stretches for miles.* **stretch** *(noun).*

strict **stricter strictest** *(adjective)*
1 If someone is **strict**, they make you
obey the rules and behave properly.
strictness *(noun),* **strictly** *(adverb).*
2 complete or total. *Our teacher
demands strict silence.* **strictly** *(adverb).*

stride **striding strode stridden**
1 *(verb)* to walk quickly, with long steps.
2 *(noun)* a long step.

strike **striking struck** *(verb)*
1 to hit or attack someone or something.
The glass broke when it struck the floor.
strike *(noun).*
2 When a clock **strikes**, it rings a bell
to show you what time it is.
3 If you **strike a match**, you light it.
4 If something **strikes** you, you suddenly
realize it or take notice of it. *It struck
me that I'd left my bag at the library.*
striking *(adjective).*
5 When people **strike** or **go on strike**,
they refuse to work because they are
not happy about something to do with
work. **strike** *(noun),* **striker** *(noun).*

string *(noun)*
1 a thin cord or rope.
2 a thin wire on a musical instrument,
such as a guitar or violin.

strip **stripping stripped**
1 *(verb)* to take something off. *Marco
stripped the paint off the door.*
2 *(verb)* to take all your clothes off.
3 *(noun)* a long, narrow piece of paper,
fabric, and so on.

stripe *(noun)*
a band of colour. **striped** *(adjective),*
stripy *(adjective).*

strode *(verb)*
the past tense of **stride**.

stroke **stroking stroked**
1 *(verb)* to pass your hand gently over
something. *Leo stroked the cat.*
2 *(noun)* a hit. *A stroke of lightning.*
3 *(noun)* a way of moving in swimming.
My favourite stroke is backstroke.
4 *(noun)* When someone has a **stroke**,
the blood supply to their brain stops for
a short time, and they can find speaking
and moving difficult afterwards.

a b c d e f g h i j k l m n o p q r s t u v w x y z

stroll (noun)
a short, relaxed walk. **stroll** (verb).

strong stronger strongest (adjective)
1 powerful, or having a lot of force.
A strong wind. **strongly** (adverb).
2 hard to break. *The new bridge
is very strong.* **strongly** (adverb).
3 full of flavour. *Strong coffee.*

struck (verb)
the past tense of **strike**.

structure (noun)
1 something that has been built
or put together.
2 the way something is organized or put
together. *The teacher said my story needs
a better structure.* **structural** (adjective).

struggle
struggling struggled (verb)
1 If you **struggle** with someone, you fight
or wrestle with them. **struggle** (noun).
2 If you **struggle** with something, you
find it difficult to do. **struggle** (noun).

strum strumming strummed (verb)
to play a guitar or other stringed
instrument by brushing your fingers
over the strings.

stubborn (adjective)
Someone who is **stubborn** always wants
to get their own way. *Jen is a stubborn
child.* **stubbornly** (adverb).

stuck (verb)
the past tense of **stick**.

stud (noun)
1 a small, round piece of metal, such
as an earring.
2 one of the small lumps on the bottom
of football, rugby or hockey boots.

student (noun)
someone who is studying, especially
a young adult at college or university.

studio (noun)
1 a room in which an artist, designer
or photographer works.
2 a place where things are made
or recorded, such as music, radio
or television programmes, or films.

Spelling tip

study   studies   studying

When you add the endings '–es' and
'–ed' to the word "study", you need to
change the 'y' to an 'i' first. But if
you add '–ing', you keep the 'y', so that
you don't end up with two 'i's in a row.

study studies studying studied
1 (verb) to spend time learning a subject
or skill. *Julia is studying ancient history.*
2 (verb) to look at something very
closely. *The detective studied the
crumpled paper.*
3 (noun) a small office or room where
someone works.

stuff stuffing stuffed
1 (noun) a substance or a material. *There
was some powdery stuff on the floor.*
2 (noun) things in general, or possessions.
Kamal is tidying up his stuff.
3 (verb) to fill something tightly. *Patrick
stuffed everything into his backpack.*

stuffy stuffier stuffiest (adjective)
1 A **stuffy** room doesn't have enough
fresh air in it.
2 A **stuffy** person is easily shocked.

stumble stumbling stumbled (verb)
1 to trip up, or to walk in a clumsy way.
Lily stumbled through the door.
2 to make mistakes when you are
talking or reading aloud.

stump (noun)
the part that
is left when
a tree is
cut down.

rings

stun
**stunning
stunned** (verb)

You can find out how old a tree was
when it was cut down by counting
the rings on its **stump**.

1 to knock a person or animal
unconscious, or nearly unconscious.
2 to shock or surprise someone very
much. **stunned** (adjective).

stung *(verb)*
the past tense of **sting**.

stunk *(verb)*
the past participle of **stink**.

stunning *(adjective)*
very beautiful or amazing.

stunt *(noun)*
a dangerous trick or act.

stupid stupider stupidest *(adjective)*
totally thoughtless, or not sensible at all.
stupidity *(noun)*, **stupidly** *(adverb)*.

sturdy sturdier sturdiest *(adjective)*
strong and firm. *A sturdy wooden bench.*

stutter stuttering stuttered *(verb)*
If you **stutter** when you speak, you
repeat sounds or words, or struggle
to say some words. **stutter** *(noun)*.

sty sties *(noun)*
a hut with a yard, where pigs are kept.

stye styes or **sties** *(noun)*
a sore, swollen area on your eyelid.

style styling styled
1 *(noun)* a way of doing something, such
as writing, dressing, building, and so on.
2 *(noun)* If someone or something has
style, they look smart and elegant.
stylish *(adjective)*, **stylishly** *(adjective)*.
3 *(verb)* If you **style** something, you shape
it or arrange it in a creative way. *Sarah
styled my hair for me.* **stylist** *(noun)*.

subject *(noun)*
1 The **subject** of a conversation, book,
and so on, is what it's about.
2 something you study, such as
geography or mathematics.
3 The **subject** of a sentence is the
person or thing that does the verb. For
example, in the sentence "Richard fell
off his bike", "Richard" is the subject
and "fell" is the verb.
4 a person who is ruled by a king
or queen.

subjective *(adjective)*
based on one person's feelings or
opinions, not facts. *This review of the
new art exhibition is very subjective.*

submarine *(noun)*
a ship that can travel under the water
for long periods.

This **submarine** is called HMS Astute.

submit submitting submitted *(verb)*
to hand something in, or put something
forward. *Bruno has submitted an entry
for the photography competition.*

subscribe
subscribing subscribed *(verb)*
to pay money regularly for a newspaper,
magazine, and so on. **subscription** *(noun)*.

substance *(noun)*
a material of some sort that you can see
and touch. Objects, powders and liquids
are substances. *There was a sticky
substance on the table.*

substitute *(noun)*
someone or something used instead of
another, such as a footballer who plays
when another player is tired or injured.
It is often shortened to "sub". *Rob came
on as a substitute in the second half.*
substitute *(verb)*, **substitution** *(noun)*.

subtract
subtracting subtracted *(verb)*
to take one number away from another.
*What do you get when you subtract
9 from 27?* **subtraction** *(noun)*.

suburb *(noun)*
an area with lots of homes on or near
the edge of a large town or city.
*My aunt and uncle have moved to
the suburbs, because it's less busy.*
suburban *(adjective)*.

subway *(noun)*
1 a covered path for pedestrians under
a road or railway. *The subway leads
to the other side of the main road.*
2 an underground railway, especially
in the US. *The New York subway.*

a b c d e f g h i j k l m n o p q r **s** t u v w x y z

Spelling tip

succeed   success   successful

In these words, the letters 'cc' make a hard 'k' sound followed by a soft 's' sound: "suk-sess", "suk-seed". This is because they are followed by an 'e'. In words where the letters 'cc' aren't followed by an 'e', they make a hard 'k' sound, such as in "occur", "hiccup" and "accuse".

succeed (suk-**seed**)
succeeding succeeded (verb)
1 to manage to do something. *Jed finally succeeded in fixing the car.*
2 to do well or get what you want.

success (suk-**sess**) (noun)
managing to do what you were aiming to do.

successful (adjective)
1 If something is **successful**, it does well, or does what it was meant to. *Our plan was successful.* **successfully** (adverb).
2 If someone is **successful**, they have done well in their life and are doing or getting what they want.

such
1 (determiner) so much. *Stefan and Drew are such good friends.*
2 **such as** a phrase used before you give examples. *I love green vegetables, such as spinach and peas.*

suck sucking sucked (verb)
1 to pull something into your mouth, using your tongue and lips.
2 to keep something, such as a sweet, in your mouth without swallowing it.
3 to pull something inside. *The vacuum cleaner sucked up my earring.*

sudden (adjective)
quick or unexpected. **suddenly** (adverb).

sudoku (noun)
a puzzle in which you write missing numbers in a grid.

suffer suffering suffered (verb)
1 to go through something unpleasant, painful, or horrible. *After the storm, the villagers suffered terribly.* **suffering** (noun).
2 If you **suffer from** an illness or condition, you get it often or have it for a long time. **sufferer** (noun).

suffix suffixes (noun)
a group of letters added to the end of a word, which change its meaning or its word class. *The suffix '-less' means "without", so "fearless" means "without fear".* See suffixes, page 352.

suffocate
suffocating suffocated (verb)
1 to die because you cannot breathe. **suffocation** (noun).
2 to kill someone by stopping them from breathing.

sugar (noun)
a sweet food that comes from plants, and can be added to food and drinks. **sugary** (adjective).

suggest suggesting suggested (verb)
to put forward a plan or idea for people to think about. *I suggested going to Wales for our next holiday.* **suggestion** (noun).

suicide (**soo**-iss-ide) (noun)
If someone **commits suicide**, they kill themselves. **suicidal** (adjective).

suit suiting suited
1 (noun) a set of smart, matching clothes, usually a man's jacket and trousers.
2 (noun) one of the four types of cards in a pack of playing cards. The four suits are clubs, diamonds, hearts, and spades. See card.
3 (verb) If a hairstyle or an outfit **suits you**, it makes you look good.
4 (verb) If an arrangement or plan **suits you**, it works well for you.

suitable (adjective)
right for a particular purpose or situation. *Those shoes aren't suitable for walking in the countryside.* **suitability** (noun), **suitably** (adverb).

suitcase *(noun)*
a large, rectangular bag that you can carry things in when you travel.

sulk **sulking sulked** *(verb)*
to be in a bad mood because you haven't got what you want. **sulk** *(noun)*, **sulky** *(adjective)*.

sultan *(noun)*
the ruler of a Muslim country.

sultana *(noun)*
a sweet, dried grape, used for snacks or in baking or cooking.

sum *(noun)*
1 an amount of money. *We need to pay the sum of one hundred pounds.*
2 a maths problem. *Fred finds sums very difficult.*
3 the total of two numbers added together. *The sum of two odd numbers is always an even number.*

summary **summaries** *(noun)*
A **summary** tells you the main points or facts about something. *Rebecca started her book report with a summary of the plot.* **summarize** *(verb)*.

summer *(noun)*
the part of the year when the weather is warmest and the days are longest.

summit *(noun)*
the top of a mountain.

sun *(noun)*
1 The **Sun** is the star that the Earth moves around, and that gives us light and warmth.

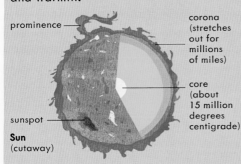

prominence

corona (stretches out for millions of miles)

core (about 15 million degrees centigrade)

sunspot

Sun (cutaway)

2 light and warmth from the Sun. *Ice cream melts in the sun.*

sunbathe
sunbathing sunbathed *(verb)*
to sit or lie in the sun to get a suntan.

sunburn *(noun)*
sore, red skin caused by staying in sunlight for too long, or without suncream. **sunburned** or **sunburnt** *(adjective)*.

suncream *(noun)*
a cream or liquid that you put on your skin to protect it from sunlight.

Sunday *(noun)*
the second day of the weekend.

sunflower *(noun)*
a tall flower with yellow petals and large seeds that are used in food and to make oil. See **flower**.

sunflower seeds

sung *(verb)*
the past participle of **sing**.

sunglasses *(plural noun)*
glasses with dark lenses that you wear to protect your eyes from bright sunlight.

sunk *(verb)*
the past participle of **sink**.

sunlight *(noun)*
light from the Sun. *Plants need sunlight to grow.*

sunny **sunnier sunniest** *(adjective)*
When the weather is **sunny**, the Sun is shining.

sunrise *(noun)*
the moment when the Sun first appears in the morning.

sunscreen *(noun)*
see **suncream**.

sunset *(noun)*
the moment when the Sun goes down and disappears in the evening. *We sat outside until sunset.*

sunshine *(noun)*
light and warmth from the Sun.

sunstroke *(noun)*
an illness caused by staying in hot sun for too long, which can give you a fever, sickness, and a headache.

suntan (noun)
If you have a **suntan**, your skin is brown because you have been in strong sunlight. **suntanned** (adjective).

super (adjective)
very good. *It was a super day out.*

superb (adjective)
excellent or wonderful. *That was a superb performance.* **superbly** (adverb).

superlative (soo-per-la-tiv) (noun)
Superlatives are adjectives and adverbs used to mean "the most". "Biggest" is the superlative of "big", and "fastest" is the superlative of "fast". **superlative** (adjective). See word classes, page 3.

supermarket (noun)
a large shop that sells food and many other things for your home.

superstitious (adjective)
People who are **superstitious** believe that certain objects or things that you do bring good luck or bad luck. *Maia is very superstitious, and will never walk under a ladder.* **superstition** (noun).

supper (noun)
a meal or snack that you eat in the evening. *We had fish for supper again.*

supply
supplies supplying supplied (verb)
to provide someone or something with what they want or need. **supply** (noun), **supplier** (noun).

support
supporting supported (verb)
1 to hold something up to stop it from falling. *These arches support the bridge.* **support** (noun).
2 to help and encourage someone. *We supported Carl when he first opened the café.* **supportive** (adjective).
3 to pay money to someone or be responsible for making sure they have what they need. *Erin has a young family to support.* **support** (noun).
4 to be in favour of something, or a fan of something. *I support my local team.* **supporter** (noun).

suppose supposing supposed (verb)
1 If you **suppose** something, you think that it is true, but you don't know for sure. *I suppose you're right. I suppose Justin will be late as usual.*
2 If you are **supposed to** do something, you are meant to do it or you ought to do it. *I'm supposed to walk the dog.*

sure surer surest
1 (adjective) certain and definite. *Are you sure it's cooked? It's sure to rain.*
2 (adjective) If you **make sure** of something, you check it or see that it happens.
3 (adjective) If you are **sure of yourself**, you are confident and believe in yourself.
4 (interjection) yes, or of course. *"Do you want to play rounders?" "Sure."*

surely (adverb)
a word you use when you think something must be true, or you would expect it to be true. *Surely you've met my brother before?*

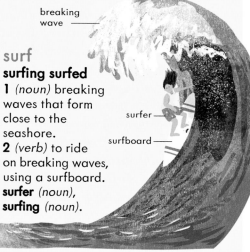

breaking wave

surfer

surfboard

surf
surfing surfed
1 (noun) breaking waves that form close to the seashore.
2 (verb) to ride on breaking waves, using a surfboard. **surfer** (noun), **surfing** (noun).

surfing

3 (verb) When you **surf** the internet, you look at different websites.

surface (noun)
the outside or top of something. *The surface of the pond was completely still.*

surfboard (noun)
a wide, flat board with a pointed end that you can use for surfing.

surgeon (**sur**-jun) (noun)
a doctor who performs operations.

surgery (**sur**-jer-ee)
surgery or **surgeries** (noun)
1 a place where people go to see a doctor, dentist, vet, and so on. *Call the surgery to make an appointment.*
2 a medical treatment that involves removing or repairing parts of a person's body. *Dad had surgery to treat his shoulder.* **surgical** (adjective).

surname (noun)
someone's last name or family name. *My surname is Murray.*

surprise (noun)
1 something you don't expect. *Matthew's present was a total surprise.* **surprise** (verb), **surprising** (adjective).
2 the feeling you have when something that you didn't expect happens. *Meg jumped in surprise.* **surprised** (adjective).

surrender
surrendering surrendered (verb)
to admit that you have lost a fight or battle. **surrender** (noun).

surround
surrounding surrounded (verb)
to be on every side of something. *The soldiers surrounded the castle.*

surroundings (plural noun)
the things around someone or something. *The surroundings of the town are also very beautiful.*

survey (noun)
a set of questions that aims to find out what people think about something. *I did a survey of my friends to find out what their favourite animals are.*

The letter 'v' is always followed by a vowel or a 'y'.

survive
surviving survived (verb)
to stay alive, especially in a difficult situation or after a dangerous event. *Only six passengers survived the crash.* **survival** (noun), **survivor** (noun).

suspect suspecting suspected
1 (suss-**pekt**) (verb) to think that someone should not be trusted. *Someone took the last carton of juice – I suspect Skye.* **suspicion** (noun).
2 (suss-**pekt**) (verb) to think that something might be wrong with a situation. *Victoria suspected that Russell had been listening to her conversation.* **suspicion** (noun).
3 (**suss**-pekt) (noun) someone who might have committed a crime. *The suspect has already spent time in jail for robbery.*

suspense (noun)
a feeling of uncertainty and excitement, caused by having to wait to see what happens. *The ending of the latest episode left me in suspense.*

suspicious (adjective)
1 If you feel **suspicious**, you think that something is wrong. **suspicion** (noun).
2 If something is **suspicious**, it makes people think that something is wrong. **suspiciously** (adverb).

swallow swallowing swallowed
1 (verb) to make food or drink go down your throat.
2 (noun) a small bird with long wings and a forked tail, that eats while flying.

forked tail

swallow

swam (verb)
the past tense of **swim**.

swamp (noun)
an area of wet, marshy ground.

swan (noun)
a very large water bird with a long, thin neck. *See* baby.

swap or **swop**
swapping swapped (verb)
to change one thing for another.

swarm (noun)
a large number of bees or other insects flying together.

swat swatting swatted (verb)
to kill an insect by hitting it quickly.

a b c d e f g h i j k l m n o p q r s t u v w x y z

sway swaying swayed (verb)
to move or swing from side to side.
The trees swayed in the wind.

swear swearing swore sworn (verb)
1 to use a rude word.
2 to make a serious promise. *I swear to tell the truth.*

sweat sweating sweated (verb)
When you **sweat**, salty water comes out of your skin because you are hot, nervous, or ill. **sweat** (noun), **sweaty** (adjective).

sweater (noun)
a warm piece of clothing that you wear on the top half of your body. It has long sleeves and no buttons up the front.

sweatshirt (noun)
a thick cotton top with long sleeves.

sweep sweeping swept (verb)
to clear away dirt using a brush.

sweet sweeter sweetest
1 (noun) a small snack made of sugar or chocolate.
2 (adjective) tasting sugary, not savoury. **sweetness** (noun).
3 (adjective) kind or cute. *Your cat is so sweet.* **sweetly** (adverb), **sweetness** (noun).

sweetcorn (noun)
a vegetable covered in small yellow seeds. Sweetcorn is sometimes called maize. *See* **vegetable**.

swell swelling swelled swollen (verb)
to grow in size. A part of your body might swell because of an injury. **swelling** (noun), **swollen** (adjective).

swept (verb)
the past tense of **sweep**.

swerve swerving swerved (verb)
to change direction quickly, usually to avoid hitting something.

swift swifter swiftest
1 (adjective) fast or rapid. **swiftly** (adverb).
2 (noun) a bird with long, narrow wings.

swig swigging swigged (verb)
to drink something in large gulps. *Joe swigged his tea.* **swig** (noun).

swim swimming swam swum (verb)
to move yourself through water. People swim by moving their arms and legs, and animals swim by moving their bodies, wings and tails. *I swim every Tuesday.* **swimming** (noun), **swimmer** (noun).

This picture shows penguins **swimming** underwater.

swimming costume or **swimsuit** (noun)
a piece of clothing that girls or women wear for swimming.

swimming pool (noun)
a large area of water that has been built for people to swim in.

swimming trunks (noun)
special shorts that boys or men wear for swimming.

swing swinging swung
1 (verb) to hang, moving from side to side or forwards and backwards. *The monkey was swinging from the branch.*
2 (noun) a playground toy, with a hanging seat that moves backwards and forwards. **swing** (verb).

switch
switches switching switched (verb)
1 to change one thing for another. *I switched my tuna sandwich for a cheese one.*
2 to change from one thing to another. *Cassie switched from French to Spanish classes.*
3 If you **switch something on or off**, you press a button to make it start or stop working. *Switch off the lights when you leave the room.* **switch** (noun).

swivel swivelling swivelled *(verb)*
to turn or rotate on the spot.

swollen *(verb)*
the past participle of swell.
swollen *(adjective)*.

swoop swooping swooped *(verb)*
to move down suddenly through the air.

swop *(verb)*
see swap.

sword *(sord)* *(noun)*
a weapon with a handle and a long,
sharp blade.

swore *(verb)*
the past tense of swear.

sworn *(verb)*
the past participle of swear.

swum *(verb)*
the past participle of swim.

swung *(verb)*
the past tense of swing.

sycamore *(noun)*
a tree that has large five-pointed leaves.

syllable *(**sil**-a-bul)* *(noun)*
a short sound in a word. *"Imagination"
has five syllables.*

syllabus *(**sil**-a-bus)*
syllabuses or **syllabi** *(noun)*
the list of things students need to learn
on a course or for an exam. *That book
isn't on the syllabus this year.*

symbol *(**sim**-bul)* *(noun)*
a design or object that stands for
something else. *A white dove is a
symbol of peace.* **symbolic** *(adjective)*.

yin and yang   recyclable   dove of peace
   symbol   symbol   symbol

three well-known **symbols**

symmetrical
*(si-**met**-ri-cul)* *(adjective)*
If a shape is **symmetrical**,
one half is the mirror
image of the other half.
symmetry *(noun)*.

a symmetrical
shape

sympathy *(**sim**-pa-thee)*
sympathies *(noun)*
understanding someone's feelings,
or feeling sorry for them because
something bad has happened. *I wrote
John a message of sympathy when
his aunt died.* **sympathize** *(verb)*,
sympathetic *(adjective)*.

symphony *(**sim**-fo-nee)*
symphonies *(noun)*
a long piece of music, usually in four
parts called movements.

symptom *(**simp**-tom)* *(noun)*
something which shows that you
have an illness. *Common symptoms
of chickenpox are itchy red spots
or blisters and a fever.*

synagogue *(**sin**-a-gog)* *(noun)*
a place where Jews go to worship.

synonym *(**sin**-oh-nim)* *(noun)*
a word that means the same or almost
the same as another word. *"Quick"
is a synonym of "fast".*

synthetic phonics *(noun)*
a way of learning to read English by
learning letter sounds and putting them
together to read words.

syringe *(sir-**rinj**)* *(noun)*
a tube with a needle on the end,
which is used to inject medicines into
people's and animals' bodies.

syrup *(noun)*
a thick, sweet liquid made from sugar
and water. **syrupy** *(adjective)*.

system *(noun)*
1 an organized way of doing things.
*Will has a system for arranging
the books on his shelves.*
2 all the parts of something which
work together to do a job. *A central
heating system.*

a b c d e f g h i j k l m n o p q r s t u v w x y z

Tt

table (noun)
1 a piece of furniture with a flat top, resting on legs.
2 numbers or information listed in rows and columns.
3 A **times table** is a list of a number multiplied by other numbers, such as 3 x 6 = 18.

tablespoon (noun)
a large spoon which you use to measure out ingredients, or to serve food. **tablespoonful** (noun).

tablet (noun)
1 a small, hard piece of medicine that you swallow.
2 a computer that you can hold in your hand.

table tennis (noun)
a game in which players hit a small, light ball over a net across a table, using round bats.

table tennis bat and ball

tabloid (noun)
a newspaper with quite small pages, and lots of photographs and stories.

tackle **tackling tackled** (verb)
1 If you **tackle** a tricky job or problem, you try to do it or deal with it. *Ben tackled his history essay today.*
2 In sport, if you **tackle** another player, you try to get the ball from them. **tackle** (noun).

tactful (adjective)
If you are **tactful**, you are aware of other people's feelings and try not to offend them. **tact** (noun), **tactfully** (adverb).

tactics (plural noun)
plans that you come up with to help you win something, especially a sports match or other contest. *The other team knows our tactics, so we need to change them.*

tactless (adjective)
If you are **tactless**, you don't think about other people's feelings when you say things. **tactlessly** (adverb).

tag (noun)
a small label on something. *Our cat has a tag on his collar in case he gets lost.*

tail (noun)
the part of an animal's body that grows out at the bottom of its back.

take **taking took taken** (verb)
1 to pick something up in your hand and hold it. *Leo took the biggest apple from the fruit bowl.*
2 to transport or move someone or something to a place. *Mum takes us to school every day.*
3 to steal something. *Helen took my swimming goggles from my bag.*
4 to swallow or drink medicine. *Gran takes her pills in the morning.*
5 If you **can't take** something, you can't bear it. *I can't take much more of this.*

takeaway (noun)
1 a meal that is cooked in a restaurant, but you take somewhere else to eat. **takeaway** (adjective).
2 a restaurant that sells meals for people to take home and eat. **takeaway** (adjective).

takeoff (noun)
the moment when a plane or other aircraft leaves the ground. *The aeroplane prepared for takeoff.*

tale (noun)
a story. *Many children love listening to fairy tales.*

Spelling tip   tail   tale

The word "tail" (the thing a dog wags when it's happy) sounds exactly like "tale" (a story). It's easy to confuse words that sound the same, so always check your spelling in a dictionary if you're not sure which word you need.

talent *(noun)*
an ability or skill. *Leah has a talent for dancing.* **talented** *(adjective)*.

talk talking talked
1 *(verb)* to say words, or to speak. *David talks a lot.*
2 *(noun)* a speech, or a lesson. *Today the teacher gave a talk on online safety.*
3 *(noun)* a chat, or a conversation.

talkative *(adjective)*
If you are **talkative**, you enjoy talking, and talk a lot.

tall taller tallest *(adjective)*
high, or higher than most things. *We climbed the tall tower.*

Talmud *(noun)*
the book containing the laws of the Jewish religion.

tambourine *(noun)*
a round percussion instrument similar to the top of a drum, with small metal discs around the rim which make a noise when shaken. *See* percussion.

tame tamer tamest *(adjective)*
An animal that is **tame** is not dangerous or frightened of people. *The hedgehog in our garden is very tame.* **tame** *(verb)*.

tan *(noun)*
If you have a **tan**, your skin has become darker, usually because you have been in the sun. *I got a tan on holiday in Cyprus.* **tan** *(verb)*, **tanned** *(adjective)*.

tandem *(noun)*
a bicycle for two people.

tandem

tandoori *(noun)*
a style of Asian cooking which uses a clay oven called a tandoor. *My favourite meal is tandoori chicken.*

tangled *(adjective)*
If something, such as hair or wires, is **tangled**, there are lots of small knots in it. *My hair is very tangled.* **tangle** *(verb)*.

tank *(noun)*
1 a glass or plastic box that can be filled with water to keep pet fish in.
2 a large army truck covered with armour, with crawler tracks instead of wheels.

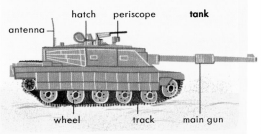

hatch   periscope   **tank**
antenna
wheel   track   main gun

tanker *(noun)*
1 a big truck that carries heavy loads.
2 a ship that carries lots of cargo.

tantrum *(noun)*
If a young child has a **tantrum**, they are very upset, and may scream, kick, and lie on the floor.

tap tapping tapped
1 *(noun)* A **tap** controls the flow of a liquid, such as water, coming out of it.
2 *(verb)* to hit or knock something gently.

tape *(noun)*
1 a strip of sticky plastic used for sticking things together.
2 a thin piece of fabric.

tape measure *(noun)*
a long strip of fabric or flexible metal, with measurements on it that you can use to see how long or tall things are.

target targeting targeted
1 *(noun)* something you aim at and try to hit or attack. **target** *(verb)*.
2 *(verb)* to focus on something.

tart *(noun)*
a pastry case with a savoury or sweet filling, often fruit.

a b c d e f g h i j k l m n o p q r s t u v w x y z

tartan – teeth

tartan *(noun)*
a pattern of coloured checks and lines crossing each other, originally from Scotland. **tartan** *(adjective)*.

task *(noun)*
a job, or something you have to do.

taste **tasting tasted**
1 *(noun)* The **taste** of a food is whether it's sweet, sour, spicy, salty, and so on.
2 *(verb)* to put food in your mouth to find out its flavour. **taste** *(noun)*.
3 *(noun)* Your sense of **taste** tells you what you are eating and what it's like.

tasty **tastier tastiest** *(adjective)*
having a nice flavour. *This pear is tasty.*

tattered *(adjective)*
old and torn, or scruffy.

tattoo *(noun)*
a picture or words that are drawn on someone's skin with permanent ink. **tattoo** *(verb)*, **tattooed** *(adjective)*.

taught *(verb)*
the past tense of **teach**.

tax **taxes** *(noun)*
money that people have to pay to the government to help pay for schools, hospitals, roads, and so on. **tax** *(verb)*, **taxation** *(noun)*.

taxi *(noun)*
a car with a driver who gets paid to take people somewhere.

tea *(noun)*
1 a hot drink made from the leaves of the tea plant. **tea bag** *(noun)*.
2 an early evening meal.

teach
teaches teaching taught *(verb)*
to show or tell someone about a subject, or how to do something. *My brother taught me to swim.* **teacher** *(noun)*, **teaching** *(noun)*.

team *(noun)*
a group of people who play or work together. *I have joined a netball team.*

London taxi

tear **tearing tore torn**
1 *(teer)* *(noun)* a drop of water that comes out of your eyes, usually when you're sad.
2 *(tare)* *(verb)* to rip a piece of paper or fabric. **tear** *(noun)*.
3 *(tare)* *(verb)* to move very quickly. *The children tore into the yard at break time.*

tease **teasing teased** *(verb)*
If you **tease** someone, you make fun of them by saying unkind things or trying to annoy them. **teasing** *(noun)*.

teaspoon *(noun)*
a small spoon used for stirring drinks, or to measure ingredients in cooking. **teaspoonful** *(noun)*.

technical *(adjective)*
1 to do with science, machines, industry, and so on.
2 using words that only experts understand. *This book on motorbikes is too technical for me.*

technician *(noun)*
someone who looks after scientific equipment or machines, or who does practical work in a laboratory.

technique *(tek-neek)* *(noun)*
a special or skilful way of doing something. *A technique for cracking eggs.*

technology *(noun)*
the use of science and machinery to do something. **technological** *(adjective)*.

teenager *(noun)*
a young person aged between 13 and 19 years old. **teenage** *(adjective)*.

teeth *(plural noun)*
the plural of **tooth**.

human teeth — lateral incisor, central incisor, canine, second premolar, first premolar, first molar, second molar, third molar

telephone *(noun)*
a machine which makes it possible for you to speak to someone who is in a different place. It is often shortened to "phone".

telescope *(noun)*
an instrument which makes things that are far away, such as stars, look nearer. **telescopic** *(adjective)*.

telescope

television *(noun)*
a machine with a screen, on which you can watch programmes and films.

tell **telling told** *(verb)*
1 to let someone know about something. *Gemma told me about the party.*
2 If you **tell** someone to do something, you order them to do it.
3 to recognize or spot. *Can you tell that he's miming?*
4 If you **tell someone off**, you shout at them because you are angry with them.

temper *(noun)*
your mood. If you have a bad temper, you are often very angry or annoyed.

temperature *(noun)*
1 how hot or cold something is.
2 If you **have a temperature**, your body is hotter than normal because you are ill.

temple *(noun)*
a building where some people worship their god, or gods.

tempo *(noun)*
The **tempo** of a song or piece of music is how fast or slow the beat is.

temporary *(adjective)*
Something **temporary** only lasts for a short time. *A temporary tattoo.*

tempt **tempting tempted** *(verb)*
1 If you **tempt** someone, you make them want something by talking about it or offering it to them. **tempting** *(adjective)*.
2 If you are **tempted**, you want to do something you probably shouldn't. *I'm tempted to eat this.* **temptation** *(noun)*.

tend **tending tended** *(verb)*
1 If a thing **tends** to happen, it usually happens. *Sally tends to be late.*
2 If you **tend to** something, you look after it. *Dad tended to the barbecue.*

tender *(adjective)*
1 sore when you touch it. *A tender bruise.*
2 loving and kind. **tenderly** *(adverb)*.
3 If food, such as meat, is **tender**, it is soft, not tough and chewy. *Tender steak.*

tennis *(noun)*
a game played by two or four players, in which they have to hit a ball over a net using rackets.

tense **tenser tensest**
1 *(adjective)* stressed or worried.
2 *(adjective)* tight and stiff. *My shoulder muscles feel tense.* **tense** *(verb)*.
3 *(noun)* The **tense** of a verb tells you when the action it's describing happens.

tennis racket

tennis ball

tension *(noun)*
1 a feeling of worry, or nervousness. *There was a lot of tension in the room.*
2 If there is **tension** between people, they're not getting on well.

tent *(noun)*
a shelter made of waterproof material, supported by poles and ropes.

tentacle *(noun)*
a long, bendy, moveable part that some animals have sticking out of their main body. For example, snails have tentacles coming out of the front of their head, with eyes at the end.

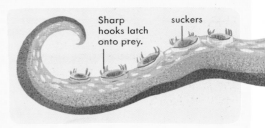
Sharp hooks latch onto prey.   suckers

The Humboldt squid has a feeding **tentacle** which it uses to grab prey.

term (noun)
1 part of the year at school or college. *Our school year has three terms.*
2 a type of word. *Technical terms are hard to understand.*

terminal
1 (noun) the building passengers leave from and arrive at in an airport or port.
2 (noun) a computer keyboard and screen.
3 (adjective) If someone has a **terminal illness**, they won't get better. **terminally** (adverb).

terrapin (noun)
a water reptile with a shell and webbed feet.

shell

terrapin

terrible
(adjective)
awful, or very bad indeed. *That is a terrible haircut.* **terribly** (adverb).

terrific (adjective)
great. *This is a terrific book.* **terrifically** (adverb).

terrify
terrifies terrifying terrified (verb)
to frighten someone very much. *That film terrified me.* **terrifying** (adjective).

territory **territories** (noun)
the land that belongs to a country, an animal, or a group of animals.

terror (noun)
great fear. *A look of terror.*

terrorist (noun)
a person who uses violence to scare people into doing what they want them to, or to try to get a government to do what they want them to do. **terrorism** (noun).

tessellate
tessellating tessellated (verb)
When shapes **tessellate**, they fit together without any gaps in between.

tessellating shapes

test (noun)
a set of questions to answer, or things you have to do, to show someone that you know something or can do something well enough. **test** (verb).

test match (noun)
a cricket or rugby match played between teams from different countries.

text **texting texted**
1 (verb) to send someone a message from a mobile phone. *I'll text Ruby to let her know we're going to be late.* **text** (noun).
2 (noun) the writing in a book or newspaper, or on a screen.

textbook (noun)
a book which you use at school or college, which contains information.

texture (noun)
the feel of something, such as whether it is rough, smooth, soft, or hard. *I don't mind the taste of mushrooms, but I hate the texture.*

thank **thanking thanked** (verb)
to tell someone that you are grateful for something. **thank you** (interjection), **thanks** (interjection), **thanks** (plural noun), **thankful** (adjective), **thankfully** (adverb).

thaw **thawing thawed** (verb)
When something frozen **thaws**, it melts and becomes soft or liquid. **thaw** (noun).

the (determiner)
a word you use when you are talking about a particular thing, for example, "The sweets that I bought earlier are all gone."

theatre (noun)
1 a large hall where people go to see plays, shows, and concerts. **theatrical** (adjective).
2 plays and acting. *My whole family enjoys theatre.*
3 An **operating theatre** is where surgeons perform operations in a hospital.

theft (noun)
the crime of stealing.

Spelling tip

their   **there**

It's easy to mix up "there" (in that place) and "their" (belonging to them). Try remembering that "there" is just "here" (in this place) with a 't' at the beginning.

their *(determiner)*
belonging to them. *Their house is really beautiful.*

theirs *(pronoun)*
belonging to a group of people that have already been mentioned. *You take your bags, and they'll take theirs.*

them *(pronoun)*
people or things that have already been mentioned. *The Smiths are nice; I like them.*

theme *(noun)*
The **theme** of a story, film, painting, and so on, is the main idea in it. *The theme of my short story is revenge.*

theme park *(noun)*
a large area full of rides and other attractions, often based on a theme.

then *(adverb)*
1 at that time. *I didn't realize then how difficult it was going to be.*
2 afterwards, or next. *We'll walk first, then eat our picnic.*
3 as a result. *If you eat all those sweets, then you'll probably be sick.*

theory **theories** *(noun)*
an idea someone has that they believe explains something. *Mum's theory is that too much television makes you lazy.*

therapy **therapies** *(noun)*
a treatment for an illness or problem, for example physiotherapy to repair a part of your body that is damaged, or psychotherapy to help with mental illnesses. **therapist** *(noun)*.

there
1 *(adverb)* a place that is not here. *I love Paris. Have you ever been there?*
2 *(pronoun)* a word used to point something out. *There is a car blocking our drive.*

therefore *(adverb)*
because of, or as a result of. *I'm tired, therefore I'm not going out.*

thermometer *(noun)*
an instrument that you use to measure the temperature of something.

thesaurus *(theh-**saw**-russ) (noun)*
a book in which you can look up a word to find other words that have the same or similar meanings.

thick **thicker thickest** *(adjective)*
1 wide, and not thin. **thickness** *(noun)*.
2 made up of a large number of things or people close together. **thickly** *(adverb)*.

thief **thieves** *(noun)*
someone who steals things. **thieve** *(verb)*, **thieving** *(adjective)*.

thigh *(noun)*
the top part of your leg, between your knee and your hip.

thin **thinner thinnest** *(adjective)*
not fat or thick. **thinly** *(adverb)*.

thing
1 *(noun)* an object, idea, or event.
2 things *(plural noun)* possessions. *I left my things on the train.*

think **thinking thought** *(verb)*
1 to use your mind to form ideas. *I need to think about what to do.*
2 to have an opinion. *Harriet thinks that this song is awful.*

third
1 *(noun)* one of three equal parts of something.
2 *(adjective)* If you come **third** in something, two people were ahead of you.

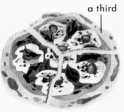

a third

This pizza has been cut into **thirds**.

thirsty – throw

thirsty **thirstier**
thirstiest (adjective)
If you are **thirsty**,
you need a drink.
thirst (noun).

Roses have
thorns.

thorn (noun)
a prickle or spike
on a plant. **thorny**
(adjective).

— thorn

thorough (adjective)
If you are **thorough**, you do things
carefully and don't leave anything out.
thoroughness (noun), **thoroughly** (adverb).

though (thoh) (conjunction)
1 even if. *Lily likes Jack, though
he's sometimes rude to her.*
2 as though like. *It looks as though
it's going to rain.*

thought (thort)
1 (noun) an idea that you have, or the
process of thinking about things.
2 (verb) the past tense of **think**. *Dad
thought there was cheese in the fridge.*

thoughtful (adjective)
1 A **thoughtful** person thinks of other
people, and their feelings and needs.
thoughtfully (adverb).
2 Something that is **thoughtful** is
well-planned and carefully done.
thoughtfully (adverb).

thoughtless (adjective)
A **thoughtless** person doesn't think
of other people and their feelings
and needs.

thread **threading threaded**
1 (noun) a strand of cotton, used
for sewing.
2 (verb) to pass a strand of cotton
through the eye of a needle, or a cord
through the middle of some beads.

threaten
threatening threatened (verb)
If someone **threatens** you, they try
to scare you by saying that they will
harm you or do something bad to you,
or to people that you care about.
threatening (adjective).

three-dimensional or **3D**
(adjective)
A **three-dimensional** shape is not flat,
but has depth. *See* shapes, *page 348.*

threw (verb)
the past tense of **throw**.

thrilling (adjective)
very exciting. **thrill** (noun), **thrill** (verb).

throat (noun)
1 the back part of your mouth and
the tubes that lead down from there.
2 the front of your neck.

throb **throbbing throbbed** (verb)
If part of your body **throbs**, you have
an aching pain in it that stops and starts
regularly, like a pulse.

throne (noun)
a very grand chair for kings and queens.

through (throo) (preposition)
1 going in on one side of something,
and coming out the other side. *There's
a path through the woods.*
2 during. *I worked through the night.*
3 If you **go through** something, you
experience something bad.

throughout (preposition)
all the way through. *This book
is exciting throughout.*

throw **throwing threw thrown** (verb)
1 to hold something in your hand and
then let it go, so that it moves quickly
through the air. *Throw me the ball.*
2 If you **throw something away**, you get
rid of it. *Mum threw my old shoes away.*
3 If you **throw up**, you are sick.

Spelling tip

threw   **through**

The past tense of "throw", "threw",
sounds the same as the word "through",
even though they are spelt differently
and have different meanings. Take
time to learn the right spellings.

thrust thrusting thrust
1 *(verb)* to push something quickly, and hard. *Beth thrust her sore hand into the icy water.*
2 *(noun)* a big, powerful push.

thud *(noun)*
the noise something heavy makes when it falls on the ground. *The watermelon hit the ground with a loud thud.*

thumb *(noun)*
the short, thick finger at the side of your hand.

thump thumping thumped
1 *(verb)* to hit someone or something with your fist. *Esme isn't allowed to use her tablet as a punishment for thumping her little sister.* **thump** *(noun).*
2 *(noun)* a dull sound. *Stanley hit the ground with a thump.*

thunder
thundering thundered
1 *(noun)* the loud, rumbling sound you sometimes hear when there's a storm.
2 *(verb)* to make a loud noise like thunder. *The trucks thundered past.*

tick *(noun)*
1 the clicking sound some clocks and watches make. **tick** *(verb).*
2 the mark (✓) that shows that something is good, or that an answer is right. **tick** *(verb).*

ticket *(noun)*
a printed piece of paper or card that proves you have paid to go on a train, plane, or bus, or to get into somewhere, such as a cinema.

tickle tickling tickled *(verb)*
to move your fingers over sensitive parts of someone's body to try to make them laugh. **ticklish** *(adjective).*

tide *(noun)*
the inward and outward movement of the sea each day. **tidal** *(adjective).*

tidy tidier tidiest *(adjective)*
neat, or in order, with everything in its place. *Hannah's bedroom is always tidy.* **tidiness** *(noun),* **tidily** *(adverb).*

tie ties tying tied
1 *(verb)* to fasten things together with string, cord, or rope. *Adam struggles to tie his shoelaces.*
2 *(noun)* a thin piece of material that people sometimes wear around their necks and hanging down the front of their shirts. *Dad has some very brightly-coloured ties.*
3 *(noun)* If two people or teams finish a race or competition in the same position, it's a **tie**. *It was a tie for first place.*

tiger *(noun)*
a large, striped animal in the cat family that is found in Asia, and is now very rare in the wild.

black stripes —

Indian tiger

tight tighter tightest *(adjective)*
1 Tight clothes fit your body very closely. *I need a new school jumper, as this one's very tight.*
2 as closely or as securely as possible. *Hollie shut her eyes tight.*
3 If you say **sleep tight** to someone when they go to bed, you mean that you hope they sleep well.

tights *(plural noun)*
thin, stretchy clothing that covers your hips, and each leg and foot.

tile *(noun)*
1 a thin piece of slate or baked clay that is used to cover the roofs of buildings.
2 a thin piece of stone, baked clay, and so on, used for covering floors and walls in some buildings.

till
1 *(preposition)* a short way of saying "until". *Wait till I tell you to let go.*
2 *(noun)* the machine where you pay in a shop. *There were queues at the tills.*

a b c d e f g h i j k l m n o p q r s t u v w x y z

time *(noun)*
1 something that we measure in seconds, minutes, hours, days, years, and so on.
2 a particular moment. *What's the time?*
3 a particular period. *Did you have a good time?*
4 If you are **on time**, you are not late.

timetable *(noun)*
a chart showing when things are supposed to happen. *Check the train timetable to see when we need to leave.*

timid *(adjective)*
shy and easily frightened. *Deer are very timid animals.* **timidly** *(adverb)*.

tin *(noun)*
1 a can of food or drink.
2 a silvery metal.

tingle **tingling tingled** *(verb)*
If your skin **tingles**, you have a slight prickling or stinging feeling.

tiny **tinier tiniest** *(adjective)*
very small. *That tiny sandwich won't be big enough for Uncle Don.*

tip **tipping tipped**
1 *(verb)* to pour or spill a liquid. *I tipped the rest of my drink down the sink.*
2 *(verb)* to knock something over, so that it's not upright any more.
3 *(noun)* the very end of something long and thin. *I have a cut on the tip of my finger.*
4 *(noun)* a useful hint. *I'll give you a quick tip for getting past this level.*
5 *(noun)* money you give to someone, such as a waiter, if you feel they've done a good job. **tip** *(verb)*.
6 *(noun)* a rubbish dump.

Spelling tip

tip   tipping   tipped

One-syllable words, such as "tip", that end with a short vowel and a consonant, double the final consonant before the endings '–ing' and '–ed' are added.

tiptoe **tiptoeing tiptoed** *(verb)*
to walk very quietly, without putting your heels down. *We tiptoed carefully past the sleeping dog.*

tired *(adjective)*
If you are **tired**, you don't have any energy and want to go to sleep. **tiring** *(adjective)*, **tiredness** *(noun)*.

tissue *(noun)*
1 soft, thin paper used for wrapping.
2 soft paper used for wiping your nose.

title *(noun)*
the name of a book, film, or painting.

toad *(noun)*
an animal that lives both in water and on land, and looks a bit like a large frog.

yellow-bellied toad

toadstool *(noun)*
a type of fungus that looks similar to a mushroom, and is often poisonous. *See* **fungus.**

toast *(noun)*
bread that has been cooked lightly on the outside, usually in a toaster, so that it is browned. **toast** *(verb)*.

toaster *(noun)*
a machine used to turn bread into toast.

tobacco *(noun)*
dried, chopped-up leaves from the tobacco plant that are put into cigarettes and cigars.

today *(noun)*
the day that is happening now. *Today is Wednesday.*

toddler *(noun)*
a very young child who has just learnt how to walk.

toe *(noun)*
one of the ten small parts of your body that are on the ends of your feet.

toffee *(noun)*
a chewy sweet made from boiled sugar and butter.

together (adverb)
1 with another person or thing. *Mum and Dad went out to the shops together.*
2 at the same time. *Cook them together.*

toilet (noun)
1 a special bowl with a seat, that you use when you need to wee or poo.
2 a building or room with a toilet or some toilets in it. *Where's the toilet?*

told (verb)
the past tense of tell.

tomato **tomatoes** (noun)
a red or yellow fruit, used in cooking, or raw in salads.

cherry tomatoes

tomb (noun)
a large grave, usually a large one for an important person.

tomorrow (noun)
the day after today. *We're going to the safari park tomorrow.*

ton (noun)
a unit of weight equal to 2,240 pounds.

tone (noun)
1 the way that something sounds. *I could tell from the tone of Will's voice that he was bored.*
2 a shade of a colour. *A pink tone.*

tongue (tung) (noun)
the soft, plump muscle inside your mouth, which you need for talking, tasting, and eating.

tonight (noun)
the evening or night that will come later today. *I have a trumpet lesson and athletics practice tonight.*

tonne (noun)
a unit of weight equal to 1,000 kilograms. *Asian elephants weigh about four tonnes.*

tonsillitis (noun)
an infection in your tonsils, that causes a very sore throat.

tonsils (plural noun)
two small lumps at the back of your mouth, at the top of your throat.

To, too or two?

You use "to" when you need to say where you're going ("**to** Canada"); "too" means "as well" ("Dad came **too**"), and "two" is the number '2' ("**two** minutes later").

---

too (adverb)
1 as well. *I'll have chips too.*
2 too much more than is needed.

took (verb)
the past tense of take.

tool (noun)
a piece of equipment that you need to use to do a particular job.

tooth **teeth** (noun)
one of the hard white structures in your mouth that you use for chewing and biting. *See teeth.*

toothbrush **toothbrushes** (noun)
a small brush that you use for cleaning your teeth.

toothpaste (noun)
a substance that you put on your toothbrush before you clean your teeth.

top
1 (noun) the highest point of something. *The top of the hill.*
2 (adjective) very good, or the best. *He's a top golfer.*
3 (noun) the lid or covering of something. *I took the top off the jar.*
4 (noun) a piece of clothing that covers the top half of your body.

topic (noun)
a subject that you study, or talk about. *Our topic this term was the pyramids.*

Torah (noun)
the sacred texts of Judaism, which are usually written on a scroll in Hebrew.

torch **torches** (noun)
a small light that you can carry with you to help you see in the dark.

a b c d e f g h i j k l m n o p q r s t u v w x y z

tore *(verb)*
the past tense of **tear**.

torn *(verb)*
the past participle of **tear**.

tornado **tornados** *or* **tornadoes** *(noun)*
a swirling column of powerful wind.

tortoise *(noun)*
a reptile that lives on land, has a thick shell, and moves very slowly.

Hermann's tortoise

torture
torturing tortured *(verb)*
to make a person or animal suffer terribly. **torture** *(noun)*.

toss **tosses tossing tossed** *(verb)*
1 to throw something without caring where it lands. *Kim tossed her cup away.*
2 to move or make something move from side to side, or up and down.

total
1 *(noun)* what you get at the end of a maths sum when you add everything up, or take it away.
2 *(adjective)* complete. *A total waste of time.* **totally** *(adverb)*.

toucan *(noun)*
a bird with a large beak that lives in Central and South America.
See **rainforest**.

touch **touches touching touched**
1 *(verb)* to put your fingers or your hand on something. **touch** *(noun)*.
2 *(verb)* to make contact with something.
3 *(verb)* to make somebody feel something. *Her sad story touched me.*
4 If you are **in touch** with someone, you are in contact with them.

tough **tougher toughest** *(adjective)*
1 strong and determined.
2 difficult. *It was a really tough choice.*
3 hard to cut and chew. *A tough steak.*

tour **touring toured**
1 *(noun)* a trip around somewhere.
2 *(verb)* to travel around an area or country. *We toured Italy last summer.*

tourist *(noun)*
someone who is on holiday in a place, and wants to look around it. *People say there are too many tourists in Paris.*

tournament *(noun)*
a competition with several stages. *Wimbledon is a famous tennis tournament in London.*

tow **towing towed** *(verb)*
to pull something behind you, usually with a rope or a chain. *The truck towed Gary's car away.*

toward *or* **towards** *(preposition)*
in the direction of. *Mr Carr walked towards the whiteboard.*

towel *(noun)*
a large, soft piece of material you can use to dry yourself when you are wet.

tower *(noun)*
a tall building that is much higher than it is wide.

town *(noun)*
a place where there are lots of buildings, shops, and so on, and where many people live, but that is not as big as a city.

toxic *(adjective)*
poisonous. Things that are toxic are often marked with a skull and crossbones sign.

toxic symbol

toy *(noun)*
a thing that children play with. *The nursery school has hundreds of toys.*

trace **tracing traced**
1 *(verb)* to put a piece of see-through paper over a picture and draw over the outline with a pencil, to copy it.
2 *(verb)* to find out where someone or something is. *The police traced the thief to an apartment in the south of the city.*
3 *(noun)* a very small amount of something. *A trace of salt.*

tracksuit *(noun)*
loose trousers and a top with long sleeves, which you can wear for doing sports.

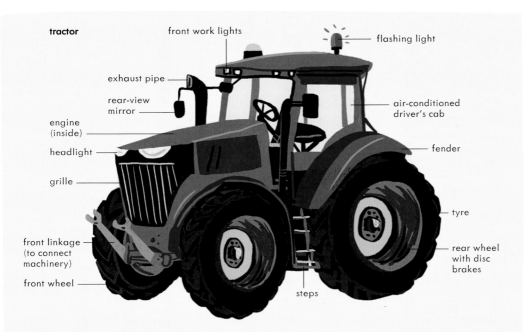

tractor — front work lights — flashing light — exhaust pipe — rear-view mirror — engine (inside) — headlight — grille — front linkage (to connect machinery) — front wheel — air-conditioned driver's cab — fender — tyre — rear wheel with disc brakes — steps

tractor *(noun)*
a powerful vehicle used on farms to pull machinery and move heavy loads.

trademark *(noun)*
a name, sign or design that shows that something is made by a particular company, and that can't be used without getting permission from that company.

tradition *(noun)*
something that people have done, or believed in, for a long time. **traditional** *(adjective)*, **traditionally** *(adverb)*.

traffic *(noun)*
1 all the vehicles on a road or network of roads.
2 A **traffic jam** is when all the vehicles on a road stop moving, or only move very slowly, for some reason.

traffic warden *(noun)*
someone whose job is to make sure vehicles only park where they are supposed to.

tragedy tragedies *(noun)*
1 something extremely sad. *The train crash was such a tragedy.* **tragic** *(adjective)*, **tragically** *(adverb)*.
2 a type of play or film in which sad things happen.

trail *(noun)*
a track or path that people can follow. *The trail led up into the forest.*

trailer *(noun)*
1 a large container that is pulled behind a car or truck, for carrying things.
2 a short advertisement that tells you about a television programme or film.

train training trained
1 *(noun)* a line of carriages or wagons containing cargo or people, which travels on rails and is pulled by an engine.
2 *(verb)* to learn how to do something, such as a job. *Jenny's training to be a pilot.* **training** *(noun)*.
3 *(verb)* to teach a person or animal how to do something. *I'm training my dog.*
4 *(verb)* to practise and prepare for a race, match, sports event, and so on. **training** *(noun)*.

trainer *(noun)*
someone who helps people get fitter, or who helps a sportsperson or a racing animal get ready for competitions. *Many celebrities have personal trainers.*

trainers *(plural noun)*
comfortable, light shoes that people wear mainly for running or doing sport.

a b c d e f g h i j k l m n o p q r s t u v w x y z

traitor *(noun)*
a person who betrays their friends, team, or country.

tram *(noun)*
a vehicle a bit like a bus, that runs on rails in the road and carries passengers.

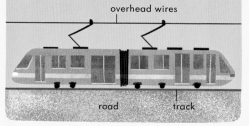

overhead wires

road   track

Trams can be powered by electricity from overhead wires.

trampoline *(noun)*
a large piece of strong, stretchy material that is fixed to a metal frame for people to bounce on.

treasure **treasuring treasured**
1 *(noun)* very precious and valuable objects, such as gold or jewels.
2 *(verb)* If you **treasure** something, you value it very highly. *I treasure the necklace my gran gave me.*

treat **treating treated**
1 *(verb)* the way you behave towards someone. *The teacher treats us kindly.*
2 *(verb)* Doctors, nurses and other healthcare workers **treat** their patients to help them get better. **treatment** *(noun)*.
3 *(noun)* something special, that you wouldn't normally do or have. *We had an ice cream as a treat.*

treble **trebling trebled**
1 *(verb)* If you **treble** something, you multiply it by three. *The raffle trebled the amount of money we've raised.*
2 *(adjective)* In music, **treble notes** are the high notes.

tree *(noun)*
a plant that can grow very large, with a hard trunk, branches, and leaves.

tremble **trembling trembled** *(verb)*
to shake and quiver, usually because you are scared or excited.

trend *(noun)*
1 a fashion that's popular at a particular time. **trendy** *(adjective)*.
2 something that more and more people are doing. *There's a growing trend for cycling into work.*

trial *(noun)*
1 a test to see how well someone or something works or does something. *A football trial.* **trial** *(adjective)*.
2 If a person is **on trial**, they are questioned in a law court about a crime they are accused of.

triangle *(noun)*
1 a three-sided shape. **triangular** *(adjective)*. See **shapes**, page 348.
2 a triangle-shaped metal musical instrument which makes a ringing sound when you hit it with a metal stick. See **percussion**.

tribe *(noun)*
a group of people who all live together, share the same traditional beliefs and customs, and usually have a leader.

trick **tricking tricked**
1 *(verb)* to make someone believe something that's not true.
2 *(noun)* something you can do that impresses people. *A magic trick.*

trickle **trickling trickled** *(verb)*
to flow slowly. *Blood trickled down Jim's leg.* **trickle** *(noun)*.

tricky **trickier trickiest** *(adjective)*
difficult, or awkward. *We've got a very tricky problem on our hands.*

trifle *(noun)*
a pudding made of layers of fruit, custard, jelly, and cream. See **dessert**.

trim **trimming trimmed** *(verb)*
to cut small bits off something so that it looks neat and tidy. **trim** *(noun)*.

trio *(noun)*
a group of three things, or three people.

trip **tripping tripped**
1 *(verb)* to stumble, or to fall over. *Zara tripped over her shoelaces.*
2 *(noun)* a journey, or a visit. *A class trip.*

The prefix 'tri-'

triangle
trio
triplet

Words beginning with 'tri–' are often to do with "three". These include "**trio**" (a group of three); "**triplet**" (one of three babies) and "**triangle**" (a shape with three sides).

triplet *(noun)*
one of three people born at nearly the same time to the same mother.

triumph *(noun)*
a great achievement or victory.
triumph *(verb)*, **triumphant** *(adjective)*.

trolley *(noun)*
a metal or plastic cart that you push and use for carrying things. You can put shopping in a trolley when you go round a supermarket.

troops *(plural noun)*
soldiers. *The troops continued fighting.*

trophy **trophies** *(noun)*
a prize, cup, or award.

tropical *(adjective)*
Tropical parts of the world are those near the equator. They are usually very hot and have a lot of rain and thick jungles full of plants and animals.

tropical fish *(noun)*
fish that come from tropical oceans, and are often kept as pets.

trot **trotting trotted** *(verb)*
When a horse **trots**, it moves at a pace between a walk and a canter.

trouble **troubling troubled**
1 *(noun)* problems or difficulty. *I'm having trouble with this homework.*
2 *(verb)* If something **troubles** you, it bothers you, and makes you worried. *We were troubled by the news of the storm.*
3 If you are **in trouble**, you have a problem you need help with, or someone is annoyed with you. *I got in trouble for eating Julia's last yogurt.*
4 If you **take trouble over** something, you do it carefully and as well as you can. *Freddie took a lot of trouble over his drawing.*

trousers *(plural noun)*
a piece of clothing that covers your legs, with a separate part for each leg.

trout *(noun)*
a fish that lives in fresh water, which you can cook and eat.

truant *(noun)*
1 someone who doesn't go to school when they should. **truancy** *(noun)*.
2 If you **play truant**, you stay away from school when you should go.

truck *(noun)*
a large, powerful vehicle which usually carries goods on the roads.

true **truer truest** *(adjective)*
accurate, correct, or happening in real life, rather than being made-up. *Is it true that octopuses have three hearts?*

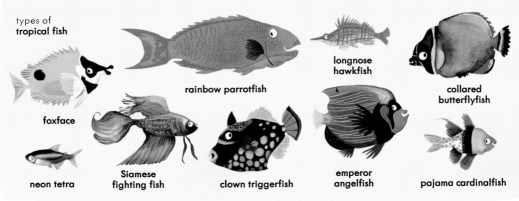

types of
tropical fish

rainbow parrotfish

longnose hawkfish

collared butterflyfish

foxface

neon tetra

Siamese fighting fish

clown triggerfish

emperor angelfish

pajama cardinalfish

a b c d e f g h i j k l m n o p q r s t u v w x y z

trumpet *(noun)*
a brass musical instrument that you blow into. *See* **orchestra**.

trunk
1 *(noun)* the hard, thick stem of a tree.
2 *(noun)* a very large suitcase.
3 *(noun)* the long, bendy nose of an elephant. *See* **elephant**.
4 trunks *(plural noun)* shorts that men and boys wear for swimming.

trust **trusting trusted** *(verb)*
If you **trust** someone, you have faith in them, and believe what they say and do. *I trust Megan to keep my secrets.* **trust** *(noun)*, **trusting** *(adjective)*.

truth *(noun)*
the facts, not something made-up. *I want to know the truth about my missing earrings.* **truthful** *(adjective)*, **truthfully** *(adverb)*.

try **tries trying tried**
1 *(verb)* to make an effort to do something. *I tried to eat all my sprouts.*
2 *(verb)* to taste something for the first time. *Mum tried snails today.*
3 *(verb)* to have a go at doing something new. *I tried snorkelling on holiday.*
4 *(noun)* In rugby, a **try** is scored when a player takes the ball over the goal line and puts it on the ground.

T-shirt *(noun)*
a piece of clothing with short sleeves that you wear on the top part of your body. *Where's my favourite blue T-shirt?*

tub *(noun)*
a deep container that is often round and made of plastic.

tubby **tubbier tubbiest** *(adjective)*
a friendly word for fat. *Our dog is a bit tubby these days.* **tubbiness** *(noun)*.

tube *(noun)*
1 a long, bendy container that you can squeeze things out of. *A tube of toothpaste.*
2 The Tube is the underground railway system in London. *Take the Tube to Piccadilly Circus.*

tuck **tucking tucked** *(verb)*
If you **tuck** a piece of material in, you push any loose bits inside.

tuft *(noun)*
a bunch of hair or grass that sticks up in a slightly messy way. **tufty** *(adjective)*.

tug **tugging tugged**
1 *(verb)* to pull something hard. *Miles tugged his sister's ponytail.* **tug** *(noun)*.
2 *(noun)* In a **tug-of-war**, two teams hold onto either end of a rope and each tries to pull the other over a line in the middle.

tuition *(tew-**ish**-un) (noun)*
training or teaching, usually given to one person, or a small group.

tulip *(noun)*
a spring flower that grows from a bulb and is shaped like a cup. *See* **flower**.

tumble **tumbling tumbled**
1 *(verb)* to fall down, rolling over and over. **tumble** *(noun)*.
2 *(noun)* A **tumble drier** or **tumble dryer** turns clothes over and over in hot air to dry them.

tummy **tummies** *(noun)*
a friendly word for your stomach.

tuna **tuna** *or* **tunas** *(noun)*
a very large fish that lives in the sea, which people catch, cook, and eat.

bluefin tuna

tune *(noun)*
musical notes arranged in a pleasant pattern. *That's a great tune!*

tunnel *(noun)*
an underground passage, usually going through a hill or under a building, river, or road.

turban *(noun)*
a long piece of cloth that some men wear wound around their head.

turkey *(noun)*
a large bird that can't fly, which farmers keep for meat.

bronze turkey

turn
turning turned
1 *(verb)* to change the way you're facing or travelling. *Laura turned and looked at me.* **turn** *(noun)*.
2 *(verb)* to move something around. *Turn the television so I can see it.*
3 *(noun)* a chance, or go. *First it's Ollie's turn, and then it's Jenny's.*
4 turn into *(verb)* to become. *The frog turned into a prince.*
5 *(verb)* If you **turn something on or off**, you make it work, or stop working. *Turn the tap off.*
6 *(verb)* If someone or something **turns up** somewhere, they arrive there unexpectedly. *My lost keys turned up in one of my shoes.*
7 *(verb)* If you **turn up** the volume on a speaker, television, and so on, you make the sound louder.

turnip *(noun)*
a round vegetable that grows in the ground.

turquoise *(noun)*
a greenish-blue colour. **turquoise** *(adjective)*.

turnip

turtle *(noun)*
a reptile that lives in the sea, and has a hard shell and flippers.

tusk *(noun)*
one of the long horns some animals have growing out of the bottom of their faces. Elephants and walruses have tusks.

tutor *(noun)*
a teacher, usually one who only teaches a small group or a single student at one time. *My cousin is a maths tutor.*

tutu *(noun)*
a female ballet dancer's skirt, which sticks out, and may be attached to a top.

TV *(noun)* *(abbreviation)*
a short way of saying television.

tweet *(noun)*
the cheeping sound birds often make.

twice *(adverb)*
two times. *Gordon sneezed twice.*

twig *(noun)*
a small, thin branch on a tree. *The bird made a nest out of twigs.*

twilight *(noun)*
the time between when the Sun goes below the horizon, and when it gets dark.

twin
1 *(noun)* one of two people with the same mother, born at nearly the same time.
2 *(adjective)* one of a matching pair of things. *The room had twin beds.*

twinkle twinkling twinkled *(verb)*
to sparkle and shine. *A twinkling star.*

twirl twirling twirled *(verb)*
to spin or twist something round and round. *Lorna twirled her hair round her finger.*

twist twisting twisted *(verb)*
to turn or bend, or to make something turn or bend. *The road twisted up into the mountains.* **twist** *(noun)*.

twitch
twitches twitching twitched *(verb)*
to make small, jerky movements. *The dog's nose twitched.* **twitch** *(noun)*.

type typing typed
1 *(verb)* to write something on a keyboard. *Type the email address.*
2 *(noun)* a kind or sort. *What type of sweets do you like best?*

typical *(adjective)*
normal or usual. *A typical day.* **typically** *(adverb)*.

tyrannosaurus *(noun)*
a large dinosaur that hunted other dinosaurs, and had very large, strong teeth and tiny front legs. *See dinosaur.*

tyre *(noun)*
the air-filled rubber circle that goes around the outside of a wheel.

a b c d e f g h i j k l m n o p q r s t u v w x y z

Uu

udder *(noun)*
the part of some female animals, such as cows and sheep, which hangs down below their bodies and produces milk.

UFO *(noun)* *(abbreviation)*
an object in the sky that cannot be identified. Some people believe that they are spaceships from other planets. UFO stands for "**U**nidentified **F**lying **O**bject".

ugly uglier ugliest *(adjective)*
not nice to look at, or not beautiful.
ugliness *(noun)*.

"Ugly" comes from an Old Norse word, "uggligr", which meant "terrifying".

ulcer *(noun)*
a sore area on your skin, or inside your mouth or stomach.

umbrella *(noun)*
a round piece of cloth stretched over a metal frame, that protects you from rain.

umpire *(noun)*
the person who makes sure players stick to the rules in a cricket or tennis match.

unable *(adjective)*
If you are **unable** to do something, you can't do it. *Sita is unable to tell the time.*

unacceptable *(adjective)*
not good enough. *The service in this restaurant is unacceptable.*

unanimous *(adjective)*
agreed by everyone. *A unanimous decision.* **unanimously** *(adverb)*.

unaware *(adjective)*
If you are **unaware** of something, you don't know that it is happening, or that it is true. *I was unaware that it was Graham's birthday today.*

unbearable *(adjective)*
very strong, or awful. *Unbearable pain.*

unbelievable *(adjective)*
1 difficult or impossible to believe.
2 surprising or amazing. *Her singing was unbelievable.* **unbelievably** *(adverb)*.

uncertain *(adjective)*
not sure. *Mum was uncertain whether to believe us.* **uncertainty** *(noun)*, **uncertainly** *(adverb)*.

uncle *(noun)*
the brother of your father or mother, or the husband of your aunt.

uncomfortable *(adjective)*
1 causing or feeling some pain or discomfort. *An uncomfortable bed.*
2 awkward or not relaxed. *The meeting was a bit uncomfortable.*

unconscious *(adjective)*
unaware of anything around you, for example because you have fainted or been knocked out.

uncontrollable *(adjective)*
impossible to control or to stop.
He was in an uncontrollable rage.
uncontrollably *(adverb)*.

uncooperative *(adjective)*
deliberately unhelpful. *The staff at the station were very uncooperative when I lost my backpack.*

uncover uncovering uncovered *(verb)*
1 to take the cover off something. *They uncovered the football pitch once it had stopped raining.*
2 to reveal. *The police uncovered a plot.*

The prefix 'un-'

unaware
uncover
unfair

Many of the words in this chapter begin with the prefix 'un-', which means "not". For example, something that is "**un**fair" is not fair, and if you are "**un**comfortable", you are not comfortable.

undecided *(adjective)*
If you are **undecided**, you're not sure what to do.

under *(preposition)*
1 below or beneath something. *The key is hidden under the mat.*
2 less than a number, or an amount. *People under 1.25m tall can't go on this ride.*

underarm *(adverb)*
If you throw **underarm**, you throw with your arm swinging under your shoulder. **underarm** *(adjective)*.

underdog *(noun)*
a person or team that is expected to be the loser.

underestimate underestimating underestimated *(verb)*
1 to think that someone or something is not as good as they really are. *We all underestimated how good the film was.*
2 to make a guess that is too low.

underground
1 *(adjective)* below the ground. **underground** *(adverb)*.
2 *(noun)* a railway system that runs under a city. *The London Underground.*

underline
underlining underlined *(verb)*
to draw a line under a word or sentence, like this.

underneath *(preposition)*
under or below something. *The dragon's cave was underneath the mountain.*

understand
understanding understood *(verb)*
to know what something means, or how it works. **understanding** *(noun)*.

understandable *(adjective)*
easy to see and agree with. *It's understandable that Mary was upset.*

understood *(verb)*
the past tense of understand.

underwater *(adjective)*
living or happening under water. **underwater** *(adverb)*.

underwear *(noun)*
clothes that you wear underneath your normal clothes, next to your skin.

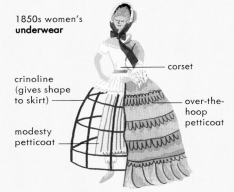

1850s women's **underwear**

corset

crinoline (gives shape to skirt)

over-the-hoop petticoat

modesty petticoat

undo
undoes undoing undid undone *(verb)*
1 to untie or unfasten something.
2 to cancel the most recent action or change using a computer keyboard.

undress
undresses undressing undressed *(verb)*
to take off your clothes.

uneasy *(adjective)*
slightly worried or unhappy. *Harvey's message made me feel uneasy.*

unemployed *(adjective)*
without a job. **unemployment** *(noun)*.

uneven *(adjective)*
not flat or smooth. *The road is uneven in some places.* **unevenly** *(adverb)*.

unexpected *(adjective)*
surprising, because you didn't expect it. **unexpectedly** *(adverb)*.

unfair *(adjective)*
not reasonable or right. *It's unfair that Mel ate all the sweets.* **unfairly** *(adverb)*.

unfamiliar *(adjective)*
If someone or something is **unfamiliar**, you haven't seen or heard about them before. *I heard an unfamiliar voice.*

unfit *(adjective)*
1 Someone who is **unfit** doesn't exercise very often, and finds exercise difficult.
2 not suitable. *That meat is unfit to eat.*

A B C D E F G H I J K L M N O P Q R S T U V W X Y Z

unfold **unfolding unfolded** *(verb)*
to open something that was folded.

unforgettable *(adjective)*
so great that you will never forget it.
Niagara Falls were unforgettable.

unfortunate *(adjective)*
unlucky. **unfortunately** *(adverb).*

unfriendly
unfriendlier unfriendliest *(adjective)*
not very kind and welcoming.

ungrateful *(adjective)*
If you are **ungrateful**, you are not
thankful for something, and don't
appreciate it. **ungratefully** *(adverb).*

unhappy
unhappier unhappiest *(adjective)*
miserable. **unhappily** *(adverb).*

unhealthy
unhealthier unhealthiest *(adjective)*
not healthy, or not good for you.
These doughnuts are very unhealthy.

unhygienic *(adjective)*
unclean, and possibly full
of germs. *Their kitchen*
is very unhygienic.

horn —

unicorn *(noun)*
an animal only found in
stories, that looks like
a horse with a horn on
its head.

The **unicorn** is the national
animal of Scotland.

The prefix 'uni-'

unicorn
unicycle
universe

The letters 'uni–' at the
beginning of a word often
mean that it has something
to do with the idea of "one".
A "**uni**cycle" only has one
wheel, and a "**uni**corn" has
one horn, for instance. The
"**uni**verse" is an enormous
group of planets and stars,
combined into one whole.

unicycle *(noun)*
a cycle with
only one wheel.

unicycle · seat
wheel · pedal

unidentified
(adjective)
If something is
unidentified, nobody
knows what it is.

uniform *(noun)*
special clothes people
wear to show they belong to an
organization, such as a school, the army,
or the police. **uniformed** *(adjective).*

unimportant *(adjective)*
not important. *Leave the unimportant*
details out of your report.

unique (you-**neek**) *(adjective)*
If someone or something is **unique**, they
are unlike anyone or anything else. *This*
necklace is unique. **uniquely** *(adverb).*

unit *(noun)*
1 a single, whole thing, which may also
be part of a larger whole.
2 In maths, a **unit** is a number between
1 and 9. In the number 46, there are
four tens and six units.
3 an amount by which you measure
something. For example, kilometres
and centimetres are units of length.

unite **uniting united** *(verb)*
to join together with other people.
The family united to welcome her home.

universal *(adjective)*
done by or affecting everyone or all
places. **universally** *(adverb).*

universe *(noun)*
everything that exists in all of space,
including all the stars and planets.

university **universities** *(noun)*
a place where many people go to study
after they leave school.

unkind *(adjective)*
not friendly or caring. **unkindly** *(adverb).*

unknown *(adjective)*
not known, or not familiar. *The cause*
of the accident is still unknown.

unless (conjunction)
You say **unless** before you say something that must happen in order for something else to happen. *I can't come unless someone gives me a lift.*

unlock unlocking unlocked (verb)
to open or get access to something that is locked with a key or a code.

unlucky
unluckier unluckiest (adjective)
1 Someone who is **unlucky** doesn't seem to have much good luck.
2 Something that is **unlucky** results from bad luck. *An unlucky defeat.*

unnecessary (adjective)
not needed. *We took wellies, but they were unnecessary.* **unnecessarily** (adverb).

unpack unpacking unpacked (verb)
to take things out of a container, such as a suitcase, and put them away.

unpleasant (adjective)
nasty. *This drink has a very unpleasant taste.* **unpleasantly** (adverb).

unpopular (adjective)
not liked by many people. *The president is very unpopular at the moment.*

unrealistic (adjective)
1 not as it is in real life. *This painting is totally unrealistic.*
2 not possible in real life. *Fiona has some unrealistic plans for her party.*

unreasonable (adjective)
not fair. **unreasonably** (adverb).

unreliable (adjective)
Someone or something **unreliable** can't be trusted or depended on.

unsafe (adjective)
dangerous, or not safe. *The plug on my hairdryer is unsafe.* **unsafely** (adverb).

unstable (adjective)
wobbly, or not staying still. *That ladder looks unstable.*

unsteady (adjective)
wobbly, or not steady. *My hands were unsteady with nerves.* **unsteadily** (adverb).

unsuccessful (adjective)
If you are **unsuccessful**, you don't achieve what you wanted or tried to do. **unsuccessfully** (adverb).

unsuitable (adjective)
1 not right for a particular purpose. *Those shoes are unsuitable for school.* **unsuitably** (adverb).
2 rude, or not appropriate. *That book is unsuitable for young children.*

unsure (adjective)
not certain, or not definite. *Carly was unsure whether she would come or not.*

untidy untidier untidiest (adjective)
messy. **untidily** (adverb).

untie untying untied (verb)
to undo knots or bows in strings, ropes, ribbons, and so on.

until
1 (preposition) only up to a certain time. *Until 2012, we lived in Oxford.*
2 (conjunction) at a specific time, or when a certain thing happens. *We'll wait until it stops raining.*

untrue (adjective)
not accurate, or not correct. *It's untrue that spaghetti grows on trees.*

unused (adjective)
never used before.

unusual (adjective)
strange, or out of the ordinary. *That's an unusual hairstyle.* **unusually** (adverb).

unwanted (adjective)
not needed or not wanted. *We gave our unwanted clothes to charity.*

unwell (adjective)
ill or poorly. *I feel unwell.*

unwilling (adjective)
If you are **unwilling** to do something, you don't want to do it. *Jess is unwilling to sing a solo.* **unwillingly** (adverb).

unwrap
unwrapping unwrapped (verb)
to take the paper or packaging off something. *Amy unwrapped her presents.*

a b c d e f g h i j k l m n o p q r s t u v w x y z

A B C D E F G H I J K L M N O P Q R S T U V W X Y Z

up

1 *(preposition)* in or to a higher place. *Darren ran up the stairs.*
2 *(adverb)* towards a higher place. *We looked up at the stars.*
3 *(adjective)* If you are **up**, you are not in bed any more. *Is Chris up yet?*
4 When you **get up** in the morning, you get out of bed. *I never get up before 9 a.m. at the weekends.*
5 If something **goes up**, it gets higher. *The price has gone up on the T-shirt I'm bidding on.*

upbeat *(adjective)*
happy and cheerful.

up-to-date *(adjective)*
containing the most recent information or technology, or in the latest style. *I changed my phone for a more up-to-date one.*

upper *(adjective)*
higher, or towards the top. *Try looking on the upper shelves for the book you want.*

upper case *(adjective)*
Upper-case letters are capital letters.

upset **upsetting upset** *(verb)*
to make someone unhappy. *Tom upset me when he shouted.* **upset** *(adjective)*.

upside-down *(adjective)*
the wrong way up, so that what was at the top of something is at the bottom.
upside-down *(adverb)*.

upside-down cake

upstairs
1 *(noun)* the floors of a building above ground level.
2 *(adverb)* on or to a higher floor of a building. **upstairs** *(adjective)*.

upwards *(adverb)*
towards a higher place. *According to the map, we need to head upwards.*

urge **urging urged**
1 *(verb)* If you **urge** someone to do something, you encourage or persuade them to do it.
2 *(noun)* a strong wish or need to do something. *I have an urge to phone Paul.*

Suffixes

use**ful**
use**less**

The ending '–ful' makes a word positive, meaning "full of", but '–less' is negative, and means "without any". Remember that the ending '–ful' only has one 'l'.

urgent *(adjective)*
needing immediate attention or action. *An urgent message.* **urgently** *(adverb)*.

use **using used**
1 *(yooz) (verb)* to do a job with something. *I use my tablet all the time.*
2 *(yuce) (noun)* the job, or one of the jobs, that something does.
3 *(yooz) (verb)* If you **use something up**, you don't leave any. *We used up the leftover vegetables.*

used *(adjective)*
not brand new. *A used car.*

useful *(adjective)*
Useful things or people help you do certain jobs. *This is a useful tool.* **usefully** *(adverb)*.

useless *(adjective)*
Useless things or people are not helpful. *This useless pen won't write.*

user *(noun)*
someone who uses something. *A road user. This program is very user-friendly.*

username *(noun)*
the name someone uses when they log on to a computer, or a website.

usual *(adjective)*
normal or regular. *We did our usual walk around the park.* **usually** *(adverb)*.

utter **uttering uttered**
1 *(verb)* to speak, or to make a sound with your mouth. *Paula uttered a moan.*
2 *(adjective)* complete, total, or absolute. *An utter waste of time.* **utterly** *(adverb)*.

Vv

vacant (adjective)
1 empty, or without anyone in it. *Is that toilet vacant?*
2 available. *The bakery has two jobs vacant.* **vacancy** (noun).

vacation (noun)
1 a break between the terms in school or college. *The Easter vacation.*
2 another word for holiday, mostly used in the US.

vaccination (noun)
an injection that protects you from getting a disease. *You should get a typhoid vaccination if you're planning to travel to India.* **vaccinate** (verb).

vacuum cleaner (noun)
see hoover.

vague (vayg)
vaguer vaguest (adjective)
not clear, or not definite. *I only have a vague idea of where we're going.*

vain **vainer vainest** (adjective)
1 Someone who is **vain** is much too proud of what they look like and interested in what people think of them. **vanity** (noun).
2 If you do something **in vain**, you don't succeed in doing it. *Michelle tried in vain to keep her shoes dry.*

valid (adjective)
1 up-to-date, or acceptable. *You must have a valid ticket to travel on a train.*
2 If you have a **valid** reason for doing something, it's a good reason.

valley (noun)
a low area between hills that makes a 'V' or 'U' shape, and which a river often flows through.

valuable (adjective)
worth a lot of money, or very important in some way. *There is a valuable painting in our local church.*

value **valuing valued**
1 (noun) the amount of money that something is worth. *What's the value of your car?*
2 (verb) to think something is important. *I really value your advice.*

vampire (noun)
a creature in horror stories that rises from its grave to suck people's blood.

van (noun)
a vehicle with a large covered area at the back, for carrying things around in.

van

vandal (noun)
someone who deliberately damages other people's property. *Vandals spoilt the new park.* **vandalism** (noun), **vandalize** (verb).

Word origin — vandal

The Vandals were a tribe from Eastern Europe who destroyed Rome in AD445. Ever since, their name has been used to describe someone who does destructive things.

vanish
vanishes vanishing vanished (verb)
to disappear suddenly. *The crowd vanished when the police arrived.*

vapour (noun)
tiny droplets of water or other liquid in the air.

variation (noun)
a slight change. *I used the same recipe, but with a small variation.*

variety **varieties** (noun)
a choice or selection. *They offered us a wide variety of breakfast cereals.*

various (adjective)
several different ones. *We have various board games.*

vary – version

vary varies varying varied *(verb)*
to change or be different.

vase *(noun)*
a container for putting flowers in.

vast *(adjective)*
massive, or stretching for a long way.
A vast forest. **vastly** *(adverb).*

vegan *(noun)*
someone who doesn't eat food made from
any animal products, including meat,
eggs, cheese, or milk. **vegan** *(adjective).*

vegetable *(noun)*
plants, or parts of plants, that you
can eat, and are good for you.

potato   sweet potato   lettuce
leek
red pepper   beetroot
carrot
parsnip
onion   red onion
asparagus   butternut squash   cucumber
sweetcorn   aubergine   cauliflower

some types of **vegetables**

vegetarian *(noun)*
someone who doesn't eat any meat
or fish. **vegetarian** *(adjective).*

vehicle *(vee-ik-ul) (noun)*
a machine that can carry people or
things from one place to another. Cars,
buses and taxis are all types of vehicles.

veil *(noun)*
a piece of material or lace worn by
some women over their faces, or by
some brides on their wedding day.

vein *(noun)*
one of the tubes that
takes blood back
to your heart
after the oxygen
it carries has been
used by your cells
and organs.

> The word "vein"
> sounds exactly like
> "vain", so try not
> to mix them up.

vending machine *(noun)*
a machine that you put money in to get
something out, such as cans of drink.

venom *(noun)*
poison that some snakes and spiders
inject into their prey with their fangs.
venomous *(adjective).*

venue *(noun)*
a place where an event is held.

verb *(noun)*
a word that describes an action or
something that happens. Verbs are often
called "action words". *See* **word classes,**
page 3 and **grammar,** *page 349.*

verbal *(adjective)*
spoken, not written. *A verbal warning.*
verbally *(adverb).*

verdict *(noun)*
1 the decision reached by a jury in a
court of law about whether someone is
guilty of a crime.
2 any decision or opinion. *What's the
verdict on my fish soup?*

verge *(noun)*
1 the strip of land at the edge of a road.
2 If you are **on the verge** of doing
something, you are just about to do it.

verruca *(noun)*
a type of wart that you get on your feet.

verse *(noun)*
a part of a poem or song. *This poem
is divided into four verses.*

version *(noun)*
a form of something, that's different from
the other ones. *A new version of the app.*

versus *(preposition)*
against. Versus is often shortened to "vs".

vertical *(adjective)*
upright, and sticking straight up.
vertically *(adverb)*.

very *(adverb)*
1 a word used before another word to make it stronger. *She is very clever.*
2 not very not much.

vessel *(noun)*
1 a ship or large boat.
2 a container for liquids.

vest *(noun)*
a piece of clothing worn on the top half of your body, under your other clothes.

vet *(noun)*
someone whose job is to treat animals that are ill. Vet is short for "veterinary surgeon". **veterinary** *(adjective)*.

via *(preposition)*
by way of. *This train goes via Manchester.*

vibrate vibrating vibrated *(verb)*
to shake with quick, small movements.
vibration *(noun)*.

vicar *(noun)*
a priest in the Church of England.

vicarage *(noun)*
the house where a vicar lives.

vice versa *(adverb)*
a Latin phrase meaning "the other way round". *You help me, and vice versa.*

vicious *(adjective)*
violent and cruel. **viciously** *(adverb)*.

victim *(noun)*
someone who suffers because of someone or something else. *A victim of bullying.*

victor *(noun)*
another word for "winner".

victory victories *(noun)*
a win, or success, in a battle or a game.

video game *(noun)*
a game played on a computer, television, or hand-held device, where you control what happens.

view viewing viewed
1 *(noun)* what you see from a particular spot. *What a glorious view!*
2 *(noun)* your opinion. *What's your view on the new Prime Minister?*
3 *(verb)* to think of someone or something in a certain way. *I view Rob as a friend.*
4 *(verb)* to look at something. *Visitors can view the new paintings in the hall.*

Viking *(noun)*
one of the people from the area that is now Sweden, Norway, and Denmark, who invaded parts of northern Europe between the 8th and 11th centuries.

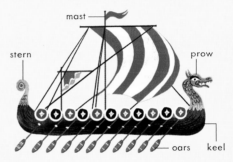

mast • stern • prow • oars • keel

Viking longships could travel along rivers as well as across the sea.

villa *(noun)*
a large house in its own garden, usually found in hot countries. *They rented a villa in Italy for their holiday last year.*

village *(noun)*
a small group of houses and other buildings, usually in the countryside.

villain *(noun)*
a bad person in a story, film, and so on.

vine *(noun)*
a climbing plant. *See grape.*

vinegar *(noun)*
a sharp, sour liquid which can be used in cooking, for example in salad dressings.

violent *(adjective)*
A **violent** person hurts or kills people.
violence *(noun)*, **violently** *(adverb)*.

violin *(noun)*
a musical instrument with four strings, that's played with a bow made from horsehair. *See bow and orchestra.*

virtual – vulture

virtual (adjective)
created by a computer to look real. **virtually** (adverb).

virus viruses (noun)
1 a kind of germ that can make you ill.
2 a program that can damage or destroy the material on your computer.

visible (adjective)
able to be seen. *The sea is visible from my room.* **visibly** (adverb), **visibility** (noun).

vision (noun)
1 the ability to see. *My great uncle's vision isn't very good any more.*
2 a picture you see in your imagination.

visit visiting visited (verb)
to go to see people or places. *We visited the Eiffel Tower.* **visit** (noun), **visitor** (noun).

visual (adjective)
to do with seeing. **visually** (adverb).

vital (adjective)
essential, or very important. **vitally** (adverb).

vitamin (noun)
one of the substances found in food that our bodies need to stay healthy.

vocabulary vocabularies (noun)
all the words you use and understand.

vocal
1 (adjective) to do with the voice.
2 (adjective) keen to tell people what you think. **vocally** (adverb).
3 **vocals** (plural noun) the singing parts of a song or in a concert. **vocalist** (noun).

voice (noun)
1 the power to speak. *I've lost my voice.*
2 the sound you make when you speak or sing.

volcano volcanoes (noun)
a mountain which sometimes erupts, throwing out ash, cinders, gas, and hot, liquid rock called lava.

volume (noun)
1 how loud something is. *Please can you turn the volume down?*
2 how much space something takes up. *The volume of this box is 100cm³.*
3 a big book, often part of a series of books. *I've only read volume one.*

volunteer
volunteering volunteered (verb)
to offer to do a job, or to help out, for no pay. *I volunteer at the local animal shelter.* **volunteer** (noun), **voluntary** (adjective), **voluntarily** (adverb).

vomit vomiting vomited (verb)
to be sick. **vomit** (noun).

vote voting voted (verb)
to choose who you want to win an election. *I voted for Sarah to be head girl.* **vote** (noun).

voucher (noun)
a piece of paper that can get you money off something you buy, or that you can exchange for something. *I have a voucher for half-price entry to the zoo.*

vowel (noun)
one of the letters **a, e, i, o,** or **u.**

voyage (noun)
a sea journey.

vulture (noun)
a big bird that eats dead animals.

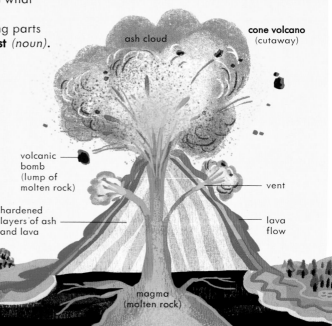

ash cloud

cone volcano
(cutaway)

volcanic
bomb
(lump of
molten rock)

vent

hardened
layers of ash
and lava

lava
flow

magma
(molten rock)

Ww

wade wading waded (verb)
to walk through water. *We waded to the other side of the stream.*

waddle waddling waddled (verb)
If you **waddle**, your bottom sways from side to side as you walk, like a duck.

wafer (noun)
a thin, crispy biscuit.

waffle (noun)
a crispy, doughy cake, with a pattern of squares on it.

Belgian waffles

wag wagging wagged (verb)
to move from side to side. *The dog wagged her tail when she saw the toy.*

wage (noun)
the money that you are paid for the job you do.

wail wailing wailed (verb)
to make a long, loud, sad sound. *The baby wailed all night.* **wail** (noun).

waist (noun)
the part of your body between your hips and your ribs, where it narrows.

wait waiting waited (verb)
to stay in a place until something happens, or someone arrives. *We waited for the bus for an hour.* **wait** (noun).

waiter (noun)
a man who serves people food and drink in a restaurant.

waitress waitresses (noun)
a woman who serves people food and drink in a restaurant.

wake waking woke woken (verb)
1 When you **wake** or **wake up**, you finish sleeping and open your eyes.
2 If you **wake someone up**, you make them stop sleeping. *Mum woke me up at 6 a.m.*

walk walking walked
1 (verb) to move forwards by putting one foot in front of the other. *My little brother has just learnt how to walk.* **walker** (noun).
2 (noun) a journey you make on foot. *The walk up the mountain was too difficult for me.*

wall (noun)
1 The **walls** of a building separate one room from another, and hold the roof up.
2 a structure made of stone or brick that shows where a piece of land, such as a garden or field, begins and ends.

wallet (noun)
a flat purse that people may carry their money and cards in.

wallpaper (noun)
thick paper that people stick onto their walls to decorate them.

walrus walruses (noun)
a large sea animal that has whiskers and two long tusks.

tusk

Both male and female **walruses** have tusks.

wand
(rhymes with "pond") (noun)
In stories, a **wand** is a stick that witches, wizards and fairies often carry, and use for doing magic.

wander
wandering wandered (verb)
to walk around with no particular aim or destination. *We wandered around the park.* **wander** (noun).

want wanting wanted (verb)
to feel that you would like something. *I want to go on holiday.*

war (noun)
fighting between countries or groups of people, in which people often die.

ward (noun)
one of the areas of a hospital containing beds, usually for patients who have similar illnesses or injuries.

a b c d e f g h i j k l m n o p q r s t u v w x y z

wardrobe *(noun)*
a cupboard for storing clothes in.

warm warmer warmest *(adjective)*
not cold, but not too hot. **warmth** *(noun)*.

warm warming warmed *(verb)*
If you **warm something up**, you heat it so that it's not cold, but not too hot.

warm-blooded *(adjective)*
Warm-blooded animals have a body temperature that stays about the same, whatever their surroundings.

warm-up *(noun)*
light exercise and stretching you do before doing sport, to avoid getting injured. **warm up** *(verb)*.

warn warning warned *(verb)*
If you **warn** someone about something, you tell them that it could be dangerous, or not as they expect. **warning** *(noun)*.

warrior *(noun)*
a brave and experienced soldier in the past.

wart *(noun)*
a small, hard lump that grows on your skin, caused by a virus. **warty** *(adjective)*.

wary warier wariest *(adjective)*
cautious and careful. *Dominic is very wary around dogs.* **warily** *(adverb)*.

wash
washes washing washed *(verb)*
1 to clean something, such as clothes or your body, with water and soap.
2 When you **wash up**, you clean the plates, pans and cutlery after a meal. **washing-up** *(noun)*.

washing *(noun)*
clothes that are going to be washed, or have just been washed.

washing machine *(noun)*
a machine that washes clothes.

wasp *(noun)*
a black and yellow flying insect that can sting you.

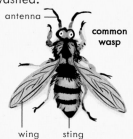
antenna
common wasp
wing   sting

waste wasting wasted
1 *(verb)* to use something badly. *Stop wasting my time.*
2 *(verb)* to throw something away that you shouldn't. *We waste too much food.* **waste** *(adjective)*.
3 *(noun)* stuff that is not used, or is thrown away. *There was a lot of waste after the meal.*

wasteful *(adjective)*
A **wasteful** person, organization or country throws things away without thinking about how they could be used, or recycled. **wastefully** *(adverb)*.

watch watches watching watched
1 *(noun)* a small clock that people wear on their wrists. *I got a new watch for Christmas.*
2 *(verb)* to look at something for a period of time. *I watched television all evening.*
3 *(verb)* to take care of someone or something, or make sure that nothing goes wrong. *Could you watch the baby while I go to the gym?*

water watering watered
1 *(noun)* a clear liquid that we need to drink to survive.
2 *(verb)* If your mouth **waters**, it produces extra spit, usually because you're hungry. *The smell from the bakery always makes my mouth water.*
3 *(verb)* If your eyes **water**, they make tears. *Onions make my eyes water.*
4 *(verb)* If you **water** plants, you pour water on the soil around them to help them grow. *You must water your plants often in summer.* **watering can** *(noun)*.

watercolours (plural noun)
paints that you mix with water before using.

water cycle (noun)
the continuous movement of the Earth's water.

Water becomes liquid and forms clouds (condensation).

clouds

rainfall

Water vapour evaporates from plants (transpiration).

Water becomes a gas (evaporation).

Water flows into rivers, lakes, and the sea.

Some water is used by plants or soaks into the ground.

the water cycle

waterfall (noun)
a place where the water in a river falls over steep rocks.

waterproof (adjective)
Something that is **waterproof** keeps water out.

water-ski
water-skiing water-skied (verb)
to be pulled behind a fast boat over water, with your feet in special skis. **water-skiing** (noun), **water-skier** (noun).

water vapour (noun)
the invisible gas that water makes when it evaporates.

wave **waving waved**
1 (verb) to greet someone by moving your hand from side to side.
2 (noun) a moving ridge of water in the sea, that breaks onto the shore.
3 (noun) the way that some kinds of energy, such as heat, sound or light, travel.
4 (verb) to move something about. *Dad waved my phone bill at me angrily.*

wax (noun)
1 a soft, smooth substance that candles are made from.
2 a soft, smooth, yellowish substance that forms inside your ears.

weak **weaker weakest** (adjective)
not strong. *I like my tea weak.*
weakness (noun), **weakly** (adverb).

wealthy
wealthier wealthiest (adjective)
If you are **wealthy**, you have lots of money, or things that are worth a lot of money. **wealth** (noun).

weapon (noun)
something that can be used to fight someone, such as a sword or gun.

wear **wearing wore worn** (verb)
1 to be dressed in something. *Valentine was wearing a tutu and tiara.*
2 If something **wears off**, it gets weaker. *The pain soon wore off.*
3 If you **wear out** your clothes, you wear them so much that you need new ones. *Josh wears out shoes quickly.*

weary **wearier weariest** (adjective)
tired. *Harry is weary after the early start.* **weariness** (noun), **wearily** (adverb).

weather (noun)
how hot or cold it is outside, and whether it is cloudy, sunny, raining, snowing, and so on. *Shall we go to the park if the weather's nice tomorrow?*

weave **weaving wove woven** (verb)
1 to make fabric or cloth by crossing threads over and under each other. **woven** (adjective).
2 to move in between things. *The cyclists had to weave between the cars.*

web (noun)
1 short for the World Wide Web, which is part of the internet. **web** (adjective).
2 a net of threads made by a spider, for catching insects to eat. See cobweb.

webbed (adjective)
Animals with **webbed feet** have skin between their toes, to make it easier for them to swim.

a b c d e f g h i j k l m n o p q r s t u v w x y z

webcam *(noun)*
a camera on a computer, that takes pictures or films that can be seen on the internet.

website *(noun)*
pages of information about someone or something on the internet. *Mum's business has a new website.*

wedding *(noun)*
the ceremony and celebration that happens when people get married.

wedge *(noun)*
a piece of something that is thick at one end and thin at the other, and often triangle-shaped. *A wedge of cheese.*

wee *(noun)*
the liquid waste that comes out of your body when you go to the toilet. **wee** *(verb)*.

weed *(noun)*
a wild plant that grows in gardens, and gardeners have to pull up. **weeding** *(noun)*.

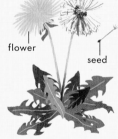
flower   seed

Dandelions are **weeds**. They rely on the wind to spread their seeds.

week *(noun)*
the seven days: Monday, Tuesday, Wednesday, Thursday, Friday, Saturday, and Sunday.

weekday *(noun)*
one of the days from Monday to Friday.

Word family

weekday
weekend
weekly

There are several words based on the word "week". A "weekend" comes at the end of a week, and "weekly" means "once a week". These patterns are common in English: look at all the words based on "water" and "wind" on these pages, for instance.

weekend *(noun)*
Saturday and Sunday. *We're going camping at the weekend.*

weekly *(adverb)*
once a week or every week. *We go swimming weekly.*

weep **weeping wept** *(verb)*
to cry a lot. *Lizzie always weeps when she watches sad films.*

weigh *(way)*
weighing weighed *(verb)*
1 to measure how heavy someone or something is. *Weigh the flour for our cake.* **weight** *(noun)*.
2 What someone or something **weighs** is how heavy they are. *This bag weighs 15 kilograms.* **weight** *(noun)*.

weird **weirder weirdest** *(adjective)*
strange or unusual. **weirdly** *(adverb)*.

welcome
welcoming welcomed *(verb)*
to greet someone in a friendly way. **welcome** *(noun)*, **welcoming** *(adjective)*.

well **better best**
1 *(adverb)* If you do something **well**, you do it skilfully. *He cooks well.*
2 *(adverb)* If something **goes well**, it's a success. *The exam went well.*
3 *(adjective)* If you are **well**, you are healthy.
4 *(noun)* a hole people dig or drill in the ground, to reach water or oil.

welly **wellies** *(noun)*
one of a pair of long rubber boots which stop your feet from getting wet. Welly is short for "wellington boot".

wept *(verb)*
the past tense of **weep**.

west
1 *(noun)* one of the four points of the compass. *See* compass.
2 *(adjective)* in or towards the west of a place. *West Wales.* **west** *(noun)*.
3 *(adjective)* from the west. *A west wind.*
4 **the West** *(noun)* The countries of Europe and the United States are sometimes called **the West**.

western
1 *(adjective)* to do with the west.
2 *(noun)* a film set in the west of the United States, often with cowboys and Native Americans in it.

wet **wetter wettest** *(adjective)*
1 soaked with water or other liquid.
wet *(verb)*.
2 not dry. *The paint is still wet.*

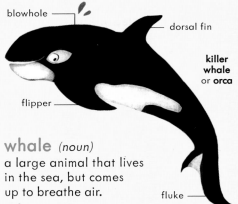

blowhole

dorsal fin

killer whale or **orca**

flipper

whale *(noun)*
a large animal that lives in the sea, but comes up to breathe air.

fluke

what
1 *(determiner)* a word used in questions, to find out information. *What time is it?*
2 *(pronoun)* a word used in questions, to find out information. *What is your name?*
3 *(pronoun)* the thing or things that. *What we need is a ladder.*
4 *(determiner)* a word used in exclamations to mean "how great" or "how much". *What a shame!*
5 You use **what about** to make an offer or suggest something. *What about a cup of coffee?*

whatever *(pronoun)*
1 everything or anything that. *I'll do whatever you say.*
2 no matter what. *Whatever he says, don't go in there.*

wheat *(noun)*
a plant grown for the grains at the top of its stalk, which can be made into flour and other foods.

wheel *(noun)*
a circular object with a pole fixed to its centre, which turns round and round and helps things to move.

wheelchair *(noun)*
a chair on wheels, used by people who can't walk, or can't walk easily.

when
1 *(conjunction)* at or during the time that. *I had blond hair when I was young.*
2 *(adverb)* a word you use to ask at what time something happened, or will happen. *When did Lucas arrive?*

where *(adverb)*
1 a word you use to ask about the location of something. *Where is the pool?*
2 the place someone or something is, or is happening. *Mum doesn't know where her glasses are.*

whereabouts
1 *(adverb)* roughly where. *Whereabouts in New York did you stay?*
2 *(noun)* the place where someone or something is. *Do you know Billy's whereabouts?*

whereas *(conjunction)*
on the other hand. *I like tennis, whereas Hayden prefers badminton.*

wherever *(adverb)*
in or to whatever place. *Meet me wherever you like.*

whether *(conjunction)*
1 a word used to show a choice between, or a doubt about, two possible alternatives. *I don't know whether to stay or go.*
2 either. *Anyone, whether young or old, can enjoy this game.*

which *(determiner)*
1 a word used to ask about one or more particular people or things. *Which gloves do you think I should buy?*
2 a word used to talk about something that has just been mentioned. *The film, which came out yesterday, is about dogs.*

whichever
1 *(determiner)* any of several. *Take whichever coat you like.*
2 *(pronoun)* any of several things that have already been mentioned.
3 *(determiner)* no matter which. *Whichever card you choose, I'll guess it.*

a b c d e f g h i j k l m n o p q r s t u v **w** x y z

Take care when spelling the words on this page that start with 'who–', as you pronounce the 'h' but not the 'w'.

whiff (noun)
a faint smell. *There was a whiff of perfume in the air.*

while
1 (conjunction) during the time that. *Grandad slept while we did some colouring.*
2 (noun) a period of time. *It was a while before we realized the film had finished.*

whimper
whimpering whimpered (verb)
to make weak, crying noises.

whine **whining whined** (verb)
to make a long, high-pitched sound. *Our dog whines when she is unhappy.* **whine** (noun), **whiny** (adjective).

whinge (winj)
whingeing whinged (verb)
to moan about something in a way that gets on everyone's nerves. *Lin wouldn't stop whingeing about being cold.* **whinger** (noun).

whip **whipping whipped**
1 (noun) a long strip of leather fixed to a handle. Whips are usually used for hitting animals, to make them go faster. **whip** (verb).
2 (verb) to beat food, such as cream or eggs, with a whisk, until they are light and fluffy. **whipped** (adjective).

whisk (noun)
a metal cookery tool, used for blending or getting air bubbles into cooking mixtures. **whisk** (verb).

whisker (noun)
one of the long, stiff hairs that many animals have on their faces.

whisper
whispering whispered (verb)
to talk very quietly. *I whispered my secret to Greg.* **whisper** (noun).

whistle **whistling whistled**
1 (verb) to blow air through your lips, to make a musical sound.
2 (noun) a small instrument often used by sports referees, that makes a high "peep" sound when you blow it.

white
1 (noun) the colour of snow. **white** (adjective).
2 (adjective) A **white** person has pale pink skin.
3 (noun) The **white of an egg** is the clear part that surrounds the yolk, which goes white when you cook it.

whizz
whizzes whizzing whizzed (verb)
to move very fast. *The motorbike whizzed down the road.*

who (pronoun)
1 a word you use to find out someone's identity. *Who are you?*
2 a word you use to talk about someone you've already mentioned. *I've got a sister who is really bossy.*

whole
1 (adjective) all of something. *Zak ate the whole pizza.*
2 (noun) a complete thing. *Two halves make a whole.*

wholemeal (adjective)
Wholemeal flour has all the wheat grain left in it, including the outside husk.

whose
1 (determiner) a word you use to ask or show which person something belongs to. *Whose hat is this?*
2 (pronoun) a word you use to ask or show which person something belongs to. *Whose is this?*
3 (determiner) belonging to whom. *Ann knows the man whose house we bought.*

Spelling tip

who's
whose

It's easy to get the words "whose" and "who's" mixed up, as they sound the same. Remember that "who's" is short for "who is", with the 'i' replaced by an apostrophe ('). "Whose" means "belonging to". Find out more about what apostrophes do on page 349.

why

1 *(adverb)* a word you use when you want an answer to a question. *Why did he say that?*
2 *(pronoun)* for, or because of which. *The reason why I didn't come is a secret.*

wicked *(adjective)*

evil and unkind. *The wicked witch is coming.* **wickedness** *(noun)*, **wickedly** *(adverb)*.

wide **wider widest** *(adjective)*

1 from one side to the other. *This road is only a few metres wide.*
2 large, when measured from side to side. *We went through a wide tunnel.*
3 including a lot of different things. *Joseph reads a wide range of books.* **widely** *(adverb)*.
4 If you are **wide awake**, you don't feel tired at all.

widespread *(adjective)*

happening in a lot of places. *Today there will be widespread thunderstorms.*

widow *(noun)*

a woman whose husband or wife has died. *She became a widow at 75.*

widower *(noun)*

a man whose wife or husband has died.

width *(noun)*

how wide something is. *What's the width of this swimming pool?*

wife **wives** *(noun)*

the woman a person is married to. *My uncle's wife comes from Japan.*

wig *(noun)*

a piece of fake hair that people wear if they have lost their hair, or if they want a different hairstyle, for example for fancy dress.

Some judges wear special **wigs** like this one.

wiggle **wiggling wiggled** *(verb)*

to make small movements from side to side, or up and down. *The jelly wiggled on the plate.* **wiggly** *(adjective)*.

wild **wilder wildest** *(adjective)*

1 natural, and not tamed or grown by humans. *There are lots of wild flowers in the fields next to our house.*
2 A **wild** animal is free, or in its natural home or habitat.
3 out of control. *The fans went wild when the band came on.* **wildly** *(adverb)*.

wildlife *(noun)*

wild animals, birds, and plants.

will **would**

1 *(verb)* a word you use to talk about something that has not happened yet, or is going to happen in the future. *I will be cross if you do that again.*
2 *(noun)* a document which says who you want your money and possessions to go to when you die.
3 *(noun)* determination or desire. *The team has the will to win.*

willing *(adjective)*

happy to help, or to do something. *Dad was willing to drive us to the cinema.* **willingness** *(noun)*, **willingly** *(adverb)*.

willow *(noun)*

a type of tree with narrow leaves. Some willows have long, drooping branches.

drooping branches

weeping willow tree

wimp *(noun)*

an unkind word some people use to describe someone who's not very brave. **wimpy** *(adjective)*.

win **winning won** *(verb)*

1 to come first in a competition, game, or race. *I won theatre tickets in a short story writing competition.* **winner** *(noun)*.
2 to gain or deserve something. *Jade won everyone's admiration for her ballet dancing.*

A
B
C
D
E
F
G
H
I
J
K
L
M
N
O
P
Q
R
S
T
U
V
W
X
Y
Z

wind **winding wound**

1 *(rhymes with "pinned") (noun)*
moving air. **windy** *(adjective)*.
2 *(rhymes with "kind") (verb)* to wrap
something round something else.
Wind the hosepipe up, please.
3 *(rhymes with "kind") (verb)* to twist
and turn. *The road winds through
the mountains.*
4 *(rhymes with "kind") (verb)* If you
wind someone up, you annoy them.
Tom really winds me up.

wind instrument *(noun)*
see woodwind.

windmill *(noun)*
a building with sails
on the front that
turn round in the
wind, making a
machine grind
grain into flour.

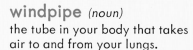
— sail

windmill

window *(noun)*
a gap in the wall
of a building or
vehicle, which has
glass in so that you
can see through it, and
can usually be opened and closed to
let air in or out. *Could you close the
window, please? I'm getting cold.*

windpipe *(noun)*
the tube in your body that takes
air to and from your lungs.

windscreen *(noun)*
the piece of glass at the front of a
vehicle that you look out of. *See* car.

windsurfing *(noun)*
a sport that involves standing on a
board with a sail and using the wind to
move across water. **windsurfer** *(noun)*.

wind turbine *(noun)*
a tall structure with blades or sails,
which turns energy from the wind
into electricity. *See* energy.

wine *(noun)*
an alcoholic drink that is made from
grapes and can be white, red, or pink.

wing *(noun)*
1 one of the parts that birds and many
insects use to fly.
2 one of the two parts on the side of
an aeroplane, that help it to fly.
3 part of a building that sticks out, or
is not in the centre. *The west wing of
the house is haunted.*

wingspan *(noun)*
the length from the tip of one wing
of a bird, plane, and so on, to the tip
of the other.

wink **winking winked** *(verb)*
to close one eye quickly as you look
at someone, either to be friendly, or
as a secret signal. *Simon winked to
show me he was only joking.*

wipe **wiping wiped** *(verb)*
1 to rub something with a cloth,
to clean it. *Please wipe the table.*
2 If something is **wiped out**, there is
none of it left. *A flood wiped out the
farmers' crops.*

wire *(noun)*
a long, thin, bendy piece of metal.
Some wires carry electricity and are
covered in plastic.

wisdom *(noun)*
knowledge, experience, and
understanding. Wisdom is something
that you get over a long time.

wise **wiser wisest** *(adjective)*
Someone **wise** has a lot of experience
and knowledge, and acts sensibly
with good judgement, whatever
the circumstances.

wish **wishes wishing wished**
1 *(verb)* to long for something, or for
something to happen, even when it's not
likely to. *I wish I could fly.* **wish** *(noun)*.
2 If you send **good wishes** or **best wishes**
to someone, you hope good things come
their way.

wit *(noun)*
1 the ability to say clever and
funny things.
2 the ability to think quickly and clearly.

Spelling tip

witch   witness

Words that end with a hissing sound, such as 'ch', 'tch', 's', 'ss', 'tz', 'x' and 'z', add '-es' in the plural. "Ox" is an exception, as its plural form is "oxen".

witch **witches** *(noun)*
In fairy stories and legends, a **witch** is a woman who has magical powers. *The witch lived in a cottage in the woods.* **witchcraft** *(noun)*.

with *(preposition)*
1 If you are **with** somebody, you are together. *Jim arrived with Mum and the dog.*
2 using. *I decorated the cupcakes with coloured sugar stars.*

within *(preposition)*
1 inside a place. *The palace was within the castle walls.*
2 inside a certain amount of time. *We'll be there within the next hour.*

without *(preposition)*
1 not having any. *I can't eat chips without salt and vinegar.*
2 not with someone else. *They went without me!*

witness **witnesses** *(noun)*
someone who sees something happen, such as an accident, and may be asked to describe what they saw in court. **witness** *(verb)*.

witty **wittier wittiest** *(adjective)*
If you are **witty**, you say clever things that make other people laugh.

wizard *(noun)*
In fairy stories and legends, a **wizard** is a man who has magical powers.

wobble **wobbling wobbled** *(verb)*
to move unsteadily from side to side. **wobbly** *(adjective)*.

woke *(verb)*
the past tense of **wake**.

woken *(verb)*
the past participle of **wake**.

wolf **wolves** *(noun)*
a fierce wild animal that lives in a group called a pack, and looks like a large dog.

woman **women** *(noun)*
an adult, female human being. *All the women wanted to walk further.* **womanhood** *(noun)*, **womanly** *(adjective)*.

womb *(woom)* *(noun)*
the part inside a woman's body where a baby can grow.

wonder **wondering wondered**
1 *(verb)* to think about something in an interested and curious way. *I wonder how that tent stays up?*
2 *(verb)* If you **wonder** what to do about something, you are not sure about it. *Sam wondered if he should tell her.*
3 *(noun)* a feeling of amazement. *The night sky filled Faye with wonder.*

won *(verb)*
the past tense of **win**.

wonderful *(adjective)*
amazing, or really great. *It was a wonderful holiday.* **wonderfully** *(adverb)*.

won't *(verb)*
a short way of saying or writing "will not".

wood *(noun)*
1 the substance that the trunk and branches of a tree are made of. **wooden** *(adjective)*.
2 an area of land covered with trees. You'll often see the plural, "woods", used. *I love to explore the wood near my house.* **woodland** *(noun)*.

woodpecker *(noun)*
a bird that lives in woods and forests and pecks trees with its beak so it can eat the insects living in their bark.

great spotted woodpecker

woodwind (noun)

instruments that you blow into to make a sound, such as clarinets and oboes. Woodwind instruments form one section of an orchestra. **woodwind** (adjective).

flute

clarinet

The first woodwind instruments were all made of wood. Today, they are made of plastic, metal, wood, or a mixture of all three. This picture shows two of the best-known woodwind instruments in an orchestra.

woodwork (noun)

1 the skill of making things out of wood. *Jack is doing a course in woodwork.*
2 the parts of a room that are made of wood. *That woodwork is very dusty.*

wool (noun)

the hair of a sheep or other animal, including some goats and rabbits, made into thread and used for weaving, knitting, and other crafts. *I'm going to knit a scarf with this yellow wool.* **woollen** (adjective), **woolly** (adjective).

word (noun)

1 a group of sounds or letters that has a meaning. *What's the longest word you know?*
2 If you **give your word**, you promise that you'll do something. *Reuben gave his word that he would come.*
3 The **words** of a song or poem are what you hear spoken or said. *I like the tune of this song but not the words.*

word processor (noun)

an electronic device or a computer program that lets you type, edit, arrange and store text. **word-processing** (noun).

wore (verb)

the past tense of **wear**.

work working worked (verb)

1 to do a job, or some studying. *Are you all working hard at school?* **work** (noun), **worker** (noun).
2 If something **works**, it does what it's supposed to do. *Does this remote work?*
3 **work out** to go to a gym, or exercise hard. **workout** (noun).
4 If you **work something out**, such as a problem or puzzle, you solve it.

world (noun)

the planet Earth, that we all live on.

worldwide (adjective)

to do with, or reaching, most parts of the world. *Pollution is a worldwide problem.*

World Wide Web (noun)

the huge network of websites containing information that people can access via the internet all over the world. It is often shortened to "www".

worm (noun)

a small, long, thin animal that lives in the ground and has no bones or legs.

tail

saddle   segment

mouth

earthworm

worn

1 (adjective) not brand new, or well-used and scruffy. *Our furniture is worn.*
2 (adjective) If you are **worn out**, you are very tired. *I was worn out after football.*
3 (adjective) If something is **worn out**, it won't work any more. *Our car is worn out.*
4 (verb) the past participle of **wear**.

worry worries worrying worried

1 (verb) to feel nervous or anxious about something. *Kate worries about her exams.* **worried** (adjective).
2 (noun) something that makes you anxious. *Our worry is that the boat will sink.* **worrying** (adjective).

worse worst (adjective)

not as good. *I feel worse than before.*

worship
worshipping worshipped (verb)
1 to pray and praise God, or a god. **worship** (noun).
2 If you **worship** someone, you admire them and think they are wonderful.

worst
1 (adjective) worse than anything else. *He's the worst referee ever.*
2 (pronoun) the one that is worse than anything else. *That excuse was bad, but this one is the worst.*

worth (noun)
1 the value of something, or how much someone would pay for it. **worth** (adjective).
2 If something is **worth** doing, it's a good thing to do, not a waste of time.

worthless (adjective)
of no value at all. *This old car is worthless.*

worthwhile (adjective)
useful and valuable.

would (verb)
1 the past tense of will.
2 a word used to say what could happen in an imaginary situation. *I would cry if I lost this bracelet.*
3 a word used to ask politely if someone will do something or wants something. *Would you like some tea?*

wound
1 (woond) (noun) a deep cut or injury on your body. **wound** (verb).
2 (rhymes with "round") (verb) the past tense of wind.

wove (verb)
the past tense of weave.

woven (verb)
the past participle of weave.

wrap **wrapping wrapped** (verb)
to cover something in paper or material. **wrapping** (noun), **wrapper** (noun).

wreck **wrecking wrecked**
1 (verb) to destroy something. *Yasmin wrecked my toy!* **wrecked** (adjective).
2 (noun) something that has been destroyed, such as a ship.

wreckage (noun)
what's left when something has been destroyed. *The wreckage of the plane.*

wriggle **wriggling wriggled** (verb)
to squirm around. *The puppies were wriggling around in their basket.* **wriggly** (adjective).

wrinkle (noun)
a small, thin line or crease. *My gran has wrinkles on her skin.* **wrinkly** (adjective).

wrist (noun)
the joint that joins your hand to your arm. *I sprained my wrist playing tennis.*

write **writing wrote written** (verb)
1 to use a computer, pen or pencil to form words on a screen or a page. **written** (adjective).
2 If you **write to** someone, you send them a letter or an email.
3 to create poetry, stories, or music. *Tom wants to make a living by writing.* **writer** (noun).
4 If you **write something down**, you make a record of it on paper.

writing (noun)
1 something that is written. *There was writing on the wall of the toilet.*
2 poems, stories, and so on.
3 the way that you write. *Lucy's writing is very neat.*

wrong (adjective)
1 not right. *Lisa always gets maths questions wrong.* **wrongly** (adverb).
2 bad, or against the law. *It's wrong to steal.*

wrote (verb)
the past tense of write.

Spelling tip

wrist   **writing**   **wrong**

On this page, you'll see lots of words that begin with 'wr-'. The 'w' is silent, and you only pronounce the 'r'.

a b c d e f g h i j k l m n o p q r s t u v w x y z

Xx

Xmas *(noun)* *(abbreviation)*
a short way of writing **Christmas**.
The lights on the outside of our house say "Happy Xmas!".

x-ray *(noun)*
a picture of the inside of a person or other object, taken using invisible waves of energy called radiation. **x-ray** *(verb)*.

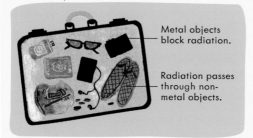

Metal objects block radiation.

Radiation passes through non-metal objects.

X-ray machines are used in airports to check for dangerous items in luggage.

xylophone (**zy**-ler-fone) *(noun)*
a musical instrument with a set of different-sized wooden bars, which you hit to play notes. *See* **percussion**.

Yy

yacht (yot) *(noun)*
a large, fast sailing boat, used for fun or for racing. **yachting** *(noun)*.

yank yanking yanked *(verb)*
to pull something hard or roughly. *Nadia yanked the cupboard door, but it was completely stuck.*

yard *(noun)*
1 an area with a hard surface, usually next to a building.
2 a measure of length or distance. One yard is about 0.9 metres.

yarn *(noun)*
thread for sewing, knitting, or weaving.

yawn yawning yawned *(verb)*
to open your mouth wide and breathe in deeply, usually because you are tired or bored. **yawn** *(noun)*.

year *(noun)*
the time that it takes the Earth to circle the Sun once. A year is 365 days long, or 366 days in a leap year.

yearly *(adverb)*
happening once a year.

yeast *(noun)*
a kind of fungus used to make bread rise, and to make alcoholic drinks.

yell yelling yelled *(verb)*
to shout or scream very loudly. **yell** *(noun)*.

yellow *(noun)*
the colour of lemons. **yellow** *(adjective)*.

yelp yelping yelped *(verb)*
When a dog **yelps**, it gives a sudden, sharp cry of pain. **yelp** *(noun)*.

yes *(interjection)*
a word you use to say that something is true, or to show you agree.

yesterday *(noun)*
the day before today.

yet
1 *(adverb)* so far, or up until now. *I haven't seen the new house yet.*
2 *(adverb)* still, or even. *Yet more people tried to get onto the train.*
3 *(conjunction)* but, or nonetheless. *James did well in his exams, yet he couldn't find a job.*

yoga *(noun)*
a form of exercise in which you stretch your body and do controlled breathing to make yourself more flexible and to relax your mind.

yoghurt or **yogurt** *(noun)*
a creamy food that is made with milk and has a slightly sharp taste. It is often eaten for breakfast or as a dessert.

Yogurt can be spelt with or without the 'h'; either is correct.

yolk *(yoke)* *(noun)*
the yellow part of
an egg. *I like my
egg yolks runny.*

yolk →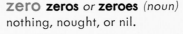

boiled egg

Yom Kippur *(noun)*
a very important Jewish
holy day, when Jews don't
eat or drink to mark
the Day of Atonement.

you *(pronoun)*
a word used to talk to another person
or group of people. *Can I help you?
Are you OK?*

young **younger youngest**
1 *(adjective)* Someone who is **young** has
only lived for a short time. *Young people
usually find learning new languages
much easier than adults do.*
2 *(plural noun)* the babies of an
animal. *Female kangaroos carry
their young in pouches.*

youngster *(noun)*
a friendly word for a young person,
especially a child.

your *(determiner)*
belonging to you, or having to do with
you. *Are these your football boots?*
yours *(pronoun)*.

yourself *(pronoun)*
1 you and nobody else. *Have you hurt
yourself? If you want to know what it
tastes like, try it yourself.*
2 by yourself on your own. *Have you
been waiting here by yourself for long?*

youth *(noun)*
1 the time of someone's life when
they are young. *My Uncle Phil was a
professional cricket player in his youth.*
youthful *(adjective)*.
2 a young person, usually a teenager.

yo-yo *(noun)*
a toy with a small,
round weight,
which you spin
up and down
a string and
do tricks with.

yo-yo

Zz

zap zapping zapped *(verb)*
a friendly word that means to shoot,
often used in a game, comic, or science
fiction film. *We need to zap 50 aliens to
get to the next level.*

zebra *(noun)*
a wild African
animal similar
to a horse, with
black and white
stripes on its body.

**zebra
crossing** *(noun)*
a place where cars
have to stop so that
people can cross the road
safely. It is shown with wide white
stripes painted on the road.

plains zebra

zero zeros *or* **zeroes** *(noun)*
nothing, nought, or nil.

zigzag *(noun)*
a line with sharp, diagonal turns.
zigzag *(verb)*.

zip *(noun)*
a fastener for clothes, made with
metal or plastic teeth that fit together.
zip *(verb)*.

zone *(noun)*
a special area that is different from the
areas around it. *They're turning part
of the forest into a conservation zone.*

zoo *(noun)*
a place where animals are kept so that
people can look at and study them.

zoom zooming zoomed *(verb)*
1 to move very fast. *Laura zoomed
off on her skateboard.*
2 to make a picture appear bigger
or smaller on a computer or camera
screen. *Helena zoomed out so that
she could see the whole page.*
zoom *(noun)*.

a b c d e f g h i j k l m n o p q r s t u v w x y z

Useful words

2D Shapes

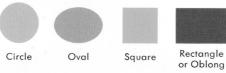

Circle	Oval	Square	Rectangle or Oblong

Diamond	Pentagon	Hexagon	Octagon

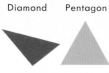

Triangle	Equilateral triangle	Isosceles triangle	Star

3D Shapes

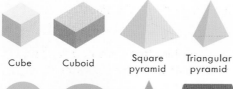

Cube	Cuboid	Square pyramid	Triangular pyramid

Sphere	Hemisphere	Cone	Cylinder

Measuring words

Measurement words often have a short form or symbol.

C	Celsius/ centigrade	m	metre
cl	centilitre	mi	mile
cm	centimetre	mg	milligram/ milligramme
°	degree	ml	millilitre
ft / '	foot/feet	mm	millimetre
g	gram/ gramme	min	minute
		oz	ounce
h	hour	lb	pound
in / "	inch	s	second
kg	kilogram/ kilogramme	t	tonne
l / L	litre		

Months

January
February
March
April
May
June
July
August
September
October
November
December

Days

Monday
Tuesday
Wednesday
Thursday
Friday
Saturday
Sunday

Numbers

1	one	1st	first
2	two	2nd	second
3	three	3rd	third
4	four	4th	fourth
5	five	5th	fifth
6	six	6th	sixth
7	seven	7th	seventh
8	eight	8th	eighth
9	nine	9th	ninth
10	ten	10th	tenth
11	eleven	11th	eleventh
12	twelve	12th	twelfth
13	thirteen	13th	thirteenth
14	fourteen	14th	fourteenth
15	fifteen	15th	fifteenth
16	sixteen	16th	sixteenth
17	seventeen	17th	seventeenth
18	eighteen	18th	eighteenth
19	nineteen	19th	nineteenth
20	twenty	20th	twentieth
21	twenty-one	21st	twenty-first
30	thirty	30th	thirtieth
40	forty	40th	fortieth
50	fifty	50th	fiftieth
60	sixty	60th	sixtieth
70	seventy	70th	seventieth
80	eighty	80th	eightieth
90	ninety	90th	ninetieth
100	one hundred	100th	hundredth

Language rules

Grammar

All languages have rules called **grammar** that you need to bear in mind. Grammar may seem difficult, but you'll already know much more about it than you think you do, because you use it every day.

Verbs and tenses

Verbs have different forms, depending on when the action they are describing happened. These forms are called *tenses*. The three main tenses are:

the present tense: I *play* the piano every day.

the future tense: I *will play* the piano tomorrow.

the past tense: I *played* the piano yesterday.

In this dictionary, wherever you see a verb, you'll see something like this:

play **playing played**

1. **play** is the name of the verb, or the *infinitive* form.

2. to use a verb with "he", "she", or "it", you usually just add an 's' on the end: She *plays* the piano.

3. the ending '-ing' is used with "be" to describe an action that is continuing: Victoria *is playing* the piano.

4. **played** is the past tense of the verb: I *played* the piano last night.

5. **played** is also used with "have", to describe something you've finished doing: I *have played* piano all night.

This form of the verb may be different to the past tense, such as:

eat **eating ate eaten**

Verbs are all different, but most follow a few simple patterns in how they make their tenses.

Punctuation

Punctuation is small marks that will help make the meaning of your writing clear. Here are the most important punctuation marks:

Full stop .
This **shows the end of a sentence**, like this one**.**

Comma ,
This **shows that there's a break in a sentence,** or between parts of it, as in this one.

Speech marks " "
You need to put these **at the beginning and end of speech** in your writing: *"Let's watch the tennis," said Caroline.*

Exclamation mark !
You use this **after expressing a strong feeling**, or a surprise: *"I love it!"*

Question mark ?
This comes **after a question**: *"Do you have any cats?"*

Apostrophe '
These can do two different jobs.
1. **They can tell you that a letter is missing**, or that a word has been shortened, for example in "it's" (short for "it is").
2. **They can show you that something belongs to someone**: *The boy's ice skates.* If something belongs to more than one person, you put the apostrophe after the final 's': *The boys' ice skates.*

Colon :
This comes **before a list or explanation**: *We need to buy: eggs, milk, and flour.*

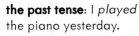

Making words plural

Plurals

Most words just add an '-s' to change from being singular (just one thing) to plural (more than one thing), but some follow different rules:

Words ending in 'f' or 'fe'

Some words that end in 'f' or 'fe' just add an '-s' in the plural:

belief	belief**s**
chef	chef**s**
chief	chief**s**
giraffe	giraffe**s**
roof	roof**s**

giraffe   **giraffes**

However, many remove the 'f' or 'fe' and add '-ves':

calf	cal**ves**
half	hal**ves**
knife	kni**ves**
shelf	shel**ves**
wolf	wol**ves**

half   **halves**

A few words ending in 'f' can be spelt with either '-s' or '-ves':

dwarf	dwarf**s** / dwar**ves**
hoof	hoof**s** / hoo**ves**
scarf	scarf**s** / scar**ves**

Words ending in 'o'

Many words that end with an 'o' just add an '-s' to become plural, but some add '-es', including:

echo	echo**es**
hero	hero**es**
mosquito	mosquito**es**
potato	potato**es**
tomato	tomato**es**

tomato   **tomatoes**

A few words can be spelt with either '-s' or '-es':

banjo**s** / banjo**es**
flamingo**s** / flamingo**es**
mango**s** / mango**es**
tornado**s** / tornado**es**
zero**s** / zero**es**

flamingo   **flamingoes**

Words ending in 'y'

Words that end with a consonant then a 'y' drop the 'y' and add '-ies':

activity	activit**ies**
baby	bab**ies**
berry	berr**ies**
lady	lad**ies**
poppy	popp**ies**

poppy   **poppies**

Words that end with a vowel then a 'y' just add '-s':

toy	toy**s**

Words ending with hissing sounds

Words that end in 'ch', 'tch', 's', 'ss', 'tz', 'x' and 'z' add '-es' in the plural:

box	box**es**
bus	bus**es**
grass	grass**es**
match	match**es**
peach	peach**es**

peach   **peaches**

One exception to this rule is "ox"; its plural is "ox**en**".

Irregular plurals

Some words don't follow a pattern when they become plural. Here are the ones you're most likely to see:

Singular	Plural
aircraft	aircraft
child	children
deer	deer
fish	fish *or* fishes
foot	feet
goose	geese
louse	lice
man	men
mouse	mice
person	people
sheep	sheep
species	species
tooth	teeth
woman	women

tropical fish

More useful words and prefixes

Pronouns

Pronouns are words you use instead of naming a person or thing. They can be used:

To talk about a person:
I/me/myself
you/yourself
he/him/himself
she/her/herself
it/itself
we/us/ourselves
they/them/themselves

To show that something belongs to someone:
mine, yours, his, hers, its, ours, theirs

To talk about objects:
this, that, these, those

To ask questions:
who, whom, which, what, whose

Prepositions

Prepositions are words that show the connection between a noun or pronoun and another word in the sentence. Here are some of the main ones:

about	beyond	opposite
above	by	outside
across	down	over
after	during	past
against	except	since
along	following	than
among	for	through
around	from	to
as	in	towards
at	inside	under
before	into	until
behind	near	up
below	of	upon
beneath	off	with
beside	on	within
between	onto	without

Conjunctions

Conjunctions link parts of a sentence together. They are sometimes called "connectives" or "linking words".

after	even if	since
although	even though	so
and	for	so that
as	however	than
as if	if	though
as long as	in case	unless
as soon as	in order that	until
as though	nevertheless	when
because	nor	where
before	once	wherever
but	only if	while
by the time	or	yet

These conjunctions are often used together:

either – or   whether – or
neither – nor   both – and

Prefixes

A prefix is a group of letters added to the beginning of a word, sometimes with a hyphen, to make a new word.

Prefix	Meaning	Example
anti-	against, opposite	anticlockwise
co-	together	copilot
de-	take away	defrost
dis-	opposite	disagree
ex-	former	ex-wife
in-/im-	opposite	incorrect
mid-	middle	midday
mini-	small	minibus
mis-	wrong, bad	misbehave
non-	not	nonfiction
over-	too much	overweight
pre-	before	prehistoric
re-	again	reread
semi-	half, partly	semicircle
un-	opposite	unable
under-	not enough	underweight

Suffixes

A suffix is a group of letters added to the end of a word to make a new word. Sometimes adding a suffix will change the spelling of the word slightly, so look in a dictionary if you're unsure how to spell it.

Suffix examples

Many suffixes are used to make nouns:

Suffix	Example	
-hood	child	childhood
-ity	regular	regularity
-ment	enjoy	enjoyment
-ness	kind	kindness
-ship	friend	friendship
-sion	divide	division
-tion	navigate	navigation

Some suffixes can make nouns that mean a person who does something:

Suffix	Example	
-er/or	dance	dancer
-ist	guitar	guitarist

The suffix '-ess' can be used to make a noun feminine:

-ess	prince	princess

The suffix '-ette' can be used to make a word that means "a small version of that thing":

-ette	statue	statuette

There are lots of suffixes that can be used to change nouns or verbs into adjectives:

Suffix	Example	
-able	comfort	comfortable
-al	music	musical
-ary	imagine	imaginary
-ful	care	careful
-ible	sense	sensible
-ic	hero	heroic
-ish	fool	foolish
-ive	attract	attractive
-less	hope	hopeless
-like	life	lifelike
-ous	humour	humorous
-worthy	trust	trustworthy
-y	ice	icy

Some suffixes change adjectives into adverbs:

Suffix	Example	
-ally	automatic	automatically
-ly	gradual	gradually
	quick	quickly

Finally, some suffixes can be used to make verbs:

Suffix	Example	
-ate	active	activate
-en	length	lengthen
-ify	pure	purify
-ise/-ize	apology	apologise/apologize

Additional design by Matt Durber.
Proofreading by Alice Primmer and Rachel Tranter.
Expert picture checking by Gerry Douglas-Sherwood, Richard Thompson and Abigail Wheatley.

First published in 2015 by Usborne Publishing Ltd., Usborne House, 83–85 Saffron Hill, London EC1N 8RT, England. Copyright ©2015 Usborne Publishing Ltd. The name Usborne and the devices ♀♔ are Trade Marks of Usborne Publishing Ltd. All rights reserved. No part of this publication may be reproduced, stored in a retrieval system, or transmitted in any form or by any means, electronic, mechanical, photocopying, recording or otherwise without the prior permission of the publisher. UKE. Printed in UAE.